THE TWO HORIZONS NEW TESTAMENT COMMENTARY

JOEL B. GREEN and MAX TURNER, *General Editors*

Two features distinguish THE TWO HORIZONS NEW TESTAMENT COMMEN-TARY series: theological exegesis and theological reflection.

Exegesis since the Reformation era and especially in the past two hundred years emphasized careful attention to philology, grammar, syntax, and concerns of a historical nature. More recently, commentary has expanded to include social-scientific, political, or canonical questions and more.

Without slighting the significance of those sorts of questions, scholars in THE TWO HORIZONS NEW TESTAMENT COMMENTARY locate their primary interests on theological readings of texts, past and present. The result is a paragraph-by-paragraph engagement with the text that is deliberately theological in focus.

Theological reflection in THE TWO HORIZONS NEW TESTAMENT COMMENTARY takes many forms, including locating each New Testament book in relation to the whole of Scripture — asking what the biblical book contributes to biblical theology — and in conversation with constructive theology of today. How commentators engage in the work of theological reflection will differ from book to book, depending on their particular theological tradition and how they perceive the work of biblical theology and theological hermeneutics. This heterogeneity derives as well from the relative infancy of the project of theological interpretation of Scripture in modern times and from the challenge of grappling with a book's message in Greco-Roman antiquity, in the canon of Scripture and history of interpretation, and for life in the admittedly diverse Western world at the beginning of the twenty-first century.

THE TWO HORIZONS NEW TESTAMENT COMMENTARY is written primarily for students, pastors, and other Christian leaders seeking to engage in theological interpretation of Scripture.

Philippians

Stephen E. Fowl

WILLIAM B. EERDMANS PUBLISHING COMPANY
GRAND RAPIDS, MICHIGAN / CAMBRIDGE, U.K.

© 2005 Wm. B. Eerdmans Publishing Co.

Wm. B. Eerdmans Publishing Co.
255 Jefferson Ave. S.E., Grand Rapids, Michigan 49503 /
P.O. Box 163, Cambridge CB3 9PU U.K.

Printed in the United States of America

10 09 08 07 06 05   7 6 5 4 3 2 1

ISBN-10: 0-8028-2551-6
ISBN-13: 978-0-8028-2551-3

www.eerdmans.com

Contents

Acknowledgments

This commentary has been a long time in the making. In between starting and completing this work many things have intervened. Shortly after agreeing to write on Philippians, I became chair of our department. This job has often required my time and attention when I had hoped to be working on Philippians. Nevertheless, it has always been one of the doctrines of our department that you need to be chair either in this life or the next. The advantage of doing it in this life is that you can be fairly certain of who your colleagues will be. We have an extraordinary group here at Loyola, and I am deeply grateful to them for their support and constant stimulation. In addition, I want to thank Jim Buckley, Dean of Arts and Sciences at Loyola. I know of no doctrines about being dean, and I was sorry when he left our department to take on this task. He does an excellent job and has also been a source of support and encouragement. I am also grateful for the Loyola College Faculty Development Summer Grants I received to work on this project.

My greatest fear in beginning this project was that I would come to loathe Philippians by the end of it. To my surprise I have come to love it even more than when I first began. In large measure this is due to the fact that I came to see Philippians' importance for the life of the church in America today. I came to appreciate this in the course of presenting my ideas about Philippians to a variety of church-based audiences. In particular I want to thank those at Point Loma Nazarene University, City Seminary in New York, The Colloquium on Excellence in Ministry that met at Duke Divinity School, and the Church of the Servant King in Eugene who listened to me talk about various aspects of Philippians. Their reception of my work and their feedback have helped greatly in preparing this commentary.

Several individuals have read through and offered advice, criticism and comment on parts of this work. In particular, I want to thank Mike Gorman,

Mark Gornik, Greg Jones, Jeff McCurry, Mike Munk, Jon Stock, and Rob Wall. They cannot be held responsible for the errors here, but there are far fewer here because of their help. In particular I need to thank Joel Green, the editor for this series. He and Max Turner are to be commended for conceiving of the series and bringing the authors together on several occasions to discuss the nature of theological commentary. Joel has read through my work with his typical care and attention. His comments have always been perceptive and reflect the enormous breadth of his scholarship. He, too, cannot be held responsible for the inadequacies of this work, but his help has been inestimable.

My wife Melinda and sons Brendan and Liam are always there to remind me that there is more to life than "reading books about God." The day-to-day joys and trials of life together have allowed me to keep the production of yet one more book in proper perspective.

In the course of reading this commentary it will become clear that I think the central task facing the Christians in Philippi is the formation of "a common life worthy of the gospel of Christ" (1:27). My friends at the Church of the Servant King in Eugene have regularly offered me glimpses of what such a common life should look like. I am quite certain that I have taken away far more from my visits with them than they have received from me. I dedicate this book to them in partial repayment of that debt.

Abbreviations

ANRW	*Aufstieg und Niedergang der römischen Welt*
Ant.	Josephus, *Antiquities of the Jews*
BAGD	W. Bauer, W. F. Arndt, F. W. Gingrich, and F. W. Danker, *Greek-English Lexicon of the New Testament*
BECNT	Baker Exegetical Commentary on the New Testament
BTB	*Biblical Theology Bulletin*
CEV	Contemporary English Version
EvQ	*Evangelical Quarterly*
HTR	*Harvard Theological Review*
JSNT	*Journal for the Study of the New Testament*
JSNTS	Journal for the Study of the New Testament Supplement
JTS	*Journal of Theological Studies*
LCL	Loeb Classical Library
LXX	Septuagint
NA26	Nestle-Aland *Greek New Testament*, 26th ed.
NAB	New American Bible
NEB	New English Bible
NICNT	New International Commentary on the New Testament
NIGTC	New International Greek Testament Commentary
NovT	*Novum Testamentum*
NPNF	Nicene and Post-Nicene Fathers
NRSV	New Revised Standard Version
NT	New Testament
NTS	*New Testament Studies*
OT	Old Testament
par.	parallel(s)
RSR	*Recherches de science religieuse*

RSV	Revised Standard Version
SBLDS	Society of Biblical Literature Dissertation Series
SNTSMS	Society for New Testament Studies Monograph Series
TDNT	G. Kittel and G. Friedrich, eds., *Theological Dictionary of the New Testament*
ThZ	*Theologische Zeitschrift*
WBC	Word Biblical Commentary
ZNW	*Zeitschrift für die neutestamentliche Wissenschaft*
ZTK	*Zeitschrift für Theologie und Kirche*

Introduction to Philippians

Writing a Theological Commentary

Having been a critic of commentaries over the years, I now find myself in the position of needing to apologize for all of the rude comments I have made in the past. Unlike a monograph which has a directed and relatively circumscribed argument, a commentary must keep a variety of different agendas in mind. In doing this, it is inevitable that certain things will be covered more adequately than others. I did not appreciate this difficulty until actually trying to write a commentary myself.

In this introduction I would like to discuss some of the specific agendas to which I have tried to pay at least limited attention. Having done that, I also need to devote some time to discussing some of the issues that typically appear in the introductions to commentaries.

First and foremost, this volume, and the entire series of which it is a part, aims to bridge some of the gaps which exist between the exegetical work typical of modern commentaries and disciplined theological reflection. There are a variety of ways to go about this task. I take it that a commentary, by its very nature, requires close, rigorous attention to the text of another. Of course, that attention can take a variety of forms; it can focus on any number of specific aspects of a text. This keeps commentary from being mere repetition of another's text. Most modern commentators on Paul's epistle to the Philippians attempt to explicate either how the first recipients of this epistle would have understood Paul's letter or what Paul intended to communicate to the Philippians. Either one of these agendas requires attention to semantics and the linguistic and social conventions operative at the time. Implications, allusions and inferences also need to be explicated. To do this, one sometimes needs to reconstruct at least some of the unspoken, but presumed elements of the situation of author and readers/hearers. Although different commentators might emphasize particular parts of this exercise, these are taken to be the basic practices of professional exegesis. To this extent, modern commentators are generally engaged in what is recognizably the same project. When people speak of historical-critical commentaries on Paul's epistles, this is the type of activity they mean.

Some, but not all, of these commentaries also have a desire to say something theological as well as exegetical. This is understandable in the light of the fact that Philippians is part of Christian Scripture and the vast majority of those who read biblical commentaries are Christians. It is not unusual, then, to find some part of a commentary devoted to theological, pastoral, or homiletic reflection on a passage which has just been commented upon in the exegetical manner noted above. To the extent that these commentaries pursue a theological agenda, theology becomes the result of exegesis done on other grounds.

This situation is so normal and widespread it is useful to note that the situation is quite different when one looks at pre-modern commentaries on Philippians or any other scriptural text. When I speak of pre-modern commentators I mean patristic, medieval, and Reformation and Catholic Reformation commentators. One way of describing and accounting for this difference would be to claim that modern commentators are primarily interested in the literal sense of a text, while pre-modern commentators (with a few exceptions) are primarily interested in figural interpretation. Although it is true that one of the signs of the rise of modern biblical criticism is the demise of figural modes of reading, I think this account misperceives the issue. The difference between modern and pre-modern commentators primarily lies in the way they understand the literal sense of Scripture. For modern commentators, explicating the literal sense of Scripture tends to be a historically determined enterprise like that charted above. Should this version of the literal sense generate theological judgments and reflections, those would be secondary and subsidiary matters. Alternatively, for the great commentators of the Christian tradition, the literal sense of Scripture was already regulated by theological concerns. For modern commentators, theology is the result of historically determined exegesis. For the pre-modern commentators, theology was more like a form of exegesis.

Let me try to illustrate some of these differences. If we look at the introductions to modern commentaries, they generally cover similar sorts of issues. Gordon Fee's commentary, which I consider to be one of the best scholarly commentaries of its type in English, is a fine example.[1] It reflects Fee's

---

1. Fee, *Philippians* (see text for pages).

great learning and skill in Greek; it manifests close attention to the text, clear and lucid exposition, and a judicious handling of secondary material. Fee's introduction addresses two basic questions: the genre of Philippians (1-23) and the occasion of Philippians (24-39). He is interested in understanding first-century epistolary conventions and in reading Philippians in the light of those conventions as they were employed and discerned by Paul and the Philippians in their very particular historical situations. He does not force Philippians into a generic or historical straitjacket, but he clearly sees these as important matters. In terms of the occasion of Philippians, Fee seeks to explain what Paul's situation was, what the Philippians' situation was, and how these two matters shape the epistle. To the extent that theological concerns bear on this discussion (46-53), they depend on a historical accounting of Paul's theological concerns and a historical accounting of the theological background of the Christians in Philippi.[2] In this, Fee's work is both typical in terms of the topics it covers and exemplary in the manner in which it covers them.

Alternatively, let us look at Thomas Aquinas's commentary on Philippians.[3] The English translation of his prologue takes up about one page. It begins with an epigram from Prov 4:18, "The path of the righteous is like the light of dawn, which shines brighter and brighter until full day." In reflecting on this text Aquinas notes that "the life of the saints is described under three aspects" (57). The lives of the saints follow a narrow path; it is a path of splendor (it shines brightly); it is a path which progresses toward an end (full day). He then goes on to note that this text summarizes the subject matter of Philippians: "For the Philippians were on Christ's narrow way, enduring many tribulations for Christ. They were enlightened by faith: 'Among whom you shine as lights in the world' (Phil. 2:15). Furthermore, they were making progress, as is clear from the entire letter." Finally, Aquinas puts Philippians into its canonical context by noting that it is fitting that Philippians comes after Ephesians. This is because Ephesians contains extensive instruction on

2. In a piece written before his Philippians commentary Fee indicates that Paul's theological concerns are very important and seeks "to come to grips with what drives him, what motivates the words and the rhetoric" ("Reflections," 389). Fee's subsequent comments clearly separate this task from making "hermeneutical observations either as to its [Paul's rhetoric] overall theological import or how it might apply" ("Reflections," 390).

3. Torrell, *Aquinas*, ch. XII, dates Aquinas's lectures on Paul to his final years of teaching in Naples (1272-73). Weisheipl, *Friar Thomas D'Aquino*, ch. VI, places Thomas's lectures on Paul during his second stint in Paris (1269-72). I have no stake in fixing the date more precisely. The "commentary" on Philippians is, strictly speaking, a *reportatio* — a work written by a secretary (in this case, Thomas's close friend Reginald of Piperno) as Aquinas lectured.

preserving the unity of the church. Hence, "it is fitting that those who best preserved it should be held up as an example of preserving the unity of the Church" (57-58).

If we take these two introductions as providing preparatory material useful for understanding the "literal sense" of the epistle, then, for Fee, it is clear that to properly (or at least better) understand Philippians one must put Philippians into its original historical context as best and as fully as one can. For Aquinas, one needs to understand Philippians in the light of Prov 4:18 as displaying the life of the saints, and in the light of the church unity advocated in Ephesians. The aims and purposes of one are historical (which may then generate theology). The aims and purposes of the other are clearly theological.

As one works through these two commentaries it is clear that both Fee and Aquinas pay close attention to textual detail. Many times they say similar things about Philippians. When they diverge, it is usually because of their differing aims and purposes. It is rare, however, for the comments of one effectively to invalidate the comments of the other. Their interests in and understanding of the "literal sense" of Philippians are simply very different. Hence, one cannot explain the difference between pre-modern and modern commentators on the basis of a renewed appreciation for the literal sense. Rather, what one sees is a change in the way the literal sense of Scripture is understood. In the modern period historical concerns regulate the theological. In the pre-modern period theological concerns regulate all others.

It appears, then, that one of the tasks of a theological commentary at the beginning of the twenty-first century is to attend to this difference between the pre-modern and the modern. In doing this, the challenge is to keep theological concerns primary rather than subsidiary to other sorts of exegesis. This is not easy as it may sound. There are cases where I would argue that an appropriate understanding of a theological point depends on knowledge of certain first-century linguistic or cultural conventions. Or, perhaps, that knowledge of certain historical data opens up important theological avenues. In particular I am thinking about 4:10-20 where Paul gives a dense theological account of the practice of giving and receiving money. The power of the theological claims here are lost apart from an understanding of the ways in which Paul addresses and in some respects undermines certain social conventions. In other places certain historical questions get in the way of theological inquiry. For example, in regard to 2:6-11 most commentaries written in the past thirty years are primarily interested in questions about the prehistory of this text and the historical background of the claims made about Christ in this passage. Pre-modern commentators

4

tend to read this text christologically in a way regulated by the church's creeds and Rule of Faith.[4]

Thus, while the distinction between historical and theological concerns is not always clear-cut, I take it that one of the challenges I face in writing this commentary is to discern how and in what ways to present historical concerns in ways that enhance rather than frustrate theological inquiry. In this light, I assume throughout the commentary that what Paul says to the "saints in Christ Jesus in Philippi" (1:1) is also meant for all saints in Christ Jesus today. Therefore, in translating and commenting upon Paul's words to the Philippians, I intend them to be taken as words for us Christians today. When it seems appropriate I will also try to explicate more specifically how Paul's claims might be embodied today by Christians in America. This seems to be particularly important when aspects of American cultural or church life seem to pose specific difficulties and challenges to Christians' abilities to order our contemporary common life in a manner worthy of the gospel of Christ (1:27). In part to remind us Christians that God aims to speak to us through Paul's words to the Philippians, I have not formally separated these comments from my comments on other aspects of Philippians.

Another challenge facing all commentators, theological or otherwise, is to attend to what has been written. This is both an intellectual and a theological discipline. It is an intellectual discipline in that it requires a willed submission to another's form of writing with the aim of making that person's work clearer to contemporary readers. The commentator's discussion, debates, and arguments derive their importance from their ability to clarify another's discussion, debates, and arguments. Commenting on Scripture is a theological discipline in that one expects that by attention to the words of Scripture one will hear the voice of God. Of course, listening to God's voice is the primary activity of prayer, too. Thus, commenting on Scripture can be a form of prayer. At their best, the disciplines of attention which lead to deep and faithful praying also apply to commentary writing as well.[5] Studying Philippians has certainly enhanced my praying. The challenge to me as a writer is to seek to open those benefits up to others. More generally, then, one of the aims of theological commentary must be to allow others to hear God's voice.

Theological commentary is but one form of theological interpretation

4. There are, of course, some modern exceptions to this. In particular I am thinking of Karl Barth's very short commentary on Philippians, which has just been reissued with introductions by F. Watson and B. McCormack.

5. This was recognized in medieval commentaries, which were often written for the formation of monks. The best example of this can be found in Bernard of Clairvaux's sermons on the Song of Songs.

of Scripture. At the end of the day, all theological interpretation of Scripture is always directed toward more faithful worship and practice so that we Christians might move toward ever deeper friendship or communion with God and each other. The final part of this commentary, "Theological Horizons," moves beyond the strict discipline of attending to the text of Philippians in the way it has come down to us. There I try to synthesize several aspects of Philippians toward a discussion of a theology of friendship. I do not take this final part of this volume to be real theology as opposed to what has preceded. Both "Commentary" and "Theological Horizons" are forms of theological interpretation. I hope both parts can fruitfully illumine each other. While it is possible to read the third section on its own, the connections between a theology of friendship and Philippians become much clearer in the light of my comments in the second.

The first task in attending to Philippians is to make a translation from the Greek to English. This task is first in the sense that it is the first part of each section of the commentary. Translation, however, is not the first conceptual or interpretive task of the commentator. Rather, translation presumes the interpretive work that formally follows it. Fortunately, the Greek of Philippians is relatively straightforward. When it is not so, or when I think the Greek conveys something important that is not easily conveyed in English, I have tried to explain this clearly and in ways that do not presume a knowledge of Greek. In particular, I want to say a few words here about the Greek word φρονεῖν/*phronein*. This word appears ten times in Philippians. It occurs only thirteen other times in the Pauline corpus. I will say more about the importance of this word in Philippians in due course. Here I want simply to note that often the English word "think" is used as a translation. This is not incorrect, but it is also not sufficient. When Paul uses this word in Philippians he is not simply referring to an intellectual activity. Rather, he is talking about a more comprehensive pattern of thinking, feeling and acting. The English phrase "pattern of thinking, feeling, and acting" and variations thereof are not particularly elegant, but I have decided to use such phrases in my translation as a way of making this clearer. This is the primary way my translation differs from those found in standard English translations of the Bible.

If commentary writing requires disciplined attention to another's writing, then it also requires attention to previous commentators. As a scholar and teacher, I think it is important to recognize and acknowledge one's intellectual debts to other scholars. As a reader of commentaries, I often get distracted or annoyed by innumerable lists detailing various interpretive options regarding a verse or phrase. Not only does this tend to obscure the commentator's own views, it also interrupts the flow of the text being commented upon. In this regard (and in many others), Fee's commentary is exemplary in balancing between a lucid discussion of the text of Philippians in the body of the commentary and various scholarly arguments in his footnotes. I hope to address a broader audience, thus my engagements with secondary literature are more limited. Nevertheless, I have tried to adhere to Fee's example of carrying on this discussion in footnotes. When I do devote time in the body of the commentary to discussing scholarly disputes it is because I consider it important for beginning students to hear and understand the different types of questions scholars bring to a text. It is also important to begin to learn how one might adjudicate different types of scholarly argument. I have tried to do some of that here, particularly around the very significant passage found in 2:6-11.

When I began this project I asked a former teacher, himself a seasoned commentary writer, for advice about how to proceed. His advice was to read widely, but converse with a select body of commentaries. I found this to be good advice and here I want to acknowledge those conversation partners, beyond the notes devoted to their work. As I have already mentioned, Gordon Fee's commentary was invaluable. Marcus Bockmuehl's commentary, as well as his several articles on Philippians, are full of provocative insights.[6] Peter O'Brien's commentary was also a reliable guide.[7] As he is one of those who first taught me Greek, my debts to Gerald Hawthorne go well beyond his commentary, which was often refreshing for its unwillingness to simply flow with the scholarly tide.[8] Although it is not strictly a commentary, Jeffrey Reed's *A Discourse Analysis of Philippians* was very helpful at the beginning stages of my work in clarifying key passages in Philippians.[9] I also tried to make regular reference to the German commentaries of J. Gnilka and E. Lohmeyer.[10] While there is much to criticize in Lohmeyer's approach, he confronted the issue of martyrdom in ways that most other modern commentaries seemed to shy away from. I also regularly conversed with the pre-modern commentary of St. Thomas Aquinas and the homilies of St. John Chrysostom.[11] I have already spoken about the importance of recovering the pre-modern commitment to the priority of theology as a method of exegesis. These two are fine examples of this. There are numerous others that I could have (and perhaps should have) regularly used. These two were easily accessible to me on a long-term basis. I do not wish to slight the works of others and

6. Bockmuehl, *Philippians,* "Form of God," and "Effective History."

7. O'Brien, *Philippians.*

8. Hawthorne, *Philippians.*

9. Reed, *Discourse Analysis.*

10. Gnilka, *Philipperbrief;* Lohmeyer, *Philipper.*

11. I have already mentioned the Aquinas text. Chrysostom, *Homilies on Philippians.*

often made recourse to them in my work. These, however, were the commentators I conversed with on a regular basis.

Integrity and Genre of Philippians

Up until fairly recently there has been a serious modern debate about the integrity of Philippians. The argument was primarily based on the appearance of the Greek word τὸ λοιπόν/*to loipon* in 3:1 and again in 4:8. This word is often translated as "finally" or "as for the rest." The argument went that each of these occurrences marked the end of an original letter. This was then used to explain the apparently abrupt introduction of warnings against "judaizers" in 3:2 and the expression of thanks in 4:10-20. In addition, the concluding expression of thanks in 4:10-20 appeared to come too late in the epistle, almost as an afterthought, to be original. These were the three central reasons that led some to conclude that Philippians is the (rather sloppy) composite of three letters: Letter A (4:10-20) thanking the Philippians for the money sent with Epaphroditus; Letter B (3:1b to some point in ch. 4) giving a polemic against false teaching; and Letter C (1:1–3:1a), which Epaphroditus brought back with him to Philippi.[12]

To my mind, Jeffrey Reed's discussion of τὸ λοιπόν/*to loipon* as part of a conventional hesitation formula, well attested in other letters, and L. C. A. Alexander's comparison of the rather loose structure of Philippians with the equally loose structure of ancient "family" or "friendship" letters, decisively put to rest any questions about the unity of the epistle.[13] Moreover, from a theological point of view, Christians have no real option but to treat the canonical form of Philippians as the basis for theological reflection. It is, ultimately, Philippians' status in the canon that demands this, not arguments for or against the literary integrity of the epistle.

The generic description of Philippians as a letter of friendship is particularly helpful in adjudicating matters of the epistle's unity. One must be cautious, however, in making too much of this designation. First, calling the epistle a "friendship letter" is a judgment about the relative formal similarity between Philippians and letters sent between friends. Such a claim does not presuppose any particular type of friendship. In the course of parts 2 and 3 I

12. An instructive survey of views on the unity of the epistle can be found in Garland, "The Composition and Unity of Philippians."

13. See Reed, *Discourse Analysis*, ch. 4. Alexander, "Hellenistic Letter-Forms." On Philippians as a letter of friendship see also Stowers, *Letter Writing,* 50-70, and "Friends and Enemies."

will note several respects in which Paul's notion of friendship in Christ differs from other types of friendship in the Greco-Roman world. Second, although Philippians and other letters of friendship share certain vocabulary and patterns of expression, it is important to recognize the particular ways in which Paul uses that vocabulary in Philippians rather than presume that two writers using the same words and phrases mean the same things. My point is not to claim that Paul's discourse is unique and discontinuous from anything that preceded it. Rather, my point is that one can make judgments about continuity and discontinuity only on the basis of an understanding of Paul's or someone else's claims. Claims about genre depend on prior understanding of the specifics; they are very clumsy tools when used to make judgments about specifics.

Paul's Imprisonment

Passages such as 1:7, 13-14, 17; and perhaps 4:14 all indicate that Paul was in prison when he wrote the epistle. Paul was imprisoned numerous times, however. Traditionally, it is thought that he wrote from Rome, where he was imprisoned (Acts 28:16-31), though Acts also relates jail time in Philippi (16:23-40) and Caesarea (23:23-26:32). Moreover, in 2 Cor 11:23 Paul speaks of numerous imprisonments.

Philippians itself offers no decisive clues. In 1:13 Paul mentions the "Praetorian guard" and in 4:22 he mentions "those of the emperor's household." These references tend to point to a Roman imprisonment. They might also fit with an Ephesian imprisonment. Rome and Ephesus are the two main options. Each has evidence both for and against it. If pressed, I would follow Bockmuehl's reasons for Rome as the place of composition. In this case, then, the epistle was probably written after the initial period of Paul's imprisonment, which Luke relates as more like house arrest (Acts 28:30-31). This would be sometime after 62 CE.[14] I would also add, however, that it is not clear that one's decisions on these matters make much interpretive difference.

Although the location of Paul's imprisonment may not make much interpretive difference, the fact of his imprisonment may, and deserves some comment. The narrative in Acts indicates that Paul's initial arrest in Jerusalem was based on the disturbance he caused in the Temple (Acts 21:27-36). Paul himself does not mention the specific charges which have landed him in prison. Instead, in Phil 1:7, 13 Paul indicates that he is in prison because of his Christianity. Moreover, Paul indicates that his life hangs on the outcome of

---

14. See Bockmuehl, *Philippians*, 25-32.

9

his trial. This would indicate that the formal charge against him was *maiestas* or diminishing the "majesty" of the emperor and people of Rome. Although this charge would certainly have applied to explicitly treasonous activity, it also appears to have been used in a fairly wide-ranging way to punish those thought to have impugned the emperor's status.[15]

Paul repeatedly speaks of his imprisonment in terms of "chains" (Phil 1:7, 13, 14, 17). It may or may not have been the case that he was constantly in chains. What this does indicate is that he was not assigned to severe confinement in a quarry *(carcer)*. Paul seems to have been under guard (cf Phil 1:13), but not necessarily chained to a guard.[16]

Paul tells us nothing of the conditions under which he is held. We do not know what or how much he ate, in what sort of place he was held, whether there were adequate light and sanitation. We do know in general that Roman prisons did not seek to rehabilitate people. They were more like holding tanks where prisoners were kept until the empire decided whether to execute them or let them go. Conditions were often quite gruesome. It was not uncommon for prisoners to take their own lives under such conditions. The support and material help of friends was crucial. At the same time, the significant stigma associated with imprisonment made it socially difficult, if not dangerous, to associate with prisoners.[17] Nevertheless, Acts 28:30-31 and Philippians both indicate that in Rome Paul had access to friends who would visit him, carry letters, take dictation, and provide him with monetary and other forms of support.

Although Paul does not tell us much about his imprisonment, he is adamant about one thing. In a world in which being in chains was dangerous and degrading, in which one became utterly dependent and easily victimized, in which control over one's future was taken out of one's own hands, the progress of the gospel cannot be impeded by Paul's imprisonment. Moreover, being in chains is not incompatible with being in Christ.

The Philippian Church and Philippi

For their part, the Philippians seem to have had a cordial relationship with Paul. They were friends in Christ and, as I have noted, Philippians is in many

15. See the discussions of Dio Cassius, Suetonius, Tacitus and Philostratus in Cassidy, *Paul in Chains*, ch 5.

16. The end of Acts seems to speak of this less severe type of confinement (28:30-31). See also Rapske, *The Book of Acts and Paul in Roman Custody*.

17. See Wansink, *Chained in Christ*, ch 1, for a discussion of Roman imprisonment culled from a wide range of sources.

respects a conventional letter of friendship. Paul reveals news about himself and others. He seeks news from the Philippians. He offers thanks and prayers for the Philippians' continued friendship with him in word and deed. As I will say repeatedly in the body of the commentary, however, as conventional as many of the motifs in Philippians are, we should not miss the fact that Paul understands his friendship with the Philippians and the conventions of friendship in a thoroughly theological way. In this respect, one might say that Paul follows his own advice in 2 Cor 10:5 and brings every thought captive to Christ. Indeed, one of Paul's purposes is to help form in the Philippians (and us) the dispositions, habits, and skills needed to understand themselves and their world in Christ.

There does not appear to be a serious theological crisis in the church at Philippi. Although Euodia and Syntyche are called to unity in 4:2-3, we have little reason to think the Philippians suffer from internal divisions similar to those of the church in Corinth. Moreover, their relationship with Paul is in good working order.

Like Paul, and because of their convictions about Christ, the Philippians face opposition (1:28). We know very little about the nature of this opposition, though Paul does talk about their suffering (1:29). Throughout the epistle Paul seems dedicated to helping the Philippians "order their common life in a manner worthy of the gospel" in a situation that is hostile to Christianity. In ch. 3 the Philippians are warned against certain characters. These seem to be members of the church, but again, we have very little information beyond what Paul says.

Although scholars have repeatedly tried to get behind the text of Philippians to a fuller historical account of the situation in Philippi, three important points must be kept in mind. First, we should follow John Barclay's advice and avoid the temptation to "mirror read" this or any other Pauline letter whenever possible.[18] We often use the Pauline letters as a mirror in which we can see reflected Paul's opponents and their arguments. In the context of a polemical letter (certainly not the case with Philippians!), Paul's concrete assertions are taken to reflect the fact that someone must have held directly opposite views. At times one needs to make such judgments, but one must be extremely cautions about taking any assertion to be directed at countering its opposite. Second, all of these reconstructions involve large amounts of speculation, and we should proportion our assent to these reconstructions in a direct relation to the amount of speculation involved. Third, while a fuller knowledge of the situation in Philippi might be of particular interest to

18. Barclay, "Mirror-Reading."

historians of early Christianity, it is not always clear that such knowledge is essential to understanding the text of Philippians. Reconstructing the history of a church in the middle part of the first century is not the same task as understanding an epistle. Thus, I will try to avoid such speculations as much as possible.

With those caveats in mind, I will note that the city of Philippi in the middle part of the first century probably had around 10,000 inhabitants. It was located in northeastern Macedonia and had a history going back to the fourth century BCE. In 42 BCE Mark Antony and Octavian (the latter of whom later became the emperor Augustus) defeated Brutus and Cassius, the assassins of Julius Caesar, in an important battle at Philippi. After Augustus secured his power over Mark Antony, he refounded Philippi as a Roman colony. At this time numerous army veterans and native Italian farmers were settled in Philippi, joining the native Thracian and Greek populace.

At this time Philippi was granted Italian legal status, exempting its colonists from various taxes and granting them citizenship and various land rights and privileges. Agriculture dominated the economy. Trade, which had a way of diffusing power in the Roman world because it demanded interaction and cooperation across ethnic groups, played a limited role in Philippi. As a result, Romans and Roman institutions exercised an unusual amount of influence. This would have included Roman religious institutions and the emperor cult in particular. In addition, a variety of other official cults seem to have been represented in Philippi as well as more popular religious movements. Outside Acts 16 we have no contemporary evidence for a Jewish population in Philippi. Moreover, the account in Acts 16 indicates that such a population would have been small indeed.[19]

Acts 16 and Philippians

For a theological commentary, this account of the beginnings of the church in Philippi found in Acts 16 will be most significant. Paul, and at least Timothy and Silas, are called into Macedonia through a vision granted to Paul. They arrive in Neapolis, the port closest to Philippi (about sixteen km. away), and from there arrive in Philippi (16:11-12). Paul and his companions go out-

---

19. One can find extensive reconstructions of social life in Philippi at this time in English in Oakes, *Philippians: From Letter to People;* de Vos, *Church and Community Conflicts;* and Bakirtzis and Koester, *Philippi at the Time of Paul.*

side the city gates to the river, to the house of prayer.[20] On their way, they begin to speak to a group of women. Among them is a Gentile woman named Lydia, who is a "God-fearer," a Gentile who worshipped the God of Israel. We also learn that Lydia is a trader in "purple cloth."

As Paul spoke to her, "the Lord opened her heart." She and her household were baptized and she offered Paul hospitality. Subsequently, as Paul and his companions are, again, on their way to the house of prayer they encounter a slave girl with a spirit of divination. She rightly divines that Paul and the others are "slaves of the most high God" and that they proclaim "a way of salvation" (16:16-17). This keeps up for several days. Finally, Paul calls the spirit out of her in the name of Jesus Christ. Her owners, seeing the profit they made from this girl going out with the spirit of divination, bring Paul and Silas before the magistrates.

They identify Paul and Silas as Jews advocating customs "which are not permissible to us Romans" (16:21). At the urging of the crowd, the magistrates have Paul and Silas beaten and then thrown into jail. Paul and Silas, displaying the joy in suffering which is so important in the epistle, are miraculously freed from their bonds. Rather than escape, Paul preaches to the jailer. This leads to the conversion and baptism of the jailer and his family. The jailer's question to Paul and Silas, "what must I do to be saved?" may reflect several different notions of salvation. At the very least, it confirms the slave girl's announcement that Paul and his companions proclaim the way of salvation.

The next day, Paul is able to rely on his own Roman citizenship to win an apology from the magistrates. After encouraging the believers in Philippi, Paul and his companions go on their way, eventually ending up in Thessalonica (17:1).

Here in Acts we can detect several points that will also be reflected in the epistle. There is the hospitable generosity of Lydia, which is reflected in the Philippians' financial partnership with Paul noted in 4:10-20. Paul is identified as a "slave of the most high God" in 4:17. In 1:1 he identifies himself (and Timothy) to the Philippians as "slaves of Christ Jesus," the one who has the name above all names (2:9-11). Paul is jailed in Philippi. Paul writes from prison to the Philippians, noting that they are in the same struggle that he is in and was in when he was with them (1:30). The civil authorities in Philippi

---

20. Luke Johnson convincingly argues that there was an actual house of prayer or synagogue here because the Greek term used for "house of prayer" in 16:16 is "virtually synonymous with 'synagogue' in Hellenistic Jewish literature." As Johnson argues, the confusion here has to do with the term "we thought" (16:13), which often, though not necessarily, refers to a mistaken assumption. In 16:16, however, Luke clearly writes as if there is a house of prayer. See Johnson, *Acts,* 292 n. 13.

seem as badly disposed toward Christianity among the inhabitants of the city (1:28-29) as they were when Paul and Silas first arrived. Finally, the joy in the midst of suffering which Paul and Silas display in the Philippian jail is precisely the joy that Paul displays for and seeks to cultivate in the Philippians in the epistle.

No claims need to be made about literary dependence here. Rather, from a theological perspective one can say that the account of the beginnings of Christianity in Philippi in Acts 16 can begin to tune our ears to hear the epistle Paul wrote to the "saints in Christ Jesus in Philippi."

Commentary on Philippians

1:1-2

1 Paul and Timothy, slaves of Christ Jesus, to all the saints in Christ Jesus who are in Philippi with the overseers and the deacons: 2 Grace to you all and peace from God our Father and the Lord Jesus Christ.

Sometimes introductions can reveal a great deal about what is to come in a text. Although there are a few hints here in these verses of themes that will re-appear later, Philippians begins in a fairly conventional way. The greeting of "grace and peace" is the way all of the Pauline letters in the NT begin. Scholars often speculate that Paul here combines the standard Greek greeting, "grace" (χάρις/*charis*), with a Greek translation of the standard Hebrew greeting, "peace" (εἰρήνη/*eirēnē* or *shalom*/שׁלוֹם). There is, however, no direct evidence for this view. Rather than explain how this standard greeting came to be, it is more important to recognize that it is a thoroughly Christian expression. It reminds us that this is a letter from Christians to Christians. Paul presumes this commonality and later in the epistle he will speak more about the nature and shape of the life he and the Philippians share in Christ.

We are further told that grace and peace come from "God our Father and the Lord Jesus Christ." Paul uses this expression in several places (Rom 1:7; Gal 1:3; 2 Cor 1:2; 2 Thess 1:2; Phlm 3; also Eph 1:2). Although this phrase is relatively common at the beginning of Paul's letters, this language also anticipates the robust christological implications behind 2:9-11. In addition, at the very beginning of the epistle we are reminded that God is source of the common life which Paul and the Philippians share in Christ. Paul will rely on the three-way nature of this relationship at several points later in the epistle.

Verse 1 identifies both the senders and the recipients of the epistle. Paul and Timothy are identified as the senders of the epistle.[1] Paul (Παῦλος/ *Paulos*) is the Greek/Latin name the apostle consistently uses in place of his Hebrew name, Saul (שָׁאוּל/*Shaul*). The change in name begins when the apostle begins his missionary activity (cf. Acts 13:9). Timothy is also listed as a sender of this epistle as in 1 and 2 Thessalonians (along with Silvanus), 2 Corinthians, Philemon, and Colossians. With the exception of Philemon and Philippians, the authors of these epistles primarily speak in the first person plural. In Philemon and here in Philippians the voice is singular and clearly Paul's rather than Timothy's.[2] Nevertheless, Phil 2:19-22 makes it clear that Timothy is well known to the Philippian Christians. Moreover, on the evidence of Acts, Timothy was present at the founding of the church (16:1, 13) and later visited the church on Paul's third missionary journey (19:22; 20:3-4).[3] It would seem, then, that Timothy is included here in the greeting of the epistle because he, too, shares in the common bond which unites Paul and the Philippians in Christ rather than because Paul seeks to buttress Timothy's authority in the light of his plans to send Timothy to Philippi.[4]

Philippians is one of the few letters where Paul does not identify himself as an apostle.[5] This may be because he has no need to assert his apostolic authority to a congregation with whom he is on such good terms. Instead, both Paul and Timothy are identified as "slaves of Christ Jesus." While many English translations prefer the word "servant," "slave" is a more accurate translation of the Greek δοῦλος/*doulos*. Readers, however, should not presume that ancient slavery was comparable with the race-based slavery practiced in the U.S. Slavery was widespread in Paul's world. Primarily, one could become a slave by being captured in battle or by falling into debt. Slaves in Paul's world

---

1. While the practice of including one's companions in the opening of a letter is quite common for Paul, it is rare in extant Greco-Roman letters. See the discussion of the evidence in Byrskog, "Co-Senders, Co-Authors," 233-36.

2. Fee, *Philippians*, 61 n. 11, is one of the most recent commentators to suggest that Timothy acted as Paul's secretary. As Bockmuehl, *Philippians*, 49, indicates, there is simply no evidence either for or against this view.

3. In addition, Acts 16:1-3 informs us that Timothy was the son of a Greek father and a Jewish Christian mother. He was from Lystra and was already a believer when he met Paul, becoming one of the apostle's closest coworkers. Eusebius identifies him as the first bishop of Ephesus (*Ecclesiastical History* 3.4). The *Acts of Timothy* (fourth century) tells of Timothy's martyrdom under Domitian in 96 C.E.

4. This is suggested by Byrskog,, "Co-Senders, Co-Authors," 246.

5. 1 and 2 Corinthians, Galatians, and, among the disputed letters, Ephesians, Colossians, and 1 and 2 Timothy all identify Paul as an apostle. Romans and Titus use the phrase "slave of Christ and apostle." 1 and 2 Thessalonians say nothing more by way of identification, and in Philemon Paul identifies himself as a "prisoner."

performed a wide variety of jobs, including working in households as well as in areas such as education and medicine.[6] One of the initial things the Philippians would want to know about any slave they encountered was to whom that slave belonged. Paul and Timothy are slaves of Christ.

This identification of Paul and Timothy as slaves of Christ is taken up in a variety of more and less direct ways in the course of the epistle. Paul's work in founding the church in Philippi was part of his service to Christ. This service provides a rationale for his care for the Philippians (1:7). Moreover, like all slaves, he is accountable to his master, who will evaluate his service. Hence, the maintenance of the Philippian congregation as a faithful witness to Christ provides a basis for evaluating Paul's service on the "day of Christ" (2:16-17).

Most importantly, however, Paul desires to see certain dispositions and habits formed in the Philippians (see especially 2:1-4, 5). These dispositions are paradigmatically exemplified by Christ, but also concretely displayed by Paul and Timothy. Hence, it is relevant that Paul and Timothy are slaves of Christ, who himself takes on the form of a slave (2:7).[7]

The recipients are initially identified here as "saints" (ἅγιοι/*hagioi*) in Christ Jesus. Indeed, with the use of "all" here Paul designates the entire congregation. This emphasis on "all" of the Philippians is picked up throughout 1:3-11 as well. The designation "saints" occurs also in the greetings of Romans, 1 and 2 Corinthians, Ephesians, and Colossians as a way of identifying the churches to whom these epistles are addressed.[8] What does this way of identifying Christian congregations tell us?

It is clear from Paul's unhesitating application of this word to the Corinthian congregations that "saints" is not primarily a reference to the moral achievements of these congregations. Rather, Paul has taken over a word used to describe Israel in the LXX and applied it to these congregations.[9] The allusions here go back to Exod 19:6; 23:22, where the Lord speaks of setting Israel apart as a "kingdom of priests and a holy nation." Further, in Leviticus the

---

6. For a useful introduction to slavery in Paul's world see Martin, *Slavery as Salvation*, and Bartchy, *MALLON CHRĒSAI*.

7. See Bockmuehl, *Philippians*, 51; also Bloomquist, *Function of Suffering*, 144. It is not clear, however, that this designation enhances Paul's credibility in the way Bloomquist thinks.

8. The use of "saints" as a form of Christian self-designation is prominent until the Montanist crisis in the late second century.

9. Interestingly, Chrysostom claims that Paul joined the term "saints" with "in Christ Jesus" to avoid any confusion with Jews (presumably in and around Philippi) who, Chrysostom thinks, would have used the term "saints" as a Jewish self-designation. See Chrysostom, *Homily* 1 on Philippians.

Lord repeatedly calls Israel to a divine holiness (11:44, 45; 19:2; 20:7, 26).[10] In part, this call is based on God's setting the people of Israel apart and delivering them up out of Egypt (11:45). Deut 7:6-8 again designates Israel as a holy people of God's own choosing and redeeming (see also 14:2, 21). Moreover, Pss 15:3; 33:9; 73:3; and 1 Macc 10:39 (LXX) also use "saints" to designate all or a part of the people of God in much the same way Paul seems to use the term.

Thus, we can say that both for the LXX and for Paul "saints" appears to designate a body of people chosen by God. The term bespeaks God's formation of a particular body of people and God's desires for them to be holy. For Paul to use this language of the Philippians is to connect them to God's activity of forming, redeeming and sanctifying a people.[11] "To us, the early Christian self-designation as 'the saints' is almost embarrassing. . . . But the word once expressed much of what was meant by 'contrast society.' The church understood itself to be the sacred people of God's possession, a people with a pattern of life which differed from that of the world."[12] In designating the congregations he addresses as "saints," Paul is indicating that they are a people set apart, not because of their moral perfection, but by the work of God.

It is important to remember, however, that the Philippians' status as "saints" is tied to being "in Christ Jesus." The real question here is what is the force of the preposition "in"? On numerous occasions Paul uses "in Christ" to speak of a distinct group or community comprised of believers.[13] In addition, recall that the use of "saints" also is tied to the formation of a particular people. This would indicate that identifying the Philippians as "saints in Christ Jesus" defines both the parameters of the community and the character of that community. Fee rightly captures both of these aspects when he notes, "That is, Christ Jesus is both responsible for their becoming the people of God, and as the crucified and risen One, he constitutes the present sphere of their new existence."[14] Being in Christ locates one within that community founded by Christ, and thereby, within the realm governed by Christ. What is not always recognized, however, is that when Paul speaks this way he is speaking in political terms. He is speaking of a community whose character and common life are defined by the lordship of Christ.

---

10. In each of these cases the phrase is "You shall be holy (ἅγιοι/*hagioi*) because I am holy (ἅγιος/*hagios*)."

11. For similar sentiments, see James's judgment in Acts 15:14 that "God is visiting the Gentiles to take out from them a people for his name."

12. Lohfink, *Jesus and Community*, 131.

13. Outside Philippians Paul uses "in Christ" in this way in at least these passages: Rom 6:11; 12:5; 1 Cor 1:2, 30; 15:22; 2 Cor 5:17; Gal 1:22; 3:28; 5:6; 1 Thess 1:1. See also Eph 1:1; Col 1:2.

14. Fee, *Philippians*, p. 65.

The next phrase of the verse geographically locates this community in Philippi. Given Philippi's status as a Roman military colony, it may be that "in Christ" and "in Philippi" can be read as setting up the two political realms vying for the allegiance of the Philippian Christians, who, ultimately, are reminded in 3:20 that their commonwealth is in heaven.

What Paul's language here simply presumes, but what contemporary Christians must remember, is that if Christ's lordship is to have any material reality in the present, then there must also be a community of people whose faith and practice, whose hopes and desires, whose very life and death, are shaped by their allegiance to their Lord. Apart from this, language about being in Christ and attempts to call Christ Lord, begin to lose their coherence. As G. Lohfink notes, "*being in Christ* means living within the realm of Christ's rule — and that realm is the church."[15] Clearly, Christians are divided over how the church should be ordered and what its constitutive practices are. This divisiveness is itself a profound wound in the body of Christ. Nevertheless, to follow Paul and to speak of the church as the body of Christ or, as in Philippians, of "saints in Christ" demands the real material presence of a community of Christians, not simply individual Christians enjoying discrete inner transactions with God. The central Christian confession that Jesus Christ is Lord calls forth and requires that community known as the church.[16]

Finally, two subgroups within the congregation are also mentioned in the greeting, the "overseers" (ἐπίσκοποι/*episkopoi*) and "deacons" (διάκονοι/*diakonoi*). This is the earliest appearance of the word "overseer" in the NT. While "elder" and "overseer" seem to be used interchangeably in other early texts such as Acts (especially 20:17-28), the Pastorals, and *1 Clement*, at least by the late second century "overseer" becomes distinct from "elder" and signifies the first of the church's three orders of ministry, bishops. But bishops did not cease to be elders. The development of the episcopate out of the presbytery was "not so much an isolated act as a progressive development, not advancing everywhere at a uniform rate, but exhibiting at one and the same time different stages of growth at different churches."[17]

15. See *Jesus and Community*, p. 127; also Fowl, "Some Uses of Story," for a similar argument about the way the phrase "in Christ" functions in Rom 6.

16. Although the context is quite different, this is, in part, what Cyprian understood when he indicated that "outside the Church there is no salvation" (*Epistle* 73.21). For a contemporary articulation of this position see Hauerwas, *After Christendom,* ch 1.

17. See J. B. Lightfoot, "The Christian Ministry," which appeared as a dissertation appended to his 1868 commentary on Philippians. The quotation is from the sixth edition (1881), 227. For a thorough account of the development of Christian ministry that notes discussions since Lightfoot see J. T. Burtchaell, *From Synagogue to Church.*

Paul is not talking about the monarchical episcopate in its later forms here in Philippians. Nevertheless, he does single out these two groups in the greeting. Although we are not likely to learn the precise nature and composition of these two groups, it is still intriguing to ask why Paul mentions them here in the greeting of the epistle. There are two basic positions that most commentators adopt here. One holds that this reference anticipates the comments of 4:2-3 directed at Euodia and Syntyche, who were clearly leaders in the congregation and were quarreling with each other. "Thus, both the 'all' with which the address begins and the addition of 'with the overseers and the deacons' at the end anticipate the problem of friction that has arisen within the community, perhaps within the leadership itself."[18] The nature and extent of the "friction" within the community, however, are extremely unclear. Equally unclear are the formal positions of Euodia and Syntyche within the leadership of the community. Hence, in regard to this proposal, one can only say "perhaps."

The other view goes back at least as far as Chrysostom. It argues that the "overseers and deacons" were the ones responsible for sending Epaphroditus to Paul.[19] One might well have expected, however, that these leaders would have again been mentioned in 4:10-20. Again, there is no strong evidence to tip the scales in the direction of either of these possibilities.

Given the very limited scope of our information, we simply have to say that while these two terms indicate offices within the church, we do not really know very much about what those offices involved in the NT period outside the discussion in 1 Tim 3:1-13. More importantly, for the purposes of understanding Philippians, we do not really know why Paul mentioned these two groups here at the beginning of the epistle. It is, however, important to note that Paul designates himself as a "slave" and not an apostle, while addressing himself to "overseers and deacons." We may not have reason to assume that these "overseers and deacons" needed to be reminded that they, too, were slaves of Christ. Nevertheless, the juxtaposition of Paul the apostle, yet slave, with the "overseers and deacons" should remind all holders of church office that "slave of Christ" is a more foundational identity marker for Christians than "apostle," "overseer," or "deacon."

Within this greeting we have the initial hints of two major theological themes in Philippians which Paul will develop in the course of the epistle. The first concerns the common bond in Christ which unites Paul, the Philippians, and God in a three-way relationship. The second theme which Paul hints at

18. Fee, *Philippians*, 69. Hawthorne, *Philippians*, 10 holds a similar view.
19. This view is also advocated by Witherington, *Friendship and Finances*, 31.

concerns the material, political visibility of the Philippian Christian community. As the epistle moves on to 1:3-8 Paul more directly discusses the nature of his relationship with the Philippians in Christ.

1:3-11

3 I thank my God because of all my remembrances of you. 4 I always make each of my prayers for you with joy 5 because of your participation with me in the gospel from the first day until now. 6 I am also confident that the one who began a good work in you will carry it through to completion at the day of Christ.

7 It is right for me to exercise this judgment about you all because I hold you in my heart, for you all are fellow sharers with me in grace, both in my chains and in the defense and establishment of the gospel. 8 For God is my witness of how I long for you all with the affection of Christ Jesus. 9 And I pray that your love may abound yet more and more in knowledge and all moral understanding 10 so that you may be able to discern and determine what is best in order that you might be people of sincerity and integrity for the day of Christ, 11 having been filled with the fruit of righteousness which comes through Jesus Christ to the glory and praise of God.

Paul regularly begins his epistles with some form of thanksgiving (see 1 Thess 1:2; 1 Cor 1:4; Rom 1:8; Col 1:3; Phlm 4) and Philippians is similar in this regard. Nevertheless, Paul is doing more than expressing thanks in these verses. For example, the structure of vv. 3-8 indicates that the entire passage is governed by Paul's expression of thanks to God.[1] While Paul begins by addressing God, it is hard to escape the implication that at least by v. 6 and perhaps by v. 5, Paul is actually addressing the Philippians, describing his recollections of them and framing his relationship to them in the course of thanking God.

Several scholars argue that in this paragraph Paul is implicitly thanking the Philippians for their financial gifts to him, which he then does explicitly in 4:10-20.[2] On the one hand, their Philippians' financial support of Paul

---

1. In Greek vv. 3-8 comprise a single sentence governed by the main verb "I thank" (εὐχαριστῶ/*eucharistō*).

2. The two strongest proponents of this view are O'Brien, *Philippians*, 56-60, and Peterman, *Paul's Gift*, 90-99. One of the first arguments Peterman makes is to note what he takes to be significant conceptual and verbal parallels between 1:3-11 and 4:10-20. It is important to remember that these parallels presuppose certain interpretive decisions and should not be used as evidence to adjudicate those disputes as Witherington, *Friendship and Finances*, 38, does. For example, if I am right that there are significant differences between the use of συγκοινωνούς in 1:7 and συγκοινωνήσαντες in 4:14, then this is not a parallel that can advance any interpretive

must be included in any account of their participation in the gospel.[3] Their past financial gifts are part of Paul's joyful recollections of them. On the other hand, the linguistic evidence in 1:3-11 simply will not support the claim that here Paul is primarily referring to the Philippians' financial assistance in the thanks he offers to God. Rather, Paul incorporates all aspects of his relations with the Philippians under the rubric of κοινωνία/*koinōnia*, which is often translated as "fellowship," "partnership," "sharing," or "communion" (see 1:5).

Paul begins this section by thanking God because[4] of his recollections of the Philippians.[5] That is, instead of thanking God for the Philippians, Paul thanks God because of his remembrance of them. Already we see Paul drawing the Philippians into his thanks to God in a way that establishes the three-way nature of this relationship. Paul's memories of the Philippians inspire

argument. Of course, if one presumes a tripartite letter with letter A (4:10-20) preceding letter B (1:3–3:1), then it is much easier to make this case. See, for example, Reumann, "Contributions of the Philippian Community," especially 441: "Having acknowledged the Philippians' gifts in Letter A, Paul need only allude to them in the prooimium in Letter B."

3. Although Peterman, *Paul's Gift*, 99-103, does tend to read v. 5 as a reference to something broader than just the financial gift, his reading of this whole passage is decisively shaped by his reading of v. 3. This is, of course, as it should be. Once a commentator takes a particular stand on a problematic verse, consistency may well demand that this decision determines the way a host of other verses are read.

4. The closest Pauline parallel here in Phlm 4. Even here, however, Paul thanks God when he remembers Philemon not because of his memories of Philemon. There is an interpretive ambiguity in this verse concerning the preposition ἐπί/*epi* ("because"). Normally, one would expect περί/*peri* ("concerning, for") to introduce the object of Paul's thanksgiving (cf. Rom 1:8; 1 Cor 1:4; Col 1:3; 1 Thess 1:2). Instead, Paul uses ἐπί/*epi* to introduce the cause of his thanksgiving. The case for the causal reading of ἐπί/*epi* is strong. In 1 Cor 1:4 and, most importantly, Phil 1:5 ἐπί/*epi* with the dative is used to express cause. Moreover, extra-biblical literature commonly uses similar constructions to the one Paul uses here to express cause for thanks. See the discussion in Reed, *Discourse Analysis*, 199-200.

5. The next interpretive ambiguity concerns the nature of the genitive "of you" (ὑμῶν/*hymōn*). Does it refer to Paul's remembrance of the Philippians (objective genitive), or the Philippians' remembering of Paul (subjective genitive)? Because it seems best to take ἐπί/*epi* as an indication of cause, those who see this as an expression of thanks for the Philippians' financial gift take Paul to be saying something like "I thank my God because of your remembrance of me." Specifically, this would be a reference to the financial gift that the Philippians sent to Paul in prison via Epaphroditus (2:25, 30; 4:10, 18).

Interpreting ἐπί/*epi* in this causal sense, however, need not entail that one interpret "of you" (ὑμῶν/*hymōn*) as a subjective genitive. In fact, the weight of evidence rather favors an objective genitive interpretation (against O'Brien, *Philippians*, and Peterman, *Paul's Gift*, 93-98). As Reed, *Discourse Analysis*, 201, decisively shows, in Greek letters when expressions of remembrance are used in this way the pronoun always refers to the person being remembered, not the one doing the remembering. Hence, the best linguistic evidence would lead one to read ἐπί/*epi* as introducing the cause of Paul's thanksgiving to God and ὑμῶν/*hymōn* as an objective genitive.

thanks to the God who is both the source and sustainer of their friendship. Recalling the Philippians not only inspires Paul to thank God, it also means that Paul's continual pattern of prayer for the Philippians is an occasion for joy. Thus in the course of offering thanks to God, Paul is at the same time conveying his own disposition towards the entire Philippian congregation.[6]

Paul's prayers for the Philippians are joyful because of their partnership or fellowship with him in the gospel. Paul and the Philippians are joined in a common enterprise that is not of their own making. Yes, their participation included their financial gifts to Paul. But it was not simply or primarily constituted by those gifts. For example, in 4:15 Paul uses similar language explicitly, but not exclusively, to speak in terms of the Philippians' financial support of his ministry.[7] Similar language is also used in Rom 15:26 and 2 Cor 9:13 to describe the Romans' and the Corinthians' contributions to the collection Paul hoped to bring to Jerusalem (see also 2 Cor 8:4). The great difference between Rom 15:26; 2 Cor 9:13; and Phil 4:15, on the one hand, and the language of 1:5, on the other hand, is that in 1:5 it is "the gospel" rather than financial gifts which governs the understanding of the Philippians' participation with Paul.[8] The question is not whether financial relationships (in the first century and today) are parts of larger networks of practices and relationships. They clearly are. Rather, the question for us is whether the financial relationship between Paul and the Philippians is the basis of their friendship and the driving force behind the epistle.

Shifting the emphasis away from a more limited reference to a financial relationship between Paul and the Philippians enables us to recognize that at

6. This is the second time in the first four verses of the epistle where Paul has used some version of "all" (πᾶς/*pas*) to emphasize the whole church in Philippi. "There is a studied repetition of the word 'all' in this epistle, when the Philippian Church is mentioned: see 1:1, 7, 8, 25; 2:17; 4:21. It is impossible not to connect this recurrence of the word with the strong and repeated exhortations to unity which the epistle contains: 1:27; 2:1-4; 4:2, 3, 5" (Lightfoot, *Philippians*, 83).

7. See the discussion in Peterman, *Paul's Gift*, 99-103, and his subsequent argument that 4:10-20 is not solely about a commercial relationship. Interestingly, Chrysostom reads 1:5 in the light of conventions of reciprocity. Christians are to follow the Philippians' example and minister to the needs of the saints, so that they will receive a share of the saints' reward. He supports this by a particular reading of Luke 16:9. Christians are to use unrighteous mammon to establish friendship with the saints so that the saints will receive them into their eternal tabernacles (see Homily 1).

8. Fee, *Philippians*, 84 argues, ". . . the best understanding of 'your *koinonia* in the gospel' is that which takes the word first of all in its 'neutral' sense to refer to their participation in spreading the gospel itself, in every possible way, which in particular includes their recent partnership in the gospel by sending him a gift while he is imprisoned for the defense of the gospel." See also Lohmeyer, *an die Philipper*, 17.

a more basic level, Paul is using the language of friendship. Within this friendship (as with most forms of Greco-Roman friendship), the giving and receiving of gifts is an important element.[9] Nevertheless, it is premature to focus too closely on that particular element at this juncture in the epistle. Paul here invokes language of friendship or fellowship in the gospel to situate his relationship with the Philippians. The gospel both establishes the relationship between Paul and the Philippians and provides a space or context within which that relationship will grow. The gospel provides the body of shared convictions and social and ecclesial conventions within which this friendship can develop.[10] As Paul develops the discussion in 1:7, 14-17, 27–2:18, it becomes clear that the gospel is not something the Philippians share in because they financially support Paul's apostolic work. Rather, this material sharing arises from and witnesses to a larger body of shared convictions and practices, which need to shape both Paul's relationship with the Philippians and the way in which the Philippians order their common life. Thus, it becomes clear that while Paul is using language and conventions associated in the Greco-Roman world with friendship, the nature of Christian friendship is going to differ from, say, Aristotelian or Stoic notions of friendship. The differences reflected in the convictions and practices provided by the gospel, and at least partially articulated in the course of Philippians, largely account for the differences between friendship in the Pauline churches and other versions of Greco-Roman friendship.

I will speak more about some of these differences in the final section of this volume. For now, let me briefly indicate one crucial difference Christian convictions and practices make for notions of friendship. Paul, the Philippians, and all their contemporaries would have recognized that one element in friendship is the giving and receiving of gifts. Within most forms of Greco-Roman friendship, this practice of giving and receiving gifts was a way in which one acquired a much more important commodity, honor. In the competitive economy of honor which framed Greco-Roman friendships, money was something one spent or gave in order to solidify or increase one's status. Giving increased one's status and put others in one's debt.[11] This is very

9. See Aristotle, *Nicomachean Ethics* 5.5.14.

10. Aristotle is perhaps the ancient writer that reflects most clearly the importance of a shared body of convictions and social conventions for the discussion and practice of friendship to even get off the ground (see *Nicomachean Ethics* 8 and 9). Obviously, however, these are not the convictions and conventions of the heavenly commonwealth.

11. Even in Aristotle's most complete form of friendship, the friendship of virtuous people, there is a "friendly" competition in virtue and the honor which may accompany it. Indeed such friends' love for each other is meant to reflect the comparative worth of the friend

different from friendships in Christ which seek to imitate Christ's refusal to use his divine status for his own advantage, and Christ's willed self-emptying on behalf of others (2:6-7). The economy of God as revealed in the life, death, and resurrection of Christ, puts the giving and receiving of gifts into a very different context. Within this context formed by the life, death, and resurrection of Christ, the circulation of gifts becomes a way in which Christians participate by analogy in the life of God. At its best, this economy is non-competitive, seeking the benefit of others rather than oneself (2:4). Moreover, unlike the economy of honor, it is driven by the superabundance of love rather than lack or absence. In Philippians 4:10-20 Paul will set the Philippians' gift to him into this christologically formed context. The point here is not that conventional Greco-Roman friendships were purely self-serving affairs. Rather, like all friendships, they were animated by assumptions about the world, humans' place in the world, and the proper end of human life. Paul's claims indicate ways in which life in Christ is animated by a different set of assumptions.

By the end of v. 5 Paul notes that the Philippians' participation in the gospel begins from the very start of the church in Philippi, and is not limited solely to the time of Paul's present imprisonment. This remark sets up Paul's comments in v. 6 about his hopes for the Philippians' future. Verse 5 introduces an unbroken continuity in the Philippians' participation in the gospel from "the first day" to "now." This continuity will be brought to its proper end in "the day of Christ." Because of the Philippians' persistent fellowship in the gospel with Paul, he is in a position to make confident judgments about the ways and extent to which God will work in them.

By the time we get to vv. 6ff. it becomes clear that although Paul is still ostensibly offering thanks to God, he is also specifically addressing the Philippians and their relationship to God. This is particularly true in the light of v. 7's claim that it is right for Paul to exercise this judgment "about you all."

Given this shift in address, Paul confidently assures the Philippians that God has both started a good work in them and will bring that work to its proper end at the day of Christ.[12] This good work could be characterized as

---

(*Nicomachean Ethics* 8.7.7). Even in such forms of friendship Aristotle notes that the friend who sacrifices money and even his life for his friends still achieves for himself something better (*Nicomachean Ethics* 9.8.20).

12. Some read both v. 5 and the "good work" mentioned here in v. 6 as referring to a financial gift. This misses the point that the "good work" is clearly what God has done in the Philippians and not anything the Philippians have done for Paul (see Gundry-Volf, *Paul and Perseverance*, 34). If one follows the "financial gift" interpretation, it is probably better to see this good work which the Philippians have done for Paul to be evidence of and testimony to the good work God has initiated in them (see O'Brien, *Philippians*, 64.).

God bringing the Philippians into the economy of salvation. While the Philippians' participation in the gospel might justify Paul's joyful prayers to God, Paul grounds his confidence about their salvation in the faithfulness of God.[13]

Paul's confidence in v. 6 is not directed toward what has happened in the past (as in v. 5) but where things are going in the future (cf. Isa 41:1-5). The God who began a good work in the Philippians is going to bring it to completion. This notion that God's work in the life of the Philippian congregation is yet to be completed complements Paul's own reflections on his own life in 3:12-14. In both instances Paul's discussion hangs on two important theological assertions. The first is that our participation in the gospel is not so much marked by a single point as by a process through which we are transformed and drawn into ever deeper communion with God and others. Within this way of thinking it becomes very difficult to draw clear temporal distinctions between "salvation" and "sanctification." Paul, and the logic of Christian doctrine more generally, presumes that joining or being incorporated into the body of Christ entails that one's allegiances, commitments, habits, thoughts, and dispositions are all submitted to Christ, the Lord. To pick up imagery that Paul will use later in Philippians, entry into the body of Christ is like changing one's citizenship. It is to enter a realm founded, shaped, and directed by God. Drawing people into this realm and sustaining them in it is God's good work in the life of the Philippian church, in Paul's own circumstances, and in the life of contemporary Christian communities.

As Paul notes here in v. 6, God is faithfully moving the life of this realm ruled by Christ toward its climax at "the day of Christ Jesus." This phrase echoes OT images of the "day of the Lord." This is both a time of judgment and consummation. For Paul, it is clearly linked with Christ's *parousia*.[14] Of course, for Christians, the *parousia* signifies an important transformation in the manner of our participation in the life of God. It does not, however, signify an end to that process in which we are drawn into ever deeper communion with God. Rather, to taste a measure of this communion with God is to develop an insatiable appetite for more. This point is made most succinctly by Gregory of Nyssa who states, "This truly is the vision of God: never to be satisfied in the desire to see him."[15]

The second theological conviction underlying Paul's claims here has to

---

13. See Gundry-Volf, *Paul and Perseverance*, 47.

14. See Rom 13:12; 1 Cor 1:8; 3:13; 5:5; 2 Cor 1:14; Phil 1:10; 2:16; 1 Thess 5:2, 4 for Pauline variations on this phrase.

15. *Life of Moses* 2.233. See below on 3:12-18.

do with God's providence. Not only does the Philippian church participate in God's good work, it is a work which God will bring to its proper end. The church is a community which has a destiny, an end, or *telos* given by God. The church is not subject to fate or indiscriminate circumstances. Paul will draw out several significant implications of this in his subsequent discussion. For example, his convictions about God's providence provide him with a different set of lenses through which he views both his and the Philippians' circumstances. Although Paul and all Christians recognize that the ways, movements, and timing of God's good work are often obscure to us, Paul is not totally in the dark about God's providential dealings with the world. These dealings are decisively displayed in the life, death, and resurrection of Jesus. Because both Paul and the Philippians participate in that body which is formed and sustained by Christ's life, death, and resurrection, they confidently hope that they, too, will participate in God's subjection of all things under Christ's rule. Because they know that God is moving the world in this way, they can narrate and describe the events around them in that light and in a manner different from those who do not recognize God's providence. This will become clearer in Paul's discussion of his own circumstances in 1:12-26 and in his reading of the Philippians' circumstances in 1:27–2:18.

Although it is possible to speculate about whether Paul's claims in v. 6 are a response to some concrete circumstances in the community,[16] it seems equally plausible to see this verse as a straightforward claim that God is the guarantor of the Philippians' future without having to claim that there were some in the congregation who doubted this. Nevertheless, given Paul's imprisonment and the indications that the community was experiencing some form of opposition, it may be that a claim such as we find here in v. 6 is designed to reassure the Philippians. Despite current opposition and suffering, God had not abandoned and would not abandon the Philippians. This sentiment does not require us to read more into the Philippians' situation than the epistle itself reveals.

Alternatively, whatever reassurances Paul's claims about God's providence might provide the Philippians, this should not be read as a form of theodicy. Paul is not seeking to justify God's goodness in the face of the Philippians' suffering. Indeed, Paul and Jesus, too, presume that suffering for

---

16. Fee, *Philippians*, 88. "While the final phrase in v. 5 undoubtedly *triggered* this clause, its form — especially the language of 'persuasion' and the emphasis on God's 'bringing to conclusion' what he has begun in/among them — suggests that its primary *raison d'etre* has to do with a larger issue brewing in the Phil. community. We may not have full certainty as to the reason for it, but several moments in this letter suggest that some of them had begun to lose the basic eschatological orientation that marks all truly Christian life."

one's Christian convictions is always a distinct possibility in a world that persistently rejects Christ. Paul does not see any disjunction here between his and the Philippians' circumstances, on the one hand, and their common convictions about God, on the other hand, which would call forth something like a theodicy.

As this passage continues in v. 7, and on into v. 8, Paul provides a justification for the thanks he has offered in vv. 3-6. In v. 7 Paul claims to be justified in his thanks to God, in his joyful recollections of the Philippians and their participation in the gospel, in his perception of the work God has started in them, and in his confidence that God will bring that work to its appropriate completion in the day of Christ.

All these activities of recollection, perception, accounting for, and hopeful anticipation, are included in the phrase translated as "exercising judgment" in v. 7. Because the Greek word behind this translation is so crucial to the argument of Philippians, I will spend a little time here discussing it.[17] Φρονεῖν/*phronein* is very difficult to translate neatly into English. Although not very common in the NT outside of Philippians, the verb and its noun form φρόνησις/*phronēsis* are quite common in Greek, particularly in discussions of the moral life. The verb occurs ten times in Philippians, often at crucial places. In 2:2 (where it is used twice) and in 4:2 it describes an activity which is essential for the Philippians to engage in if they are to be unified in the ways Paul wishes. In 2:5 it reflects the patterns of thinking, feeling, and acting the Philippians are to embody in conformity to Christ. In 3:15-19 φρονεῖν/*phronein* occurs 3 times, again to talk about a comprehensive pattern of judgment that involves thinking, feeling, and acting. In 4:10 it occurs twice in reference to the Philippians' disposition toward Paul, particularly their habit of sending him financial gifts.

The English phrase "practical reasoning" is often used in scholarly literature, especially in reference to ancient moral philosophy, as a description of the activities noted by φρονεῖν/*phronein* and φρόνησις/*phronēsis*. Sometimes we simply find an English transliteration like *phronesis* used. Other times the English word "prudence" is used, following the Latin *prudentia,* which is what Aquinas uses to translate φρόνησις/*phronēsis* in Aristotle. If, however, one is not familiar with the Thomistic usage, the English word "prudence" seems old-fashioned. For the purposes of Phil 1:7 it seemed most adequate to use the

---

17. Regarding the importance of this word for the argument of Philippians as a whole Wayne Meeks notes, "Although Paul does not use the noun, we may say with some cogency that this letter's most comprehensive purpose is the shaping of Christian *phronēsis*, a practical moral reasoning that is 'conformed to [Christ's] death' in hope of his resurrection" (Meeks, "The Man From Heaven," 333).

phrase "exercise judgment." That is, Paul is claiming to be justified in his judgments about the Philippians and about God's action among them. At other places I will translate the verb slightly differently to convey more adequately what I take to be Paul's particular point.

As the present context makes clear, however, this form of judgment is not a strictly intellectual matter. Remember, Paul expresses his judgments about God's work in himself and in the Philippians in the context of prayer and thanksgiving. Judgment in this respect is not separated from prayer and thanksgiving. Moreover, Paul's judgment is supported by the fact that he holds them all in his heart.[18] Paul can exercise this particular judgment about God's activity in the life of the Philippian church because he holds them in his heart. I will say more about the connection between love, prayer, knowledge, and judgment in a moment.

The Philippians occupy this special place in Paul's heart because he and they are participants together in grace.[19] The subsequent phrase, "both in my chains and in the defense and establishment of the gospel," describes the manner in which the Philippians are partakers with Paul in grace. Given the end of Acts, it seems that Paul was indeed chained to a soldier. Nevertheless, it is probably best to take his mention of his chains here as a metonymic reference to his overall captivity.[20] The Greek terms translated "defense" and "establishment" are most at home in a legal context, but are not confined to such a context.[21] Interestingly, although Paul is in chains, it is the gospel which is under attack, requiring "defense and establishment." This separation of Paul's circumstances and the ultimate progress of the gospel becomes a crucial element in understanding 1:12-26. Here, in v. 7 he makes that initial separation, opening up the prospect that God's providential advance of the gospel is not directly tied to one's estimation of Paul's circumstances. Of course, since the Philippians are

---

18. Although there may be some initial ambiguity about the subject and object of this clause, Jeffrey T. Reed has shown that in an infinitive construction followed by two accusatives, as here in v. 7, the first accusative is the subject and the second is the object (Reed, "The Infinitive").

19. The Greek here is a bit ambiguous. I have taken the first person pronoun (μοῦ/*mou*) as modifying "fellow sharers" (συγκοινωνούς/*synkoinōnous*) rather than "grace" (χάριτος/ *charitos*), following Fee, *Philippians*, 91 n. 88; Lightfoot, *Philippians*, 85. O'Brien, *Philippians*, 70, offers the best reasons for this. The difference is the claim that the Philippians are "fellow sharers with me in grace" rather than "fellow sharers in my grace."

20. See Rapske, *The Book of Acts and Paul in Roman Custody.*

21. The first term, ἀπολογία/*apologia*, refers to a defense that one would make in the light of an accusation (see Acts 25:16; 2 Tim 4:16; also Acts 22:1; 1 Cor 9:3 in oppositional but not strictly legal contexts and 1 Pet 3:15). The second term, βεβαίωσις/*bebaiōsis*, is used to refer to a guarantee or security given against a promise (Heb 6:16 uses it of an oath).

fellow participants with Paul in grace, they, too, will need to learn to understand the implications of this separation in the light of their own context.

Thus, the second part of v. 7 asserts that Paul is justified in the judgments about the Philippians which he articulates in the previous verses. This justification stems from the fact that he holds the Philippians in his heart. His affection is tied to the fact that he and they are fellow sharers in grace. Their fellowship is thus cast in terms of Paul's chains and the defense and confirmation of the gospel.

Although commentators agree about the force of Paul's comments here, they are divided in their assessment of the practices and the situations that lie behind Paul's claims. Some argue that the Philippians, by means of their financial provision for Paul, have become fellow participants in Paul's chains and defense and confirmation of the gospel. They take the reference in v. 7 to being "fellow sharers" with Paul in grace as a reference to this financial gift.[22] The primary support for this view comes from the use of "fellow sharers" in 4:14 to refer to the Philippians' financial provisions for Paul. Since the same word is used here in 1:7, this must also be a reference to the Philippians' financial gift to Paul.

Several arguments tell against reading v. 7 as such a narrow reference. First, in 4:14 the term refers to someone providing something for another.[23] The point of v. 7, however, is to note that Paul and the Philippians have been joint recipients of something (cf. the usage in Rom 15:27). "In 1.7 the Philippians definitely receive a share in the grace. Any attempt to make the συγκοινωνούς ['fellow sharers'] of 1.7 perform both functions, meaning 'shared' in the sense of 'provided' (which is the meaning in 4.14) and 'shared' in the sense of 'receiving', looks like exegetical slight of hand. 1.7 seems unequivocally to mean 'received, alongside me, a share of grace'. Even if Paul is thinking about financial support rather than suffering, we cannot draw in 4:14 as an explanation of his language."[24]

We will better understand v. 7 if we focus on the "grace" in which Paul and the Philippians are fellow participants or sharers. In this respect 1:27-30 give us some further insight. There we learn that the Philippians have been given grace not only to believe in Christ but to suffer for Christ (1:29). Further, in 1:30 Paul links the Philippians' suffering to his own. Thus, not only is the Philippians' faith in continuity with Paul's, their suffering is also analogous to his own.

22. Most notably, O'Brien, *Philippians*, 70.
23. Compare the similar usage in Rom 12:13.
24. Oakes, "Jason and Penelope," 164.

Given the way this point is developed in 1:27-30, we should, therefore, read 1:7 as Paul's initial attempt to draw a parallel between his chains and his defense and confirmation of the gospel, on the one hand, and the common life and mission of the church in Philippi, on the other. It is primarily in this respect that Paul sees the Philippians as fellow participants with him in grace. Yes, the Philippians' financial gift to Paul would be included under this more general account, but it is included indirectly and by implication.

Rather than focusing on the Philippians' gift to Paul, this verse introduces what I take to be a theologically more significant aspect of Philippians. This has to do with the type and manner of judgment which Paul exercises here in v. 7 as he begins to connect his situation to that of the Philippian congregation. Paul claims to be thankfully confident in the Philippians, as he is in himself (1:12-14, 19), because he and they are fellow participants in similar situations for Christ's sake. Therefore, they will, Paul hopes, act in analogous ways. Paul's abilities to narrate his and the Philippians' situations in such a way as to demonstrate their similarities are an essential element in making this judgment. On the basis of these similarities, he can then argue that the Philippians should adopt similar or analogous patterns of life.

In v. 8 Paul reiterates his expression of affection which he began in v. 7. This verse expands the notion of having the Philippians in his heart. Paul "longs" for the Philippians. Paul uses this same expression to express his longing for other churches as well (see 1 Thess 3:6; Rom 1:11; 2 Tim 1:4). It is also the term used in 2:26 of Epaphroditus's longing for the Philippians. In addition to deepening the notion of Paul having the Philippians in his heart, the longing here is given christological focus by the phrase, "with the affection of Christ Jesus." Thus, Paul's longing is not simply a personal yearning. Rather, it reflects the love Christ has for the Philippians.

In these verses Paul expresses his heartfelt thanks to God for the Philippians and for their common friendship in the gospel. At the same time, Paul strengthens the bonds between himself and the Philippians by, at least indirectly, addressing them through his prayer to God. As will become clear, this is more than just cultivating the good feeling that convention demands from a letter of friendship. Paul is going to propose that his friends in Philippi adopt the pattern of life worthy of the gospel (1:27). That pattern will draw its coherence from the story of Christ narrated in 2:6-11 and will be exemplified by Paul, Timothy, and Epaphroditus. Here in 1:3-8 Paul establishes for the Philippians the plausibility of such a pattern of life because he and they are already fellow participants in the gospel.

Having mentioned his disposition to pray for the Philippians in v. 4, Paul actually presents a prayer for them in vv. 9-11. He begins by praying that their love may abound yet more and more. The use of a present tense verb here denotes a continuous growth in love.[25] As Chrysostom notes, growth in love is a "good of which there is not satiety."[26]

The object of the Philippians' abounding love is left undefined. In a similar passage Paul explicitly prays that the Thessalonians may "abound in love for one another and all people" (1 Thess 3:12). Further, in Phil 2:2 Paul urges the Philippians to have "the same love." In 2:2 it seems clearer that the focus of this love is the love they have for each other. Hence, it seems reasonable to read the prayer in 1:9 in this light.

The abundant love Paul prays for is to be accompanied by "knowledge"[27] and "moral understanding."[28] This phrase indicates the manner in which their love is to abound. These verses are "the New Testament's most profound and precise statement about the influence of *agape* from the intellectual and moral point of view, in this world or in the next."[29] It is theologically interesting to note here that knowledge arises out of love and not the other way around. Drawing from 1 John 2:27 and John 16:13 Aquinas indicates that the Spirit with which believers are anointed provides them with knowledge and truth, and that the Spirit is charity or love. This would indicate that charity (via the Spirit's presence in the lives of believers) gives rise to knowledge (the truth into which the Spirit leads believers). Aquinas then goes on to explain how love concretely gives rise to knowledge. "The reason for this is that when a person has a habit,[30] if that habit is right, then right judgment of things pertaining to that habit follows from it. . . . Now all things that are done by us must be informed by charity. Therefore a person with charity has

---

25. Both the manuscript evidence and the context strongly favor the present over the aorist. See Lightfoot's comments, *Philippians*, 86.

26. *Homily* 2.

27. In the introductory thanksgivings of so-called captivity letters Paul consistently prays for "knowledge" (ἐπίγνωσις/*epignōsis*) for those to whom he is writing (see Eph 1:17; Col 1:9-10; Phlm 6). In these contexts the word seems to indicate a conceptual grasp of a truth about life in the Spirit. See O'Brien, *Philippians*, 76.

28. The word here translated "moral understanding" (αἴσθησις/*aisthēsis*) does not occur elsewhere in the NT. In the LXX the word occurs 28 times, all but 6 of them in Proverbs. In Proverbs it is often used in parallel with "wisdom," "conscience," and "practical wisdom" (φρόνησις/*phronēsis*) (Prov 1:7; 2:3, 10; 3:20; 8:10; 18:15; 19:25; 24:4). This would seem to indicate that the word implies not simply knowledge but a sort of moral wisdom. This fits with the secular Greek usage of the word to indicate insight and experience which lead to and reflect moral understanding. See BAGD, 25.

29. Spicq, *Agape*, 2:277.

30. The English "habit" is used here to translate the Latin *habitus*. A *habitus* is a settled disposition to act in a certain way. In this case, charity is seen as a *habitus*, see Aquinas, 62.

a correct judgment both in regard to things knowable; . . . and in regard to things to be done."[31]

If we are to follow Aquinas and, ultimately, Paul in this, we will have to shift our notions of love away from the overly romantic and sentimentalized versions of love so common in our current culture. Instead we should see love as a "habit." Love needs to become an established disposition within us. This does not simply happen overnight. Rather, love becomes a habit for us as we undergo spiritual formation. Over time through prayer, contemplation, and action we become loving people. To the extent that such a disposition becomes stable within us, we have developed that habit of love. Then that love informs our judgments and actions so that they generate knowledge and moral wisdom. In this way abounding love leads to knowledge and moral wisdom. Paul's claim in v. 7 also demonstrated this. Remember that Paul's wisdom and judgments about the Philippians and God's action in their lives are expressed in the context of prayer and thanksgiving and supported by the love he has for them.

It should thus become clear that love, prayer, knowledge, and the wisdom needed to live faithful lives are not separable components of the Christian life. Rather they are a set of interconnected habits that we must seek to cultivate and nurture over a lifetime. Growth in one of these habits will as a matter of course lead to growth in the others. Failure or frustration in one will ultimately manifest itself in more comprehensive forms of failure and frustration. The following verses will also have more to say about this.

As the prayer continues, Paul desires that such growth in wisdom will allow the Philippians to discern, test, and determine what is worthwhile. Paul uses similar vocabulary in Rom 2:18, where this idea of determining what is superior is linked to knowledge of God's will. As Paul's prayer here develops, we see that abounding love leads to knowledge and wisdom, which lead to an ability to discern those things which are good and worthwhile. As the prayer continues, it becomes clear that this ability to make moral discriminations will result in the Philippians leading lives of absolute integrity.[32] Fee may well

---

31. Aquinas, *Philippians*, 63.

32. Paul uses two adjectives to describe this integrity. The first, "sincerity" (εἰλικρινῆς/ *eilikrinēs*), occurs only here in Paul (the only other NT occurrence is 2 Pet 3:1). Paul uses the noun in 1 Cor 5:8; 2 Cor 1:12; 2:17. In all of these cases the word denotes sincerity. Moreover, in 2 Corinthians Paul uses the term to defend his ministry in a context where Paul's motives were either unclear or suspect. In Phil 1:10 "sincerity" is coupled with "integrity." The Greek word here, ἀπρόσκοπος/*aproskopos*, seems to be used in the light of 1 Cor 10:32, where Paul speaks of actions that do "not give offense" (with Fee, *Philippians*, 102, and contra Lightfoot, *Philippians*, 87, who reads εἰλικρινῆς/*eilikrinēs* in relation to Acts 24:16, taking the word intransitively as "without stumbling").

be right in claiming that "The behavior of some appears to have the latent possibility of 'mixed motives,' or at least is a potential source of offense."[33] We should not, however, move from Paul's prayer that the Philippians' lives be characterized in a certain way to an assumption that there were some in the congregation lacking in this respect. The purity and integrity Paul desires for the Philippians is not a one-time achievement. Rather, it denotes their proper end. It is to mark their lives "for the day of Christ."[34] Thus, we see that the spiritual formation represented by the cultivation of love, knowledge, prayer, and moral wisdom in the previous verses is wholly directed toward preparing us for our ultimate end in Christ, holiness.

The prayer concludes with Paul's desire that the Philippians might be filled with the "fruit of righteousness." It would appear from the way the definite article is placed in the Greek that the phrase is a way of indicating that Paul is praying for the Philippians to be filled with the fruit which is righteousness and which comes through Jesus Christ.[35] This notion should be read in the light of the contrast Paul draws in 3:6-9 between the righteousness found in the law and the righteousness which comes through faith in Christ which is the righteousness of God. Just as it is Paul's desire for himself that he may be found to have the righteousness of God, so he desires this particular fruit for the Philippians. As 3:10 makes clear, however, Paul's desire to be found "in Christ," having the righteousness of God, is integrally tied to Paul's desire to know Christ and the power of his resurrection, to share in Christ's sufferings, and to be conformed to Christ's death. In the light of the way this notion of righteousness gets spelled out in Paul's own life and tied to the example of Christ as narrated in, for example, 2:6-11 and in the light of the sorts of behavior Paul seeks to establish in Philippi, this prayer can be seen as a foreshadowing of many of the significant themes of the rest of the epistle.

The passage concludes by noting that the fulfillment of the prayer will issue in glory and praise to God.[36] "Finally, all these things — St. Paul's

---

33. Fee, *Philippians*, 103.

34. The phrase translated "for the day of Christ" occurs only here and in 2:16 in Paul. In view of the way the phrase is used in Eph 4:30, Fee argues that Phil 1:10 indicates the *telos* toward which the Philippians are moving. "Thus he prays that they might be pure and blameless 'for the day of Christ,' that is, with the day of Christ as their ultimate goal" (Fee, *Philippians*, 102).

35. The same Greek phrase rendered here in English as "fruit of righteousness" appears in the LXX in Amos 6:12; Prov 3:9; 11:30. In all of these cases the phrase is equally unclear. It also appears in Jas 3:18, "The fruit of righteousness is sown in peace by those who make peace."

36. There is an interesting textual variant here. Some mss. read "to the glory and praise of Christ" (D*); others read "to the glory and praise of me," that is, of Paul (F, G); and p[46] has "to

prayer, richer charity, deeper knowledge of God, more sensitive moral perception, active and informed prudence, the innocence and beauty of the Christian life — all contribute to the glory and praise of God."[37]

Paul's initial address here to the Philippians lays bare some of the presumptions that underlie all forms of Christian friendship. I will mention a few of these here, but I will take them up in more detail in the final section of this volume. While Paul recognizes that he and the Philippians are fellow participants in grace, the depth of feeling and the richness of Paul's desires for the Philippians indicate that there is already a deep communion here between him and them. This communion enables and, indeed, requires a high level of accountability among Christian friends. Paul is able to express his longing for the Philippians and his desire for their continued and ongoing transformation. Like many friends in the ancient world Paul is able both to encourage and to help direct the Philippians toward their proper end. What is distinctive here is that the proper end for these friends is found in Christ. Moreover, as his final comments in v. 11 make clear, God is both the one who draws Paul and the Philippians to their proper end in Christ and the one who is glorified when this good work is brought to completion at the day of Christ. As Paul's comments here intimate, Christian friendship is never simply a relationship between two parties. Rather, it is always a three-way relationship in which friends are drawn into deeper communion with each other and with God.

1:12-26

12 I want you to know, brothers and sisters, that, contrary to what one might expect, my circumstances have worked to advance the gospel, 13 so that it is recognized among the whole Praetorian Guard and by everyone else that my bonds are in Christ. 14 Moreover, most of the brothers and sisters, having been made confident in the Lord by my imprisonment, now speak the word with greater boldness and without fear. 15 Some, however, preach Christ from envy and a spirit of strife, while others preach from pure motives. 16 These proclaim Christ out of love, knowing that I have been appointed for the defense of the gospel. 17 The others preach out of a selfish ambition. They are insincere, intending to deepen the pain of my

---

the glory and praise of God and me." While there is ample evidence for preferring the accepted text (see Metzger, *Textual Commentary*, 611), it is interesting that the latter two variants show that it was not inconceivable that the fate of the Philippian congregation might in some way reflect on Paul. This notion is made explicit in 2:16, and I will discuss it further in my account of that verse.

37. Spicq, *Agape*, 2:284.

imprisonment. 18 What should one make of all this? Just this; in every way, whether by false motives or true, Christ is proclaimed. In this I will rejoice.

Yes, and I will continue to rejoice, 19 because I know that this will result in my salvation through your prayers and the provision of the Spirit of Jesus Christ and 20 because it is my eager expectation and hope that I will in no way be disgraced. Rather with all boldness, as I have always done, Christ will be magnified in my body whether I live or die. 21 For to me, to live is Christ; to die is gain. 22 If I am to remain in the flesh this will lead to fruitful labor for me. I do not know, however, which I will choose. 23 I am torn between two options. I would much rather die and be with Christ. 24 It is much more beneficial for you, however, that I remain in the flesh. 25 And I am convinced that I will remain and continue with all of you for your progress and joy in the faith 26 so that when I come to visit you again, I might share in your abounding boasting in Christ Jesus.

Stylistically, this section is united by its first person narration. It is best to see it as comprised of two paragraphs, one consisting of vv. 12-18a and the other of vv. 18b-26. In terms of its content, this section focuses on Paul's situation in prison and, more importantly, how he views that situation. The section begins by Paul claiming that he wants the Philippians to know how things are with him. It soon becomes clear that there is nothing self-evident about Paul's imprisonment. In fact, much about Paul's situation and his view of that situation runs counter to what we (or the Philippians) might expect. Thus, the most significant aspect of this passage is its demonstration of Paul's ability to see his circumstances in a particular way. Paul has developed the skill of accounting for his situation in such a way that he is able to see God at work and to see the gospel advancing in the midst of what others (perhaps others in Philippi) might have viewed as disastrous and humiliating circumstances.

After discussing the various components of this passage it will become clear that Paul has not only developed the ability to see his situation in a certain light, but that this habit of seeing, this pattern of judgment, enables him to live in particular ways. Hence, even though Paul does not use the verb φρονεῖν/*phronein* in this passage as he did in 1:7, he is displaying a similar pattern of perception, judgment, and action. It will also become evident that one of the aims of presenting an account of his circumstances (of making things known) to the Philippians is so that they can begin to develop similar patterns of perception, judgment, and action for themselves.[1] This aim becomes

---

1. See Engberg-Pedersen, *Paul and the Stoics,* 107, who makes a similar argument about Paul's purposes in Philippians.

explicit in 2:5 when Paul again makes recourse to the verb φρονεῖν/*phronein*, urging the Philippians to adopt a Christ-focused pattern of perceiving, judging, and acting.

Verse 12 begins with what is almost a formulaic phrase, "I want you to know. . . ."[2] In this case Paul wants the Philippians to know about his circumstances. This passage about Paul's circumstances will lead into the discussion of the Philippians' circumstances in 1:27. On the surface, it would appear that Paul is engaging in the conventional sharing of news characteristic of letters of friendship. Although the initial language is formal and conventional, Paul is, nevertheless, introducing matters of significance. He is not simply relating news about himself. He is trying to shape the way the Philippians view that news. While recognizing this, we must be careful not to equate Paul's rhetoric here with that of any contemporary "spin doctor." In seeking to shape the ways in which the Philippians view his circumstances, Paul is not trying to make himself look good. Indeed, we will see in the course of this passage that Paul often displaces himself as the subject of his account. Instead of making himself look good, Paul is displaying a theological skill. That is, he is presenting a pattern of perception that should characterize those in Christ. Paul habitually views things this way, and it will become clear that he desires the Philippians to view things in this way, too.

Paul's task would be easier if he were not in such apparently wretched circumstances. The fact that his circumstances appear so awful leads him to begin by noting that, despite his imprisonment, the gospel has advanced.[3] One can easily imagine several ways in which the gospel might have been hindered in the light of Paul's chains. Instead, it has "advanced."[4] Interestingly, this sentence does not identify the agent advancing the gospel. Paul does not claim to have advanced it himself. Indeed, what progress has been made occurs despite his circumstances. Presumably, the implied agent here is God.

---

2. T. Y. Mullins identifies this disclosure form, which is conventional in Koine letters. See Mullins, "Disclosure," 44-50.

3. The Greek word μᾶλλον/*mallon* introduces an idea that runs contrary to expectation, see Lightfoot, *Philippians*, 87. Fee, *Philippians*, 111 n. 20, translates the word as "really." Collange, *Philippians*, 53, correctly notes that the adverb contrasts "two conflicting views about the actual consequences of the events in question."

4. Paul uses the word προκοπή/*prokopē* to talk about the gospel's advance. This term has a rich heritage in Stoicism. Paul's usage here, however, conforms more closely to 2 Macc 8:8 and Josephus, *Ant.* 4.59, where the word is used in a nonphilosophical sense of progressive movement toward an objective. See Engberg-Pedersen, *Paul and the Stoics*, 70-73, for the dual senses of the term in Stoicism. While the Stoic notion may not come into play when thinking about the gospel's progress, it may be much more relevant when considering the Philippians' progress in 1:25.

Thus, although most people in Paul's world would assume that imprisonment would inhibit the spread of the gospel, God has, nevertheless, caused the gospel to be advanced.

In terms of the next few verses it would seem that the progress of the gospel is manifested in the fact that many have learned that Paul's imprisonment is the result of his life in Christ and not the result of a straightforwardly criminal act. In addition, many, who might have otherwise been silent, have been emboldened to proclaim the gospel in Rome. There is, however, little Paul can do to control the contours of this situation. Instead, he narrates God's work in this situation to manifest, contrary to expectation, the advance of the gospel. God is the agent who advances the gospel and forms Paul in such a way as to see progress in circumstances that might lead others to see God's purposes as being frustrated.

Having claimed that the gospel has been advanced through his circumstances rather than frustrated, Paul begins to explain why this is the case in v. 13. He first mentions the effect of his confinement on unbelievers. Paul claims that "the whole Praetorian Guard and everyone else" recognize that his bonds are "in Christ." In Matt 27:27; Mark 15:16; John 18:28, 33; 19:9; and Acts 23:35 the word "praetorium" (πραιτώριον/*praitōrion*) is used to describe the official residence of a provincial governor. Although here it might refer to the imperial palace in Rome, such usage is otherwise unattested. In fact, no place in Rome is called by this name. Paul probably uses the term to note the body of men forming the praetorian guard.[5] If this is so, there would have been about 9000 men in this guard. It is unlikely that Paul would have been known to them all, much less "everyone else." It seems best to take this as a not very precise reference to a large number of people.[6]

However many praetorian guards Paul has in mind, what they have learned is that Paul's bonds are "in Christ." The terse phrase "in Christ" here must imply a great deal. The context here does little to determine which of several possible lines of implication to pursue. Moreover, Paul uses the phrase similarly in 2:1, 5, where again the context does not help much to determine its precise implications.[7]

At the very least, "in Christ" indicates that Paul's imprisonment is the result of his life in Christ, his convictions about the crucified and resurrected Jesus, rather than of some base criminal act. "In Christ" must stand for a body

---

5. See Lightfoot's discussion of this, *Philippians*, 99-104. Also O'Brien, *Philippians*, 93.

6. So Fee, *Philippians*, p. 112 n. 25; O'Brien, *Philippians*, 93; Lightfoot, *Philippians*, 88.

7. In 3:3, 14; 4:19, 21 Paul also uses "in Christ." In these cases, however, the context works to determine the way one ought to take the phrase.

of convictions about Christ (or a narrative account of the person and work of Christ as in 2:5-11). Moreover, one would also have to say that the practices entailed by sharing these convictions account for why Paul ends up in prison. Presumably, this phrase also ties Paul to others sharing similar convictions and practices. Hence, the phrase also stands as a sort of verbal shorthand for the body of believers who are "in Christ" and the manner of life appropriate to that body (2:1). It would have been Paul's membership in this body which landed him in jail.

Another implication of this clause is that being in chains is not inconsistent with being "in Christ." That is, Paul's current circumstances are not only consistent with his convictions about Christ, but are the sorts of circumstances one who shared those convictions might also expect to share. In this context there is little one can rely on to help narrow the range of possible implications of this phrase. Alternatively, it is not clear why one needs to narrow down what is an extremely illusive phrase when the context leaves a variety of possibilities open. Would the Praetorian Guard or other unbelievers have understood Paul's chains in all of these ways? Probably not. Would the Christians in Rome have noted all the possible ways to take Paul's claim? Perhaps, but we have no way of knowing. Recognizing the ways in which the Philippians and we Christians should understand this phrase is theologically more important. In the light of the way the rest of the epistle runs, it is probably best to note that all of these different implications of being "in Christ" resonate throughout the argument of the epistle. Ultimately, it is important for the Philippians and us to develop the abilities to understand and embody what it means to be "in Christ." Paul's specific concerns for the Philippians are sharpened in the light of the fact that Paul sees them in an analogous situation to his own (1:29-30).[8]

In v. 14 Paul shifts his attention to the way his situation has resulted in the progress of the gospel among believers in Rome. He claims that the majority of the brothers (and sisters) have become confident in the Lord[9] on ac-

---

8. See Fee, *Philippians*, 114, who notes, "Paul's concern would be to encourage the Philippians in their own current suffering, resulting in part from their lack of loyalty to the emperor. To the world — and especially to the citizens of a Roman colony — Caesar may be 'lord'; but to Paul and to the believers in Philippi, only Jesus is Lord (2:11), and his lordship over Caesar is already making itself felt through the penetration of the gospel into the heart of Roman political life."

9. Although it is possible to take "in the Lord" with the phrase "most of the brothers," most take "in the Lord" to describe the source of this new-found confidence (with Lightfoot, *Philippians*, 88; Fee, *Philippians*, 115; O'Brien, *Philippians*, 94; Hawthorne, *Philippians*, 35; Bockmuehl, *Philippians*, 76).

count of Paul's chains to speak the word boldly. "To speak the word" is not a common Pauline phrase. It occurs often in Acts, sometimes explicitly referring to the word of God.[10] In these cases it refers to the apostolic preaching, and this is probably how it should be read here in Philippians. This conforms to Paul's usage in 2:24; Rom 14:14; and Gal 5:10, where he also speaks about being confident "in the Lord." Thus, Paul claims in v. 14 that God has used his circumstances to make others more confident to speak the word.

Having made the bold assertion that God has used his bonds, contrary to expectation, to advance the gospel, Paul also recognizes some problems in the newfound boldness that some have to proclaim the word. More precisely, some are preaching Christ from "envy and a spirit of strife" (1:15).[11] Given Paul's claims in v. 17, it seems clear that this envy and strife are directed at Paul. As Lightfoot says, "The mainspring of their activity is a factious opposition to the Apostle, a jealousy of his influence. They value success, not as a triumph over heathendom, but as a triumph over St. Paul."[12]

In addition to these, however, there are those who preach Christ "from pure motives." Unlike those who preach from envy and strife, it is less clear that these pure motives are directed at Paul, though that is one way to take the phrase.[13] Since the envy and strife depicted here are clearly directed at Paul, there would be some symmetry in viewing these benevolent motives as also directed to Paul. It is not, however, exactly clear what pure or benevolent motives toward Paul would be other than, perhaps, sympathy. It is, therefore, preferable to see Paul's judgment about motives here to be about purity of motives directed toward God.[14] Thus, Paul here describes the goodwill from which a worthy act is generated (cf. Rom 10:1).[15]

As v. 16 goes on to elaborate, those who preach Christ from "pure motives" are the ones who operate out of love or *agapē*, having seen that Paul is imprisoned for the defense of the gospel. Hence, the emboldened preaching of these Christians stems from having perceived that Paul's circumstances are both the result and the manifestation of his defense of the gospel.

---

10. See Acts 4:29, 31; 11:19; 13:5, 7, 44, 46; 14:25; 16:32; 17:13; 18:11.

11. The two Greek terms translated here as "envy" (φθόνος/*phthonos*) and "spirit of strife" (ἔρις/*eris*) occur together, though not as a pair, in the vice lists of Gal 5:20-21 and Rom 1:29, describing characters who will not inherit the kingdom of God. These terms (along with others) appear in 1 Tim 6:4 to describe certain teachers. Their desire for controversy or disputation stems from envy and strife (among other things).

12. Lightfoot, *Philippians*, 89. So also Fee, *Philippians*, 120; Bockmuehl, *Philippians*, 80.

13. So Fee, *Philippians*, 120.

14. So O'Brien, *Philippians*, 100.

15. This is Gnilka's view, *Philipperbrief*, 61.

In phrasing the matter this way, Paul makes a subtle transition. It is the gospel, rather than Paul, which is on trial and in need of defense. Again, we see a displacement of Paul as the subject of what is ostensibly his discussion of his own circumstances. In 1:12 Paul speaks of the gospel progressing through God's agency. Here it is the gospel, rather than Paul, which is on trial. In 1:12 Paul, rather conventionally, began to make known the disposition of his own circumstances (more exactly, "the things concerning me"). It turns out, however, that these things are only indirectly about Paul. Clearly, here, as in many other places in the epistles, Paul and his story are integrated so thoroughly into the story of Christ that it becomes difficult to separate the two. Paul has learned to see that his circumstances are part of this larger ongoing story. Hence, in talking about himself he quite naturally ends up talking about the progress of that story. If one sees the aim of the life of discipleship as growing into ever deeper communion with the triune God and with others, then one of the things that contemporary Christians can learn from Paul is this habit of being able to narrate the story both of one's past and one's present circumstances from the perspective of those who have learned their place in Christ's ongoing story.

In v. 17 Paul returns to discuss those who preach from envy and strife. In contrast to those who preach Christ "out of love," the others proclaim Christ from "selfish ambition."[16] In 2:3 the same word appears. There it describes that disposition which contrasts with the disposition of seeking the benefit of others in humility. In this light, the "selfish ambition" described here would reflect a self-absorption which is ultimately destructive of a common life.

As Paul sees it, the aim of such characters is to deepen the pain of his imprisonment. In this particular context it is unlikely that those who preach Christ from selfish motives have fomented a deliberate plot to exacerbate Paul's physical sufferings or to cause actual bodily harm. Instead, the aim would be to create an "inward annoyance,"[17] or in Lightfoot's words, "to make my chains gall me."[18]

Despite the intentions of those who aim to trouble Paul, he rejoices. This is because Christ is preached. The motives of the preachers, while important, seem secondary to the act of proclamation. It appears that Paul pragmatically prefers to see the gospel preached than to wait until everybody's

---

16. The Greek word translated as "selfish ambition" (ἐριθεία/*eritheia*) is an obscure word. Prior to the NT the word occurs only in Aristotle, where it denotes self-serving pursuit of political office by unfair means. Within the NT "selfish ambition" (ἐριθεία/*eritheia*) occurs in Rom 2:8; 2 Cor 12:20; Gal 5:20; and James 3:14, 16 in addition to here in 1:17 and 2:3. See BAGD, p. 309.

17. So O'Brien, *Philippians*, 102.

18. Lightfoot, *Philippians*, 90.

motives are pure. I do not think Paul sees the choice in quite this way. Ultimately, because Paul is convinced that God is directing both his personal circumstances and the more general spread of the gospel, he need not be overly concerned about the motives of any particular set of preachers. Paul is able to see that, despite appearances and contrary to expectations, God is advancing the gospel. Rather than expressing a preference for preaching from selfish motives over no preaching at all, this phrase is an expression of faith in God's providential oversight of the gospel's progress.

From a theological perspective it is important to note that a very particular doctrine of providence underwrites Paul's account here. As we have already seen, Paul is confident that God will bring the good work started in his own and the Philippians' lives to its proper completion (1:6). This is not, however, the willed blindness displayed by someone like Dr. Pangloss in Voltaire's *Candide,* proclaiming through ever more serious disasters that this is the best of all possible worlds. Paul, more than most, directly and willingly endured suffering because of his convictions about the crucified and resurrected Christ. Yet, he does not attempt to call such suffering a good in itself. Suffering is what the followers of Christ may expect as they negotiate their way through the same sort of world that crucified Jesus. Paul's view of God's providence leads him to fit himself and his various circumstances into a larger on-going story of God's unfolding economy of salvation. Within this larger context, and only within this context, Paul's circumstances can be seen as advancing the gospel. This view of providence enables Paul to displace himself as the one who is guiding and directing his own life. Thus, one might argue that Paul's self is de-centered in certain important respects. I do not mean to say that Paul lacks a notion of self or that his life lacks a center or focal point. Instead, Paul's sense of himself now attains its coherence and intelligibility from being part of the larger movement of God's economy of salvation. The crucified and risen Christ provides both the central point for the drama of God's salvation and central focus for Paul's own life. Of course, the fact that one may speak of Paul's self as de-centered does not mean that Paul or any other disciple is free from being responsible for his actions. Paul's is a self in which God is at the center, ordering and opening courses of action in the light of the ends and purposes of God's economy of salvation. Instead of controlling and directing circumstances, the primary tasks for these theologically de-centered selves have to do with perceiving the movements of this larger drama into which they have been drawn and appropriately fitting themselves into that drama in word and deed.

Verses 16-18 have become an occasion for scholars to speculate both about the identity of those who preach Christ from selfish motives and about the nature of Paul's relationship to them. The scholarly opinions as to the identity of these self-serving preachers range from Judaizers[19] to Gnostics.[20] All such identifications go well beyond the information available in the text.[21] My own preference (following O'Brien) is to chalk the opposition up to personal rivalry, thus displaying factions within the Roman church. "Some were antipathetic to Paul and preached Christ from a spirit of envy and rivalry, with no worthier motive than to rub salt in his wounds and so add to the sense of frustration that he might well feel in his restricted situation."[22] This view best fits the wider context of Philippians.

If one follows this account, it does, however, raise the question of why Paul spends so much time conveying information about Christians in Rome to Christians in Philippi. Of course, in a letter of friendship it is conventional and expected that Paul would convey news about himself and others. The interesting question is: why convey this news about strangers (presumably) in this way? The answer must be that Paul's primary concern here is to relate his own disposition to this situation, laying the groundwork for his later attempts to shape the Philippians' disposition to their own situation. This will become clearer in 1:19-26 and even more explicit in 1:27–2:13. In addition, the repetition of "selfish ambition" in 2:3 and Paul's more general comments in 2:1-4 about seeking the benefit of others rather than oneself, indicate that he is telling the Philippians things about the Christians in Rome that might be relevant to the dispositions and practices he seeks to see formed in the Philippians.

In 1:18 Paul ends his discussion of various types of preachers with an expression of joy. Most modern commentators note that 1:18a closes off one thought, and 1:18b begins another.[23] Clearly, the future tense verb in v. 18b is

19. This position is argued by Koester, "The Purpose of the Polemic."

20. This position is argued by Schmithals, "Die Irrlehrer."

21. Robert Jewett, "Epistolary Thanksgiving," offers a less speculative proposal. He argues that Paul's imprisonment is an embarrassment and not appropriate for a powerful apostle. Paul's situation was humiliating and reflected the inadequacy of his gospel. This leads to Paul's emphasis on suffering in the epistle. This would tend to reflect the sort of opposition encountered in 2 Corinthians. O'Brien, however, raises some telling criticisms of this view. First, these people are recognized as Christian preachers. Paul does not condemn the substance of their message. Second, if they are embarrassed by Paul's situation, why does he note that they have been emboldened by his chains to proclaim the gospel even more boldly? If they are truly enemies of the cross of Christ (3:18), how can Paul assert that they preach Christ sufficiently clearly to lead him to rejoice in that despite their motives? See O'Brien, *Philippians*, 103-4.

22. O'Brien, *Philippians*, 105.

23. So, Fee, *Philippians*, 129; Gnilka, *Philipperbrief*, 65; O'Brien, *Philippians*, 108. NA26 begins a new paragraph at 18b.

connected to the rejoicing in v. 18a. It also, however, leads into v. 19.[24] In v. 18, then, we learn that Paul rejoices now in the fact that the gospel is proclaimed despite the motives of some of the proclaimers. Further, he commits himself to continued rejoicing in the future. This commitment is based on a certain knowledge Paul has. The two subsequent clauses, one here and one in v. 20, each introduced by "because," explain the basis for this knowledge. The first clause is a verbatim quote of the LXX of Job 13:16, "This will result in my salvation." Paul does not introduce this quote with any of his standard introductory phrases. Moreover, the claim is certainly intelligible to anyone who does not know the text of Job.[25] As Richard Hays has noted, however, for someone who does pick up and identify the quote, there are some "intriguing resonances."[26]

In Job 13 Job is in the midst of defending his integrity in the light of his "friends'" accusations that his situation is the result of some hidden sin in his life. He claims in 13:16 both that he will ultimately be vindicated before God and that those who have spoken falsely will not be welcomed into God's presence.[27] In 13:18 Job again proclaims that his judgment is near and he "will be shown to be righteous."

In Philippians Paul takes on Job's voice "to affirm confidence in the favorable outcome of his affliction; thereby, he implicitly transfers to himself some of the significations that traditionally cluster around the figure of Job."[28] One may even ascribe some of the implicit judgment which Job predicts for his false-speaking friends to those seeking to make Paul's bonds more painful than they already were.[29]

Of course there are differences between Job and Paul. Most important are their respective stances before God. For Job, God is both adversary and vindicator. Paul sees God only in terms of vindicator. Nevertheless, the quota-

---

24. We would do well to follow O'Brien's reasoning here: "But without wishing to deny the links between the two halves of v. 18 — the repetition of the verb χαίρω [rejoice] makes such a conjunction plain — it does appear that the two particles ἀλλά and καί are combined in a progressive sense, meaning 'further' so that the words introduce a fresh point" (O'Brien, *Philippians*, 108).

25. Gnilka, *Philipperbrief*, 66, for example, notes that the Philippians would probably not have recognized the quotation. While this may or may not be true, it is, as I argue below, a separate issue.

26. See Hays, *Echoes of Scripture*, 21-24. For much of the following I am indebted to Hays's work.

27. See also 13:7: "Do you all not speak before the Lord? But you speak before him falsely." See also Hays, *Echoes of Scripture*, 22.

28. Hays, *Echoes of Scripture*, 22.

29. So Hays, *Echoes of Scripture*, 23.

tion from Job seems to indicate that Paul sees his situation as analogous to Job's. This analogy of situations helps to generate and sustain in Paul a similar sort of hope to that which Job expresses in 13:6. Given that Paul's admonitions to the Philippians depend to a large degree on the Philippians' abilities to see the similarities between their situation, on the one hand, and Paul's situation (cf. 1:29-30), the story of God's activity in Christ (cf. 2:5-11), and the actions of Timothy and Epaphroditus (cf. 2:19-30), on the other hand, we might well take this allusion to Job as one further example of the patterns of judgment and perceptual habits which Paul wishes to see formed in the Philippians.

Were all of these allusions circulating in Paul's mind? We can never know. Would the Philippians have picked them up? Again, we cannot really know. Even if it is probable that they would not have picked up these allusions, that is a separate matter from whether Christians today should allow these texts from Job to resonate in their ears when they listen to Philippians. In regard to this latter question, the answer must be yes. Christians should read Philippians in the light of all of Scripture. One need not determine in advance what that entails for the interpretation of any particular verse. Nevertheless, when there is a direct quotation from Job in Phil. 1:19 and attention to the larger context of Job can provide a theologically edifying context in which to read Philippians, Christians would be unwise willfully to cut themselves off from such edification.

Paul goes on to state that he is confident that the prayers of the Philippians and the provision of the Spirit will result in his "salvation." There seems to be a fruitful ambiguity in Paul's use of the term "salvation." On the one hand, this term clearly reflects Paul's expectation that he will be vindicated before God.[30] On the other hand, when this term appears in other types of letters, it is a reference to physical well-being.[31] Indeed, Paul may be playing on both of these meanings in order to undermine any excessive desire on the Philippians' part to be delivered from physical suffering taken on in Christ.[32]

Having indicated in 1:3-11 that he prays for the Philippians, Paul now implicitly asks for their prayers for him. The structure of the Greek indicates

---

30. This is the way O'Brien, *Philippians,* 110, among others takes it.

31. Silva, *Philippians,* 76-78, seems to have decisively shown that the term cannot simply refer to release from prison.

32. See the arguments for this view in Reed's *Discourse Analysis,* 212-215. Fee, *Philippians,* 131-33, moves in a similar direction. This view gains further support from 2:14, where Paul urges the Philippians to avoid "grumbling and dissension," using language that evokes Israel's response to physical hardships.

that Paul here is talking about the support and aid he will receive from the Spirit as the result of the Philippians' prayers.[33] In the light of Paul's confidence in v. 20 that he will not be disgraced, it would appear that he is quite specifically asking for the Spirit's aid as he comports himself as a disciple in custody, and as he appears before the authorities to make his defense. Paul's request here can be read in the light of Matt 10:16-21 par. Mark 13:9-12 where Jesus promises his followers that the "Spirit of your Father" will speak through them when they are brought before the authorities to give an account of their faith in Christ.

We read of a second reason for Paul's joy in v. 20. Paul will continue to "rejoice" because "his eager expectation and hope" is that he "will in no way be disgraced." On the one hand, it would appear that hope and eager expectation are simply appositional phrases. Aquinas, however, notes a difference between them and his comments are worth noting at length:

> But isn't hope the expectation of future happiness? I answer that hope is a movement of the appetite toward an arduous good; and this can occur in two ways: sometimes a person hopes to obtain something by himself; and then there is hope without expectation; but sometimes he hopes to obtain something through someone else, and then there is hope with expectation.[34]

The imprisoned Paul has set his desires on the arduous good of magnifying Christ in his body in either life or death. He realizes, however, that this hope can be achieved only through the prayers of the Philippians and God's supplying of the Spirit. Hence, he combines hope and expectation.

Paul's language here about being "disgraced" is quite common in the LXX (cf. Isa 50:7). In the LXX "disgrace" does not so much reflect an inner feeling of shame as a failure of faith (in word or deed) which brings with it a certain disgrace.[35] Rather than being disgraced, Paul plans, with all boldness,

---

33. The word "provision" (ἐπιχορηγία/*epichorēgia*) is used only here and in Eph 4:16, where it has medical overtones, referring to a ligament which supports something. The verbal form is used in relation to the Spirit in Gal 3:5, where the context makes it clear that the verb talks about God supplying the Spirit to the Galatians. There is some debate about whether "of the Spirit" is objective or subjective. Is the Spirit the giver or the gift? Lightfoot, *Philippians*, 90, argues to keep both options open. Gnilka, *Philipperbrief*, 67, and O'Brien, *Philippians*, 111, argue that it is subjective; Silva, *Philippians*, 79; Fee, *Philippians*, 133; Bockmuehl, *Philippians*, 84, all take it as objective. The use of similar language in Gal 3:5 to clearly speak of the Spirit as God's gift should direct us to read Phil 1:19 in a similar way.

34. Aquinas, *Philippians*, 68.

35. See especially Pss 24:3; 68:7; 118:80, 116; Jer 12:13.

and as he has always done heretofore, that Christ will be magnified in his body. The notion of "magnifying the Lord" has strong links to the Psalms.[36] Luke uses the same word in the Magnificat where it ascribes glory to God. The passive voice of the verb allows Paul to make a significant distinction. While it is Paul who might be disgraced, it is Christ who will be magnified in Paul's body whether the apostle lives or dies. Because the quotation from Job in 1:19 speaks of a heavenly vindication, there is a tendency among commentators to think that Paul here is also talking about a confidence directed toward the eschaton.[37] Such an eschatological view, however, seems to miss some important points. First, Paul's discussion of Christ's being magnified in his body notes not only that such magnification will happen in the future, but that Christ is regularly magnified in Paul's body. This is the force of "as I have always done." Paul's confidence is not primarily about the eschaton but about his ability to continue, with the Spirit's help, in circumstances of extreme adversity, a practice he has carried on for some time.

Paul's claims imply that whether he dies or lives there is, in each instance, an opportunity for magnifying Christ or disgracing himself. In dying Paul could either be disgraced or magnify Christ; in living he faces the same option. Magnifying Christ in life, however, will require a different set of practices than magnifying Christ in death. Aquinas recognizes this when he observes, "Christ is honored in our body in two ways: in one way, inasmuch as we dedicate our body to his service by employing our bodies in his ministry . . . ; in another way by risking our body for Christ. . . . The first is accomplished by life, the second by death."[38]

Paul understands that in this particular matter his body will display the disposition of his character whether he lives or dies.[39] For example, in dying in a way that disgraces himself — by recanting under torture — Paul's body would display something crucial about his character.[40] He understands what

---

36. See LXX Pss 33:3; 34:27; 39:16; 56:10. In this light, the usage here conforms more to Paul's use of this same vocabulary in 2 Cor 10:8 rather than Rom 1:16.

37. O'Brien, *Philippians*, 113, is a good example of this: "In other words, what is eagerly expected is the consummation of God's purposes. Here at Phil 1:20 Paul's confident expectation and hope have to do with that consummation, and his future vindication by God will be in accordance (κατά) with it."

38. Aquinas, *Philippians*, 69.

39. This is a point that is missed both by those who, following Bultmann, *New Testament Theology*, 1:190-226, wish to translate Paul's "body" terminology into a reference to some sort of existential or anthropological essence and by Robert Gundry, who in trying to counter Bultmann's influence limited Paul's "body" language to the physical body alone. Gundry's views can be found in *Sōma in Biblical Theology*, especially 37.

40. As Chrysostom comments on this passage, "For if fear of death had cut short my

47

virtually all ancient moral philosophers would have recognized — bodily actions and bodily responses to specific situations display elements of a person's character. It is not simply Paul's death that is being discussed here. Rather, it is the manner of his death and Paul's abilities to describe that death as something which might give glory to God or which might bring shame on himself. In this respect Paul's claims are not particularly surprising.

On the other hand, Paul was in a situation where his control over his body was restricted. Moreover, he was facing a situation in which he might be expected to lose all control over his body. In the context of imperial imprisonment, the prisoner's body becomes the text on which the empire's power is inscribed.[41] In a situation where the Roman Empire would be expected to exert a great deal of control over Paul's body, Paul counters that Christ will be magnified by the way in which he comports himself. Whether he lives or dies, Paul's body will be, as he has always been, Christ's text rather than the empire's.

Paul's claims here remind us that our actions display aspects of our character as Christians. Christians in America may appear to have far greater control over their bodies than the imprisoned Paul had over his. We would do well to recognize, however, that at the beginning of the twenty-first century all Americans are under unprecedented and minute levels of surveillance. Americans' purchases, reading materials, and the form and content of their communication are under the scrutiny of an extraordinary number of interested parties. At the very least, most of these parties seek to create and manipulate the desires of all of us and to offer alternative narratives into which we all might be tempted to fit our lives.

In the light of the aims and purposes of the Roman Empire, Paul indicates that his regular practice is to magnify Christ in his body. If we, too, are called to magnify Christ in our bodies as a regular practice, in the face of all the forces seeking to exert some control on us, then we, too, must be as intentional about all aspects of our life as Paul was. The desires we manifest, our patterns of consumption, the ways in which we get, hold, and distribute wealth, can all be occasions where either we are disgraced or Christ is magnified.

Surprisingly, the specific aspect of life in which Paul confidently thinks Christ can be magnified in his body is his death. Because he, like most subsequent Christians, recognized that he had no control over the moment of his

---

boldness, death would have been worthy of shame, but if death at its approach cast no terror on me, no shame is here; but whether it be through life I shall not be put to shame, for I still preach the Preaching, or whether it be through death I shall not be put to shame; fear does not hold me back, since I exhibit the same boldness" (*Homily* 3).

41. This general point in regard to imprisonment and punishment was first made by Foucault in *Discipline and Punish*.

death, Paul understood the importance of living each day of his life in a way that would make his death a fitting culmination, should it come that day. Because of the great advances in medical technologies in America, we appear to be offered a great deal of control over the time, place, and manner of our deaths. This tempts us to treat death as an event that is discontinuous with the rest of our life. Thus, for many, death is simply presented as the last great opportunity to exert an autonomous consumer choice, rather than an occasion on which Christ might be magnified in our bodies. One of the challenges facing contemporary American Christians, then, is to reflect theologically about death in the light of advances in death-denying, or death-delaying technologies.

Having confidently asserted that whether he lives or dies he intends to continue to glorify Christ in his body, Paul now turns to reflect at greater length on what is at stake in living and dying. In v. 21 Paul claims that "for to me, to live is Christ; to die is gain." "To live is Christ" is further described in v. 22 as continuing earthly life, magnifying Christ and engaging in fruitful labor for Christ.[42] Life results in fruitful labor in Christ's service. This may involve a variety of different apostolic activities. Particularly, in the light of v. 24, where Paul claims such labor is more beneficial to the Philippians, it would appear that this labor involves building up congregations. Further, in v. 23 Paul indicates that the benefit of death is an enhanced union with Christ.

Verse 22 begins an intriguing part of the paragraph. Paul begins to reflect on his own preference for death over life and actually speaks of having a choice in whether he lives or dies. A substantial part of any interpretation of vv. 22-26 depends on how one understands particular words and phrases. Hence, part of my discussion here will require that I both explain how and why I translated these key terms as I did and justify those decisions in the light of other options.

Once he has clarified the consequences of life in the flesh, Paul notes that he does not know which he will choose.[43] There are several difficulties in understanding this clause. First, the phrase translated "I do not know" is somewhat problematic for commentators. While a translation like "I do not know" makes the most sense, this is not the way Paul normally uses the Greek verb γνωρίζω/*gnōrizō*. There are, however, numerous examples outside the NT to support a translation like "I don't know."[44] Normally, Paul uses this

42. O'Brien, *Philippians*, 121.

43. Following the future reading "I will choose" (αἱρήσομαι/*hairēsomai*) against the subjunctive read by p[46], B, and others.

44. See Philo *Joseph* 165; *De Confusione Linguarum* 183; Josephus *Ant.* 2.97; *Life* 420. Also Amos 3:3; Prov 3:7b; 15:10 (LXX).

verb to speak of disclosure — often in regard to God's mysteries (cf. Rom 16:26; 1 Cor 15:1; 2 Cor 8:1; Gal 1:11). Thus, the verb is often translated "to make known." In the light of this typical Pauline pattern, Lohmeyer argues that God's mind had not yet been revealed to Paul. Hence, this clause indicates that Paul cannot make known to the Philippians which he shall choose because Paul does not yet know God's choice in the matter.[45] The problem with this is that by v. 25 Paul does know which he will choose. He also explicitly notes why he made the choice to "remain," and it has nothing to do with a direct revelation from God.

Alternatively, Fee thinks the idiom "I can't tell" comes fairly close to what Paul is expressing. But he does not see Paul as having a real choice, so he must add the following gloss, "His point, of course, is that if he really *had* a choice, the alternatives would put him in a genuine quandary, since *from a given perspective either is to be preferred.*"[46] It is not clear whether Paul overestimates his control of the situation. Paul's words, however, indicate that he has a real choice and does not yet know which he will choose. Thus, in the light of the overall context of this passage the best alternative is to take the Greek as "I don't know."

We should also be clear that in v. 22 the use of "I will choose" raises another sharp interpretive issue. Many (including the NRSV) translate the Greek as "prefer" or treat the word as if Paul were primarily talking about a preference rather than a choice. The word is not common in the NT. It is used in 2 Thess 2:13 and Heb 11:25 to indicate a choice. This usage is confirmed by extrabiblical uses of the term. Often, the choice is based on a preference, but this can be misleading. Clearly, preference and choice are related in that one often chooses what one prefers. Choice and preference are not, however, the same. Understanding this becomes quite important by vv. 23-25, when Paul explicitly chooses a course he does not prefer but which is more beneficial for others. In fact, in the light of the dispositions Paul advocates in 2:1-4, it is crucial for him to display here that he is choosing to follow what is most beneficial for others and not what he prefers for himself.

Nevertheless, in v. 23 Paul makes it clear that this is not an easy choice. The Greek conveys an image of being pressed together, as in Lightfoot's rendering "I am hemmed in on both sides."[47] The English idiom of being "torn" between two options rightly gives the sense of being faced with two possibili-

---

45. Lohmeyer, *Philipper,* 60-61. O'Brien, *Philippians,* 127-28, seems to agree with this view.

46. Fee, *Philippians,* 145.

47. Lightfoot, *Philippians,* 93.

ties, each of which has a certain appeal. In addition, the idea of being torn (or hemmed in) recognizes the fact that one cannot opt for both possibilities at the same time.

Although at this point Paul has yet to reveal his choice, he clearly has a personal preference. That is, he desires to die, "to depart and be with Christ."[48] There is a great deal of literature devoted to fitting Paul's implicit claim that upon death he will be with Christ into an account which also follows 1 Cor 15:51, 52 and 1 Thess 4:14 in speaking of Christians who have died as being asleep, awaiting a general resurrection of the dead.[49] In addition, later, in 3:20, 21, Paul seems to hold the view that there will be some sort of subsequent transformation of Christians which will prepare them for heaven. Clearly, if Paul expected to remain in some undetermined state, death would have had less appeal. Paul here expects death to issue in some sort of deeper union with Christ.[50]

One way of managing these differences is to distinguish texts such as this one and 2 Cor 5:6, 8, which speak in spatial metaphors of being with Christ as if it were a place, from texts which speak in metaphors relying on a temporal sequence moving from sleeping and then waking. Both are attempts to speak about a mystery toward which humans can only gesture with a variety of different metaphors and analogies. It is not possible to produce a conceptually neat package of them all without allowing one of these metaphors or analogies to take precedence over the others.

In addition, both *1 Clement* and Polycarp indicate that Paul, among other martyrs, was removed from this life and went directly into the presence of the Lord.[51] This notion is also reflected in Rev 6:9-11, where the martyrs under the altar seem to have special access to the Lord prior to a general resurrection. (Of course, being in the presence of the Lord is also a metaphorical way of speaking about this mystery.) If Paul is reflecting here on his possible death as a martyr, he may not be presenting a general picture of what happens to Christians when they die. Rather, he would be simply anticipating entering God's presence as the result of dying a martyr's death.[52]

These two possibilities are not mutually exclusive. Whether or not martyrs enjoy the presence of God in a way that anticipates that which all Chris-

---

48. The word ἀναλύω/*analyō* is widely used as a euphemism for death and should not be taken as a technical philosophical term as Plato uses it. See the references in BAGD.

49. See the discussion in Fee, *Philippians*, 145-51; O'Brien, *Philippians*, 135-37, discusses various views.

50. See Lincoln, *Paradise Now*, 104; O'Brien, *Philippians*, 130.

51. *1 Clement* 5; Polycarp, *Philippians* 9.

52. Not surprisingly, Lohmeyer, *Philipper*, 63, makes this point.

tians will enjoy, one must always keep in mind that all our speculations in this area are provisional. They are motivated by a well-grounded hope in God's resurrecting power, but constrained by our human finitude and ignorance in this area. Nevertheless, it is important to keep a number of theological considerations in mind here. God's love for us will not allow God to offer us anything less than God's self. Christians have described this in various ways such as the beatific vision or communion with God. Christians have also traditionally maintained that one's life in Christ on earth is both a foreshadowing of and a training ground for one's eschatological life with God. Thus, for example, growth in charity in this life increases one's capacities to take in the beatific vision. Or, to follow someone like Gregory of Nyssa, who is relying primarily on Phil 3:13, the training in virtue one gains here on earth prepares one for a life of ever deeper growth in virtue resulting in ever deeper communion with God. Each advance into deeper communion with God simply creates a desire for more.[53]

Returning to Paul's reflections on whether he will choose life or death, he makes the decisive judgment in v. 24 that "remaining in the flesh" is more necessary or beneficial for the Philippians. Remaining in the flesh will also result in fruitful labor on behalf of the Philippians. It is important here to recall that Paul is comparing two alternatives. To be with Christ is better *for Paul*. For Paul to remain and engage in fruitful labor for Christ is better *for the Philippians*. That is, contrary to Paul's own personal preference to die, he has decided to live because it would be more beneficial to the Philippians. As I already indicated, this pattern of seeking the benefit of others is crucial for the argument of the epistle.

As 2:5-11 will make clear, it is precisely this activity of seeking the benefit of others which God has decisively displayed to the world in the life, death, and resurrection of Jesus. When faced with the choice of life or death, Paul opts for life. This is not because life is obviously superior to death. For Paul, this is far from the case. Rather, Paul's choice here analogously replicates the climactic movement in the divine economy of salvation. Seeing his situation as part of that larger story provides Paul with a compelling exemplar of how he should comport himself in his imprisonment.

In the end, then, Paul claims that he has decided to live and remain with the Philippians because it is more beneficial for them and will advance their "progress and joy in the faith" (v. 25). Verses 25-26 make the transition from Paul's discussion of his affairs to his direct discussion of the Philippians' affairs in 1:27. He does this by bringing his affairs and their affairs into the same story.

---

53. See Gregory of Nyssa, *Life of Moses*, 2.219-55. See also my comments on 3:13.

While this transition is accomplished explicitly by 1:30, in 1:25-26 Paul introduces this transition, at the same time making several verbal connections to themes he has already introduced in ch. 1. For example, the phrase "I am convinced of this" in v. 25 introduces a bold statement about how Paul's situation will work itself out for the Philippians' advantage — they will advance and have joy.[54] It also recalls the bold statement in 1:6 ("I am convinced of this very thing") about God's continued work in the life of the Philippian congregation.

Further, in 1:12 Paul introduces the discussion of his circumstance in prison by asserting that, contrary to expectation, his circumstances have worked to advance the gospel. In 1:18 Paul notes that, despite the motives of some, he rejoices in the advance of the gospel. In v. 25 Paul asserts that his remaining with all the Philippians[55] will lead to their advancement and joy in the faith.[56]

Moreover, the verbal connections noted above remind us that from the very first part of the epistle, Paul has asserted his conviction that God has worked and will continue to work in the lives of the Philippians. This indicates that Paul has already been reading the Philippians into the narrative of God's economy of salvation in much the same way he has read himself into that story. His claims in v. 25 simply resume that activity. In reading the Philippians into his account of the divine economy from the beginning of the epistle, Paul is laying the groundwork for the claim he is going to make in 1:30 that he and the Philippians are engaged in the same struggle. This claim is essential for the larger aims of Paul's argument. If Paul can establish that he and the Philippians are in similar circumstances, then he can argue that the Philippians ought to act as he does. Moreover, as Paul offers an account of the Philippians' situation in a way that both ties their situation to his and accounts for their circumstances in the light of the larger movements of the divine economy, he is implicitly encouraging them to learn how to see their situation in a similar way. By the time the argument reaches the explicit claim in 3:17 that the Philippians should be "fellow imitators" of Paul, he has already laid so much conceptual and rhetorical groundwork that the claim should come as no surprise.

---

54. Lightfoot, *Philippians*, 94, and O'Brien, *Philippians*, 138, note that this phrase is an expression of confidence, not a claim about prophetic knowledge (contra Lohmeyer, *Philipper*, 66-67).

55. Again, this is another occasion when Paul uses πᾶς/*pas* to emphasize the whole of the Philippian congregation.

56. The use of "progress" (προκοπή/*prokopē*) here is similar to the Stoic use of the term to speak of the progress one makes once one has started to order one's life in the light of wisdom. See the explanation of this usage in Engberg-Pedersen, *Paul and the Stoics*, 72-73.

Paul goes on to express the hope that by remaining in the flesh, he will be able to visit the Philippians. Such a result leads to abundant "boasting" in Christ Jesus. Almost all of the occurrences of "boasting" in the NT are Pauline (55 of 59). In the Greco-Roman world, boasting is quite compatible with a cultural system based on honor and shame. It is a way of rightly locating honor.[57] Of course, locating honor or boasting in one who suffered a slave's death would have struck many in Paul's world as foolishness. This is made quite clear in 1 Cor 1:18-31, which concludes with a citation of Jer 9:23-24.[58] As the passage from Jeremiah makes clear, this practice of boasting or giving glory, if done in the right way and for the right reasons, is the paradigmatic activity of the believer. If done in the wrong way or for the wrong reasons, it is fundamentally destructive of a believer's relationship with God. In 1:26 the grounds for boasting are in Christ Jesus, and, more precisely, what Christ Jesus has done through Paul.[59]

This displacement of himself as the ground and focus of "boasting" is consistent with the pattern noted above. Paul is not the object of his own or the Philippians' boasting. Rather, Christ is the object; Paul's circumstances provide the occasion. If it is the case that Paul's presence with the Philippians is the result of his active and successful defense before his judges (see below), it is not to be an occasion to glory in Paul's skill and courage. Rather, it is the result of Christ's providential care of the apostle.

In this passage Paul has consistently displaced himself as the primary actor in a story which is ostensibly about himself. Thus, Paul's account here makes it clear that his story is part of a larger story, the story of God's economy of salvation. In the light of Paul's persistent emphasis on the fellowship or communion which he shares with the Philippians, he starts to draw them into this larger story as well. Paul makes this explicit in 1:5, where he claims that he and the Philippians are fellow sharers in the gospel. It is also explicit in 1:30, where Paul claims that he and the Philippians are part of the same struggle. It is further evident in Paul's expression of thanks in 4:10-20. Hence, both preceding and following the arguments in 1:12-26 Paul explicitly notes that he and the Philippians share a common situation.

Within 1:12-26 Paul reflects about his own life and death. He claims that

---

57. See Witherington's discussion of this issue, *Friendship and Finances,* 47-49.

58. In regard to Phil. 1:26, Fee, *Philippians,* 54, helpfully points to Jer 9:23-24 as the passage which makes this clear. Here the wise person boasts in "the Lord" and not in "wisdom, might, or wealth."

59. As Witherington, *Friendship and Finances,* 47, notes, "Paul is trying in part in this discourse to de-enculturate his audience from such values by indicating that they are part of a different commonwealth, holding a different sort of citizenship."

his views and plans are shaped not only by his commitment to continue magnifying Christ in his body, but also by what is most beneficial to the Philippians. These claims implicitly indicate that he and the Philippians share a common situation. Further, he has indicated that his future joy and boasting in the Lord are intimately connected to the destiny of the Philippian community, a point he makes explicit in 2:12-18.

In vv. 22-25 Paul makes some rather bold claims about his future and the choices he faces. However else one may seek to make sense of this paragraph, one must, at least initially, take seriously Paul's claim to be faced with the choice of whether to live or to die. *A Noble Death*, written by James Tabor and Arthur Droge, argues that in Phil 1:21-26 Paul is contemplating suicide or voluntary death. They note that there is no explicit biblical prohibition against suicide. Many of Paul's contemporaries found the idea of suicide quite acceptable. Death was often seen in the Greco-Roman world as a release from a miserable life.[60] Nevertheless, since Paul as a slave of Christ was not free to do with his body as he wished, he would need God's approval to take his own life.[61] Given this, however, Droge and Tabor argue that Paul could conceive of killing himself and of glorifying God with his body by doing so.[62] Hence, although Paul would rather die/take his own life and be released from his misery, he will continue to live because it is useful to the Philippians. "Given the widespread acceptance of voluntary death among Paul's contemporaries, whether pagan or Jewish, is it so surprising that he would espouse a similar view?"[63]

Although there are certainly examples in the Greco-Roman world of those who view death as a release from a miserable life, Droge and Tabor's explanation cannot account for the persistent theme of joy running through Philippians. Paul sees his current situation as an occasion for joy. He expects to rejoice when he sees the Philippians (or hears about them). Although he is in prison and often mentions his chains, he could at the same time speak of the joy he has in the midst of prison. To the extent that Paul sees death as an advantage, it is not because it releases him from the misery of prison. Rather, it unites him with Christ. In this respect Paul's suicide would undermine his rhetoric in 1:12-26.

Moreover, while it might be conceivable in an abstract sense that one

---

60. Socrates and Antigone are the two prime examples for Droge and Tabor. They also cite Musonius Rufus who argues in a like manner to Paul that one should not desire death if one can be useful to others by remaining alive.

61. Droge and Tabor, *A Noble Death*, 124.

62. Droge and Tabor, *A Noble Death*, 124.

63. Droge and Tabor, *A Noble Death*, 125.

could both take one's own life and glorify God in one's body, this does not seem to be the case for Paul. Clearly, although it is an enemy, death is not the ultimate evil for Paul. Nevertheless, the ways in which one faces death play a major role in evaluating whether or not God is glorified by the disposition of one's body. Droge and Tabor simply have not made it clear how this might be so in Paul's case.

Criag Wansink in his book *Chained in Christ* offers a more precise accounting of these verses.[64] He also takes Paul's language in 1:21-26 seriously. That is, he takes Paul's discussion about having a choice about life or death in a straightforward way. But his argument is superior in that he is able to fit an account of Paul's claims here into a larger account of the argument of Philippians. Moreover, he points to a close epistolary parallel to Paul's rhetoric in Phil 1:18b-26 in a letter of Cicero to his brother Quintus (*Ad Quintum Fratrem*).

Writing as he stands accused of a crime, at two points in his letter Cicero indicates that he has contemplated taking his own life.[65] First he considered taking his life to save his brother from further shame and humiliation and from seeing Cicero in such reduced circumstances. That is, Cicero thought that by taking his life he would be benefiting his brother. He claims that he was "called back from death" by those who argued that his death would actually be worse for Quintus (1.3.1-2). What is consistent in Cicero's reflections here about his own life and death is that he desires to act primarily out of concern for Quintus rather than his own desires.

Later in 1.3.6 Cicero indicates that as soon as Quintus no longer needs him, he will not seek to remain alive. It is clear that while he remains alive, Cicero is dependent upon others. "By emphasizing that he had desired to kill himself in the past, Cicero protects himself from potential criticism that he was exploiting others for whatever financial support he was receiving."[66]

This is such a striking parallel to Phil 1:18-26 because, like Cicero, Paul expresses a clear preference to die (for very different reasons from Cicero's). Nevertheless, for the sake of others, both men seek to remain alive. They seek the benefits of others rather than their own preferences. In making his views known to the Philippians, Paul is beginning to develop a theme which will run through the entire epistle.[67] This theme is more explicitly devel-

---

64. Wansink, *Chained in Christ*.

65. Wansink, *Chained in Christ*, 107-12, gives a full analysis of 1.3.

66. Wansink, *Chained in Christ*, 111.

67. Wansink, *Chained in Christ*, 125, writes: "In Phil. 1.18b-26, Paul is not simply musing out loud on whether he would 'prefer' life or death. Rather, Paul is referring to a situation where he has a choice. By employing the rhetoric of voluntary death, by letting his readers know that

oped in 1:27–2:11. Paul expressly calls the Philippians to "walk in a manner worthy of the gospel of Christ." It becomes clear that the health of the Philippian congregation, in its current adversity, will depend on their abilities to unite and stand firm in the gospel. Such steadfast unity entails learning to look after the interests of others rather than their own individual interests (2:4). In 2:5-11 Paul will give this practice christological density. In ch. 2 he will note that Epaphroditus and Timothy exemplify this practice. Here in 1:18b-26 Paul implicitly presents his disposition regarding his own situation as a primary example of the sorts of activities to which he will call the Philippians.[68] This implication is brought to the surface when in 1:30 Paul links the Philippians' situation to his own. This requires the Philippians to develop patterns of judgment which will enable them to see their own circumstances as similar to Paul's (and Christ's) and to discern how to act in the appropriate ways.

Given that this is the theological import of Paul's discussion of both his preference for death over life and his decision to remain for the benefit of the Philippians, one might well ask to what extent Paul actually had a choice and what that choice was. Was Paul's choice a choice between committing suicide and not committing suicide?

Some time ago and in regard to a different case, Alasdair MacIntyre noted that the language we use to describe a specific death will decisively shape the evaluation we offer of that death. That is, to use the single term "suicide" to cover all occasions in which one takes one's own life simply does not provide the narrative density needed to describe and evaluate a particular action. MacIntyre contrasts the self-inflicted death of Minamoto no Yoshitsune in twelfth-century Japan with the death of an anonymous Japanese person today. Yoshitsune's death was performed to preserve his honor in the face of imminent defeat and done in accordance with Buddhist scriptures, whereas MacIntyre's modern Japanese person takes his own life because he is unable to cope with the burdens of trying to succeed. Given a sufficiently developed narrative framework into which to fit these actions, one can see Yoshitsune's death as a triumph over imminent defeat while the modern Japanese person's is a reflection of total defeat. The former is an act that can express the achievement of a supreme good, while the latter ex-

---

he does have a choice — with a preference which, for their sake, he will not choose — Paul presents a pattern of behavior which he expects the Philippian community to follow. Paul is talking about making a choice, against his own preference, for the sake of others. He expects his readers to do the same."

68. This, of course, stands in sharp contrast both to those who preach the gospel out of selfish motives (1:15-17), and the vices of selfishness and vanity proscribed in 2:3.

presses the total frustration of an individual's practical reasoning by external circumstances.[69]

I use this example to indicate that discussions over whether or not Paul contemplated suicide or even voluntary death tend to miss the point unless they can provide a sufficient narrative context into which such an act might fit. As Droge and Tabor note, there is no explicit prohibition of suicide in the OT that Paul might have violated. Even though Acts seems to indicate that initially Paul was in a relatively light form of custody, such a situation provided an abundance of physical, material, and mental trials. Moreover, should his situation have changed and he was actually put in a more severe form of confinement, these trials would have intensified dramatically. As Wansink's work makes clear, Roman jails and other places of confinement were horrific places devoid of much hope. Further, imprisonment brought great shame in a culture much more attentive to matters of honor and shame than our own. People often took their lives when faced with the prospect of prolonged imprisonment. On the other hand, what could one make of Paul's hopeful claim in 1:6 (and 2:13) about God's continued working in the lives of the Philippians in the midst of their adversity if Paul took his own life in hopeless despair over God's abandonment of him in prison? Clearly, the claim that Paul makes in 1:20 that Christ will be magnified in his body now as always would be falsified by any failure of cruciform courage on Paul's part — either in seeking to preserve his life in inappropriate sorts of ways or by taking his life.

Although there is much we do not know about Paul's imprisonment, it seems safe to presume Paul did not anticipate any action which would have rendered his claims in 1:6, 20 and elsewhere problematic. Wansink proposes that Paul might choose death by not defending himself in court.[70] In the ancient world there are numerous accounts of those who brought death on themselves in this way.[71] More importantly, the Synoptic Gospels present Jesus as being uncooperative during his trial. When faced with various charges, Jesus refused to answer them before Pilate (Mark 15:2-5; Matt 27:11-14; Luke 23:2-7 and Jesus' similar response to Herod in Luke 23:8-11). Many martyrs "chose death" by imitating Christ in their own trials.[72] Of course, the other

---

69. See MacIntyre, "Positivism, Sociology and Practical Reasoning," 96-97. L. Gregory Jones and I discuss this issue further in *Reading in Communion,* 8-9.

70. Wansink, *Chained in Christ,* 121.

71. Xenophon (*Apology* 9) and Epictetus (*Dissertationes* 1.9.22-24) both portray Socrates' death in this way. See also the discussion in Wansink, *Chained in Christ,* 121.

72. See, for example, Droge and Tabor, 129-58, on the *Martyrdom of Polycarp.* This chapter, unlike the previous chapter on Paul, shows much more theoretical sophistication in addressing the issue of how to use terms like "martyr" and "suicide."

option facing Paul would have been to make a vigorous defense of himself and the gospel for which he was in chains (cf. 1:13) as he does in Acts 22:1-21; 24:10-21; 26:1-29. Given the ways in which he resolves his dilemma in Phil 1:22-23, it seems most likely that Paul anticipates pursuing this option.

1:27-30

27 Do this one thing: Order your common life in a manner worthy of the gospel of Christ so that when I learn of your circumstances (either by coming and seeing for myself or by hearing of them) I will know that you are standing steadfast in one Spirit, with one soul striving together for the faith of the gospel. 28 Do not in any way be intimidated by your opponents, which will be a sign to them of destruction, but it is your salvation and this is from God. 29 For you have been granted not simply the grace of believing in Christ but to suffer for his sake. 30 For you now have the same struggles which you once saw I had and now hear that I have.

This passage is a linchpin in the argument of the epistle. Paul has just finished talking about his own situation and his disposition toward that situation (1:12-26), demonstrating a form of what one might call christologically dense irony. That is, Paul has raised the prospect that his situation appears to be frustrating both him and the advance of the gospel only to argue that, ironically, such a view misapprehends Paul's imprisonment, the power of the gospel, and the workings of God's providence.

This Christ-focused perspective on his sufferings allows Paul to see his imprisonment as leading to the providential advancement of the gospel. Moreover, in the light of this perspective, Paul decides that remaining in the flesh would be more beneficial to the Philippians. Hence, he will seek to remain in the flesh even though he would prefer to die and be with Christ.

By 1:27 Paul shifts the ground of his theological reflection from his own sufferings to the sufferings of the Philippians. In 1:27-30 Paul advocates that the Philippians adopt both a particular way of life and a particular disposition toward their sufferings. Both the pattern of life and the disposition toward suffering are analogous to those Paul has just reflected in his account of his own imprisonment. Indeed, by the end of this passage Paul will explicitly note that the Philippians' struggles are the same as his own (1:30). Because they are engaged in the same struggle Paul is, they, too, should see their circumstances in the light of the divine economy of salvation. Thus, they should comport themselves in a manner similar to Paul's. Paul's display of a life "worthy of the gospel of Christ" can be a model for the Philippians as they struggle to manifest a common life worthy of the gospel.[1] The Philippians are to stand firm in the face of their opponents. To their enemies, this steadfast adherence to the gospel will appear to seal the Philippians' doom. Instead, their fidelity is a sign of their salvation.

In 1:27 Paul makes it clear that he anticipates learning of the Philippians' circumstances. He will either see them face to face or learn of them from Timothy (cf. 2:24). How Paul learns of the Philippians' circumstances is less important than what he learns. Paul urges the Philippians to order their common life in a manner worthy of the gospel of Christ. In calling them to a pattern of life worthy of the gospel, Paul enjoins them to act in a manner consistent with or appropriate to the community's identity in God (cf. Eph 4:1; 1 Thess 2:12).

The real interpretive and theological focus of this injunction, however, depends on how one understands the single Greek verb πολιτεύεσθε/*politeuesthe*, which I have translated with the phrase "order your common life." As is often observed, this verb is not the normal way Paul speaks about the conduct of believers. It would be much more common for Paul to use a verb like "walk" (cf. Rom 13:13; Eph 4:1; Col 1:10; 1 Thess 2:12; 4:12). It appears then that Paul must be doing something more than urging a particular pattern of individual behavior. The question is, what more does Paul mean by using this word?

In his 1954 article R. Brewer made the case that πολιτεύεσθε/*politeuesthe* is a way of speaking about discharging one's obligations as a citizen. He combined this account of the verb with judgments about Philippi's status as a Roman colony with full legal standing to argue that Paul is urging the Philippians to continue to discharge their duties as citizens and residents of Philippi, while recognizing that their ultimate allegiance is to their heavenly "commonwealth" (πολίτευμα/*politeuma;* cf. 3:20).[2] The particular (and decisive) problem with this view is that, while Brewer has made a case that Paul's language here refers to discharging one's obligations as a member of a specific polity, he incorrectly infers that this implies the particular polity represented by Rome. For example, in the LXX this verb is widely used to refer to the practice of a Jewish (as opposed to Gentile) way of life (cf. Esth 8:13; 2 Macc 6:1; 11:25; *3 Maccabees* 3:4; *4 Maccabees* 2:8, 23; 4:23; 5:16). This is also the way the term is basically used in Josephus, *Vita* 1.2; *Letter of Aristeas* 31; and Acts 23:1.[3]

---

1. "Just as the apostle read his own circumstances in the light of the gospel's progress, so now he desires that the Philippians' behaviour be entirely worthy of the same gospel of Christ resulting in their contending together with one accord for the faith of the gospel" (O'Brien, *Philippians*, 145).

2. See Brewer, "The Meaning of *Politeuesthe*," 82-83.

3. See Miller, "Πολιτεύεσθε in Philippians 1.27."

Further, as Bockmuehl notes, in these particular contexts such a notion is clearly "a politically relevant act, which in the context is distinguished from alternative lifestyles that might have been chosen."[4] In the case of Esther and 2 Maccabees this is particularly poignant since in each case Jews are under threat because of the ways they conduct themselves.

Hence, it seems that rather than speaking of the Philippians' obligations as citizens of either Philippi or Rome, Paul is speaking about the ordering of the common life of the Philippian Christians. As the context makes clear, the standard against which this ordering takes place is not Rome or Jewish law. It is the gospel of Christ. "The rhetorical force of Paul's language is to play on the perceived desirability of citizenship in Roman society at Philippi, and to contrast against this the *Christian* vision of enfranchisement and belonging."[5] This seems especially clear in the light of Phil 3:20 where Paul notes that the Philippians are citizens of a heavenly commonwealth. Taken in this light, there seems to be an implicit contrast here between Roman citizenship and being a citizen of the gospel of Christ. "Paul interposes a counter-citizenship whose capital and seat of power are not earthly but heavenly, whose guarantor is not Nero but Christ."[6]

There seems to be a tendency to take Paul's claims here as a call to the Philippians to recognize their dual citizenship, that they are citizens of Philippi (or Rome) and the heavenly commonwealth. There are two significant problems with this dual citizenship argument. The first is that it is historically unlikely that many (if any) of the Philippian Christians would have been citizens.

The second problem is theological. The dual citizenship reading seems to underplay the contrast between Rome and Christ that Paul both bodily and rhetorically displays for the Philippians. Remember, Paul is in a Roman prison for the sake of Christ (1:13). Further, the opponents of the Philippians mentioned in 1:28 would appear to be the Roman citizens of Philippi (see also Paul's claim in 1:30 that the Philippians are engaged in the same struggle as Paul). Clearly, Paul is not advocating violent opposition to the empire here. Nevertheless, he makes it very clear that the interests and aims of the church are different from and largely at variance to the interests and aims of the empire.

More generally, once this notion of dual citizenship is applied in a contemporary theological context it starts to demonstrate a tendency toward a

4. Bockmuehl, *Philippians*, 97.
5. Bockmuehl, *Philippians*, 98.
6. Bockmuehl, *Philippians*, 98.

posture of accommodation to the modern state. Christian life then becomes a matter of private transactions between believers and God, while the state exercises control over the public lives of Christians. As Paul persistently makes clear both to the Philippians and to contemporary Christians, belief in Christ joins us to a "contrast society."[7] Notions of dual citizenship with Christ on the one hand, and either the Roman Empire or the modern nation state, on the other hand, will always tend to distort the physically and materially weaker side. As modernity has so powerfully shown, this results in a privatizing of Christian convictions so that they can coexist alongside one's loyalty to the state. This allows the state effectively to discipline the church, to destroy the church's identity as the material body of Christ in the world, to co-opt the bodies of believers for service to the state and, ultimately, to erase the possibility of Christian dissent that might be substantial enough to create martyrs.[8] While Christians will need to discuss and discern together the concrete shape of a common life worthy of the gospel in the light of the particular secular orders they find themselves under, they must avoid thinking of themselves as holding dual citizenship. They have one Lord and serve only one master.

As the rest of vv. 27-28 unfolds, it is clear that ordering their common life in a manner worthy of the gospel will require that the Philippians engage in a set of interrelated practices. They are to "stand steadfast in one spirit"; "with a single soul they are to strive together for the faith of the gospel"; they are not to be intimidated by their opponents.

Paul wants to learn that the Philippians are "standing steadfast in one spirit."[9] The main interpretive dispute in this clause concerns Paul's reference to the one spirit. Is it a common, unified disposition which is the precondition of steadfastness, or the Holy Spirit, which would be the power enabling steadfastness? Those who take this reference to a single spirit as a reference to a unified disposition within the community primarily rely on reading this phrase in the light of the two words which immediately follow in the clause, "one soul." "Spirit" and "soul" occur in parallel like this in Luke 1:46-47 and clearly refer there to a human spirit. Moreover, in Phil 4:23 "spirit" unambiguously refers to the common spirit of the Philippian congregation.[10]

---

7. The phrase "contrast society" comes from Lohfink's *Jesus and Community*.

8. See Cavanaugh, "'A Fire Strong Enough to Consume the House"; *Torture and Eucharist*.

9. When the verb στήκω/*stēkō* is used in similar contexts in the NT (e.g., 1 Cor 16:13; Gal 5:1; Phil 4:1; 1 Thess 3:8; 2 Thess 2:15) it refers to a steadfast disposition. This would seem to be its force here as well.

10. Those who see the issue this way include Hawthorne, *Philippians*, 56-57, and O'Brien, *Philippians*, 149.

Those who take this as a reference to the Holy Spirit cite, for example, the use of "the fellowship of the Spirit" in 2:1 as support of their view.[11] There are also references to the "one spirit" in 1 Cor 12:9, 13 and Eph 2:18; 4:3-4. Of these, only Eph 4:3-4 is directly relevant to an understanding of Philippians. The context of Eph 4:1-4 is quite close to Phil 1:27–2:4.[12] The references to the singularity of the Spirit in Ephesians come in a section which begins with a call to walk worthily. Walking worthily entails that the members of the body display certain types of habits, dispositions, and practices toward one another (several of which are also noted in Phil 2:1-4). Living in a manner appropriate to the Ephesians' calling will result in a unified peaceable body. The unity of the body, thus, testifies to the singularity of the Spirit (4:1-4). It is not the case that the oneness of the Spirit is dependent upon the lives of believers. Rather, the nature of the single Spirit from the one Lord enables a particular manner of living. Such a common life, then, reflects and bears witness to the character of the Spirit.

If the sole interpretive issue is what Paul intended to convey, the evidence for Philippians is inconclusive. Theologically, it is probably preferable to allow Eph 4:1-4 to influence our reading of this passage. That passage nicely illustrates that a common unified disposition, which is the result of a common life worthy of the gospel of Christ, reflects and bears witness to the power of the Spirit. "Standing firm in one Spirit" would point both to the common disposition of the community and the singular Spirit which enables such steadfastness and whose character is testified to in such a steadfast common life.

The second manifestation of a common life worthy of the gospel will require the Philippians to "strive together for the faith of the gospel." The Philippians have a common task, and they are to struggle together in their common task "with one soul."[13] The unity found in their common life, and the dispositions such a life fosters, are the means by which they can struggle together. Indeed, it is the failure of such dispositions in Euodia and Syntyche in 4:3 that leads to Paul's admonition in 4:2-3 and his reminder that they have in the past manifested the unity required of fellow strugglers in the gospel.

Paul does not elaborate here on the nature of "the faith of the gospel." Within the context of the epistle as a whole, such a faith would involve holding a variety of convictions: convictions about the God who is at work in the lives of Paul and the Philippians (e.g., 1:12-26; 1:6), convictions about Christ

---

11. See Bockmuehl, *Philippians,* 99, and Fee, *Philippians,* 164-66.

12. Aquinas, *Philippians,* 73, makes reference to Eph 4:3 in his comments on Phil 1:27.

13. This is one of the two occurrences of συναθλέω/*synathleō* (strive together) in the NT. The other is in Phil 4:3, again in regard to "the gospel." In both places the verb speaks of struggling together in a common task.

(most obviously displayed in 2:6-11), and convictions about the nature of Christian community and friendship (e.g., 2:14-30; 4:1-7). It is equally clear, however, that holding these convictions also entails a variety of practices (most concisely stated in 1:27 and 2:1-4). Here in 1:27, however, "struggling together for the faith of the gospel" indicates that faith refers both to the reason for the Philippians' common struggle and to the end toward which that struggle is directed.

As v. 28 makes clear, the Philippians have opponents. Moreover, it is the Philippians' commitment to the gospel that has generated opposition. Further, the Philippians' ability to maintain their commitment in the face of opposition testifies to the power of the gospel. Thus, the third practice which Paul ties to the Philippians' manifestation of a common life worthy of the gospel requires that the Philippians not be intimidated by their opponents. Such courage in the face of opposition is what standing steadfast requires. Paul's admonition to courage recalls his earlier claim to magnify Christ in his body whether through life or through death (1:20). As v. 30 makes clear Paul sees the Philippians in an analogous situation to his own, and his convictions and practices ought to be theirs, too. The sort of courage Paul advocates here is not the only component of lives and bodies which magnify Christ, but it is a necessary element, particularly in the face of opposition which may have the power to kill.

A large amount of ink has been spent on trying to identify the adversaries mentioned in this verse. One particular question concerns the relationship between these characters and those mentioned in ch. 3. Despite the fascination this and other similar questions may hold for us, it is very important in this regard not to say more than the evidence indicates, and the evidence does not allow one to say very much here.

From the claims in 1:29 it would appear that the Philippians' opponents can inflict suffering on them. This would indicate that the opponents are outside the church and thus different from those characters addressed in ch. 3.[14] In 1:30 Paul makes a connection between his current struggles and his past struggles in Philippi on the one hand, and the Philippians' current struggles on the other hand. This would indicate that the Philippians, like Paul, are under pressure from the authorities because of their Christian confession. There is certainly a body of evidence indicating that Christianity was seen as a threat to political harmony and stability.[15] Moreover, in Acts 16:20 this is the charge

---

14. This goes against Collange, *Philippians*, 75, and Hendriksen, *Philippians*, 87, among others, who see the opponents in 1:28 as identical with those addressed in 3:2.

15. In addition to material in the NT see, for example, Origen, *Contra Celsum* 5-7; also the

brought against Paul in Philippi. In addition, 2 Cor 8:1-2 suggests that Christians in Macedonia were being persecuted. All this would argue that the opponents in 1:28 are those from the local population who see Christianity as a threat to the harmony and stability of this imperial outpost.[16] While it would appear that at least some Philippian Christians were under threat of imprisonment and even death, we should not necessarily assume that this was the only opposition faced by Christians in Philippi. For example, opponents of Christianity could have brought a number of economic pressures on Philippian Christians ranging from firing Christian workers to refusing to buy from Christians. Given that it is most likely that the economic circumstances of the majority of Philippian Christians would have been extremely fragile, such economic pressures would have put a tremendous burden on individual Christians as well as the community.[17] Indeed, in the light of Paul's explicit commands in 2:1-4, economic pressures would have provided the Philippians with a concrete occasion in which they would be tempted to seek their own benefit rather than the benefit of others, thus threatening the unity of the church. While economic opposition is a possible and neglected consideration in regard to this verse, we can simply note that this is a possibility.

Even so, we should not lose sight of the fact that Paul's emphasis on magnifying Christ in his body, his reflection on his own imprisonment and his assertion in 1:30 that he and the Philippians are in the same situation indicate that at least some in the church were facing arrest, imprisonment, and even death.

At this point we come upon the problematic part of 1:28. The concluding phrase of this verse is relatively easy to translate in a formally exact way: "which is to them a sign of destruction, but it is your[18] salvation. And this is from God." Despite this, it is not very clear what Paul is getting at. Indeed, all attempts to make sense of this verse end up having to supply words or concepts which are not directly expressed, but perhaps implied, in these two

---

narratives related in Musurillo, *The Acts of the Christian Martyrs;* Robert Wilken, *The Christians as the Romans Saw Them.*

16. See deVos, *Church and Community Conflicts.* Also Bormann, *Philippi,* 218, and, in particular, Oakes, *Philippians,* ch 3. This is also basically the position of Bockmuehl, *Philippians,* 100; Fee, *Philippians,* 167 n. 50 and O'Brien, *Philippians,* 153.

17. See Oakes, *Philippians,* ch. 3, for a strong argument for the primary form of the Philippians' suffering being economic.

18. Some later mss. read ὑμῖν/*hymin* (to you) here. Though the evidence is against the originality of this variant, it does rightly capture the sense that the distinctions made in this verse are between ways of interpreting the sign and not between destruction and salvation. This is explicitly against Beare, *Philippians,* 68.

clauses. My interpretation here will try to take the best account of the evidence that is there, unpacking its inferences in a way consistent with the argument of the epistle as a whole and without requiring unusual leaps of logic.

The sentence which began in 1:27 with the demand that the Philippians order their common life in a manner worthy of the gospel goes on, by means of the following participial phrases, to elaborate the specific practices Paul thinks are essential to this ordering. Paul then claims that the Philippians' faith, a faith which generates and sustains steadfast courage in the face of opponents, is a sign to their opponents.[19] Their faith is, therefore, something which stands as a concrete demonstration of what is the case.[20] The rest of the verse explains what type of sign it is and to whom it is directed.

The text is quite clear that, whatever else it is, the Philippians' steadfast adherence to their faith is a sign of destruction to their opponents. What sort of destruction is this and who is destroyed? Recent commentators tend to try to answer this question by focusing on the nature of "destruction" and the "salvation" mentioned here. The common way in which Paul (and the Bible generally) uses these terms is to refer to eternal damnation and eschatological salvation.[21] There is no real reason to think otherwise here. To make real progress in our understanding, however, it will be important to shift attention for a moment. Instead of focusing on the nature of the destruction mentioned here, we need to clarify who the object of this destruction is. By focusing on this question I think we can get a better answer to the nature of the destruction (and the salvation) mentioned here.

The majority of the recent commentators and recent English translations take it that Paul is claiming here that the Philippians' steadfast faith in the face of opposition is a concrete manifestation to their opponents of the opponents' destruction.[22] In fact, however, the syntax of this clause neither

---

19. There is some ambiguity about the antecedent of the feminine relative pronoun "which" (ἥτις/*hētis*). Most recent commentators argue — with some plausibility — that this feminine relative pronoun takes its gender by attraction to the feminine noun "sign" (ἔνδειξις/*endeixis*). While this is not the only solution, it is the one most commentators adopt. See, for example, Fee, *Philippians*, 169 n. 53; O'Brien, *Philippians*, 154. Also see the earlier commentaries of Lightfoot, *Philippians*, 106, and E. Lohmeyer, *Philipper*, 76.

20. Although Fee's preference for "omen" is well defended (*Philippians*, 168 n. 53), as is O'Brien's (*Philippians*, 154) preference for "proof," I think my account makes the same point without overtones of either something overly mysterious or a logical proof.

21. See in particular the pairing of the verbal forms of these two words in 1 Cor 1:18. See also the survey of different passages in O'Brien, *Philippians*, 156-57.

22. See Bockmuehl, *Philippians*, 101; Fee, *Philippians*, 168; Hendriksen, *Philippians*, 89; O'Brien, *Philippians*, 156-57; Witherington, *Philippians*, 56. In addition, the RSV, NRSV, NEB, CEV, and NAB are just some of the English translations which translate the verse this way.

demands nor indicates this. Moreover, such a reading makes it much more difficult to make sense of the clause.

How exactly would the opponents recognize this sign? Of the modern commentators, Beare at least treats this as a serious interpretive problem. He comes up with an account of how the Philippians' behavior would at least subliminally affect the opponents' psyches,[23] even though we have no way of knowing what was going on in the opponents' psyches. Nor is it really clear that Paul knows or cares about this. Indeed, if we take Paul's own reflections on his role as persecutor of Christians, he suffered no psychic distress. As Paul explicitly notes in Phil 3:4-11, his role as persecutor of Christians was a mark of virtue. It was a concrete manifestation of his commitment to Judaism. He was sinfully misguided in this perception, but there is no evidence that he suffered from psychic turmoil. Indeed, he notes that as to the righteousness found in the law he was blameless (3:6). Furthermore, if the Philippians remain steadfast in their faith in the face of opposition from pagans who see Christianity as a threat to the empire, or at least to the harmony and stability of Philippi, we should not expect the opponents to characterize the Philippians' attitude as steadfast courage. Rather it will be a mark of stubbornness, a stubbornness that will result in their justifiable punishment at the hands of the authorities.

These difficulties do not arise if we take the Philippians' steadfastness in the face of opposition as a sign to the opponents of the Philippians' destruction. There are numerous occasions in Scripture when the enemies of the faithful take the persecution, misfortune, or death of the so-called faithful as a sign that God has rejected these people (e.g., Psalms 22; 41:4-10; Isa 36; 52:13–53:12, and, of course, Job). Indeed, such a fate confirms the persecutors' suspicions that the faith and practice of such people were not really "faithful" at all. The most obvious example here is the way Jesus' opponents evaluate the crucifixion (see Matt. 27:32-44 par.). The stories of Christian martyrs often relate that this is precisely the position held by those who put Christians to death. The unwillingness of Christians to apostatize is viewed as irrational, impious, superstitious, willful and worthy of death.[24] It is a concrete manifestation to the opponents of the Christians' impending destruction, a destruction that would have entailed more than just physical death, but also the judgment of the gods.[25]

23. See Beare, *Philippians*, 68. Hendriksen speaks of the opponents' "dim awareness" of their destruction. See *Philippians*, 89.

24. See the paradigmatic account of the death of Macellus of Tangier in *The Acts of the Christian Martyrs*.

25. For a discussion of Roman attitudes toward the early Christians see Wilken, *The*

Paul, however, asserts that the Philippians' fidelity to the gospel in the face of opposition results in their salvation. Thus, while the Philippians' steadfast unity in the gospel in the face of persecution is a sign to the persecutors of the Philippians' destruction, such fidelity is, rather, a concrete manifestation of their salvation. That is, from the Philippian Christian perspective, steadfast adherence to the faith is a concrete manifestation of their salvation to those who are able to interpret the economy of God's salvation properly.

Thus, in this verse Paul is displaying two competing evaluations of the Philippians' adhering to their faith in the ways Paul admonishes. To the opponents, it is willful flaunting of Roman authority and a harbinger of the Christians' imminent destruction. In reality, it marks the salvation of the Christians.[26] On this account, debates about whether the destruction/salvation pairing here refers to the temporal or eternal realm simply miss the point. The opponents view the Philippians' physical destruction as testimony to their eternal perdition. For Paul and the Philippians, their steadfastness demonstrates their salvation whether they live or die. It is simply the way they magnify Christ in their bodies (cf. 1:20). The final clause in this verse, "and this is from God," works to offer divine authorization for the perspective Paul is advocating. Of course, the fuller account of God's authorization of this perspective is laid out in the account of God's dealing with Christ's steadfast obedience and fidelity in 2:6-11.

In addition to avoiding unconvincing explanations of how the opponents come to recognize their own damnation in the Philippians' behavior, this account of 1:28b fits with a general pattern of Paul's argument thus far. Opponents of the gospel tend to misperceive the difficult circumstances in which Christians find themselves. In 1:12-26, Paul relates how his circumstances have worked to advance, rather than frustrate the gospel. Those who seek to increase Paul's tribulation ironically work to advance the gospel, and this leads to Paul's rejoicing (1:17-18). Those seeking to secure political harmony and stability by destroying Christians provide an occasion for Christians to demonstrate their salvation and the grace they have been given to suffer for Christ (1:28-29).

Further, in ch. 3 Paul relates for the Philippians his own dramatic change of perspective. Although Paul never says it in these words, it is precisely this christologically dense, ironic perspective that Paul seeks to form in

---

Christians as the Romans Saw Them, especially chapter III. There are also numerous occasions when the faithfulness of the people of God in the face of imminent danger is a sign to the faithful of their enemies' demise (e.g., Exod 14:13-14; Joshua 4–6; 1 Samuel 17, etc.).

26. As Hawthorne, *Philippians*, 60, notes, the real contrast here is between two different perceptions of the Philippians' behavior.

the Philippians. It is only within this perspective that one could even consider being a friend rather than an enemy of the cross (3:18-20). This is because through attentive contemplation and reflection upon the gospel of the crucified and risen one, Christians learn that, despite the signs to the contrary, the cross of Christ does not signify God's or the world's destruction of Jesus: rather it is a concrete manifestation of salvation.

The practices Paul presents as requisites of a common life worthy of the gospel, practices which might lead to persecution and even death, will tend to result in competing evaluations of those very acts of steadfast fidelity. Further, the differences in these competing evaluations cannot simply be resolved when one party is subdued by the other. As Stanley Hauerwas notes, "Rome could kill Christians but they could not victimize them. The martyrs could go to their death confident that the story to which their killers were trying to subject them — that is, the story of victimization — was not the true story of their death. To Rome, Christians dying for their faith, for their refusal to obey Caesar, was an irrational act. For the martyrs, their dying was part of a story that Rome could not acknowledge and remain in power as Rome."[27]

As the argument moves on to 1:29, Paul offers a justification for his claims about the result of Philippians' "ordering of their common life in a manner worthy of the gospel of Christ." It is not simply the Philippians' faith in Christ which is a gracious gift, their suffering for Christ's sake is also a gracious gift.

Paul has already noted that he and the Philippians (as part of the good work God has started in the Philippians) are fellow partners in Paul's commitment to and proclamation of the gospel (1:6-7). In this passage Paul shows that the Philippians are also his fellow participants in suffering for Christ's sake and that their suffering is the direct result of their commitment to Christ.[28]

This claim closely links the formation and maintenance of a common life worthy of the gospel of Christ with being granted the opportunity of suffering for one's commitments to that gospel. The Philippians' suffering is not

---

27. *After Christendom*, 38.

28. The use of the preposition ὑπέρ/*hyper* to speak of the Philippians' suffering for Christ's sake is similar to that found in 2 Cor 12:10; Acts 9:16; and (less directly) Col 1:24b. In all these cases the preposition works to distinguish suffering that is the result of one's commitments to Christ from other types of suffering. Fee, *Philippians*, 170-71. See also Bockmuehl, *Philippians*, 102: "While Christians saw this perspective uniquely fulfilled and vindicated in Christ, that did not prevent them from seeing their own sufferings *on behalf of* Christ as also making a positive, albeit derivative and participatory, contribution within the redemptive plan of God."

the result of a failure to walk worthily, but is a gracious gift that results from a common life worthy of the gospel.

The use of the passive voice in this clause presumes that God is the subject of the verb. The same God who began a good work in the Philippians and who will bring that good work to completion, is also the one who grants them the opportunity of suffering for their faith. Throughout this first chapter, and in the assertions of 1:29 in particular, Paul manifests great confidence in God's providential ordering of events — in both his life and the Philippians'. This is, in part, due to the similarity of their circumstances, a point which Paul explicitly makes in the next verse.

In 1:30 Paul draws a parallel between his ongoing struggle, which the Philippians have known both firsthand and via reports, and the situation of opposition and suffering which the Philippians currently face. In this context Paul's "struggle" would seem to refer to the pagan opposition which Paul often encountered both when in Philippi (Acts 16:16-24; 1 Thess 2:2) and now in his current imprisonment.

Paul and the Philippians are engaged in "the same struggle." Presumably, the Philippians were aware of Paul's situation. They certainly were aware of their own situation. What is the point of noting their sameness? Throughout his account of his own circumstances in 1:12-26 Paul has consistently argued that despite his "struggles" the gospel has advanced. Moreover, his convictions about God's providential working in his situation have led him to manifest a particular set of dispositions and practices (1:19-26) in the face of imprisonment. In 1:27-30 he has initiated an argument that the Philippians are to have a parallel faith in God's providential ordering of their situation. He wants them to "read" their situation as he "reads" his own. He also calls on them to manifest a similar set of dispositions and practices in their common life. Here at the end of the chapter the reason he gives for this is that he and they are in the same struggle. Paul's pattern of life here is particularly exemplary for the Philippians because his situation is so much like theirs.

Indeed, one of the crucial moves Paul makes here is that he narrates and names both his suffering and the Philippians' suffering as a gracious gift from God. This surely must strike modern ears as very strange. Paul here is not making a general claim about all suffering. Rather, his remark is about suffering willingly taken on because of one's convictions about the crucified and resurrected one. Moreover, Paul did not, and he does not, advise the Philippians to seek out suffering. Rather, suffering is the result of being obedient to God in a world that cannot abide such obedient ones. Paul is quite clear that the primary activities of the Christian are focused on forming and maintaining a common life worthy of the gospel. Such a life both calls forth and results in a steadfast unity, empowered by the Spirit, in which Christians struggle together in this common vocation. Whether this results in suffering is largely out of our hands. To the extent, then, that such suffering is a gift from God, it is so because our common life has been worthy of the gospel. The world (particularly nation states), being the sort of place it is, is threatened by the presence of those who find their security in God and give their allegiance to God alone.

In addition, it is clear that Paul's call to a common life worthy of the gospel, lived in fidelity to the Lord, will tend to generate opposition. In the face of opposition, Christians in Philippi and elsewhere are to remain steadfast and courageous. Of course, the point is not to be oppositional, but to be faithful. Nevertheless, the question then becomes whether Christians in America or elsewhere testify in word and deed to a faith substantial enough to provoke opposition from powers that are either indifferent or hostile to the triune God. Christians in the U.S. should not assume that the church here does not suffer state-sponsored opposition because of the benevolence of our government or the protective powers of our constitution. I suspect that it is much more the case that the common life of most churches is so inadequate to the gospel and our disunity so debilitating that the state has nothing to fear from us. I am also confident that should substantial numbers of Christians in America, under the Spirit's guidance and provocation, repent and take Paul's words to the Philippians seriously, then we, too, may find that we have been given that gracious gift of not simply believing in Christ but also suffering for his sake.

In this section Paul presents united, courageous, and steadfast fidelity as both an essential practice of a common life worthy of the gospel of Christ and a sign of the worthiness of the life of Christian communities. This is clearly not the only practice of a common life worthy of the gospel. Nevertheless, Paul's claims here offer a set of probing questions directed at the common life of all contemporary Christian communities. Do Christians in America, for example, consider (with Paul) unity an essential practice of the Christian life? Have we been so schooled in the habits of individualism that we are no longer willing to form our lives in Christ in common with other believers?

Answering this question will require both a brief account of the difference between a united church in which there are disagreements, and a longer account of the divided church in America. Neither of these accounts will be the last word on these matters. I hope, however, they will provoke further thought and action.

It is important to understand Paul does not desire a monochrome church. He recognizes varieties of theological views, styles of worship, and exercise of gifts in ministry. Pauline notions of unity rely on the harmonious in-

71

terrelation of diverse Christians rather than a unity that is achieved through homogeneity. In this respect Paul's views are sharply at odds with many contemporary strategies of church growth.[29] Moreover, Paul's churches can sustain a measure of debate and disagreement without sacrificing unity. We can see an example of this in a passage I will treat in greater detail later, but which will also be useful to speak about now.

In 3:15 Paul wraps up a long plea to the Philippians to adopt a pattern of thinking, feeling and acting that is focused around the patterns displayed to them by the crucified and resurrected Christ. This pattern of thinking, feeling, and acting will lead the Philippians to do certain things and avoid other things, all of which Paul lays out in some detail. These will enhance the Philippians' prospects of attaining their true end in Christ. Paul then turns to himself. He does not claim that he has attained this end yet. Rather, he presses on to the finish line so that he might win the prize of the heavenly call of God in Christ Jesus. These are some of the most elevated lines in the entire New Testament. Rather than stopping there and moving on to something else, Paul adds, "If any of you are inclined to adopt a different pattern of thinking, feeling, and acting, God will reveal to you the proper mindset to adopt." After this impassioned plea, Paul seems willing to allow that others may think differently. This is not because Paul is a good liberal and thinks that in matters of faith people should be allowed their own opinions. Rather, he can display a certain detachment from his own argument because he is convinced that God is directing and enabling the advancement of the gospel. Paul does not have to coerce the Philippians into adopting his pattern of thinking, feeling, and acting because he is confident that God will bring both him and the Philippians to their proper end in Christ. It is this steadfast conviction about God's providence that enables Paul to be patient when the result he seeks is not immediately achieved. Again, Pauline patience stands in sharp contrast to the practice of many American Christians who eagerly join small group Bible studies only to leave the group as soon as their views are questioned, challenged, or disciplined. As Robert Wuthnow's research indicates, these groups retain their unity only to the extent that the members refuse to disagree openly with each other.[30]

29. See the discussion of homogeneity in congregations in Kenneson and Street, *Selling Out the Church.*

30. See Wuthnow, *Sharing the Journey.* Wuthnow found that over half of the small groups he surveyed were organized around Bible study. This, however, did not actually significantly help people learn more about the Bible or its interpretation. In fact, people tended to leave a Bible study as soon as their interpretation was challenged by another. Some small Bible studies counter this by forbidding anyone to criticize the interpretation of another.

The practices of unity which Paul advocates for the Philippians allow for a measure of disagreement and diversity. Paul could not, however, understand the divisions which mark our churches today, divisions in which Christians recognize each other as Christians and yet are unable to share the eucharist or recognize each other's orders of ministry. To the extent Paul could understand these matters, they would grieve him deeply. The question facing contemporary American Christians concerns whether we have become so used to a divided and fragmented set of Christian churches that we no longer feel the sting of division. To gloss the words of George Lindbeck, does the eucharist taste bitter to us in the midst of our divisions?[31]

To understand why the eucharist *ought* to taste bitter in our mouths we need to begin with an account of salvation. Christian accounts of salvation often speak of being drawn into communion with God, whose very being is characterized as the communion of Father, Son, and Holy Spirit. 2 Peter 1:4 indicates that we are called into "communion with the divine nature." 1 John 1:3, likewise, claims that "our communion is with the Father and his Son Jesus Christ." Moreover, 1 John links our communion with God to our communion with each other. Jesus' prayer in John 17 is that his followers "may be one just as we are one." In addition, as 1 Cor 11:17-34 makes plain, Paul sees our communion with each other as integrally connected to our communion with God.

All this indicates that the unity or communion of believers is intimately tied to our salvation or communion with God. Thus, if salvation is a gift of God's grace, then the unity of the body of Christ is also a gift of grace. This understanding of the unity of the church would also make sense of Paul's assumption that Christ cannot be divided (1 Cor 1:13; Eph 4:4). This all implies that ". . . the unity of church is a reality we cannot destroy. A person or community may leave this unity but cannot divide it."[32]

Both Phil 1:27-30 and the logic of Christian accounts of salvation indicate that unity is an essential component of a common life ordered in a manner worthy of the gospel of Christ. At the same time, Christians live in a world marked by church divisions. How can these theological truths about the unity of the church stand alongside our manifest divisions? On the one hand, they are simply contradictions. "We can understand the contradiction of unity and division as the halting of a movement or trajectory before that movement

31. This is the title of a talk given by Lindbeck and reprinted in *Spectrum*, the Yale Divinity School bulletin. The title is tied to Radner's chapter in *The End of the Church*, "Vinegar and Gall: Tasting the Eucharist in a Divided Church."

32. Root, "Why Care about the Unity of the Church?" 104. My argument here draws extensively from Root's work.

or trajectory has reached its natural goal. We are given a unity in Christ and the Spirit but fail to live out that unity in a way that unity itself demands."[33] It would appear, then, that our initial task has to be focused on how to understand the contradiction of church division.

This is a very different issue for us than it was for Catholics, Lutherans, Calvinists, and others in the sixteenth century. At that point the issues were focused on where the true church is located and how to know this. Once the true church was found, all other options simply were not church. There is a real sense that the sixteenth century did not need to address the issue of a divided church, because one's opponents were not really part of the Church in the first place. The problems of a divided church as we know it today are really the result of ecumenism. The more Catholics and non-Catholics, for example, recognize each other as true Christians, the greater the problem of their division, the sharper the pain of this fracture.

To understand our contemporary divisions we should begin by looking at stories of divided Israel.[34] The division of Israel into northern and southern kingdoms provides us with a closer analogy for our current situation than either divisions within Pauline churches, such as the ones in Corinth, or the divisions arising out of the Reformation. Israel's division is one of the results of Israel's persistent resistance to the Spirit of God (cf. Psalm 106; Jer 3:6-15). Division is simply one manifestation of this resistance along with such things as grumbling against God and Moses in the wilderness, lapses into idolatry when Israel occupies the land, and the request for a human king. Interestingly, each of these manifestations of resistance becomes a form of God's judgment on Israel.

Let me explain this a bit more. Take the example of Israel's request for a human king in 1 Samuel 8. Although Samuel takes this as a personal affront, God makes it clear that it is simply part of a pattern of Israel's rejection of God's dominion which has carried on from the moment God led the Israelites out of Egypt. This rejection of God results in the granting of a king. The granting of this request becomes the form of God's judgment on Israel as kings become both oppressively acquisitive and idolatrous (cf. 1 Sam 8:10-18; 12:16-25).

We see here that one of the forms of God's judgment is giving us what we want. If we treat division in this light it becomes clear that division is both a sign that we are willing to, and even desire to, live separate from our broth-

33. Root, "Why Care about the Unity of the Church?" 108.
34. In doing this I am following the invitation of Ephraim Radner in his very challenging book, *The End of the Church,* chapter 1.

ers and sisters in Christ and it is also God's judgment upon that desire. Our failure to love, especially to love our brothers and sisters with whom we are at odds, lies at the root of our willingness and desire for separation. This separation in the form of church division is God's judgment on our failure to love as Christ commands.

One of the by-products of Israel's resistance to God's Spirit is that their senses become dulled so that they are increasingly unable to perceive the workings of God's Spirit. Isaiah makes this particularly clear in 6:10; 28:9; 29:9-13. This sort of stupefaction and blindness is a precursor to judgment. At those times when Israel is most in need of hearing God's word and repenting, they have also rendered themselves least able to hear that word. Judgment, however, leads to restoration. Importantly, it is restoration of a *unified* Israel as noted in passages such as Jer 3:18 and Ezek 39:21-29.

If we read the divided church in the light of biblical Israel and its division, then we face several conclusions. First, division is one particularly dramatic way of resisting the Spirit of God. Such resistance further dulls our senses so that we are less able to discern the movements and promptings of God's Spirit. Thus, we become further crippled in reading God's word. The response called for throughout the prophets to this phenomenon is repent. Whether our senses are so dulled that we cannot discern the proper form of repentance, whether God's judgment is so close at hand that we cannot avoid it, one cannot say. Instead, we are called to repent and to hope in God's unfailing plan of restoration and redemption in Christ.

The second set of scriptural texts we might look at are those NT passages which deal with unbelieving Israel, and Romans 9-11 in particular. It seems to me there are a right way and a wrong way to read our current divisions in the light of this passage. The wrong way is to devote time and energy to figuring out which part of the divided church is the natural vine, which parts are grafted in, and which are cut off. Instead, we should remember that the God who grafts in can also lop off. There is no place for presumption or complacency here. Instead, we should in our divisions try to provoke our divided brothers and sisters through ever greater works of love to return to the vine. As Cardinal Ratzinger notes, "Perhaps institutional separation has some share in the significance of salvation history which St. Paul attributes to the division between Israel and the Gentiles — namely that they should make 'each other envious,' vying with each other in coming closer to the Lord (Rom 11:11)."[35]

---

35. Ratzinger, "Anglican-Catholic Dialogue: Its Problems and Hopes," in *Church Ecumenism and Politics*, 87.

In each of these passages we see some of the consequences of church division for believers: Division is seen as a form of resistance to the Spirit of God. It dulls believers' abilities to hear and respond to both the Spirit and the word, which, in turn, generates further unrighteousness. Division provokes God's judgment and is not part of God's vision for the restoration of the people of God. While both presumption and complacency are real temptations, neither is an appropriate response to division. Rather, we are called to sustained forms of repentance, "vying with each other in coming closer to God" with the aim of drawing the other to God.

At the beginning of Ephesians we are told that God's plan for the fullness of time is that all things shall be gathered together under Christ's lordship. Just as God's restoration of Israel brings a reunion of the divided Israel and the infusion of Gentiles, so in Christ, God will bring all things together in their proper relationship to Christ. It is important to note that this includes those principalities and powers which are not yet under Christ's dominion (1:10).

For Paul's purposes, the paramount activity of Christ's gathering of all things is the unification of Jews and Gentiles in one body through the cross and resurrection of Jesus. Ephesians 2 is focused on just this activity by which those near and those far off are brought together into one. This is and always has been God's providential plan for the redemption of the world. Paul calls this plan the "mystery which was made known to me by revelation" (Ephesians 3:2). It is, in short, the good news which Paul has been commissioned to proclaim. Then in 3:9-10 he makes a claim upon which I want to focus briefly. Paul is reflecting on his commission to proclaim this gospel of the unification of Jew and Gentile in Christ. He claims that God has given him the charge "to make everyone see what is the plan of the mystery hidden for ages in God who created all things: so that through the church the riches of God's wisdom might be made known to the principalities and powers in the heavenlies." The church, by its very existence as a single body of Jews and Gentiles united in Christ, makes God's wisdom known to the principalities and powers. As it appears here in Ephesians the church's witness to the principalities and powers is integrally connected to and may even depend upon its unity.

What do we make of this in the light of our current situation of division? The most extreme way of putting the matter is to say that the church's witness to the principalities and powers is falsified or undermined by division. At the very least, one must say that the church's witness to the principalities and powers is hindered and frustrated by division.

Each of these passages requires a different style of reading. One reads Israel and its resistance to the Spirit as a figure of the church to call the divided church to repentance. Romans expands on this to provide admonitions, by way of analogy, about how to live in a divided church. Ephesians implicitly warns of some of the consequences of division for the world at large, especially the principalities and powers.

Paul's argument in Phil 1:27-30 is that a common life worthy of the gospel both generates and depends on (among other things) the practice of unity among the Philippians. If Christians in America are to take this admonition to heart, the first and essential step in confronting the contradiction of our divisions is to begin to understand it and to see it in all its ugliness. If church division represents a series of wounds to the one body of Christ, then we must stop anesthetizing ourselves to this wound. Until large numbers of Christians feel the pain of this wound, we will not seek healing. Out of that pain, our response is to be repentance.

2:1-4

1 Therefore, if in Christ there is any encouragement, if any solace of love, if any fellowship of the Spirit, if any compassion and mercy, as, of course, there is, 2 then make my joy complete by manifesting a common pattern of thinking and acting, having the same love, being bound together by this common way of thinking and acting. 3 You must avoid selfish ambition and vain conceit. Instead, in humility consider others as your superiors. 4 Do not attend to your own interests but rather to the interests of others.

At the close of ch. 1 Paul indicated that if the Philippians order their common life in a manner worthy of the gospel, remaining steadfast in the face of suffering, they will secure their salvation. Achieving this will require two interrelated things of the Philippians. First, they need to be able to see that, despite what their opponents think, their steadfastness is a sign of their salvation. Perceiving things in this way requires attention to God's providential economy of salvation within which the Philippians have been granted the grace not only to believe but to suffer for Christ's sake. In 1:12-26 Paul has already given a "reading" of God's economy in relation to his own imprisonment. He implicitly invites the Philippians to learn a similar pattern of reading God's economy because they are engaged in the same struggle he is (1:30). He will make this invitation more explicit in 2:2-4. Second, the salvation of which Paul speaks in 1:28 entails that the Philippians manifest a certain sort of common life or politics. That is, this salvation will call forth and require the presence of a community living in a manner worthy of the gospel and not intimidated by its opponents. Such an outward disposition will require the Philippians to order their common life in certain ways, which Paul discusses briefly in 1:27-30.

As ch. 2 begins, Paul further outlines the shape of this common life. In a very general sense this passage is about friendship and political concord among friends. Concord was often seen as the basis for friendship and was also a very common topic of ancient political treatises.[1] Nevertheless, as I will try to show, although concord is a common political idea, Paul's understanding of both the nature of such concord and how the Philippian Christians might achieve and maintain it, is rather different from views that would have been common among the citizens of Philippi. We can see this by examining Paul's specific admonitions to the Philippians regarding their life together.

2:1-4 is clearly connected to 1:27-30, where Paul commands the Philippians to order their common life in a manner worthy of the gospel of Christ in the midst of opposition and suffering.[2] Paul appeals personally to the Philippians in 2:1-4 as he begins to spell out the character of that common life. Paul begins with four "if" clauses leading to an entreaty to "make my joy full." This plea seems to provide Paul some purchase on the demands he will go on to make in vv. 2-4. The structure of this passage, however, reminds us that these are not so much the commands of an officer to troops as the directives of one Christian friend to other Christian friends based on their common vocation to live in a manner worthy of the gospel.

If read aloud in Greek, these "if" clauses carry a certain rhythm and, perhaps, convey Paul's personal passion here. As they are laid out on a page in English, however, they can convey just the opposite. That is, these conditional clauses may seem to indicate that Paul is somehow unsure about the bonds which he and the Philippians share in Christ.[3] To see that this is not the case, one can compare 2:1 with the grammatically parallel passage in 2 Cor 5:17. In that context the clause is not conditional ("should anyone be in Christ") but inclusive and indefinite ("whoever is in Christ"). In regard to Phil 2:1 Bockmuehl writes, "If the conditional sense is in any sense to be retained here, this could be in terms of ironic understatement: 'if Christ means any encouragement at all . . . [as of course he does].'"[4]

---

1. Plato says that friendship is "concord" in *Alcibiades* 126-27. See also the discussion in Stowers, "Friends and Enemies," 111-12. See the discussion of the rhetoric and ideology of concord in Martin, *The Corinthian Body*, 39-47.

2. In the Greek this is made clear by the use of the conjunction οὖν/*oun* in 2:1.

3. See Hawthorne, *Philippians*, 64.

4. Bockmuehl, *Philippians*, 104-5. Bockmuehl also has a persuasive explanation for the occurrence of the singular τίς/*tis* used with the plural σπλάγχνα/*splanchna* (105).

Moreover, 2:1 makes it clear that Paul shares all of these bonds with the Philippians because they and he are "in Christ." In this particular context, with its focus on the common life of the Philippian congregation, it is important to recognize the political and communal nuances of being "in Christ." As with Rom 6:1-14, being in Christ is a way of talking about one's citizenship within the realm shaped, determined, and ruled by Christ (cf. Phil 1:1). Further, this phrase applies to all four of the clauses in this verse. In fact, as the repetition of the phrase in 2:5 indicates, this issue of life "in Christ" never really moves from the forefront of Paul's discourse.

Paul uses four phrases to describe the benefits or blessings that the Philippians and he share by virtue of their commitments to life in Christ. These are "encouragement," "the solace of love," "fellowship in the Spirit," and "compassion and mercy." The combination of these aims to speak of a single comprehensive effect rather than four sharply distinguishable attributes.

In addition, it is crucial to recognize that all of these attributes apply to the community and not to individuals. Paul's admonitions here flow from his call to the Philippians in 1:27 to order their common life in a manner worthy of the gospel of Christ. He is, therefore, speaking about how a community whose common life is founded and sustained by the crucified and risen Christ should live together. Paul's discourse is both communal and christocentric. In his profound little book, *Life Together,* the German pastor/theologian Dietrich Bonhoeffer makes this point about the christocentric nature of Christian community:

> Christianity means community through Jesus Christ and in Jesus Christ. No Christian community is more or less than this. . . . We belong to one another only through and in Jesus Christ.
>
> What does this mean? It means, first, that a Christian needs others because of Jesus Christ. It means, second, that a Christian comes to others only through Jesus Christ. It means, third, that in Jesus Christ we have been chosen from eternity, accepted in time and united for eternity.[5]

Further, all these specific characteristics of life in Christ (solace of love, fellowship enabled by the Spirit, compassion and mercy) are relational. That is, all of these characteristics can really be displayed only in relation to others. They require a community for their proper expression. To see this, let us look more closely at each of them.

---

5. *Life Together,* 21.

Commentators are divided over whether "encouragement" or "comfort" is the best way to translate παράκλησις/*paraklēsis*.[6] Certainly, in the context of the Philippians' situation, they would receive courage and edification in the midst of opposition by virtue of being in Christ. Paul uses the same Greek term in Rom 15:5 with the sense of "encouragement." Alternatively, in 2 Cor 1:3-7; 7:4, 7 Paul uses the term with the sense of comforting the afflicted. While the Corinthian and Philippian contexts are different, the Philippians certainly experience afflictions for which they would receive comfort due to their life in Christ. Thus, both "comfort" and "encouragement" seem possible here. Nevertheless, if there is any point in making a distinction here, it would seem better to opt for "encouragement" as the next phrase, "solace of love," carries the sense of comfort.

"Solace" aptly translates the only NT appearance of παραμύθιον/ *paramythion*.[7] Paul's point here would seem to be that the bonds of love uniting the Philippians (and Paul) in Christ are the basis for comfort in the midst of suffering. The character of that love and by implication the quality of the comfort it provides are shaped, determined, and manifested by Christ. Thus, it is important to understand that such comfort in affliction will not necessarily remove or obviate the affliction. The one who comforts is himself the crucified one. The source of Christian comfort lies in the grace of finding Christ present in affliction.

The "fellowship of the Spirit" should be read as a reference to the Holy Spirit. While "spirit" is used in 4:23 to refer to the common spirit of the Philippian congregation, there are sufficient parallels here in 2:1 with Eph 4:3-4 to see this as a reference to the Holy Spirit. Moreover, in keeping with the notion that the benefits mentioned here are all "in Christ" it seems best to see this fellowship or partnership of the Spirit as a reference to a fellowship of people in Christ enabled and empowered by the Holy Spirit (or, in the light of 1:19, "the Spirit of Jesus Christ").

Paul has already used the term "compassion" to indicate the affection he has for the Philippians in 1:8. Here in 2:1 he uses the combination of "compassion and mercy" (σπλάγχνα καὶ οἰκτιρμοί/*splanchna kai oiktirmoi*) to characterize the common life of those in Christ. There is some debate among commentators regarding the specific objects of this compassion and mercy.[8] Is this the compassion and mercy the Philippians have received from God? Is it a

6. Fee, *Philippians*, 177; Collange, *Philippians*, 77; Lohmeyer, *Philipper*, 82, opt for "comfort." Bockmuehl, *Philippians*, 107; Hawthorne, *Philippians*, 65, and Lightfoot, *Philippians*, 107, opt for "encouragement."

7. παραμυθία/*paramythia* appears in 1 Cor 14:3.

8. See Fee, *Philippians*, 182, for the views of various scholars.

disposition they are to show each other? Is it an emotion Paul wants the Philippians to extend to him as he has extended it to them? Given that all of the benefits mentioned in 2:1 are part of being "in Christ," it would appear that these dispositions are to characterize the common life of those in Christ (cf. Col 3:12). In addition, as 1:8 and 2:6-11 indicate, these dispositions which the Philippians (and Paul) are to display received their definitive embodiment in the person of Christ.

Further, if we read this passage in the light of Col 3:12, where similar vocabulary is used, we are reminded that this compassion and mercy are necessary if Christians are to exercise forbearance and forgiveness. For Christians, this is crucial because the quality of common life in Christ is not simply judged by the holiness of believers' lives (though that is to be encouraged). Rather, Christian community is more definitively judged by the forgiveness that enables and calls Christians to be reconciled and reconciling people. Indeed, it is this quality that is most attractive to a broken and alienated world.

In 2:2 we find the result of these grammatically conditional clauses in 2:1. Given all of the benefits which are theirs in Christ, the Philippians are to make Paul's joy complete by displaying a common pattern of thinking and acting. What does it mean to complete Paul's joy? In thinking about this matter we should avoid two extremes. One is the view that "Paul is concerned with his own feelings only as a by-product."[9] The other is the view that the incompleteness of Paul's joy is somehow direct evidence of serious and widespread problems in the Philippian church.[10] Instead, in a letter between friends this sort of appeal is quite natural and serious.[11] Moreover, if Paul and the Philippians are Christian friends embarked on a similar journey, engaged in the same struggle, the sustained and continued advancement of one friend would be both a cause for joy and the basis for strengthening the friendship. Because this friendship is first and foremost a friendship rooted and sustained in God, their joy is founded on what God has done in the lives of their friends in Christ (cf. 1:11).

At the same time, if we are to take 2:16 seriously, Paul has a deep personal and theological stake in the destiny of the Philippian congregation.[12]

---

9. Hawthorne, *Philippians,* 67.

10. This is Peterlin's view, *Paul's Letter to the Philippians,* 59-65. Pointing to Paul's assumption of the Philippians' obedience in 2:12, Caird, *Paul's Letters from Prison,* 117, posits that the "warnings of vv. 1-4 were occasioned by the behaviour of the Christians in Rome and not by what Paul heard of those in Philippi."

11. Bockmuehl, *Philippians,* 108.

12. Fee, *Philippians,* 183, says, "His own life and apostleship are deeply bound up with his converts' well-being, and especially with their perseverance. . . ."

Nothing would raise sharper questions about the wisdom and truthfulness of Paul's reading of the divine economy, as well as about Paul's own endurance of suffering, than for the Philippians to fail to meet the challenges posed by their suffering. As Paul sees it, it is not suffering itself which raises questions about the coherence of God's continuing action in the common life of the Philippian church. Instead, it is the potential failure of the Philippians to maintain a common life worthy of the gospel in the face of suffering that would undermine the assertions about the continuity of God's work made in such passages 1:6 and 2:13. While the perseverance of the Philippians is a central personal and theological concern for Paul, there is very little evidence that the Philippians as a group were failing to meet those challenges. No doubt Paul's comments here in 2:2 anticipate, to some degree, the direct warnings he offers in 4:2-3. The admonitions in ch. 4, however, bespeak serious but specific and limited problems.

In the rest of this passage Paul indicates both what the Philippians should do and what they should avoid in order to make his joy full. Thus, the real interpretive question concerns exactly what these things are. We can begin with the rest of v. 2, which lays out the positive disposition(s) the Philippians are to manifest. The picture here builds on the unity first mentioned in 1:27. In 2:2 there are three clauses, the first and third using the verb φρονεῖν/*phronein,* the second calling on the Philippians to "have the same love."

The English phrase "manifest a common pattern of thinking and acting" is the way I have translated the Greek phrase τὸ αὐτὸ φρονεῖν/*to auto phronein.* The same Greek phrase appears in Rom 12:16; 15:5; 2 Cor 13:11; and Phil 4:2. In all these cases the phrase refers to the unity that is achieved by coming to hold the same perspective, by seeing things the same way. There is clearly an intellectual component to this activity. Equally important for understanding this phrase, however, is the assumption that such a common perspective will generate, direct, and sustain a particular course of action.[13] Hence, if Paul wants the Philippians to pursue a common course of action, such as standing firm in the Spirit (1:27), they will need to be "like-minded." If Paul wants the Philippians to see that God's salvation is found as they remain

---

13. This is why in literature outside the NT the noun φρόνησις/*phronēsis* is so often translated "practical reasoning," "practical wisdom," or "prudence." The term is particularly prominent in Aristotle. See *Nicomachean Ethics* 6.4.6-7: "It therefore follows that Prudence [φρόνησις] is a truth-attaining rational quality, concerned with action in relation to the things which are good for human beings" (LCL translation). Also, as Wayne Meeks notes, the word plays a central role in Greco-Roman moral philosophy ("The Man from Heaven in Paul's Letter to the Philippians").

steadfast in the face of opponents who see them as stubborn people bound for destruction (1:28-29), then they will need to read God's economy the same way (i.e., the way Paul does). If the Philippians are to order their common life in a manner worthy of the gospel of Christ (1:27), then they will have to share a common perspective. Paul is calling both for a common perspective or way of thinking about things and for a common pattern of action flowing from that pattern of thinking.

Given that the command to "have the same love" comes between the two clauses urging the Philippians to manifest a unified common mind or perspective, it is reasonable to assume that this command is also related to the formation of a unified body in Christ. Having the same love "must mean to share the kind of love which has the same source (love's consolation is 'in Christ', v. 1), motivation and object."[14] The third clause here, "being bound together in this common pattern of thinking and acting," again invokes the verb φρονεῖν/*phronein* which speaks of this common practical wisdom to which Paul calls the Philippians and which he sees as the essential element of their unity in Christ.

Each of the components of this clause is part of a call to concord within the political and ecclesial space designated as "in Christ." At a formal level, then, Paul is not calling for anything different than many political commentators of his day. Concord is a central political virtue within Paul's world. A call to concord, however, is not the same as a call to self-erasing homogeneity. Paul is not asking everyone to think in an isomorphic way. They do not all have to wear gray and eat gruel at every meal.[15] What is required here are a common disposition, perspective, and comportment toward each other that will enable them to believe, worship, and act in concert so that their common life will be worthy of the gospel.

Christians should understand this common mind in a manner analogous to the triune life of God. The life of the one God is characterized as the communion of Father, Son, and Holy Spirit. The three persons are not dissolved into one, nor do they struggle competitively for dominance over the others. Instead, this communion of persons is singular, existing in peaceable harmony, characterized by self-donation in love. On analogy with the triune life of God, unity within Christian communities neither requires self-erasure, nor does it result in the competitive and violent struggle between isolated selves each seeking their own advantage at the expense of others. Rather, the

---

14. Bockmuehl, *Philippians,* 109.

15. As Troels Engberg-Pedersen notes, "There is no principled denial of the self in this passage." "Radical Altruism in Philippians 2:4," 13.

unity of Christian communities should be understood in terms of a peaceable harmony characterized by self-donation in love.

Just as this common disposition requires the Philippians to display certain communal virtues, they will also need to avoid certain vices. In 2:3 Paul warns against these vices. "Selfish ambition and rivalry" are what he noted and condemned in 1:17 as destructive practices evident in Rome. The term "vain conceit" (κενοδοξία/*kenodoxia*) does not occur elsewhere in the NT. This word, however, is common in Greek, used of those with an inflated sense of themselves.[16] This disposition and the actions it generates are ultimately destructive of the virtue of a common pattern of thinking and acting which is required for the sort of unity Paul desires for the Philippians.

As this verse continues, Paul sets out an alternative to these vices, introducing dispositions and habits which will enhance the Philippians' prospects of manifesting a unified perspective. In humility[17] they should consider others as their superiors.[18] Within the OT, God manifests a distinct concern for the humble and lowly (e.g., Pss 17:27; 33:18; 81:3; 101:17; Prov 3:34; 11:2; Zeph 2:3 [LXX]). In addition, the Qumran Community Rule views humility as a crucial virtue for the unity of the group.[19] Paul and the rest of the NT seem to be heirs of this positive account of humility.

In the pagan world, however, humility was regarded as a base disposition appropriate to slaves.[20] According to the common political wisdom, concord depended on people understanding their status and knowing who was superior, who was inferior, and giving to all what was due to them based on their status. On this view of things, for those of high status, humility would have been, at best, inappropriate and, at worst, socially destabilizing.

This widely-held perspective on humility provides a sharp contrast with Paul's claims about Christ in 2:6-8. In addition, this wisdom of the world runs directly counter to Paul's claim in 2:3 that the political vitality of the Christian community depends on the humility of all as each reckons the

---

16. The term κενόδοξος/*kenodoxos* is found in Gal. 5:26 conveying much the same meaning. See especially Wis 14:4; 4 *Maccabees* 2:15; 8:18, and Hawthorne, *Philippians*, 69.

17. Dative τῇ ταπεινοφροσύνῃ/*tē tapeinophrosynē* most likely indicates the manner in which others are to be considered superior to oneself. This is Fee's view, p. 187. While Fee does not give reasons for this judgment, I would argue that it can be based on Col. 2:23, the only other NT use of dative ταπεινοφροσύνῃ/*tapeinophrosynē* without a preposition.

18. It is probably better to translate ὑπερέχοντας/*hyperechontas* as "superior" rather than "better" as NRSV does. The term primarily indicates status and not a moral quality as is clear from the two NT occurrences of the participial form outside Philippians (Rom 13:1; 1 Pet 2:13).

19. 1QS 2:24; 3:8-9; 4:3; 5:25. See also Hawthorne, 70.

20. See W. Grundmann, "ταπεινός," *TDNT* 8:1-4.

other as "superior."[21] The term "superior" primarily indicates status and not a moral quality. Within a status-conscious empire (wherever such empires may be found), Paul makes the bold assertion that the political concord appropriate to being "in Christ" requires a humility that regards others to be of higher status. Paul further specifies the nature of this disposition in the next verse where he explicates how one acts when considering others superior to oneself. One looks out for or attends to the concerns of others rather[22] than one's own. The upshot is that directing one's attention towards others in humility is supposed to lead to a particular course of action, which is attending to the needs and concerns of others.

While many commentators note that this disposition to seek the benefit of others is paradigmatically displayed by Christ as related in 2:6-11, only a few have noted how manifestations of this disposition resound throughout the epistle. In 1:24 when Paul is faced with a decision about whether or not to "remain in the flesh," the decisive consideration for him is that remaining in the flesh is "more necessary" for the Philippians. In Paul's comments about Timothy in 2:19-24, Paul characterizes Timothy as someone who is deeply concerned about the Philippians' welfare in contrast to those who seek their own benefit rather than the things of Christ (2:20-21). Further, Paul praises Epaphroditus as one who both ministered to Paul's needs and is deeply concerned for the Philippian congregation (2:25-30). Hence, the Philippians have a number of friends who already display for them the disposition of attending to the needs of others rather than their own. Without question, the actions of Paul, Timothy, and Epaphroditus all are formed by attention to the actions of Christ as related in 2:6-11. Moreover, while virtually all would agree that 2:6-11 forms the center of Philippians, it is important to see that Paul has been laying the ground work for his presentation of the story of Christ related in 2:6-11 from the beginning paragraphs of the epistle.

It is quite common to note that in this passage and elsewhere in Philippians, Paul seems to be relying on conventional notions of friendship in

---

21. In 2 Cor 10:1-2 Paul explicitly contrasts these competing conceptions of the importance of humility.

22. In 2:4 the word καί/*kai* is omitted by mss. in the Western tradition. This yields a translation like "Look not to your own interests but those of others." The inclusion of καί is supported by the best textual evidence. The tendency, however, is to translate the clause as Fee, *Philippians*, 175, does: "Each of you should look not only to your own interests but also to the interests of others," taking καί/*kai* to have the force of "both/and." Recently, however, Engberg-Pedersen, "Radical Altruism in Philippians 2:4," has argued on the basis of J. D. Denniston's *Greek Particles*; Sophocles, *Ajax* 1313; Plato, *Phaedrus* 233B; and Lysias 6.13 that "Clearly the force of *alla kai* is to turn attention *away from* A and *instead* towards B."

addressing the Philippians. We should be wary, however, of seeing too close a connection here between common Greco-Roman notions of friendship and politics on the one hand, and the sorts of friendships and politics Paul commends, on the other. Clearly, there are some very general conceptual parallels here. It is far more striking, however, to note that the practices and dispositions that form and sustain concord and friendship in Christ are sharply at odds with the practices and dispositions needed for concord and friendship in the Greco-Roman world more generally.[23] For many Greco-Roman commentators on friendship, the common striving of friends is essentially a competition for honor.[24] Within this economy of honor, friendship reflects a competitive movement of selves each seeking their own advantage. Paul's comments in 2:3 about considering others superior to oneself as well as the image of Christ's willed self-emptying in 2:7 directly undermine the economy of honor on which this sort of Greco-Roman friendship stands. Hence, while Paul (especially here in 2:1-4) uses language that is commonly found in discussions of friendship and political concord, it should become increasingly clear that Paul is proposing a very different economy of friendship and a politics sharply at odds with that of the citizens of Philippi.

From at least 1:12, Paul has offered a reading of the divine economy and how his situation fits into that larger narrative of God's action. On the basis of his understanding of God's action and how he fits into that economy, he has acted in particular ways, and formed his desires and plans in the light of God's providence. Moreover, he has offered the Philippians an account of their situation in the light of God's economy. As they find themselves in the same struggle that he is in, graced not only with faith, but the opportunity of suffering for Christ's sake, he encourages them to act in ways analogous to the ways he has acted. He urges them (and us) to form their desires and plans and their common life in such a way that they will be able to continue, like him, to live in a manner worthy of the gospel. The central virtue which will enable this sort of common life is the formation of a common perspective, a common pattern of thinking and acting which will enable them to understand rightly their place in God's economy and to act accordingly. Forming and maintaining this common perspective will result in a united body capable of manifesting a politics worthy of those "in Christ."

23. On this score see in particular Peterman's criticisms of White, *Paul's Gift*, 114-17.

24. This is nicely captured in Peterman's citation of Aristotle, "Also the virtuous man is ready to forgo money if by that means his friends may gain more money; for thus, though his friends get money, he himself achieves nobility and so assigns the greater good to his own share" *Nicomachean Ethics* 9.7.9, also 8.1.1. See Peterman, *Paul's Gift*, 114-16, for a thorough critique of the straightforward application of friendship language to Philippians.

Paul's Christ-focused ecclesial politics was, on a formal level, similar to the political wisdom of his day. It emphasized concord and friendship as the keys to a successful common life. Once one scratches beneath the surface, however, it becomes clear that the shape and nature of concord and friendship within a church founded on the crucified and resurrected Christ would have seemed odd to Paul's non-Christian contemporaries. In a very real sense, Paul proposes a Christian counter-culture. At a formal level, it would have been recognizable to most of Paul's pagan contemporaries as a culture. Nevertheless, they could not have recognized the truthfulness of this culture without at the same time undermining the foundations of their own imperial culture.

From a contemporary perspective, however, Paul's ecclesial politics are no less strange. Although this passage reflects the depth of the friendship between Paul and the Philippians in a way we might both understand and admire, it also reflects an extraordinary level of accountability. Paul presumes that he has obligations to the church in Philippi and he certainly makes it clear that they have obligations to him. He and they can make demands on each other's lives because he and they are in Christ. Their common participation in the body of Christ sets them on a shared journey in which they can and must engage each other as fellow pilgrims, offering help when needed, making demands when called for, exhorting and praying for each other as they move into ever deeper communion with God. I will say more about this in the final section of this volume.

For the vast majority of Christians in the U.S. (and Europe) this sort of common life is largely unimaginable. Moreover, when we do imagine it, we often find it repellant. We have been so deeply schooled in individualism, that the ecclesial life to which Paul and the Philippians call us can only sound alien and frightening. I suspect that to the extent that we can imagine this sort of ecclesial accountability in our particular churches, we can also only imagine this as an oppressive form of Christianity.

It would go well beyond the scope of this commentary to try tell the story of how the ecclesial common life which Paul saw as essential for the Philippians if they were to resist the pressures of their opponents came to be seen as oppressive by contemporary Christians. Again, a full account of how this situation might be changed would also be a monograph in its own right. Nevertheless, I will offer a few brief observations. In late capitalist democracies such as the U.S. we are encouraged to view our selves as independent individuals who seek first and foremost our own benefits and security. Our relationships to others are purely voluntary and exist to meet our felt needs. Those to whom we do not extend these sorts of considerations are viewed as threats or competitors.

Christians understand, however, that people are created by God for friendship with God and with each other. In this respect, our lives are never fully our own until they have been given back to God. We are neither independent nor disconnected from others. This recognition should lead us to view others as gifts rather than competitors.

Moreover, Christians share connections that are forged in our baptism. These are not voluntary. Just as we do not get to choose our biological siblings, we do not get to choose our brothers and sisters in Christ. In addition, our baptism starts us on a journey into ever deeper communion with God and each other. Moreover, the further we advance in this journey the more clearly we see that our lives are caught up into a larger drama of God's dealings with the world. This story has its climactic moment in the life, death and resurrection of Jesus and reaches its finale when all things are put into their right relationship to God. This drama is what Christians call God's economy of salvation. If we are to unlearn our commitments to individualism and to begin to embody the sort of common life to which Paul and the Philippians call us, we must come to share with them the sense of being caught up into the movement of God's economy of salvation. At its roots the friendship, and thus, the accountability, between Paul and the Philippians comes from their conviction that they have been made fellow participants in God's gracious redemption of the world in Christ. Unless and until we can see our lives as having been incorporated into that larger drama of redemption, we will never be able to see the necessity for the sort of ecclesial common life Paul urges on the Philippians. In the following section of the epistle (2:5-11) Paul explicitly lays out the crucial climactic element of this drama of redemption. Although this is roughly the middle of the epistle, everything that has preceded and all that will follow draws its coherence from this passage.

2:5-11

5 Let this be your pattern of thinking, acting, and feeling, which was also displayed in Christ Jesus, 6 who, being in the form of God, did not consider equality with God as something to be used for his own advantage. 7 Instead he emptied himself, taking the form of a slave, being born in human likeness. 8 And being found in human form, he humbled himself and became obedient even to the point of death — a death on the cross. 9 That is why God highly exalted him and gave him the name above all names, 10 so that at the name of Jesus every knee should bow, in heaven, on earth, and under the earth, 11 and every tongue should confess that Jesus Christ is Lord to the glory of God the Father.

This passage is the climax of the argument of the epistle. In saying this, I mean that the arguments both preceding and following draw their force from this passage, which poetically narrates Christ's status and activity.

In addition to being a crucial component of the epistle as a whole, this is one of the most theologically significant passages in the New Testament. Although I will indicate various ways in which this is so in my interpretive comments on the passage, I will also devote more space to some of the constructive theological aspects of this passage in the final section of this volume.

Few other passages in the NT have generated more scholarly literature.[1] Much of that scholarly literature has focused on the form of this passage and whether the passage had some sort of prior life in the worship of the first Christians. Scholars have also shown an intense interest in the conceptual and religious background of the phrases and images used here to describe Jesus. Many of these issues are not of direct relevance to the task of commentary writing. Nevertheless, they are significant matters for students of the New Testament. I address these issues in greater detail in an excursus below. There I will lay out some of the standard scholarly claims and assumptions regarding the form and background of Phil 2:5-11. Moreover, I will articulate what I take to be the crucial questions that must be answered by anyone making these standard claims and assumptions. In suggesting answers to these questions, I expect that my own (rather skeptical) views on these matters will become clear. My hope is that even those who disagree with my findings will need to sustain their disagreements by providing better answers to these questions than I have. Most importantly, however, I hope that students who, when faced with the enormity of the secondary literature on this passage, tend to fall in with the scholarly consensus, will find my discussion here useful for sorting out one view from another regarding the form and background of this passage. Having said this, it is time to turn to comment directly on 2:5-11.

Phil 2:5 provides the transition between the demands of 1:27–2:4 and the story of Christ related in 2:6-11. The question is what sort of transition is being made. The obscurity of the syntax in Greek means that almost any translation into English is also going to be an amplification. My translation is no different in that respect.

The demonstrative pronoun "this" points backward, summarizing the habits of thinking, acting, and feeling Paul desires for the Philippians, as laid out in 1:27–2:4.[2] Paul then uses the imperative form of the verb φρονεῖν/

---

1. See R. P. Martin, *Carmen Christi*; O. Hofius, *Der Christushymnus*; R. P. Martin and B. Dodd, *Where Christology Began*.

2. L. A. Losie has made the strongest argument for reading the pronoun as pointing for-

phronein, which played such an important role in 2:1-4.[3] Thus, in this first clause of 2:5 Paul is urging the Philippians to adopt that common *phronēsis,* or practical reasoning, that he has argued for in 2:1-4. This pattern of practical reasoning involves a common perspective on their situation and how it fits into the divine economy and the practical implications of that perspective. We might do well to follow Wayne Meeks's paraphrase: "Base your practical reasoning on what you see in Christ Jesus."[4] In my translation I have amplified this to note that practical reasoning is a pattern of thinking, feeling, and acting.

In Greek the second clause lacks a verb. The vast majority of commentators supply some form of the verb "to be."[5] This is what I have done also.

Paul's previous discussion provides a general outline of what he thinks will be crucial to the practice he urges in v. 5. The common practical reasoning he has urged in 2:1-4 requires a particular perspective on, or reading of, God's plans for the world generally and for the Philippians in their current situation in particular. Such a common reading of the divine economy should lead the Philippians, so Paul argues, to adopt a specific set of practices. Such practices include addressing the needs and concerns of others rather than one's own. In addition, Paul has already asserted two crucial points in regard to adopting this practical reasoning. First, it is what is required to manifest a common life worthy of the gospel (1:27). Secondly, this disposition will assure their salvation in the face of opposition (1:28). The story of Christ that follows in vv. 6-11 provides the decisive display of this practical reasoning focused on attending to and participating in the divine economy. In this verse, then, Paul is urging the Philippians to adopt a pattern of practical reasoning that is displayed to them in and by Christ.

As we move to examine the story of Christ related in vv. 6-11 it becomes

---

ward to vv. 6-11. See L. A. Losie, "A Note on the Interpretation of Phil. 2,5." The preponderance of evidence, however, is against this. The following verses in Philippians use τοῦτο/*touto* to point backward to previous points: 1:7; 1:22; 1:25; 3:7, 15 (2x); 4:8; 4:9. See also O'Brien, *Philippians,* 204 n. 7, and Fee, *Philippians,* 199 n. 25, who offer decisive arguments against Losie's view.

3. If one reads γάρ/*gar* after τοῦτο/*touto* here with some early mss., then φρονεῖτε/*phroneite* will not be read as an imperative. Rather the indicative would indicate that the Philippians already think this way. As Bockmuehl, *Philippians,* 121-22, notes, however, this would work against Paul's argument in 1:27–2:4 that the Philippians are to do something they have either not yet done or not done sufficiently yet. After all, Paul's joy is not yet complete (2:2).

4. See "The Man from Heaven in Paul's Letter to the Philippians." This is in line with the readings of C. F. D. Moule, "Further Reflections," 265; Fee, *Philippians,* 200.

5. Of course, in Greek the verb "to be" is often unstated, but assumed. It is, strictly speaking, only the English which requires this. Fee, *Philippians,* 201; Moule, "Further Reflections," 265; O'Brien, *Philippians,* 205; Bockmuehl, *Philippians,* 123-24, all move in this direction.

clear that v. 6 is crucial for the way one reads the entire passage. Once one takes positions on this verse, the requirements of consistency will work to circumscribe the available options with regard to subsequent verses. Unfortunately, the terms and phrases in 2:6 are rather obscure. The key issue concerns what it means to speak of Christ as being "in the form of God" (ἐν μορφῇ Θεοῦ/*in morphē Theou*). Moreover, the way one comes to understand "form" (μορφή/*morphē*) here must be compatible with the way the same word is used in v. 7.[6] Obviously the form of God stands in contrast to the form of a slave. Nevertheless, how one describes this contrast must account for "form" being used in roughly the same way in both places.

In its most conventional sense, the Greek term refers to something visible or perceptible about an object; thus, the "form" of an object indicates something about an object's appearance. It notes an object's perceptibility and visibility.[7]

Of course, the OT strongly resists any visual representations of God (Exod 20:4). When Moses asks for a vision of God, he is told that no one can see the face of God and live (Exod 33:20; cf. also Deut 4:12). In the NT John 1:18; Rom 1:20; and Col 1:15 all refer to the invisibility of God. How, then, should we interpret this phrase in a way that both takes "form" in its conventional sense of "appearance" (since we have no basis for taking it otherwise) and explains what it might mean for Paul to assert that Christ is "in the form" of the invisible, unrepresentable God of Israel in ways that would not be deeply problematic?

Since attempts to understand what it means to speak of Christ being in

---

6. Both Fee, *Philippians*, 204 n. 49, and Hawthorne, "In the Form of God," 99-100, use this criterion as a way of arguing against those who see Christ's being in the "form of God" as connected to the glory of God. As long as one is not making the erroneous claim that μορφή/*morphē* is synonymous with δόξα/*doxa*, however, it seems plausible to claim that if the μορφή/*morphē* of God designates something visible about God, then it is not without merit to claim that within the OT one way of talking about the visibility of God is to refer to the glory of God by which God is made manifest to humanity (see Exod 16:10; 24:16; 33:17-23; 1 Kgs 8.11; Isa 6:3, and Paul's similar uses of δόξα/*doxa* in Rom 1:23; 1 Cor 11:7; 2 Cor 3:18; 4:6). For a fuller account of this view see Fowl, *The Story of Christ*, 53-55; also O'Brien, *Philippians*, 208-9. My views now are much closer to those of Bockmuehl, "'The Form of God,'" discussed below.

7. Within the LXX see, e.g., Tob 1:13; Job 4:16; Wis 18:1; Isa 44:13; Dan 3:1, 7, 11, 12, 14, 19; 4 Maccabees 15:4. See also the numerous listings in Behm, "μορφή," 742-44. Moreover, when one looks at the phrase μορφή Θεοῦ/*morphē Theou* in such texts as the *Corpus Hermeticum* or the *Sibylline Oracles* it becomes clear that God's μορφή/*morphē* is taken to refer to something visible about God, or better, God's visible appearance. See Steenburg, "*Morphē and Eikōn*," 81-85; Fowl, *The Story of Christ*, 53-54. This is also the case in pagan literature when the μορφαί/*morphai* of the gods are spoken of.

the "form" of God need to span the gap that appears to exist between the conventional notion of "form" and the insistence on the invisibility of the God of Israel, it will be important to note any Jewish texts that speak of God having a form (μορφή/*morphē*). Josephus and Philo each provide us with such an example. In *Contra Apionem* 2.190 Josephus writes that God is perceptible to humans through his deeds and benefits. Alternatively, God's "form" and greatness are hidden. This passage importantly asserts, then, that God has visible "form"; it is simply not perceptible to humans.

Philo, for his part, uses "form" in its conventional sense of "appearance" in numerous cases.[8] When he speaks about what Moses saw in the midst of the burning bush in Exodus 3, he describes it as "a most beautiful form (μορφή/*morphē*), not like any visible object, an image supremely divine in appearance, shining with a light more brilliant than that of fire. One might suppose this to be the image of him who is; but let us rather call it an angel" (*Life of Moses* 1.66). "Philo clearly goes beyond the LXX in suggesting that what Moses saw in the bush was something which, although on balance best regarded as an angel, nevertheless manifested a visible 'form' which in every significant respect could easily be taken to be that of God."[9]

These texts indicate that it is not completely incoherent to speak of the God of Israel having a "form." Given this possibility, what might the "form" of God refer to? I want to suggest two different but related answers. Throughout the LXX the visible manifestation of God is associated with God's glory, δόξα/*doxa* (Exod 16:10; 24:16-17; 33:17-23; 40:34-38; 1 Kgs 8:11; Isa 6:3; Ezek 1:28; 43:3; 44:4; 2 Macc 2:8; 3 *Maccabees* 4:18; also 1 *Enoch* 14:21; *Testament of Levi* 3:4; *Ascension of Isaiah* 10:16). This is a conceptual connection based on the LXX's description of the appearance of God to humans in terms of God's glory; I am not claiming that "form" is synonymous with "glory."

Moreover, Paul uses similar language to speak of the visible manifestation of God's majesty in Rom 1:23; 1 Cor 11:7; 2 Cor 3:18; 4:6.[10] In this light, the "form" of the God of Israel would be a reference to the glory, radiance, and splendor by which God's majesty is made visible to humans. By locating Christ in this glory, Phil 2:6 places Christ within that aspect of God's identity which is most visible to humans. In this regard, Paul's description fits neatly with John 17:5, in which Christ shares in God's eternal glory (cf. Heb 1:3).[11]

This view of "form" is compatible with v. 7 in that just as Christ is

8. See Bockmuehl, "The Form of God," 15, for some of these citations.

9. Bockmuehl, "The Form of God," 15.

10. See also Luke 2:9; Rev 15:8; 21:23.

11. This view is closest to O'Brien, *Philippians,* 210-11; Hawthorne, "In the Form of God," 101.

known to be a slave because he takes on the appearance of a slave, he is also known to be God because he has the appearance of God as one who shares in God's eternal glory. Indeed, it may be the case that it is precisely Christ's taking on the "form" of a slave which definitively makes God's glory visible to humans. This view also anticipates 3:21, which speaks of Christ's body of glory, into whose likeness believers will be transformed.

Marcus Bockmuehl has proposed a similar solution to this issue, locating the notion of God's "form" in a tradition of Jewish visionary mysticism, "in which it was possible to speak of the Lord's majesty and greatness by alluding to the inconceivable size and beauty of his bodily appearance."[12] This view is evident in a variety of Jewish and Christian texts.[13] One of the best illustrations of this comes from a striking passage in the pseudo-Clementines which speaks of angels who behold the face of God. They can do so because God "has shape (μορφή/*morphē*), and he has every limb primarily and solely for beauty's sake and not for use" (*Homily* 17:7).

Bockmuehl then tries to connect Paul and Phil 2:6 to this way of thinking in several ways. First, Paul stands, to some extent, in the visionary tradition of his ancestors, and one should not needlessly downplay the impact of his vision(s) of Christ on his theology. Of course, it is difficult to pin down the direct impact of Paul's visionary experiences on his theology. Moreover, since we know so little about these experiences, it seems quite possible to overestimate their impact. Second, the Jewish mystical literature to which Bockmuehl refers has an interest in the name of God as well as the beautiful form of God's body. Phil 2:9 ascribes to Christ the name above all names. Alternatively, however, Isa 42:8 explicitly links God's glory and God's name in ways that would support the notion that God's "form" is related to God's visible glory. Third, Phil 3:21 refers to Christ's body of glory into which our humiliated bodies will be transformed.

Bockmuehl's interpretation is capable of reading "form" consistently in vv. 6 and 7. In both verses "form" refers to the visible appearance of something. The contrast between the verses is achieved by the contrast between the appearance of God and the appearance of a slave.

Although Bockmuehl is not able to muster a conclusive case for this reading as the one that would have been most obvious to Paul and/or the Philippians, it is certainly one possibility. Moreover, this interpretive approach is theologically powerful and is nicely represented in Bernard of Clairvaux's homilies on the Song of Songs:

12. Bockmuehl, "The Form of God," 19.
13. See Bockmuehl, "The Form of God," 19.

How beautiful you appear to the angels, Lord Jesus, in the form of God, eternal, begotten before the daystar amid the splendors of heaven, the radiant light of God's glory and the perfect copy of his nature, the unchanging and untarnished brightness of eternal life! How beautiful you are to me, my Lord, even in the very discarding of your beauty! When you divested yourself of the native radiance of the unfailing light, then your kindness was thrown into relief, your love shone out more brightly. . . .[14]

Thus the claim that Christ was in the "form" of God can be taken as a reference to Christ's sharing in the eternal glory of God and making that glory visible. It may *also* indicate that the best way to think of Christ's manifestation of the glory of God is in terms of Christ's beautiful body, a beauty that is not diminished but enhanced by taking on the "form" of a slave.

In interpreting the next part of this verse, "he did not consider his equality with God as something to be used for his own advantage," everything hangs on the way one interprets the Greek word ἁρπαγμός/*harpagmos*. Although this term has generated a long scholarly debate, it now appears that there is a consensus emerging, which is that in contexts such as this one we should understand the word indicating something that is used for one's own advantage.[15]

There are several things to note about this way of taking the verse. First, while it does not precisely specify the nature of Christ's equality with God, the most obvious way to take this is in the light of the previous clause, which identifies Christ as participating in the eternal glory of the God of Israel. Moreover, instead of arguing for Christ's equality with God, this phrase presumes it. Based on this presumption, the emphasis of this clause is to assert Christ's disposition toward his equality with God, not to specify the precise nature of that equality. Thus, precisely because Christ was in the form of God, he did not consider equality with God as something to be used for his own advantage. This claim, which is a powerful assertion of the highest sort of christology, is also primarily a negative claim. It asserts what Christ did not do. The positive account of what it meant for Christ not to consider his equal-

---

14. Bernard of Clairvaux, *On the Song of Songs* 49:5, cited in Bockmuehl, "The Form of God," 23.

15. For a survey of the differing views see N. T. Wright, "Jesus Christ Is Lord: Philippians 2:5-11," in *The Climax of the Covenant*, 56-98. This chapter is an expanded version of an essay which first appeared in *JTS* 37 (1986). The key essays in resolving this issue are R. W. Hoover "The Harpagmos Enigma," and W. Jaeger, "Eine stilgeschichtliche Studie zum Philipperbrief." Wright follows Hoover as well. J. C. O'Neill offered some objections to Hoover's argument, which have not generally persuaded critics ("Hoover on *Harpagmos* Reviewed"). See Wright's rebuttal of O'Neill in "Jesus Christ Is Lord," 85 n. 119. Fee, *Philippians*, 206, offers no real objections to Hoover, but some appropriate cautions.

ity with God as something to be used for his own advantage receives a narrative explication in the verses which follow.

If the end of v. 6 indicates what Christ did not do (use equality with God for his own advantage), v. 7 begins with an assertion of what Christ did. This verse continues to explicate the dual assertions that Christ was in "the form of God" and "equal to God." The first thing we learn about this one who did not consider equality with God something to be used for his own advantage is that he "emptied himself."

One conventional way of interpreting the Greek verb κενόω/*kenoō* is with the sense of emptying something of its contents. Instead of thinking of emptying a bucket of water, however, Paul rather consistently uses the metaphor of "kenosis" or emptying with the sense of nullification or making void (cf. Rom 4:14, which claims that unless Abraham is reckoned righteous by faith, the promise is emptied or voided; 1 Cor 1:17, which claims that wise words nullify or empty the cross of its power; 1 Cor 9:15 and 2 Cor 9:3, where boasting is nullified or emptied of its force).[16]

What might this mean for the notion of Christ's self-emptying? Clearly, the following clauses emphasize Christ's willingness to take on flesh. This leads to the notion that self-emptying is a single choice taken on by the Son in the incarnation. Read in this light, it is easy to see that, when Christians were trying think through and order claims about Christ's full humanity and full divinity in the fourth and fifth centuries, this verse would come to play a significant role. The primary role Phil 2:7 can play in this discussion is that of catalyst. The image of Christ's self-emptying raises, or perhaps sharpens, questions about the relationship between the Son's two natures. On its own, however, this verse does not provide the answer to those questions.[17] Nevertheless, there seems to be little doubt that 2:7 can be interpreted in the light of an orthodox Chalcedonian christology. Understanding Christ's self-emptying in terms of its relationship to the incarnation can be comprehended within the assertions of Christ's full humanity and full divinity.

To claim, as many biblical scholars do, that Paul never would have thought in such metaphysical terms is not in itself theologically relevant.

---

16. See Collange, *Philippians*, 101; Fee, *Philippians*, 211 n. 79. Other possible metaphorical uses of κενόω/*kenoō* can be found in Jer 14:2; 15:9; Philo, *Legum Allegoriae* 3.226. Joachim Jeremias's attempt to establish a linguistic connection between this phrase and the Hebrew of Isa. 53:12 has been roundly criticized and rightly rejected. See Jeremias, "Zu Phil. ii.7," 182-89. For the criticisms see G. Bornkamm, "Zum Verständnis der Christus-Hymnus Phil. 2,5-11," 180; Fowl, *The Story of Christ*, 58; Gnilka, *Philipperbrief*, 118.

17. See Frances Young's *From Nicea to Chalcedon* for a fuller accounting of the figures and concerns involved here.

Later creeds and confessions are best understood as scripturally disciplined ways of coherently ordering claims, inferences, and implications of scriptural language about God, the world, and God's purposes for the world. Scripture by its very diversity requires such an ordering. The question is not whether Paul thought this way himself. Rather, the question is whether one uses historical-critical, sociological, philosophical, or Christian theological categories for ordering that diversity.

Moreover, Christ's self-emptying illumines his disposition against using equality with God for his own advantage. In this respect self-emptying does not primarily represent a decision on the part of the preexistent Christ prior to incarnation. Rather, self-emptying displays something crucial about the character of God. In refusing to use his participation in the glory of the God of Israel for his own advantage and adopting, instead, the disposition of self-emptying, which includes incarnation, obedience, crucifixion, and ultimately exaltation, Christ is actually displaying the form of God, making the glory of God manifest to humans.[18] This fits with Paul's claims about the wisdom of the divine economy in 1 Cor. 1:18-25 as well as the Johannine theme that, "in the uttermost form of a slave, on the Cross, the Son's glory breaks through, inasmuch as it is then that he goes to the (divine) extreme in his loving, and in the revelation of that love."[19] Along these lines the theologian Hans Urs von Balthasar notes, "What [kenosis] does mean . . . is that the divine 'power' is so ordered that it can make room for a possible exteriorization, like that found in the Incarnation and the Cross, and can maintain this exteriorization even to the utmost point."[20] Further, "in the Incarnation the triune God has not simply helped the world, but has disclosed himself in what is most deeply his own."[21] In worlds such as ours and Paul's where power is manifested in self-assertion, acquisition, and domination, Christ reveals that God's power, indeed the triune nature, is made known to the world in the act of self-

18. "The real humiliation of the incarnation and the cross is that one who was himself God, and who never during the whole process stopped being God, could embrace such a vocation. The real theological emphasis of the hymn, therefore, is not simply a new view of Jesus. It is a new understanding of God." Wright, "Jesus Christ Is Lord," 84.

19. H. U. von Balthasar, *Mysterium Paschale*, 29.

20. See Balthasar, *Mysterium Paschale*, 29.

21. Balthasar, *Mysterium Paschale*, 29. In the subsequent pages Balthasar shows how this view makes sense of a variety of patristic and medieval approaches to kenosis. In subsequent writing Balthasar seeks to modify Hilary's position by insisting that the proper starting point for thinking about kenosis is with inner-trinitarian relations rather than with God's undifferentiated essence (the position he attributes to Hilary). This is the only way to assure that the cross is a real demonstration of God's power as willed powerlessness, rather than just an apparent powerlessness. For this further explication see *The Glory of the Lord*, 7:213-15.

emptying. Self-emptying is not so much a single act as the fundamental disposition of the eternal relationship of the Father, Son, and Spirit. The incarnation, life, death, and resurrection of Jesus become the decisive revelation to us of that "self-emptying" that eternally characterizes the triune life of God.

As the passage moves on, it becomes clear that Christ's self-emptying entails a particular mission, a mission first characterized as taking the "form" (as in v. 6, the Greek word is μορφή/*morphē*) of a slave. Requirements of consistency really compel interpreters to take "form" here in v. 7 basically the same way as in v. 6 — that is, as a reference to someone's visible appearance. What would have been the visible appearance of a slave? This is less clear than one might think. Some slaves in the Greco-Roman world were quite wealthy and of relatively high status. Their physical appearance might have been more impressive than many free persons'. Other slaves were both visibly impoverished and of very low status.[22] Physical appearance need not immediately identify one as either slave or free. That which did mark all slaves, however, is that they were all under obedience to a master. This could only be visible in a slave's relationship to another.

In v. 7, then, Christ's taking the "form" of a slave is a way of referring to his submission to the will of a master. Interestingly, however, no master is explicitly named here. One way of understanding Christ's taking the form of a slave is to recognize that Paul saw all humanity as in bondage (cf. Rom 6:12-14; Gal 4:3; Col 2:20, etc.) and the human Christ as subjected to the various powers seeking to control the world (Rom 6:9; 8:3). Moreover, as the verses to come situate Christ's activity within the human realm, one might think that Christ's taking the form of a slave is a reference to the incarnation, in which Christ became subject to the things to which humanity is subject, including, ultimately, death.

This might seem to be further supported by v. 8, which further specifies the nature of Christ's obedience. This, however, reflects a misunderstanding of some of the older English translations of v. 8 which declare that Christ was obedient "unto death."[23] The Greek here indicates the extent of Christ's obedience, not the object to which Christ is obedient (hence NRSV's "obedient to the point of death").

Thus, it becomes clear that in his obedience, even to the point of death, Christ was being obedient to God.[24] Further support comes from vv. 9-11,

22. See Dale Martin's *Slavery as Salvation*, chapter 1, for further information.

23. Thus, e.g., the RSV and KJV.

24. So L. Hurtado, "Jesus as Lordly Example in Philippians 2:5-11," 122-32; also Bockmuehl, *Philippians*, 139.

where God is clearly the subject who acts to exalt the obedient Christ. This systematic obedience to God is the way in which Christ manifests the appearance of a slave.[25] That is, rather than using his status as equal to God for his own advantage, Christ empties himself, becoming obedient to God. This disposition both reflects the character of God (since it is the disposition of the one who is equal to God) and exemplifies the habit of seeking the benefit of others rather than oneself, as Paul urged the Philippians in 2:4. In manifesting the appearance of a slave through his obedience to God, Christ not only becomes the decisive actor in the economy of salvation, he also demonstrates the appropriate ways in which to attend to God's economy. This reflects a crucial sense in which the Philippians are to manifest the *phronēsis* that is found in Christ Jesus (2:5).

The following clauses, "being born in human likeness, and was found in human form," are, in one sense, relatively straightforward. They talk about the humanity of the one who took on the appearance of a slave, but they do so in ways that do not really help us answer our questions about the precise nature of Christ's humanity. The crucial Greek words here translated as "likeness" and "form" do not have sufficient precision to help with this question.[26] Further, this particular context does not give us much aid in adjudicating between the ranges of meaning for each of these terms.

Therefore, it is important to recognize that on grounds of grammar, syntax, and semantics alone these two clauses support neither a docetic nor an orthodox account of Christ's humanity. The inner logic of Christian accounts of salvation demands a fully human Christ. We, in our humanity, can be saved only by a God who fully takes on that humanity. As Gregory Nazianzus famously put it, "The unassumed is the unhealed."[27] It is this logic of salvation rather than strictly formal considerations that require Christians to read these verses in a way that is compatible with Christ's full humanity

25. Obviously, there are numerous gospel passages which narrate Jesus' service to his disciples and others (cf. John 13:3-17). This is true service, but is probably not the sense in which this passage is concerned with Christ's taking the appearance of a slave (against Hawthorne, *Philippians*, 87; Fee, *Philippians*, 212-13 holds a similar view, as does Chrysostom, *Homily* 7). To read the passage this way seems to connect God's vindication and exaltation of Christ to Christ's service to others rather than to Christ's obedience to God (which generated service to others).

26. For example, a term like ὁμοίωμα/*homoiōma* (likeness) is used to reflect a range of relationships, from those that border on identity (Deut 4:16) to those that reflect loose analogy (Rev 9:7). Likewise, the term σχῆμα/*schēma* (form) can be used to indicate outward appearance and inner nature. See J. Schneider, "ὁμοίωμα," *TDNT* 5:191-98. Moreover, the use of εὑρεθείς/*heuretheis* (was found) indicates that what is in view is not a quality of a thing in itself, but a quality as it is recognized by others (see Martin, *Carmen Christi*, 208; O'Brien, *Philippians*, 226).

27. See Gregory Nazianzus, *Epistles* 101.32.

and full divinity. Straightforward exegetical explication cannot substitute for the reflective theological logic required here. This is a good example of letting Christian theological convictions rather than sociological or historical-critical concerns govern a theological reading of Scripture.

These two clauses introduce the primary activities of the one who took on the appearance of a slave. The clauses that follow further explicate the nature of Christ's freely willed self-emptying. That is, being found in appearance as a human, "he humbled himself." This clause echoes the language of 2:3-4, where Paul articulates the common perspective and pattern of action he desires for the Philippians, and the language of v. 7 with its use of the reflexive pronoun. In addition, the reflexive pronoun reminds us that Christ's humiliation here is self-willed. It is not the result of fate or misfortune. The subsequent clause, "he became obedient to the point of death, even a death on the cross," explicates the nature of Christ's willed humiliation.[28]

Crucifixion was the most humiliating form of state-sponsored execution, a form of death reserved for slaves.[29] It is clear that, from Rome's perspective, those who were crucified were not simply humiliated, but humiliated by Roman power. The public display of the crucified body served both as testimony to Rome's power over all bodies and as a public warning against future transgression.

The possibility that crucifixion might be the extent to which one humbled oneself in obedience to God struck at the very roots of the power Rome sought to display in crucifying someone. If Christ's life was freely offered up to God in obedience, then although Rome can take the life, Rome cannot make Christ its victim. Ironically, they become unwitting agents in God's economy of salvation. On the cross Christ's body becomes the site where Rome's pretensions to dominion are overwhelmed by the power of God, a power which is revealed in weakness.

This perspective parallels Paul's perspective on his own circumstances in 1:12-26 and on the Philippians' circumstances in 1:28-29. The imprisoned Paul is not a victim; rather his imprisonment has provided occasion for the advance of the gospel and an opportunity to magnify Christ in his body. Indeed, Paul can seriously adopt this perspective only in the light of his reading

28. The phrase "even a death on the cross" is taken to be a Pauline gloss by those who view this passage as a previously formulated composition. As a result, scholars have tended either to overemphasize or to ignore this phrase, depending on their interests. Within the passage as it stands now it is clear that Christ's death on the cross is testimony to the extent of his obedience which testifies to his humiliation. For a thorough discussion of the relation of this phrase to an original hymn see O. Hofius, *Der Christushymnus,* 3-17.

29. See Hengel, *Crucifixion,* 54.

of the economy of salvation worked by God in Christ and decisively displayed in 2:6-11. Of course, if the story of Christ ended at v. 8 then Paul's perspective is deluded. Rome's account of Christ's death as a story of victimization and as a bodily testimony to imperial power would be true. This is why vv. 9-11 play a crucial role in any attempt the Philippians might make to adopt the patterns of thinking, feeling, and acting displayed by Christ Jesus.

If the claims of v. 8 implicitly subvert Roman imperial power, they also raise interesting theological questions about God's will in relation to Christ's death. These concerns can be summarized in this question: Does the Father will the death of the Son? In this regard, it is important to remember that the emphasis in 2:8 is on obedience. Of course, Christ's obedience ultimately leads to death. God could, however, will the obedience without directly willing the death. It would seem best to formulate the matter this way: God wills Christ's perfect obedience. The Son, as an expression of love for the Father, willingly takes on human life, becoming fully human and revealing God's deepest desires for the world. The world, being the sort of place it is, cannot abide the obedient one and kills him. As Anselm wrote, "Therefore, God did not compel Christ to die, when there was no sin in him, but Christ himself freely underwent death, not by yielding up his life as an act of obedience, but on account of his obedience in maintaining justice, because he so steadfastly persevered in it that he brought death on himself."[30]

The transition from v. 8 to v. 9 marks a theological and grammatical shift in this passage. In vv. 6-8 Christ has been the subject of all the finite verbs. At v. 9 the subject shifts to God. Further, I have translated the double Greek conjunctions, διὸ καί/*dio kai,* as "that is why" to indicate that there is a causal relationship between the actions narrated in vv. 9-11 and those of vv. 6-8.[31] The exaltation mentioned here in v. 9 is causally connected to Christ's not using his equality with God for his own advantage, to his self-emptying, and to his self-humiliation. The important interpretive question, then, concerns the nature of this causal link.

One way of looking at this is to see God's exaltation of Christ as a reward for Christ's obedience. This way of understanding the causal connection between vv. 6-8 and 9-11, however, misses several key points. The first is internal to the story related in vv. 6-11. If, as I have argued, these verses display a crucial aspect of the character of God by complexly tying the manifestation of God's

---

30. Anselm, "Why God Became Man," 9. See also Aquinas, *Summa* III.47.1-3, who notes that the sacrifice of Christ's passion and death proceeded out of obedience. For a further set of reflections along this line see Herbert McCabe, *God Matters,* chapter 8.

31. O'Brien, *Philippians,* 233, also translates the phrase "that is why."

glory to Christ's self-emptying, his humiliation, and his unstinting obedience, then it will be important to understand that God's exaltation of Christ also primarily displays something about the character of God. Christ's death on the cross is not the last word on the relationship between God and the Christ who both shares God's glory and manifests the appearance of a servant in his incarnation and obedience. Christ's willed suffering in obedience to God can truly display the glory of the God of Israel only if that suffering is vindicated. If the circle which begins with glory and equality with God and then moves to servitude, humiliation, and death is not closed by an account of God's vindication, then the God whose character is displayed in these verses cannot rightly be identified as the God of Israel. Moreover, on the same grounds, Jesus cannot rightly be identified as the Christ. Hence, our ability to identify the two chief characters of vv. 6-11 depends on the vindication related in vv. 9-11.

The second element which is glossed by seeing vv. 9-11 as God's "reward" of Jesus' obedience is external to vv. 6-11 but crucial to the argument of the epistle as a whole. That is, Paul's ironic readings both of his own and of the Philippians' situation in the light of his understanding of God's economy of salvation depend on God's pattern of ultimate vindication (rather than reward) of those who suffer in steadfast obedience to the gospel. Unless one takes vv. 9-11 as the appropriate, albeit surprising, response to the manifestation of God's glory in the form of a slave, then Paul has no christological basis for the ironic perspective he adopts.

Finally, on trinitarian grounds, Christians must avoid reading these verses as a crude transaction between Christ and God where obedience is offered in exchange for exaltation. To read vv. 6-11 in this way would be to portray the inner life of the Trinity on the basis of a straightforward exchange of gifts in which one person's gift effectively coerces a reciprocal gift. Such a structure inscribes both a hierarchy and a struggle within an economy of lack into the life of the Trinity. Alternatively, Christians understand that within the life of God there is no lack. To the extent that we want to think of the relations between the three persons in terms of gift-giving, it would have to be in terms of an uncoerced circulation of gifts flowing from a super-abundance of love rather than lack.[32]

In short, then, although vv. 9-11 are causally linked to vv. 6-8, it is not the case that Christ's activity in vv. 6-8 coerces or provokes God's activity in vv. 9-11. Rather, it is fitting that God's activity in vv. 9-11 follows Christ's obedient self-emptying because that is the nature of the triune God.

---

32. In recent theology this argument has been made most strongly by John Milbank. See "Can a Gift Be Given?" and "Can Morality Be Christian?"

Having said this, it will be useful to examine what these verses say about the scope and nature of God's vindication of Christ's obedience. Grammatically, vv. 9-11 are a single sentence with God as the subject of the two main verbs. First, we learn that God "highly exalts" the crucified Christ.[33] Verse 9 further explicates the nature of this exaltation by noting that God gave Christ the name above all names. The Greek verb here translated as "gave" (ἐχαρίσατο/*echarisato*) recalls 1:29, where it was said that the Philippians were given the gift of both believing in Christ and suffering for Christ's sake. Here in 2:9 the gift that is given to Christ is the "name above all names." What is this name? Most scholars recognize that the name given to Jesus is that acclaimed in v. 11, "Lord" (κύριος/*kyrios*).[34] This is the designation used in the LXX for the personal name of the God of Israel. As Richard Bauckham reminds us, "the name itself is not Lord [κύριος/*kyrios*], which is not the divine name or even a Greek translation of the name, but a conventional Greek reverential *substitute* for the name. However, the fact that it was a substitute — evidently among Greek-speaking Christians *the* substitute — for the Tetragrammaton is certainly relevant to the meaning of the passage. It connects the unique identity of God (YHWH) closely with his sovereignty [κύριος/*kyrios*] as a key identifying characteristic of his uniqueness."[35] More on this in a moment.

The next two verses (vv. 10-11) explain the purpose of God's exaltation of Christ and of the gift that God bestows on Christ. The purpose of God's

---

33. Some scholars have tried to read this verb comparatively, reflecting the idea that Christ is exalted to a higher position than he had in v. 6. Some who do this are Kennedy, *Philippians*, 438; Lohmeyer, *Philipper*, 97. There is, however, no evidence to indicate that ὑπερυψόω/*hyperypsoō* by itself has a comparative force. For example, see the use of ὑπερυψόω/*hyperypsoō* in Ps 96(97):9; throughout the "song of the three men" in Daniel 3; also Dan 4:34; 11:12. When the verb is used of God's superiority to any other exalted being, the preposition is used to make the comparison (cf. Ps 96:9). In Acts 2:33; 5:31 it is used of Christ's exaltation to the place of highest honor. Rather, in both conventional use and in its particular application to Jesus (cf. Acts 2:33; 5:31) the verb is used in a superlative sense. See Beare, *Philippians*, 85; Collange, *Philippians*, 106; Gnilka, *Philipperbrief*, 125; Martin, *Philippians*, 240-43; O'Brien, *Philippians*, 236.

34. O'Brien, p. 238, lists four reasons for this majority view: (1) In the subordinate clause of vv. 10-11 Jesus is identified with κύριος/*kyrios* (*Yahweh*), the one to whom universal homage is given (Isa. 45:23). (2) It is best to view "the name Jesus" and "the name above all names" as juxtaposed. (3) For a Jew such as Paul the superlative name was *Yahweh*. (4) κύριος/*kyrios* gives a symmetry to the passage: θεός/*theos* (God) becomes δοῦλος/*doulos* (slave) and is exalted to κύριος/*kyrios* (Lord). The minority view, most strongly advocated by C. F. D. Moule, is based on the beginning of v. 10 and claims that the name above all names is "Jesus." "Because of the incarnation, the human name, 'Jesus', is acclaimed as the highest name; and the Man Jesus thus comes to be acclaimed as Lord, to the glory of God the Father" (Moule, 270).

35. See Bauckham, "The Worship of Jesus in Phil. 2:9-11," in *Where Christology Began*, 131.

exaltation of Christ is that "at the name of Jesus every knee shall bow."[36] The image of bowing of the knee is taken from Isa 45:23. In the context of Isaiah, and also here in Philippians, it signifies the recognition of authority, and it is a way of offering homage to Jesus.

As Bockmuehl notes, "Bowing one's knee 'in the name of' Christ is comparable to raising one's hands 'in the name of' God (LXX Ps 62:5). The meaning of the phrase, in other words, is equivalent to Isa 45:23."[37] In Rom 14:11 Paul also quotes Isa 45:23 to support his claim of God's universal rule and God's subsequent judgment of all things. In this respect, it is interesting to note that the authority and power Paul attributes to God in Romans he here attributes to Christ by citing the same OT text.

The subsequent phrase, "in heaven, and on earth, and under the earth," breaks from the quotation of Isa 45:23 but is clearly in line with the sentiments expressed there. Thus it would be a mistake to treat these terms as specifications of particular and limited groups of humans or angels or spiritual powers. Rather, we should read this text as Chrysostom does: "It means the whole world, and angels and men, and demons; or both the just and the living and sinners."[38] Thus, instead of seeking to separate out certain beings, this clause asserts the universal scope of the homage paid to Jesus (cf. Rev 5:13).

This acclamation continues into v. 11, announcing that "every tongue will confess that Jesus Christ is Lord." This resumes the language of Isa 45:23.[39] The larger context of Isa 45:18-25 speaks of a time when all of creation will acknowledge the saving power of *Yahweh*. So, too, 2:11 speaks of some eschatological point when all of creation confesses that Jesus Christ is "Lord." As Bauckham notes, "the worship of Jesus in Philippians 2 should be understood within the context of the Jewish monotheistic tradition, in which worship is recognition of the unique identity of the one God as sole Creator and Ruler of all things, and in which God's sole deity is expected to come to be acknowledged in worship by the whole creation."[40]

---

36. Where I have translated "at" in this clause, the Greek uses the preposition normally translated "in." The exact function of the preposition ἐν/*en* is debated. Does it refer to the object of worship or the medium? The LXX usage would suggest that worship "in the name of" God is worship offered to God (see 1 Kgs 8:44; Pss 43:8; 62:5; 104:3; also Bockmuehl, *Philippians*, 145).

37. Bockmuehl, *Philippians*, 145.

38. *Homily* 7.

39. The manuscript evidence is about equally divided between the aorist subjunctive ἐξομολογήσηται and the future ἐξομολογήσεται. In fact, however, both forms can be used to express an action occurring in the future.

40. Bauckham, "Worship of Jesus," 136.

Finally, v. 11 frames all this activity by concluding that it leads to the "glory of God the Father." Although doxological claims like this are common in the NT, this passage makes the striking assertion that the acclamation of Jesus as "Lord" serves to enhance rather than compete with the glory of the God who says, "I am the Lord, that is my name; my glory I give to none other" (Isa 42:8). Just as 2:6 identifies Christ with God in terms of "appearance" and "equality," 2:11 identifies Christ with God in that the worship reserved for Yahweh alone is directed to Christ, without diminishing or competing with the glory of God the Father.

The vast majority of modern commentators treat the granting of the name as an event subsequent to Christ's death on the cross. In a sense, the flow of the narrative supports this. Hence, most commentators simply make a few remarks seeking to avoid treating Christ's exaltation as a reward and move on as if that were sufficient. To simply treat this passage as a straightforward narrative in which one event creates the conditions for the next event, would raise serious questions about the theological logic of the passage that should, at least, be noted.

Simply to follow the flow of the narrative without further comment would also indicate that the Christ who was identified with God in terms of appearance and equality in v. 6 was still lacking something that is completed with the granting of the name in v. 9. Such a view cannot avoid the impression that Christ is somehow promoted into the name "Lord," a name that was not applicable prior to the incarnation. Even commentators who affirm Christ's preexistence in this passage can become implicated in this view. As David Yeago has made clear, however, "If relationship to Jesus of Nazareth is *intrinsic* to the identity of YHWH, if Jesus is not 'other' than YHWH in the sense of Isaiah 45, then it is impossible to fix *any* moment as the moment when that relationship began."[41] This assertion, however, raises another question. If, as is theologically necessary, Christ is eternally "Lord," then what is the point of bestowing this name that was already Christ's?

In thinking about this very issue, Aquinas gives two theological solutions.[42] First, one can say that what happens in vv. 9-11 is the deification of Christ's human nature. The Father brings what is distinct from God's nature, that is, Christ's human nature, into union with his divine nature. Aquinas attributes this view to Ambrose. The second view, which Aquinas attributes to Augustine, is that the granting of the name above all names in the presence of all creation makes known to creation what has been true eternally. In this

41. Yeago, "The New Testament and Nicene Dogma," 92.
42. See Aquinas, *Philippians*, 85.

light, vv. 9-11 do not describe a filling up of what was lacking in Christ's "equality with God." Rather, these verses describe the revelation to creation of what has always been the case. In the light of Augustine's interpretation, Aquinas goes on to read this passage through Acts 2:36, "Let all the house of Israel therefore know assuredly that God has made him both Lord and Christ, this Jesus whom you crucified." The revelation to the "house of Israel" is not Christ's promotion, but the coming of knowledge of what has eternally been the case. Aquinas treats both of these explanations as appropriate to the text and so should we.

Moreover, within the political context of Philippi the ascription of the name "Lord" to Christ is equally striking. Such naming is in direct competition with Caesar's claims: ". . . one who says 'Jesus Christ is *Lord*' cannot also agree that 'Caesar (or any other human potentate) is Lord': a Christian is forbidden to render to other powers, or to require from them, allegiance that belongs to Christ alone. This conviction is unmistakable in the accounts of the early Christian martyrs."[43] As we have already seen in 1:12-26, Paul views his circumstances and those of the Philippians in terms of an alternative story of the way the world works. Here in 2:6-11 the basis for that alternative view is laid out. It serves as a direct counter to the claims of the empire. These verses account for the nature and scope of Christ's dominion in ways that make it impossible for one also to acknowledge Caesar's claims to dominion. At the same time, these verses lay the foundation for the counter-politics that Paul desires the Philippians to embody in their common life.

This returns us to Paul's demand in 2:5 that the Philippians are to display the patterns of thinking, feeling, and acting which they see in Christ. The christological richness of this passage should not lead us to forget that Paul is ultimately concerned with the shape of the common life of the Philippian church. While someone like Irenaeus will make ready reference to this passage to correct christological errors, this is not Paul's primary concern. There is no sense in the epistle that the Philippians have any qualms about what this passage asserts about Christ. Rather, Paul wants them to see that what this passage asserts about Christ has deep and profound implications for the ways in which they order their life together. The habits, dispositions, and actions Christ displays in 2:6-11 are precisely the habits, dispositions, and actions Paul wants the Philippians to display toward each other.

Paul's distinctive language here shows that he is trying to form in the Philippians the intellectual and moral abilities to be able to deploy their knowledge of the gospel in the concrete situations in which they find them-

---

43. Bockmuehl, *Philippians*, 147.

selves, so that they will be able to order their common life in a manner worthy of the gospel of Christ (1:27). Thus, I agree with Wayne Meeks that "the letter's most comprehensive purpose is the shaping of a Christian *phronēsis,* a practical moral reasoning that is 'conformed to [Christ's] death' in hope of his resurrection."[44]

We can see this by placing this passage in the larger context of the epistle. In 1:12–2:4 Paul has offered comments and judgments about his own situation of imprisonment and what he takes to be the Philippians' parallel situation (cf. 1:30). His conviction that God is at work in both his life and the Philippians' common life is based on the way he reads the divine economy of salvation. That economy is decisively displayed in 2:6-11. Moreover, an understanding of Christ's manifestation of that economy leads Paul to adopt a certain course of action in his imprisonment (1:19-26) and to urge a particular course of action in the life of the Philippian congregation (2:1-4). In this respect, the story of Christ in 2:6-11 functions as an exemplar for Christians from which they can draw analogies to their own situations in order to order their common life in a manner worthy of the gospel. Thus, if the Philippians will unite in a steadfast adherence to the gospel (which will entail the practices mentioned in 2:2-4), even in the face of opposition, then God will vindicate them in the same way God vindicates the obedient, humiliated Christ in 2:6-11. Paul's admonition in 2:5 is a call to recognize this, a call to apply to their common life the precedent that is theirs by virtue of the fact they are "in Christ." To do this requires practical moral reasoning, the developed habit of thinking, feeling, and acting in particular Christ-formed ways.[45]

Many previous modern treatments of 2:5-11 which tried to present this passage as an ethical example tended to exhibit two serious problems. First, there is really no way for humans to imitate vv. 6-7. Secondly, most "ethical example" interpretations tended to ignore vv. 9-11.[46] My presentation here avoids these two pitfalls. First, it avoids the claim that Christians are to imitate Christ in any sort of isomorphic way. Clearly, Christians cannot do exactly what Christ did. This passage does not treat Christ as an example to be imitated in anything other than an analogical sense. Christians participate in

---

44. See "The Man from Heaven in Paul's Letter to the Philippians," 333. Meeks's essay, which appeared at the same time as my *The Story of Christ in the Ethics of Paul,* makes the same sort of arguments about Paul's moral reasoning.

45. As I noted above, Meeks claims that 2:5 with its use of φρονεῖν might well be translated "Base your practical reasoning on what you see in Christ Jesus" ("The Man from Heaven in Paul's Letter to the Philippians," 332).

46. These pitfalls were noted and sharply criticized by E. Käsemann, "Kritische Analyse von Phil. 2,5-11."

the economy that Christ reveals, but their participation is guided by analogy rather than isomorphic imitation. Second, my presentation treats vv. 9-11 seriously. If 2:9-11 demonstrate the character of God in the light of Christ's self-emptying and humble obedience, then Christians can expect God to act in character and in analogous ways in their lives of humble obedience. This does not entail that Christians will never suffer. Indeed, it almost seems to presuppose that they will.

Paul's analogical extension of the story of Christ in 2:6-11 to the common life of the Philippian church will be extended further in 2:12-18 by means of further admonitions to forsake factionalism (2:14) and encouragements to stand firm in the midst of hostile surroundings (2:15-16). Here we will also get further assurances that God is at work in the lives of the Philippians (2:13). Again, the point is not simply to calm the Philippians but to make strong assertions about the character of God, assertions based on Paul's attention to the divine economy displayed in Christ. Paul seems to recognize that his imprisonment and the opposition faced by the Philippians raise questions about the coherence and even the presence of God's work in the world. Paul's point in 2:14-18 (and 1:28-29) is that it is not suffering and opposition as much as the Philippians' possible failure to remain faithful that threatens to render God's world incoherent.

Further, within this context, Paul's "news" about Timothy and Epaphroditus in 2:19-30 is not meant simply to reassure the Philippians, but to offer them further models of those who do not seek after their own interests but the interests of others.[47] Paul's practical moral reasoning, based on 2:6-11, can provide him, and the Philippians, with the basis for commending the actions of Timothy and Epaphroditus and for admonishing Euodia and Syntyche in 4:2 to employ a common Christ-focused practical reasoning (again the Greek verb φρονεῖν/*phronein* is used).

In a much more systematic way than in 1:19-26, Paul will offer an account of his own life in 3:2-16 as a manifestation of a form of practical reasoning based on the story of Christ in 2:6-11. As his account will show, one of the primary tasks of practical reasoning is learning how to view things in the right way. Once one does this, then one can draw the appropriate types of analogies and act in appropriate ways. Throughout 3:2-16 Paul will seek to counter those whose practical reasoning is set on earthly things (3:19).[48] The contrast is not between judgments that rely on practical reasoning and those that do not. Rather, the contrast is between practical reasoning appropriate to

---

47. See Meeks, "The Man from Heaven in Paul's Letter to the Philippians," 334.
48. See Meeks, "The Man from Heaven in Paul's Letter to the Philippians," 332.

those whose commonwealth is in heaven and to those whose *phronēsis* is directed by earthly concerns. In this light, Paul's account of his life in 3:2-16 is really an account of how his perspective was transformed through his encounter with Christ. This transformation enables Christ-focused practical reasoning, which works to form a life that "knows the power of [Christ's] resurrection, is capable of sharing in his sufferings and becoming like him in his death" (3:10). The call to become fellow imitators of Paul, his associates, and those who live in a similar way (3:17) is primarily a call to understand what God has done in Christ in the way Paul has understood, embodied, and articulated it. From this one can then walk as someone who is a friend of the cross.

There is an enormous amount of secondary literature devoted just to Phil 2:5-11. One need not read very far in the modern literature on this passage to see that scholars regularly try to determine what sort of history this passage may have had prior to its incorporation into Philippians and what sort of texts and ideas formed its "background." There are a variety of different scholarly positions on these issues and it is well beyond the scope of this commentary to address them. Nevertheless, these issues of form and backgrounds are major preoccupations of modern scholarship on this passage. Hence, students should at least come to grips with a few of these proposals. In doing this, students can come to see what scholars are doing in this regard and begin to form some of their own ideas and interpretive habits. Hence, here I will examine questions about whether Phil 2:6-11 is a "hymn" and attempts to read Phil 2:6-11 in the light of Paul's so-called Adam christology. Those who are reading this commentary for other purposes can easily skip over this discussion.

Form: Hymn?

It is a critical commonplace to refer to this passage as a hymn. This view became part of the accepted set of assumptions of scholars working on this text by the time of Lohmeyer's *Kyrios Jesus* (1928) and probably earlier.[49] Once one subjects this critical commonplace to much scrutiny, however, two things become clear. First, there is a remarkable imprecision in the use of the term "hymn" in regard to this passage (and others). Secondly, once one gives the term "hymn" some sort of precision, there is very little evidence to support the application of the term to this passage.[50]

The term ὕμνος/*hymnos* (hymn) in the Greek of Paul's day seems to have two possible uses. First, in general Hellenistic usage it indicates a type of encomium prais-

---

49. Some of the early precursors to this view were J. Weiss, "Beiträge zur paulinischen Rhetorik," and A. Seeburg, *Der Katechismus der Urchristenheit.*

50. This, in short, was the position I argued in chapters 1 and 2 of *The Story of Christ in the Ethics of Paul.* Of the commentaries which have come out subsequently, Fee is the one who most thoroughly questions the use of the term "hymn" in regard to this passage.

ing the gods.[51] If this relatively precise notion of "hymn" is used, there are several reasons why it should not be applied to Phil 2:6-11. The most obvious reason is that while it is about a divine being, the Philippians passage is not an expression of praise. Further, "hymns" begin by someone justifying the need to praise.[52] Moreover, this type of hymn regularly ends in a petition to the gods while Phil 2:6-11 does not. Of course, this passage and "hymns" both poetically relate the activities and/or virtues of divine figures. As numerous encomia share this characteristic, this similarity, on its own, is not a sufficient reason to call Phil 2:6-11 a "hymn."[53]

The second, more precise understanding of ὕμνος/*hymnos* is found in the LXX. Here the majority of occurrences of "hymn" designate songs of praise to God (e.g., 2 Chron 7:6; Neh 12:24, 46, 47; Judith 15:13; Pss 99:4; 118:171; 148:14; Sir 44:1; 1 Macc 4:33). No doubt, in the LXX the objects of praise would have differed from pagan "hymns" and the LXX would use different stylistic conventions.[54] Nevertheless, that these "hymns" are also expressions of praise indicates that someone operating with this notion of hymn would not have used the term in regard to Phil 2:6-11.[55] Hence, if one uses "hymn" to describe a distinct literary genre comparable to what a first-century Greek speaker would have meant by ὕμνος/*hymnos*, then one has to say that Phil 2:6-11 is not a "hymn."

---

51. See Menander 1.331; also K. Berger, "Hellenistische Gattungen im Neuen Testament," 1150 for other citations. Berger also notes some occasions where ὕμνοι are addressed to humans or places. See also E. Krenz, "Epideiktik and Hymnody."

52. See Berger, "Hellenistische Gattungen," 1151, and also Philo, *De Vita Mosis* 2.239.

53. "Neither the Christ-hymns (such as Phil. 2:6-11; 1 Tim. 3:16) nor the hymns of the Apocalypse could be classed within the ancient genre ὕμνος" (Berger, "Hellenistische Gattungen," 1151; see also pp. 1153, 1167, and 1171 for similar comments).

54. It may well have been something much like these LXX ὕμνοι to which Pliny referred in his famous observation about Christians singing songs to Christ as to a God (see *Epistulae* 10.96-97).

55. There are a few exceptions to this use of ὕμνος/*hymnos* which might be relevant here. On the occasions when the phrase ἐν ὕμνοις/*en hymnois* is used in the titles of Pss 6, 53, 54, 60, 66, and 75 (also *Psalms of Solomon* 10) the psalms that follow are not expressions of praise. In fact, the only thing these psalms seem to have in common is that they are all addressed to God. In addition, in the NT ἐν ὕμνοις/*en hymnois* occurs in Col 3:16-17 and the parallel passage Eph 5:19-20 paired with ψαλμός/*psalmos* and ᾠδὴ πνευματική/*ōdē pneumatikē* in such a way that the context would not allow one clearly to distinguish a "psalm" from a "hymn" from a "spiritual song." These general uses of ὕμνος/*hymnos* in this particular construction may indicate that in certain circumstances the term could be used in a general way to refer to some sort of distinct formal expression addressed to God. In this respect Phil 2:6-11 as it currently stands would not be a ὕμνος/*hymnos* since it does not stand as a distinct text on its own. Moreover, even if one posits (on the basis of yet to be determined evidence) that some earlier form of 2:6-11 existed as a distinct formal expression directed to Christ or God, calling such a text a ὕμνος/*hymnos* in this general sense of the term would not be particularly enlightening, since there would be no basis for saying anything further about the reconstructed passage that would allow one to speak with any precision about its prior form or function.

This does not invalidate the use of the term "hymn" in regard to Phil 2:6-11. Rather, it suggests that in calling this passage a hymn it might be better to use the term "hymn" in the standard form-critical sense used by modern scholars. In this case, one would be using a term that is the construction of later biblical critics and not a straightforward translation of ὕμνος/*hymnos* in either its specific or generic sense.[56]

This use of the term "hymn" goes back to Gunkel's form-critical work on the Psalms.[57] According to Gunkel's classification, a hymn is a song of praise to God. It normally begins with an introductory phrase, which usually is an exhortation to rejoice and sing. The main body of the hymn then poetically recounts some of God's actions and attributes. A recitation of the motive for praising God accomplishes the transition from the introduction to the body of the hymn.[58] A hymn often closes with some type of concluding formula.[59]

Gunkel's analysis has often been expanded beyond the Psalter and finds obvious NT applications in both the Lukan birth story and the Apocalypse.[60] As widespread as this phenomenon seems to be, it is still not possible to call Phil 2:6-11 a hymn in this sense of the term. The same basic reason holds here. On Gunkel's view a hymn is an expression of praise directed by an individual or group toward God. This is clearly not the case with Phil 2:6-11. While all scholars seem to recognize that Phil 2:6-11 speaks of the activities of God and Christ in poetic style or elevated prose, this recognition does not make a passage a hymn in the relevant sense of the term.

Having accepted this, one might still claim that although this passage as it stands now is not a hymn, it is a quotation from a preexisting text which one might reasonably call a hymn in one of these senses.[61] Indeed, the majority of modern scholars believe that Phil 2:6-11 represents preexisting material that Paul is quoting and/or redacting. Without surveying all of the various views on this, I want to raise several questions about this critical consensus. First, I want to examine the reasons for viewing this passage as a quotation. Second, if one finds sufficient reason for seeing

---

56. This means that one cannot rely on the ambiguity between "hymn" as a translation of ὕμνος/*hymnos* and hymn as a form-critical designation to equate this passage with the ὕμνοι/*hymnoi* mentioned in Colossians and Ephesians as a means of saying something about the worship of the earliest Christian communities. Two works which tend to do just this are M. Hengel, "Hymn and Christology," and R. P. Martin, "Some Reflections on New Testament Hymns."

57. See H. Gunkel and J. Begrich, *Einleitung in die Psalmen* (2nd ed., Göttingen: Vandenhoeck und Ruprecht, 1966 [1st ed. 1933]).

58. See the discussion which begins in Gunkel, *Einleitung in die Psalmen*, 32.

59. See Gunkel, *Einleitung in die Psalmen*, 56.

60. Gunkel himself wrote an essay on the hymns in Luke, "Die Lieder in der Kindheitsgeschichte Jesu."

61. G. Schille, *Frühchristliche Hymnen*, 11, is quite explicit about this. This also seems to be the view of J. Sanders in *The New Testament Christological Hymns*, 1-5. K. Wengst, *Christologische Formeln und Lieder*, 11, also recognizes that the "Formeln" and "Lieder" of the NT need to be reconstructed. R. Deichgräber's comments (*Gotteshymnus und Christushymnus der frühen Christenheit*, 21 n. 3) also lead him this way.

this text as a quotation, what does that tell us about the role this passage might have played in the life of the church? Finally, how and in what ways are answers to these questions relevant to understanding the text of Philippians?

Unlike numerous other places in Paul where he explicitly recounts what another has said or written (e.g., 1 Cor 11:23; Gal 3:10) there is no such specific statement in Phil 2:5-11. Neither do we have another text with which a comparison could be made to show that Paul is quoting something else (as with the Synoptic Gospels).

Some might argue that the very presence of these poetic passages, which presumably took a great deal of reflection to compose, in the midst of epistolary discourse would indicate that such a passage was not composed with the rest of the epistle.[62] This view is plausible if one can account for the fact that Paul is not hesitant to note when he is citing previously formulated material.[63] Further, one would have to account for the existence of poetic material such as Rom 11:33-36, which seems to have been composed with the rest of the epistle. In fact, a passage like Rom 11:33-36 argues for the possibility of the composition of poetic speech in the midst of epistolary discourse. To decide this question we would need to have a fairly clear idea of the composition process in regard to Paul's letters generally and Philippians in particular. This information, of course, is hidden from us. Hence, further criteria would be needed to support the view that these passages are quotations.

The two criteria which scholars invoke most often are uniqueness of vocabulary and evidence of redaction based on stylistic abnormalities.[64] Clearly, there is unusual vocabulary in Phil 2:6-11. It is less clear that this means that the passage is a quotation from previously existing material. It seems no less likely that Paul would use unusual words in a poetic passage than that he would quote them. The appearance of unusual vocabulary adds to the distinctiveness of the passage. It does not necessarily indicate that someone else wrote it first. Further, even to make a probability judgment in regard to this we would have to develop a more detailed profile of the linguistic abilities and tendencies of an author than can be obtained from the Pauline corpus.

The criterion of redactional activity indicated by stylistic abnormalities in a passage has greater potential for indicating that these passages are quotations. This criterion, however, presupposes a standard of what is stylistically conventional. Previous scholarship has generally relied on the work of E. Norden to provide an account of both Hellenistic and Jewish stylistic conventions.[65] Of course, our knowledge of these conventions has advanced markedly since 1912.

62. See Martin, *Carmen Christi*, 44-46, for those who make this point.

63. As Richard Hays, *Echoes* has shown, Paul does allude to OT texts without explicitly citing them, and OT texts often echo throughout portions of his letters unannounced. In these cases, however, there is always a prior text with which to compare, an original voice whose echoes are heard in Paul's letters. It would be difficult to make a similar sort of argument here in Phil 2:5-11.

64. See W. H. Gloer, "Homologies and Hymns in the New Testament," 125-32; Martin, *Carmen Christi*, 42; Kim, *The Origin of Paul's Gospel*, 144-49.

65. See Norden's *Der Antike Kunstprosa* and most importantly, *Agnostos Theos*.

With regard to the poetic conventions operative in Jewish literature, scholarship has focused on formal characteristics and parallelism in particular. Works by Kugel, Watson, and others have moved our understanding of parallelism well beyond the ideas of *parallelismus membrorum* supported by Norden.[66] Using these findings as a new standard, it would be difficult to say with any precision what a stylistic abnormality would look like, since parallelism would be conceived of either as one general type — "A, and what's more B" — or a hundred types.[67] In theory, however, one could make such a case. In fact, this has yet to be done.

Further, if one were to apply more recent accounts of the stylistic standards of pagan Hellenism to Phil 2:6-11 the results would hardly be decisive for determining on the basis of redactional activity whether this passage is a quotation. As Berger notes, "The extensive structuring of the comparable New Testament prose texts ('hymns') by means of anaphoric elements (repetition of relative pronouns, and connecting words) is without analogy in the poetic and prosaic hymns and encomia. The New Testament texts are in this sense a separate group."[68] This is a crucial comment. If there are no pagan Hellenistic analogies to the stylistic features of these passages as a whole, it is hard to see how using pagan Hellenistic conventions as a standard could indicate the sort of stylistic abnormalities necessary for claims about redactional activity, and hence, quoted material.

Hence, in regard to my first question noted above, the primary piece of evidence for the claim that Phil 2:6-11 is a quotation drawn from preexisting material seems to be the scholarly consensus that this is so. In the absence of further evidence, however, I suggest that scholars simply drop this claim. The reason that scholars are loath to do this seems to be that, if this passage was drawn from preexisting material, then we would have some evidence from that period of Christianity between the death and resurrection of Jesus and the writing of Paul's epistles, and we would eagerly like to know more about this period.[69] Of course, having a desire and being able to fulfill that desire are two different things.

In order to proceed to my second question, let us assume that we somehow develop criteria that would allow scholars to make a convincing argument that Phil 2:6-11 is drawn from a piece of preexisting material. What might that tell us about the role of this reconstructed text in the life of the earliest church? The answer to this question depends on how the text is reconstructed. One could, for example, add an introduc-

---

66. See *Agnostos Theos,* 260ff. Norden relies on the work of R. Lowth, *De Sacra Poesi Hebraeorum.* See also J. Kugel, *The Idea of Biblical Poetry,* and W. Watson, *Classical Hebrew Poetry.* The fact that these conventions appear in Greek texts is not unusual. See Sirach 51; Judith 16; the Greek additions to Daniel; also S. Segert, "Semitic Poetic Structures in the New Testament," 1432.

67. See Kugel, *The Idea of Biblical Poetry,* 58.

68. Berger, "Hellenistische Gattungen," 1168.

69. M. Rese shows that this was one of the primary motives for the earliest research into NT "hymns." See "Formeln und Lieder im Neuen Testament," 75-95. See also Hengel, "Hymn and Christology," 173, 189.

tory expression of praise and call to praise along with a motive clause to reconstruct a text that could quite plausibly be called a hymn in the form-critical sense of that term. There might be some reason for reading this reconstruction in the light of one of the descriptions of early Christian worship to then argue what we now have is a text that comes from the liturgical life of the earliest church.[70]

It is not clear, however, why this particular reconstruction should be preferred over other, equally possible (because equally arbitrary) reconstructions. A different reconstruction might yield an original confession or a piece of catechetical material from which Phil 2:6-11 is a quotation. That is, from the material we actually have, one could just as plausibly reconstruct an assertion of belief as an expression of praise. In theory any number of reconstructions might be possible, each of which would have played a different role in the life of the earliest church. Hence, even if one grants that Phil 2:6-11 is a quotation, the reconstruction of any particular form of the original text is an arbitrary choice. It is really only on the basis of this arbitrary choice that one might be able to say anything substantial (though completely speculative) about the earliest church.

This leads to my final question. If one could convincingly argue that Phil 2:6-11 was a quotation from previously existing material that played a specific role in the life of the earliest church, would that be relevant to discussing this passage as it occurs in Philippians? At a general theoretical level the answer must be no. The function of an utterance is determined by the specific context in which it is used. This is now a commonplace among philosophers of language and others.[71] How one understands an utterance or a text depends on its context and is independent of other contexts in which the utterance or text might have been used. One obvious exception to this would be if one could show that Paul was quoting from preexisting material that was known to the Philippians. In this case, the presupposed common knowledge between Paul and his audience would be part of the context in which the passage is quoted. Hence, it would be important for a third party, such as a commentator on Philippians, to know this if such a person wished to comment on how Phil 2:6-11 should be understood in its current context.

Of course, any judgment about an audience's previous knowledge about Phil 2:6-11 is not necessarily tied to judgments about the particular role of that text in the life of the earliest church. One could simply argue that Paul quoted a text that the Philippians already knew in some form. This would free one from having to balance unwarranted assumption on unfounded speculation, but there is no explicit indication that the Philippians did already have some knowledge of the material in 2:6-11. Neither is there any evidence that, as in 2 Corinthians, Paul is addressing himself to an issue he has previously discussed. Moreover, since the passage is relatively intelligible in its current context we are not justified in assuming that Paul presumes the Philippians' prior exposure to it.

---

70. For some of these descriptions see Martin, *Carmen Christi*, 1-16.

71. The most enjoyable and edifying argument for this is to be found in J. L. Austin's *How to Do Things with Words.*

Background: Adam Christology?

Form-critical studies of this passage have converged with history-of-religions concerns to generate a pattern of scholarship that has tried to articulate the history-of-religions background to the pre-Pauline hymn lying behind Phil 2:6-11. As I have just indicated, the form-critical studies have proceeded in the absence of persuasive evidence. Without reliable form-critical studies, there is really no way to develop a scheme of development for the concepts ultimately presented in 2:6-11. Nevertheless, it is possible, and common among scholars, to view Phil 2:6-11 in its current form in the light of other textual material to see what light each text might shed on the other without, at the same time, making questionable historical arguments about how a concept might have developed.

One of the most persistent issues to which scholars have attended over the past thirty years has to do with the relationship between this text and Paul's "Adam christology." The most vigorous proponent of this view has been J. D. G. Dunn.[72] On Dunn's view, Phil 2:6-11 offers an implicit contrast between Adam, who grasps at equality with God and fails, and Christ, who does not grasp, but is exalted by means of his obedient death. Adam's grasping fundamentally alienates people from God. This alienation is rectified by the human Christ's activity related in 2:6-8. Within the larger argument of *Christology in the Making*, Dunn's points about "Adam christology" in Phil 2:6-11 are used to undermine the notion that this passage imagines Christ's preexistence. This supports Dunn's larger argument that notions of Christ's preexistence developed relatively late. As will become clear below, however, one can argue both that some sort of "Adam christology" lies behind this passage and that the passage strongly asserts Christ's preexistence.

In the light of a substantial body of criticism Dunn has pointed out that his claims are only about implications and allusions within this passage. He admits there is no explicit reference to Adam in these verses.[73] This, however, does not really address the problems in his position. The implications and allusions Dunn finds in this passage hinge on the way he reads the linguistic evidence — and his reading of the Greek term ἁρπαγμός/*harpagmos* (translated above as "something to be used for his own advantage") in particular, and his account of the way Adam was viewed in Second Temple Judaism. If Dunn's reading of the evidence is flawed, and many have made this case, then there is no reason to claim that there are probable allusions to Adam in this passage.[74]

N. T. Wright also vigorously asserts that 2:6-11 is an example of Paul's Adam christology. But he distinguishes his view from Dunn's in several ways. In Wright's Adam christology, Adam, Israel, and Christ are closely connected. Adam perfectly displays God's intentions for humanity. Through Adam's disobedience, that harmonious

---

72. Dunn's views were first laid out in *Christology in the Making*.

73. See "Christ, Adam and Preexistence."

74. For critiques of Dunn's views see Fowl, *The Story of Christ*, 71-75; Hurst, "Christ, Adam and Preexistence, Revisited"; J. R. Levison, *Portraits of Adam in Early Judaism*, 20-21.

relationship between God and humans is damaged (though not destroyed). As part of God's dramatic restoration of the relationships characteristic of Eden, Israel is chosen to display God's intentions for humanity to the world. "Israel is God's true humanity. . . . Israel will be given the rights of Adam's true heir."[75] As Paul develops this view, Christ as the Messiah fulfills this role:

> That which was purposed in Genesis 1 and 2, the wise rule of creation by obedient human beings, was lost in Genesis 3, when human rebellion jeopardised the divine intention, and the ground brought forth thorns and thistles. The Messiah, however, has now been installed as the one through whom God is doing what he intended to do, first through humanity and then through Israel. Paul's Adam-christology is basically an Israel-christology, and is predicated on the identification of Jesus as Messiah in virtue of his resurrection.[76]

When it comes to reading Phil 2:6-11, Wright is quite clear that Adam and Christ are contrasted, though not in a rigid parallelism. Hence, he is able to read v. 6 in accordance with the best linguistic evidence as a reference to Christ's preexistence, thus avoiding Dunn's conclusion that the passage says nothing about preexistence because of its links to Adam.[77] As Wright sees it, Phil 2:6-11 contrasts Adam and Christ in the following way:

> Christ's obedience is not simply the replacement of Adam's disobedience. It does not involve merely the substitution of one sort of humanity for another, but the solution to the problem now inherent in the first sort, namely sin. The temptation of Christ was not to snatch at a forbidden equality with God, but to cling to his rights and thereby opt out of the task allotted to him, that he should undo the results of Adam's snatching.[78]

Wright goes on to claim that 2:9-11, with its clear reliance on language from Isa 45:23, "credits Jesus with a rank and honour which is not only in one sense appropriate for the true Man, the Lord of the world, but it is also the rank and honour explicitly reserved, according to scripture, for Israel's God and him alone."[79] This shows clearly the further points at which Christ might be contrasted with Adam without there being a strict parallelism.

Throughout his chapter on Phil 2:6-11, Wright argues not only that the passage should be read in the light of and as an example of Paul's Adam christology, but that this passage is closely linked with Rom 5:12-21. It is here that I wish to raise some questions. My point is not to criticize Wright's Adam christology as a whole.[80] I also do

---

75. Wright, *The Climax of the Covenant*, 24.

76. Wright, *The Climax of the Covenant*, 29

77. See Wright, *The Climax of the Covenant*, 92.

78. Wright, *The Climax of the Covenant*, 91-92.

79. Wright, *The Climax of the Covenant*, 94.

80. Levison, *Portraits of Adam in Early Judaism*, 22-24, is critical of Wright's treatment of Adam in post-biblical Jewish literature.

not wish to argue that the views of Christ in Romans 5 and Philippians 2 are incompatible. I do, however, want to note some significant differences between these two passages which tend to be glossed over by Wright. The obvious point of contact between these two passages is their emphasis on Christ's obedience. In Romans 5 Christ's obedience is specifically contrasted with Adam's disobedience. The importance of this contrast is to show how the damage caused by Adam's sin is reversed by Christ's obedience, thus redeeming humanity and demonstrating the righteousness of God. That is, the Adam-Christ contrast in Romans has an explicit soteriological emphasis. Philippians 2 makes no such direct soteriological statement. Further, in Romans 5 Adam's trespass allows the regnant power of sin to enter the cosmos, bringing death with it. To the extent that Phil 2:9-11 articulates the cosmic effects of Christ's obedience, it does so along different lines.

Romans 5 explicitly emphasizes sin's entry into the world through Adam and how Christ defeats the power of sin through his obedience. If this is presupposed in Phil 2:6-11, it certainly is not emphasized or made explicit there. Instead, 2:6-11 initially focuses on the preexistent Christ's disposition toward his equality with God and Christ's subsequent obedience. Unlike Romans 5, Philippians 2 says something about the character of that obedience: it is obedience manifested in willed self-emptying, and humiliation; it is obedience that extends as far as the cross. In Romans 5 one might claim that since Paul speaks about sin and death as powers (5:14, 21), Christ's death could be seen as a form of submission to these powers in order to bring about their ultimate defeat (cf. 6:2-14). In this way Christ becomes obedient unto death. This is not, however, what is stated in Phil 2:8.[81] Death is not portrayed as a personalized power to whom Christ is subject. Rather death — death on a cross — is the extent to which Christ is obedient to God. Finally, in Romans 5 Christ's obedience results in humanity's justification. In Phil 2:9-11 Christ's obedience results both in the world recognizing his exaltation and in the glorification of God — points that (as Wright indicates) have no real analog in Romans 5.

Let me be clear; I am not arguing that there are inconsistencies between the pictures of Christ presented in Romans 5 and Philippians 2. They clearly identify one and the same character. Further, I have no doubt that one can fit both passages into a coherent Pauline christology. My point is simply that there are some very real differences of emphasis between the two that ultimately must temper any claims that Phil 2:6-11 exhibits some sort of Adam christology. Romans 5 emphasizes Christ's obedience as part of a larger account of how God's saving activity counters the disobedience of Adam. The explicit aim here is to narrate and summarize the story of human disobedience that Paul begins in 1:18, showing how Christ's obedience works to restore God's intentions for the world first displayed in Eden, and then reiterated with the call of Abraham and the formation of the people of Israel. The upshot of this is to reveal the righteousness of God (cf 1:16-17).

---

81. Wright, *The Climax of the Covenant*, 92, seems to hold the view that 2:8 speaks of death as the object of Christ's obedience, not its extent.

Rather than fitting Christ's obedience into a narrative that is primarily about salvation, Phil 2:6-11 focuses on the quality of Christ's obedience as we follow his descent from equality with God to the humiliation of the cross. Through its focus on God's exaltation of the obedient crucified one we are told something about the character of God. It is just these points — emphasized in Phil 2:6-11 and not in Rom 5:12-21 — which are taken up by Paul and applied to the life of the Philippians in the rest of the epistle. Given these considerations, it appears that there are few conceptual parallels between Paul's view of Adam and the account of Christ in Phil 2:6-11.

On the one hand, it is not necessary to provide a precise conceptual background to this or any other passage in order to understand it. Indeed, useful parallel texts can be suggested only on the basis of a fairly substantial understanding of this passage. On the other hand, if I were forced to do so, I would argue that Jewish texts discussing the suffering servant/righteous one provide a more adequate conceptual background against which to illumine Phil 2:6-11. Most particularly, the servant passages of Isaiah seem to resound throughout Phil 2:6-11. The problem which tends to ensnare modern attempts to read Phil 2:6-11 against this background is that they tend to draw the background too finely, extending textual parallels too far, and in ways easily refuted. This is particularly the case when scholars try to make direct connections between Phil 2:6-11 and very specific texts.[82] These linguistic enterprises have been roundly criticized.[83] Their rejection has moved scholars away from such passages as a possible background for Phil 2:6-11.

If, however, one is concerned to find conceptual backgrounds for 2:6-11 and not direct literary sources, there is much to commend Isaiah 53. Indeed, Richard Bauckham has recently argued that Phil 2:6-11 could be read as an early Christian interpretation of Isaiah 40–55 and especially Isaiah 53.[84] Bauckham is particularly helpful in pointing out the close connections between the servant's exaltation and the claims made about Christ. On the other hand, the servant's sufferings are related to the forgiveness of sins, which is not directly a part of Phil 2:6-11. Further, there is in Philippians an emphasis on Christ's free choosing of humiliation that is not apparent in Isaiah. Nevertheless, Paul and the earliest Christians would have found much in Isaiah 53 as well as Psalms 8:6 and 110(LXX 109):1 which would have helped them articulate their convictions about God's economy of salvation revealed in Christ.

---

82. One finds a good example of this in Jeremias's attempts to show that ἑαυτὸν ἐκένωσεν/*heauton ekenōsen* is a direct translation of the Hebrew of Isa 53:7 and that δοῦλος/*doulos* in 2:7 is a translation of עֶבֶד/*'ebed* in Isaiah 53. See "Zu Phil. ii.7," 182-89.

83. See M. Hooker, *Jesus and the Servant*, and Bornkamm, "Zum Verständnis der Christus-Hymnus Phil. 2, 5-11," 180.

84. See *God Crucified*, 47-54; "The Worship of Jesus."

2:12-18

12 So then, my beloved, just as you have always obeyed, not only in my presence, but now much more in my absence, work out your salvation with fear and trembling. 13 For God is the one working in you, both to will and to bring about God's good pleasure for you. 14 Do all things without grumbling and foolish reasoning 15 in order that you may be blameless and innocent, children of God without blemish in the midst of a crooked and perverse generation, in which you shine as lights in the world 16 as you hold fast to the word of life, in order that I may boast in you on the day of Christ that I did not run in vain or work for nothing. 17 Even if I am being poured out as a drink offering on your sacrifice and service, which is your faith, I rejoice and rejoice together with you. 18 Likewise you all should rejoice and rejoice together with me.

Paul began chapter 2 by urging the Philippians to adopt a variety of practices designed to sustain a common life worthy of the gospel of Christ. He then presented a story about Christ emphasizing the dispositions and actions that marked Christ's relationship of love and obedience to God. This story of Christ provided the Philippians with an exemplar of the sorts of habits, dispositions, and actions Paul had urged them to adopt in their relations with each other. In 2:12-18 Paul returns to admonishing the Philippians in a way that both presumes what has already been argued and points toward further implications and inferences.

Paul begins by addressing the Philippians as "my beloved." This term is certainly appropriate in the light of the cordial relationship Paul seems to have with them. On the other hand, Paul uses the same term in addressing the Corinthian congregation, with whom his relations are much more strained (cf. 1 Cor 10:14; 15:58; 2 Cor. 7:1; 12:19). He also uses it with the Romans, whom he has not met (12:19). In all these cases Paul invokes the relationships of love that bind these communities to him as a way of making various moral demands of the congregation. Hence, in addition to reminding us of the cordial relations between Paul and the Philippians, this phrase signals that Paul is going to make some demand regarding the conduct of their common life.

Paul calls on the Philippians to "work out" their salvation. This call, however, is set within the context of obedience, an obedience that has, according to Paul, always been characteristic of the Philippians. It is important to recognize Paul is not calling them from disobedience to obedience. Rather, he is urging a continuation of the obedience they have heretofore displayed.

The verb "obey" echoes the adjective "obedient" in 2:8. Here as there the one who is obeyed in not made explicit. Is Paul calling the Philippians to obey him or to be obedient to God? But since vv. 9 and 13 both insert God as the one who is acting on the obedient subject (Christ and the Philippians respectively), one can infer that it is God who is the object of the obedience, here as in v. 8.

Alternatively, Paul's recognition that the Philippians have always been obedient indicates that the real issue is not obedience as such. Rather, the issue concerns the precise nature and shape of the Philippians' obedience. That is, the issue does not seem to be the Philippians' willingness to form a common life worthy of the gospel of Christ, but what that common life should look like in their particular situation. To address this, Paul generates a rather detailed answer, drawing first on his disposition toward his imprisonment, then moving to discuss the habits, practices, and dispositions the Philippians should manifest, and finally bringing this discussion to its climax by basing it on the story of Christ narrated in 2:6-11. Hence, the obedience Paul calls for is also obedience to him, to Paul's particular account of the economy of salvation and to how both he and the Philippians are to live in the light of that economy. To the extent that the "working out" of the Philippians' salvation runs along the lines Paul has advocated, it is obedience to him and to his vision of the way God has worked and will continue to work in the world. Nevertheless, to the extent that God is the primary agent at work in Paul's life, the lives of the Philippians and in the story of Christ, then it is God who is the ultimate object of obedience.

In this respect then, there is no substantial difference between obedience to Paul and obedience to God. This is a bold claim, full of both promise and pitfalls. The history of Christianity is littered with the false claims of those who asserted that obedience to God was identical with obedience to them. The most dangerous variation on this is when the modern nation state claims that obedience to God entails obedience to the state. In the light of this history, Christians are right to be skeptical of those who claim too close a connection between their will and the will of God.

Paul, too, would also urge caution in evaluating the claims of those who speak in God's name. He would, no doubt, concur with the Johannine admonition to test the spirits (cf. 1 John 4:1). Nevertheless, the need for such discernment already implies the necessity and the presence of people speaking in the name of God. The need to test the spirits presumes the presence of people who will assert at particular points in time that there is no significant difference between obedience to their words and obedience to God. Paul, along with the rest of the NT writers, assumes the importance of people making such claims and that Christians should submit to these claims when the light of wise discernment has validated them.

This need to submit to one another will prove most troublesome for contemporary Christians. This is particularly true of those Christians who have been more deeply schooled in the habits and practices of American individualism than the habits and practices of the gospel. For Paul and the earliest Christians, discerning how to form a common life worthy of the gospel required concrete figures who could speak authoritatively to the rest of the community. Paul and the Philippians already assumed that their common life depended on the testimony and admonition of others about how God was leading them. Of course, they needed to discern and discriminate between various testimonies and admonitions. They also, however, realized that they could not survive if they, in principle, ruled out submitting to each other's authority. If we Christians today are chilled by Paul's bold presumption that there is no significant difference between obedience to him and obedience to God in specific matters, it may well be because the common life of our particular congregations is so impoverished that we cannot imagine either how to test the spirits or how we might submit to each other without risking obliteration. In such cases Paul's claims here will sound like little more than crude power plays.

Paul modifies his call to obedience in two particular ways. First, Paul refers to his former visit with the Philippians and calls for them to show the sort of obedience that characterized that time even though he is not now with them. Secondly, they are to obey in "fear and trembling."[1] The first relies on the past obedience of the Philippians as the basis for further obedience. The second, "with fear and trembling," is typically used in the NT as an almost idiomatic expression indicating a virtuous attitude of submission that people exhibit toward those of higher status (cf. Eph 6:5; 2 Cor 7:15). In one sense, this seems to fit well with Paul's admonition in 2:3 that the Philippians are to consider others superior to themselves.

Ironically, however, Paul has already identified himself as a "slave" of Christ (1:1). Hence, any status that Paul may have has to do with the status of his master, who himself took the appearance of a slave. We cannot escape the fact that in this verse Paul is exercising a certain type of power here. As we saw in 1:12-26, however, there is an almost ironic displacement of Paul as the source of his own power. Here in 2:12 Paul relies on his prior presence in Philippi and his friendship with the Philippians in order to seek their obedience.

---

1. Grammatically these two phrases could modify either "obey" or "work out." It seems best to take them as together modifying a common verb. There are, however, no absolutely decisive arguments for tying them to one verb rather than the other. I have tied them to "obey" because the other occurrences of "with fear and trembling" in the NT appear in connection with "obey" (see Eph 6:5 and 2 Cor 7:15; cf. 1 Cor 2:3). Hence, it makes sense to take this phrase as a modifier of "obey" here.

Paul's call to obey leads to his command to the Philippians to "work out your own salvation." Taken on its own, this phrase seems to re-open the polemics of the sixteenth century regarding justification.[2] In the context of Philippians, however, this verse merely reiterates a central presumption of Paul's entire argument. If God were not at work among the Philippian congregation, then the suffering they will face at the hands of their opponents would be senseless; their steadfastness would indeed signify their destruction — as their opponents already think — and not salvation (1:28); the story of Christ in 2:6-11 would have no obvious relevance to them. In the same way that God worked to exalt and vindicate the humiliated, obedient Christ, God will also work to accomplish the salvation "worked out" by the Philippians.

In a culture that stresses the salvation of individual souls based on personal decisions, it is significant to note that Paul is not talking here about individual Philippian Christians so much as the salvation of the Christian community in Philippi. Obviously, Paul is often concerned about the spiritual health of individuals (see 4:1-3). Generally, however, this is not his primary focus. It certainly is not his focus here.

Rather than treating this verse as a threat to a doctrine of grace, it is better to see this claim as the affirmation of God's continuing work among the Philippians. Indeed, this verse closely echoes Paul's earlier judgment in 1:6. God's work in the lives of the Philippians is God's good pleasure. That is, this is God's deepest desire for the Philippians, not a gift grudgingly given.[3] The conviction that God's deepest desires for humans both inspire and provide the *telos* for the economy of salvation stands behind almost everything Paul has argued for thus far. Here in 2:13 it is made explicit.

The lack of any conjunction or connecting particle closely ties vv. 14-18 to the preceding claims about God's aims and desires for the Philippians and God's continued working in their midst. There are a striking number of OT allusions in these verses. Paul seems to read the Philippians situation in the

---

2. Günter Bornkamm calls this an "oddly paradoxical phrase." See "Der Lohngedanke in Neuen Testament," in *Studien zu Antike und Urchristentum*, 92. Aquinas (88-89) notes that in this verse Paul excludes four false opinions: (1) that humans can will their own salvation apart from God's help, (2) that humans lack free will altogether, (3) that humans provide the will and God provides the accomplishment of that will, and (4) that God accomplishes good in us through our merits.

3. Thus I am taking the Greek phrase ὑπὲρ τῆς εὐδοκίας/*hyper tēs eudokias* to refer to God's disposition toward working in the lives of the Philippians (with Beare, *Philippians*, 91; Fee, *Philippians*, 239; Gnilka, *Philipperbrief*, 150; O'Brien, *Philippians*, 288). This is against the view that it refers to the goodwill Paul seeks in the common life of the Philippian church (so Collange, *Philippians*, 111; Hawthorne, *Philippians*, 101).

light of Israel in the desert, urging them not to replicate the Israelites' response.

In the light of Paul's claims about God's continued care and activity among the Philippians in 2:13, he hastens to add in 2:14 that they should "do all things without grumbling and dissension." The key allusive phrase here is "without grumbling." The only other time Paul uses this phrase is in 1 Cor 10:10, where he cites the grumbling of the Israelites as a negative example to be avoided by the Corinthians. The Greek word for "grumbling" is used a number of times in the LXX for Israel's grumbling against God and Moses.[4] This rather straightforward allusion is a puzzle for modern commentators because it does not seem to have any direct application to the Philippians' situation in the same way it does for the Corinthians.[5] In the case of 1 Corinthians, it is quite clear that Paul reads the current life of the Corinthian church in the economy of salvation through the positive and negative examples of God's dealings with Israel in the desert. In Philippians Paul engages in a similar activity. In fact, in these verses he is displaying the same form of practical reasoning he has displayed throughout the epistle. That is, he interprets the movements of God's economy of salvation in a way that allows him to draw analogies and spell out implications for the common life of the Philippians. The analogy would look something like this: When faced with political and material hardship and opposition, the Israelites grumbled, doubting that God (through Moses) had led them thus far and would lead them out of their present difficulties. It is precisely this attitude that Paul has tried to frustrate throughout the epistle. In 2:13 he reiterated his conviction that God has and will continue to work in the lives of the Philippians. The Philippians, therefore, are to avoid the response of the Israelites when they are in a similar situation. By alluding to the Israelites in the desert, Paul is not seeking to counter present behavior as much as a possible response from the Philippians.[6]

The second habit that Paul wants the Philippians to purge is character-

---

4. Exod 16:7-12 (six occurrences); 17:3; Num 14:27-29 (three); 16:41; 17:5 (two), 10. "Grumble" also occurs in these passages.

5. Some point to the fact that Paul elsewhere addresses internal dissension in the Philippian congregation (4:1-3) to suggest that, rather than alluding to grumbling against God, Paul is using this term to talk about internal dissent. The language in 4:1-3, however, is different. Moreover, such a suggestion seems deaf to the LXX overtones of "grumbling."

6. Chrysostom seems to be on the right track in taking this passage as a warning about future possibilities rather than a direct admonition about current realities. He rightly contrasts the situations of the Corinthians, where the grumbling is real and the allusion to the Israelites is direct and explicit, with the Philippians, where grumbling is a possibility to be avoided and the allusion is, correspondingly, less explicit. See *Homily 8*.

ized as "foolish reasoning." Paul uses this term elsewhere for a false sort of reasoning, the reasoning of those who may seem wise but are foolish in the light of divine wisdom.[7] In the case of Philippians and its rather persistent emphasis on the formation of a Christ-focused *phronēsis* or practical reasoning, "foolish reasoning" would be the very opposite of the practical reasoning Paul desires to see formed in the Philippians. If we stick with the OT allusion to Israel in the desert suggested by "grumbling," then "foolish reasoning" would be the habit of reasoning displayed by the Israelites. When faced with the hardships of the desert, they grumbled against God and Moses, doubting that God was the one working among them. The term thus suggests a disposition to dramatically misread the economy of salvation, thereby generating unfaithful actions. This line of interpretation is bolstered by the allusion to Deut 32:5 in the next verse.

Avoiding "grumbling and foolish reasoning" will enable the Philippians to be "blameless and innocent,[8] children of God without blemish[9] in the midst of a crooked and perverse generation, in which they shine as lights in the world." The conjunction of "blameless," "innocent," and "without blemish" gives the very clear impression that Paul is describing the final end toward which God is moving the church at Philippi. He is looking forward to that time when God's ultimate "good pleasure" is brought to fruition in them, to that time when the purposes for which God first called them are achieved. Moreover, Paul contrasts this holiness toward which God is moving the Philippian Christians with the crookedness and perversity of the present age. On its surface, then, this verse indicates that by avoiding grumbling and foolish reasoning, the Philippians will be brought to that state of holiness for which God called them in contrast to the pagan society around them.

Beneath this surface, however, the clause "children of God without

---

7. See Rom 1:21; 14:1; 1 Cor 3:20; 1 Tim 2:8.

8. Paul uses the Greek term translated as "blameless" (ἄμεμπτοι/*amemptoi*) in 3:6 to describe himself as blameless according to the righteousness found in the Law. It is tied to holiness in 1 Thess 3:13. In Luke 1:6 it is part of a series of adjectives describing the blameless state of Zechariah and Elizabeth. The LXX uses the word to speak of God's desire that Abraham walk before God and be "blameless" (Gen 17:1). It is also used to describe Job. Fee, *Philippians*, 244, however, probably reads too much into this word when he suggests that Paul is alluding to the renewal of the covenant with Abraham in Gen 17:1.

The term translated as "innocent," ἀκέραιοι/*akeraioi*, is used by Jesus to contrast the wisdom of serpents and the innocence of doves (Matt 10:16). Paul uses it to call the Romans to wisdom in knowing what is good and to innocence with regard to what is evil (Rom 16:19).

9. Here the Greek adjective is ἄμωμα/*amōma*. It is used in Col 1:22 and Eph 1:4; 5:27 of the holiness for which God has destined the church. In the LXX the term is commonly used to designate an animal "without defect" and therefore acceptable for sacrifice.

blemish in the midst of a crooked and perverse generation" echoes Deut 32:5 with some rather interesting results. While the syntax of the LXX of Deut 32:5 is obscure, the general thrust of the passage is clear.[10] Israel has failed to perceive God's economy of salvation; they have failed to attend to God's saving deeds and their implications. Hence, in their foolishness, they have ultimately sinned against themselves. Thus they have become a crooked and perverse generation (cf. Deut. 32:1-14). In alluding to this verse, Paul is not claiming that the church in general and the Philippians in particular have replaced Israel.[11] Rather, as in 2:14, he invokes the negative example of Israel as something for the Philippians to avoid if God's best purposes for them are to be fulfilled. Unlike Israel, the Philippians should attend wisely to God's economy of salvation. In doing this, they will both avoid grumbling and foolish reasoning and become holy and blameless children of God in the midst of those who do not rightly recognize and understand God's mighty acts of salvation.

The next two clauses (which actually run into the beginning of v. 16) further display the Philippians' position in a "crooked and perverse generation."[12] Paul claims that in the midst of this corrupt generation the Philippians "shine as lights in the world." This image fits with several others throughout Scripture where the people of God are spoken of as lights in the midst of an unbelieving world. In Isa 42:6 and 49:6 redeemed Israel shines as a light to the Gentiles, drawing them to God. These same verses are glossed by Simeon in Luke 2:29-32 to prophesy the blessings that come to both Israel and the Gentiles through Christ. In Acts 13:47 Paul and Barnabas quote Isa 49:6 to justify their mission to the Gentiles.

Both Fee and Bockmuehl make the interesting suggestion that this clause in 2:15 echoes Dan 12:3, where, in an apocalyptic vision of the resurrection, Daniel is told that "those with understanding shall shine like the brightness of the heavens." And "Those who strengthen my words will be like the stars of heaven forever."[13] If we take this allusion seriously, it further supports Paul's claims that those who manifest the proper understanding of God's saving activity will be brought to their proper end. Further, the phrase "holding

10. A wooden translation of the LXX might read, "They sinned not against him, children of blemish, a crooked and perverse generation." See Bockmuehl, *Philippians*, 156-57, for a discussion of this passage.

11. Bockmuehl, *Philippians*, 157, rightly sees that Moses is not claiming that God has disowned Israel and that Paul is not claiming that the church has replaced Israel.

12. I am following Bockmuehl, *Philippians*, 159; Fee, *Philippians*, 246-47; Gnilka, *Philipperbrief*, 153; and O'Brien, *Philippians*, 297, who connect the participle "holding fast" in v. 16 with the finite verb "in order that you might be" in v. 15.

13. See Bockmuehl, *Philippians*, 158; Fee, *Philippians*, 247-48.

fast to the word of life" at the beginning of v. 16 might be seen as an explication of "strengthening the words" of God in the second part of Dan 12:3.[14]

In these verses Paul has been concerned with keeping the Philippians from following the negative example of Israel in the desert, misreading the signs of God's activity and thereby falling to "grumbling." The aim of avoiding this situation is so that God can lead the Philippians to their true end, holiness. In the course of reaching this end, the Philippians will shine in the midst of an unbelieving and hostile world as they order their common life in a manner worthy of the gospel of Christ (remember that this whole section is an outworking of 1:27). The Philippians will hold fast to the word of life as they obediently work out their salvation.

One might well ask whether the Philippians themselves would have perceived the force of Paul's allusive language here in 2:14-16 (or in 1:19). There are really two types of answer to that question. First, we should take seriously the fact that levels of literacy in Paul's world would have been quite low (probably ten percent).[15] Moreover, it is not clear that the Philippians would have had ready access to texts of Exodus or Deuteronomy in whole or in part. In addition, Paul does not explicitly note that he is quoting from Scripture, as he often does. Finally, each of these passages is relatively intelligible without the allusions. All of these factors might lead one to argue that the Philippians would not have heard or understood the sorts of allusions I have noted here.[16]

Of course, this judgment assumes that the Philippians had a relatively static relationship to this epistle and those who conveyed it. If we grant that the Philippians probably read/heard and subsequently reread/reheard Paul's letter several times and that those delivering the letter could well have instructed the Philippians in the OT allusions here, then we must grant that in time they, too, might have detected these allusions. Obviously these latter considerations do not answer the question. They merely make it more probable that over time the Philippians might have come to see the connections between their situation and Israel's.

Second, regardless of how one answers this first question about the epistle's first audience, Christians today must take these allusions seriously. It

---

14. So Fee, *Philippians*, 247 n. 33.

15. This is based on the work of William Harris and cited in Gamble, *Books and Readers*, 4-6. Although Gamble raises some good questions about the notion of "literacy" in early Christianity, I do not see any reason to assume the numbers of readers in the Philippian congregation differed from Harris's projection.

16. These sorts of reasons are invoked by C. Stanley, *Paul and the Language of Scripture*, though not in regard to this passage.

would be extremely odd to argue that despite the fact that attention to these allusions will probably enhance Christian life and practice in the present, Christians should not attend to these allusions because the epistle's first audience might not have recognized them. No matter how one resolves the historical questions, commenting on such allusions and reflecting on them would seem to be an essential element of a theological commentary. Moreover, cultivating the familiarity with Scripture that will enable one to "hear" these and other allusions is a foundational practice of the Christian life. This is not because it enhances one's prospects of being a cleverer reader of Scripture. Rather, such habits of reading Scripture enhance one's prospects of engaging Scripture in ways that will deepen one's communion with God and others.

In these verses Paul continues to reflect on how the Philippians are to order their common life in a manner worthy of the gospel of Christ. Specifically he has called them to attentive obedience to God's desires for them. He is convinced that even in times of external hostility and perhaps persecution, God's desires for the Philippians have remained constant. Moreover, and despite appearances to the contrary, God will bring those desires to fruition in the life of the Philippian church. In this respect Paul is extending by analogy the pattern of God's activity in Christ as narrated in 2:6-11 to the life of the Philippian Christians. At the same time he cautions the Philippians against misunderstanding the movements of God's economy of salvation and thereby frustrating God's desires for them. In this, Paul's allusions to Israel in the desert provide a negative example for the Philippians. Attention to the ways in which Israel misapprehended the movements of God's economy and, as a result, fell to grumbling and foolish reasoning can serve as a cautionary warning to the Philippians. Paul here presumes some sort of analogy between Israel's sojourn in the desert, somewhere between slavery and the Promised Land, and the Philippians' situation. Life in the desert calls for a particular sort of practical wisdom. The same wisdom will enable sojourners in Philippi to manifest a common life worthy of the gospel by attending to the *telos* toward which God is directing them.

Paul's discussion here is not limited to the common life of a Macedonian Christian community in the first century. Any Christian community seeking to order its life together in a manner worthy of the gospel of Christ must learn how to discern rightly their particular place in the economy of salvation in the light of the end toward which God is directing all things. As the negative example of Israel in the desert indicates, failure in discernment results in grumbling and, subsequently, foolish reasoning. What makes this situation dangerous for the Israelites, for the Philippians, and for Christians today is that this sort of "grumbling" is not simply to be equated with annoying complaint and whining. As Paul's discussion makes clear, grumbling is the pattern of life to which the Philippians would fall prey should they become convinced (as many of the Israelites were) that God was no longer leading them. Such a conviction cannot help but result in foolish reasoning.

If Paul's language here strikes us as alien, it may well be because we have lost the sense of being pilgrims or sojourners. We may well find that we have become so acclimated to our current situation that we no longer see the yawning chasm between our comfortable lives and God's deepest desires for us. Whether we characterize those deepest desires in terms of holiness (as Paul does here) or communion with God or a messianic banquet, unless we sense the extraordinary difference between our world and God's desires, we will always feel too much at home to conceive of ourselves as pilgrims and of our life together as a journey. If that is the case, Paul's allusions to Israel in the desert will not resonate with us. This is not due to any of the historical factors mentioned above. It is simply due to our unwillingness to be called away from the fleshpots of Egypt into a journey of obedience to God such as Christ undertakes in 2:6-11.

In such a situation, we will both miss the urgency in Paul's discourse and be offended by the stake that he has in the life of the Philippian church. As vv. 16-18 indicate, Paul sees the course of his work as bound up with the success or failure of the Philippian congregation. Should the Philippians attend properly to the work of God in and around them, they will avoid grumbling and foolish reasoning. God will bring them to their proper end. They will shine as lights in the world, and Paul "will boast in them at the day of Christ." Paul's boasting in the Philippians at the coming day of Christ parallels the Philippians' boasting in Paul in 1:26. In each act of boasting, the focus is on what God has done.

Should the Philippians fail to manifest a common life worthy of gospel, however, Paul does not propose that this will reflect badly on God. Rather, it will indicate that Paul has "run in vain or that his work has been for naught." Here in v. 16 Paul relies on images of running a race or working toward a particular goal as a way of describing his ministry among the Philippians.[17] It also does not appear that Paul thinks it likely that this ministry will amount to nothing. Nevertheless, the ecclesial and eschatological assumptions behind this verse deserve some further reflection. For Paul and the Philippians to en-

---

17. Bockmuehl makes the interesting observations that in the Servant Songs of Isaiah, the servant fears that he has labored in vain (49:4), that the servant's task is to bring light to the Gentiles (49:6), and that he pours out himself unto death (53:12). In the light of these connections, Bockmuehl suggests that Paul, too, may be reading his situation in the light of Isaiah (*Philippians*, 159).

gage in reciprocal boasting in God's work in each other's lives already presumes a level of connection and accountability between them which would be foreign in most American churches today. Paul and the Philippians are engaged in each other's lives to such a degree that they can bear each other's burdens and rejoice in each other's successes. Moreover, Paul recognizes that he is accountable before God for the state of the Philippian church. For people thoroughly schooled in the habits of individualism in all aspects of our lives, it is difficult to imagine being held accountable for our participation in the life of a local Christian community. For most American Christians, it is inconceivable that we might be held accountable before God for the lives of our fellow believers. Of course, we do not precisely share in Paul's apostolic call. Nevertheless, it also seems implausible that Paul, and only Paul, is to be held responsible for the churches he founded while other believers can simply focus on the state of their own souls through a series of privatized transactions with God.

The section that began in 1:27 with Paul's admonition to walk in a manner worthy of the gospel of Christ concludes here in vv. 17-18 with an assertion of Paul's joy over his relationship with the Philippians and a call for them to rejoice as well, regardless of how his present circumstances work out. Paul's suggestion here that, "Even if I am being poured out as a drink offering on your sacrifice and service, which is your faith, I rejoice and I rejoice together with you," employs complex collection of images. They seem to come from the OT sacrificial system, in which the priest makes a daily drink offering to God (see Exod 29:38-42; Num 28:1-8).[18] In addition, the Philippians' faith is seen as a sacrificial offering as well.[19] Despite the obscurity of these images taken singly, commentators recognize that Paul is reflecting on his devotion to God as exemplified in his willingness to minister to the Philippians and others no matter what the personal cost. This ministry is closely tied to the Philippians' own ministry. In many respects these images simply reassert the three-way partnership or friendship in the gospel into which God has called both Paul and the Philippians.

Most recently, scholars have struggled over whether this passage is a reference to Paul's impending martyrdom or a more general reference to his sufferings.[20] On the one hand, drink offerings were offerings of wine, not blood.

---

18. See Bockmuehl, *Philippians*, 160-61, and Fee, *Philippians*, 250 n. 51, for some of the linguistic evidence for this claim.

19. See Lightfoot, *Philippians*, 118-19, and Bockmuehl, *Philippians*, 160-62.

20. Lohmeyer, *an die Philipper*, 112-13, not surprisingly, favors a reference to martyrdom. Fee, *Philippians*, 252-54, and Collange, *Philippians*, 113, following A. Denis, "Verse en libation (Phil. 2,17)," read this phrase as a more general reference to apostolic hardships.

Hence, they might not appear as a very apt metaphor for death. Alternatively, Christ's own use of wine in the Last Supper might serve as a precedent for Paul's analogous use of "wine" to refer to the shedding of his own blood. In addition, the two subsequent occasions when this language is most clearly taken up, 2 Tim 4:6 and Ignatius, *Romans* 2:2, refer to Paul's death.

This particular debate, however, seems to miss the point. In Rom 12:1-3 Paul uses sacrificial language to talk about the lives of believers being offered to God. Such a notion is also evident in the Psalms (50:14; 51:17; 119:108) and elsewhere. The sacrificial imagery here seems primarily to speak of offering one's life back to God so as to more faithfully pursue and serve God's purposes. Paul's claim here that he is being poured out as a drink offering on the sacrifice and service of the Philippians' faith seems to be yet another way of reflecting on the three-way nature of his relationship with the Philippians. By devoting himself to the formation and nurture of the Philippian congregation (among others), Paul is exemplifying one of the ways in which he has offered his life back to God as a living sacrifice. In offering his life back to God in the ways in which he does, in a context largely hostile to Christianity, Paul has come to the attention of the empire and is now in prison. If the empire should put him to death or if he should continue to work among the Philippians, his life will equally be poured out on behalf of the Philippians. Paul cannot control the empire's response.[21] He can only continue his customary practice of magnifying Christ in his body (1:20). As Paul understands but commentators forget, martyrdom is not an end in and of itself. Obedience and fidelity are appropriate goals for Christians. The lives of the faithful can be seen as sacrifices whether they result in death or not.

This is, in fact, the only way to account for Paul's joy and his call to the Philippians to rejoice with him. Death is not a cause for joy. As Paul notes, death is an enemy who will be defeated (1 Cor 15:54-58). Fidelity in the face of death or any other enemy is a cause for joy. Thus, Paul concludes this section by expressing his own joy and calling the Philippians to participate in his rejoicing. The great temptation for believers here is to reduce joy to happiness. When believers manifest lives worthy of the gospel of Christ, it is an occasion for joy. Such lives, however, may well entail pain, hardship, and deprivation. These can frustrate one's sense of well-being, but must not frustrate one's ability to rejoice. Paul will reflect on this issue more deeply in ch. 4.

From 1:27 to 2:18 Paul has focused on the common life of the church in Philippi. He has offered direct admonitions, narrated an account of Christ to

---

21. To make this point Aquinas notes, "But sometimes tyrants mingle the blood of the offerers with their sacrifices as in Luke [13:1]" (90).

serve as an exemplar for the church members, and urged them to remain constant in their obedience to God. In the next section Paul shifts to speak about Timothy and Epaphroditus. His discussion of the activities and character of these two men, however, makes it clear that he still has the Philippians' common life in view.

2:19-30

19 I hope in the Lord to send Timothy to you as soon as possible in order that I might be encouraged by learning about your circumstances. 20 I do not have anyone else who both shares my loves and desires and genuinely loves and cares for you all. 21 Everyone else is concerned with their own interests rather than the interests of Jesus Christ. 22 You, however, know Timothy's proven character, how, as a son toward a father, he has served me in the gospel. 23 I hope to send him to you as soon as I learn what will happen next with me. 24 Indeed, I am confident in the Lord that I myself will soon come.

25 I consider it necessary to send you Epaphroditus, my brother, fellow worker, and fellow soldier and your emissary and minister to my need. 26 He has been longing for you all and has been distressed because you heard that he had been sick. 27 Indeed he was sick, so sick he almost died. But God had mercy on him, not only on him, but on me, too, so that my sorrows would not be multiplied. 28 I am eager, therefore, to send him to you, so that you all may rejoice again at seeing him and so that I may be less anxious. 29 Welcome him, therefore, in the Lord with all joy and honor all such people 30 because he came close to death doing the work of Christ, risking his life in order to fill up what was lacking in your service to me.

Ch. 2 concludes with two brief paragraphs in which Paul speaks of his plans to send Timothy and Epaphroditus to the Philippians (2:19-30). While it appears that Epaphroditus is to precede Timothy (cf. 2:25, 28), the sending of Timothy is mentioned first. As Fee suggests, this may have to do with the logic shaping 1:12–2:18. Paul's initial reporting about his situation has led to his concern for the Philippians and their circumstances. The prospect that Timothy will be able to give Paul news of the Philippians' circumstances (2:19) follows well from the course of the discussion thus far.[1]

In vv. 19-30, we find a sharing of news, hopes, and plans for the immediate future. These are some of what sometimes concludes ancient letters, including some of Paul's (see Romans, 1 Corinthians, Colossians, and Phile-

1. Fee, *Philippians*, 260.

mon).[2] While these verses do convey news of Paul's future plans and hopes in a way similar to the endings of those other letters, this is only one of the purposes these verses serve. More importantly, they serve to commend Timothy and Epaphroditus to the Philippians. This practice is also common in Paul's letters (see Rom 16:1-2, commending Phoebe; 1 Cor 16:15-18, commending Stephanus, Fortunatus, and Achaicus; 2 Cor 8:8, 16-24, commending Titus; 1 Thess 3:2-3, 9, commending Timothy). But here these commendations serve a larger purpose. They point out to the Philippians concrete examples of the type of life that Paul has commended throughout 1:27–2:18, examples of the practice of attending to the concerns of others above one's own concerns.[3] In this passage Paul further defines this practice as attending to the "things of Jesus Christ" (2:21). In witnessing to the lives of Timothy and Epaphroditus in the ways he does, Paul presents both of them as manifestations of the specific command to display the practical reasoning found in Christ Jesus (2:5). Thus, Paul's commendation of Timothy and Epaphroditus finds its basis in the story of Christ narrated in 2:6-11.

Paul begins this section by noting that he hopes "in the Lord" to send Timothy to the Philippians. The point of hoping "in the Lord" (both here and in 2:24) is to recognize that the Lord is the one who both directs Paul's planning and will bring it to fruition.[4] Thus, this assertion is not meant to convey either vagueness or weakness of conviction. Rather, it reflects the strong conviction that Paul's plans are in accord with the Lord's desires.[5] I have translated the Greek adverb ταχέως/*tacheōs* with the English phrase "as soon as possible" rather than "quickly," which is often used. This recognizes that the word conveys a sense of urgency rather than the sense that Timothy will begin his journey immediately (see similar usage in 2:24; 1 Cor 4:19; 2 Tim 4:9). In this particular case, Paul makes it clear that he will wait until

2. It is not altogether surprising, then, that several scholars think that 2:19-30 mark the close of an original letter to Philippi which has been merged with a second letter beginning at 3:1. Ultimately, I am not convinced by these suggestions. For two particularly helpful studies of Philippians in the light of ancient epistolary conventions see L. C. A. Alexander, "Hellenistic Letter-Forms and the Structure of Philippians," and D. Watson, "A Rhetorical Analysis of Philippians."

3. See Meeks, "Man From Heaven," 334; also Fee, *Philippians*, 263.

4. With Bockmuehl, *Philippians*, 164-65.

5. O'Brien, *Philippians*, 317, reads this phrase in the light of 1 Cor 16:7, where Paul hopes to visit the Corinthians "if the Lord permits." Fee, *Philippians*, 264 nn. 18-19, suggests that this phrase alludes to 2:9-11. He also notes the numerous times variations on the phrase "in the Lord" occur in Philippians. It is not exactly clear, however, what one is to make of this aside from the notion that Paul conceives of the entirety of his life within the sphere governed by the Lord.

he has further news of how his circumstances will work out before sending Timothy (2:23).

Timothy is in some sense the coauthor of the letter (1:1). He is Paul's closest coworker at this time. Paul's epistles reflect several occasions when Timothy is sent as a messenger to various Pauline churches (cf. 1 Thess 3:1-5; 1 Cor 4:17). He can be relied on both to represent accurately Paul's views and to provide Paul with a reliable account of the state of the congregations. Indeed, it is precisely for this purpose that Timothy is to be sent to Philippi. He will encourage Paul by bringing him news of the Philippians' circumstances.[6] Timothy can also bring the Philippians news of Paul's circumstances, which, Paul expects, will encourage them (2:23).[7]

Having stated the reason for sending Timothy, Paul proceeds to commend Timothy to the Philippians. In this case, there is no reason to assume that Paul's commendation of Timothy is designed to counter questions or accusations against Timothy.[8] If there were serious questions about Timothy's character, it would be odd for him to be listed as one of the epistle's senders. More importantly, such explanations seem to miss the particular character of this commendation. Paul's description of Timothy's character casts him as an exemplar of the very behavior Paul has urged on the Philippians. The commendation does not reflect some lack in Timothy or Paul. Rather Paul commends Timothy as a concrete example of a life that is worthy of the gospel.

In fact, Timothy is unique in certain respects. Although the language Paul uses to describe him is not as precise as we might like, in this context it would seem that Paul is saying that Timothy can be expected, like no other, to reflect the concerns, love, and attention of Paul.[9] In addition to Timothy's in-

---

6. Here Paul uses a version of the same construction he used in 1:12 to speak about his own circumstances.

7. The emphatic "I also" (κἀγώ/*kagō*) indicates that Paul expects the Philippians to be encouraged by Timothy's account of Paul's circumstances. The verb translated here as "encourage" (εὐψυχέω/*eupsycheō*) does not appear elsewhere in the NT. Fee, *Philippians*, 265 n. 25, however, is surely right to compare the usage here with Josephus's in *Antiquities* 11.241, where it refers to making someone glad. We do not learn how exactly Paul will hear from Timothy about the Philippians. The widespread assumption is that Timothy will return to Paul. The text, however, is silent on this matter.

8. This is against Collange, *Philippians*, 116, who thinks that this indicates deep and grave problems within the Philippian congregation. This view really has no evidence to commend it. O'Brien, *Philippians*, 320, and Silva, *Philippians*, 150-51, both propose that by offering this particular commendation, Paul is explaining why he is not sending Timothy sooner.

9. I have used an extended phrase, "who shares my loves and desires," to translate the single Greek word ἰσόψυχον/*isopsychon*. No single English word seems suitable to convey the intimacy between two friends conveyed by this one word. In the LXX it is used just once, as part of

timate connection with the concerns, loves, and passions of Paul, he is also deeply concerned for the Philippians and their circumstances. He manifests both a genuine heartfelt love as well as an active concern for them. In short, Paul's description of Timothy here reflects that particular virtue of concern for the needs of others rather than one's own advocated in 2:3-4.

Having characterized Timothy as one who is concerned over the Philippians' welfare, Paul contrasts him with those who pursue their own interests. In addition, when Paul contrasts pursuing one's own interests with pursuing the "things of Jesus Christ," he implicitly connects concern with the welfare of others with concern for the things of Jesus Christ. Paul claims that, with the exception of Timothy, "all are pursuing their own interests rather than those of Jesus Christ." This raises the issue of who stands behind this sweeping reference to "all." Does Paul really mean to condemn all his coworkers who are with him? Clearly, this does not include Epaphroditus. If Paul is in Rome, "all" includes, according to Phlm 23-24, Luke, Aristarchus, Epaphras, and Mark. Paul commends all of these (see also Col 4:10, 14). Thus, it would be odd if Paul were referring to them.

One interpretive option is to suggest that these specific characters are no longer in Rome. Hence, when Paul claims that he has no one like Timothy and that all the others pursue their own interests rather than Christ's he is really only talking about the relatively small number of people available to him at that time.[10] Several things tell against this suggestion. First, it assumes that Paul seriously considered sending someone other than Timothy and reads v. 20 as an attempt to bolster Timothy's position rather than noting that Timothy exemplifies the particular disposition Paul has been urging the Philippians to adopt. Second, in 1:14 and 4:21-22 Paul speaks warmly of his coworkers in Rome. Why would he slander them here?

Alternatively, given that Paul's characterization of Timothy in 2:20 indicates that he exemplifies the practices commended in 2:3-4 and avoids those proscribed in 2:3, here in 2:21 Paul may well be pointing to those who do things from "selfishness and vain ambition" (2:3). If this is the case, then the obvious candidates are those in Rome described in 1:15-17.[11] The weakness of this view is that it is a rather circumscribed view of "all." Despite such a weakness, this reading makes better sense of the verse in its current context. More-

---

an extended description of the intimacy of friends in God (Ps 54:13). The Psalm emphasizes this intimacy to sharpen the pain felt when a friend, rather than an enemy, betrays.

10. See O'Brien, *Philippians*, 322.

11. Note the appearance of "selfish ambition" (ἐριθεία/*eritheia*) in 1:17 and 2:3 — two of the three times Paul uses the word.

over, it does not have to suppose that so many of the coworkers Paul obviously thinks highly of have left the scene.

While the precise referent of "all" is difficult to determine, the more significant move in v. 21 is Paul's connection of concern with the needs of others rather than one's own interests with "seeking the things of Jesus Christ." In this way Paul further draws together his own disposition toward his circumstances, the common life he desires for the Philippians, Timothy's disposition toward the Philippians, and the story of Christ narrated in 2:6-11.

Seeking the benefit of others is not a uniquely Christian disposition. For example, on the account offered by Troels Engberg-Pedersen, Stoicism ultimately moves toward other-directed behavior.[12] Of course, what counts as "seeking the benefit of others" is usually contested. It assumes answers to what the end or the good for humans is and to how specific actions might advance someone toward that end. For example, the parent who tells a child that the child is about to be hit for the child's own good could be said to be seeking the benefit of others.

By connecting this disposition with the practice of "seeking the things of Christ," as Paul does here in v. 21, he ties this more general disposition to the dispositions and actions of Christ. The most obvious textual witness for Christ's dispositions and actions would be 2:6-11. For Christians, then, the practice of seeking the benefit of others will receive its scope and direction from Christ's own activities.

In contrast to those who seek after their own affairs, Timothy's proven character is well known to the Philippians. According to Acts 16, Timothy was with Paul when he first preached in Philippi, so the Philippians already knew him. Indeed, Paul says that Timothy has served with him "as a son with a father." While the image conveys the intimacy between the two men, in this particular context the image seems to draw on the role of a father teaching a trade to his son. This is important if Timothy is to serve as an exemplar of the dispositions, habits, and actions Paul himself displays and which Paul wants to see formed in the common life of the Philippians. Ultimately, Paul's language here conveys the conviction that Timothy will be an accurate reflection of these dispositions, habits, and practices.

Given Timothy's obvious suitability for this particular mission, Paul here reiterates his desire to send him. He is simply waiting until he has a clearer view of his circumstances regarding his imprisonment and trial. Until this is known Timothy cannot really convey much news to the Philippians. At the same time, Paul also expresses his firm conviction that he himself will

---

12. See his *Paul and the Stoics*, especially 1-130.

soon come to the Philippians. As v. 19 began with Paul hoping "in the Lord" to send Timothy, this paragraph closes with Paul convinced "in the Lord" that he will soon be able to be with them.[13]

As v. 25 begins we learn that Paul is sending Epaphroditus before Timothy.[14] Although Paul claims that he "considered it necessary to send Epaphroditus" to the Philippians, we should not assume that this is due to a failure on Epaphroditus's part. Paul says nothing that might substantiate that judgment. Moreover, it is especially hard to sustain in the light of the fulsome praise Paul heaps on Epaphroditus in this paragraph. Further, such a suspicious reading between the lines seems to be based primarily on the strength of the commendation. That is, the reasoning runs, if Paul is saying such nice things about Epaphroditus, then there must be something negative he is trying to counter. This type of "mirror reading" is questionable as an intellectual exercise and fails to take account of the relatively clear role Paul's commendation plays in the argument of the epistle. Rather, in its current context, that Paul considers it "necessary to send Epaphroditus" already explains why Epaphroditus is arriving before the result of Paul's trial is known.[15]

Verse 25 offers an extremely positive description of Epaphroditus. He is Paul's "brother, coworker, and fellow soldier." The first two attributes conform well to other sorts of designations Paul uses for those he sends to various congregations.[16] "Fellow soldier" is less common.[17] Using this image to describe a Christian from Philippi, a Roman military colony, may well invoke the contrast between God's army and Caesar's.

All these terms situate Epaphroditus within Paul's mission. We are then told of his role as part of the Philippians' service to Paul. Paul calls Epaphroditus the Philippians' "apostle." Paul is using the term in a non-specialized sense of one who is set apart for a specific task, an "emissary."[18]

13. This along with 1:26 would indicate a change in Paul's travel plans from Rom 15:22-29. As Bockmuehl, *Philippians,* 95, suggests, this is not inconceivable, as Paul seems to be able to adapt his plans to changing circumstances.

14. Fee, *Philippians,* 272; Hawthorne, *Philippians,* and O'Brien, *Philippians,* seem justified in assuming that Epaphroditus is carrying the epistle back to Philippi. The assumption is that vv. 29-30 imply this. Such an implication can only be very indirect. The circumstantial evidence, however, points in this direction.

15. So Fee, *Philippians,* 274.

16. See "brother and coworker of God," of Timothy in 1 Thess 3:2; "beloved child and faithful in the Lord," of Timothy in 1 Cor 4:17; "beloved brother, faithful servant, and fellow slave in the Lord," of Tychicus in Col 4:7; and "beloved brother and faithful servant in the Lord," of Tychicus in Eph 6:21. See also the terms used in Romans 16.

17. It is used of Archippus in Phlm 2.

18. This is Bockmuehl's translation (*Philippians,* 171).

This task is defined more precisely when Paul calls Epaphroditus a "minister" (λειτουργός/*leitourgos*) of my needs." In view of the way Paul uses this term elsewhere, it would appear that he is characterizing the care Epaphroditus showed to Paul's material needs as a form of priestly ministry.[19] Even if Paul's confinement is relatively light, as described in Acts 28:16, he still has substantial material needs in prison. In addition, the companionship of friends is also a very real need that Paul would know. Indeed, when Christ speaks of serving the imprisoned in Matt 25:36, it is in terms of visiting them, of being present with them. Paul's characterization of Epaphroditus has already shown him to be someone more concerned with the needs of others rather than his own needs. As we saw with Timothy, Paul presents Epaphroditus to the Philippians as a concrete example of the habits and dispositions he has already advocated.

Having thus described Epaphroditus, Paul gives his reason for sending him back to the Philippians. Epaphroditus has been "longing" for them. There is nothing in the text to indicate that he is being sent home because he is homesick.[20] Moreover, Paul describes his own longing for the Philippians in exactly the same terms (1:8).[21] Thus, rather than pointing out some flaw in Epaphroditus, Paul's language here seems to tie Epaphroditus's dispositions tightly to his own.

We further learn that Epaphroditus has been "distressed" because the Philippians have heard of his illness (v. 26). The only other times the verb translated here as "distressed" appears in the NT it refers to Jesus' anxiety in Gethsemane before his arrest (Matt 26:37; Mark 14:33).[22] Hence, it would appear to describe a deep emotion but not an obvious character flaw.[23]

---

19. Paul uses this term in Rom 15:16 to refer to himself as a "minister" among the Gentiles. There he further characterizes this ministry as a "priestly service to the gospel of Christ." Further, in Phil 4:18 when Paul specifically speaks of the Philippians' financial gift which Epaphroditus brought to Paul he refers to it in sacrificial imagery as "a fragrant offering and a pleasing sacrifice to God." So Hawthorne, *Philippians*, 117; also Collange, *Philippians*, 120, who says, "the worship acceptable to God is that which shows itself in the practical solidarity of those who strive for the advancement of the Gospel."

20. Against Hawthorne, *Philippians*, 117; Plummer, *Philippians*, 61.

21. Those who take this clause as a sign of Epaphroditus's mental distress base their claim on what they take to be the imperfect periphrastic form of the verb, indicating a persisting action. Even if this is so, it does not really support the claim that the verb indicates in 2:26 that Epaphroditus was suffering from some mental distress, but in 1:8 it denotes the virtuous longing of one friend for another. O'Brien, *Philippians*, 307, noting that the periphrastic construction is very rare in Paul, argues that the participle is adjectival.

22. Indeed as J. Moffatt has shown, the same term is used in a second-century papyrus relating a soldier's concern that his mother had learned that he was sick. See J. Moffatt, "Philippians II.26 and 2 Tim IV.13."

23. This verse is often used to support an Ephesian provenance of Philippians because of

Paul confirms that Epaphroditus was indeed sick. In fact, the illness was life-threatening. Paul says nothing else about the timing or cause of the illness. Although knowing these things would be useful to us, they are secondary to Paul's concern to note the extent to which Epaphroditus was concerned for the needs of another rather than his own. We then learn that God was merciful to Epaphroditus, who recovered.[24] Paul's assertion about God's mercy clearly situates Epaphroditus, his mission, and its ultimate success within God's economy.

Moreover, Epaphroditus is not the only recipient of God's mercy. In healing Epaphroditus God was also showing mercy to Paul, lest his "sorrows be multiplied." Interestingly, in his homily on this passage Chrysostom rhetorically wonders how Paul could both affirm that to die and be with the Lord is better than living (1:21) and that Epaphroditus's recovery could be seen as an act of mercy.[25] In response Chrysostom echoes Paul's claim in 1:24 that to remain in the flesh, engaging in fruitful labor, is more beneficial to the Philippians. Chrysostom rightly picks up here the formal parallels between Paul and Epaphroditus that emerge in the course of Paul's commendation here. This characterization further works to establish Epaphroditus as an exemplar of a life worthy of the gospel of Christ.

In the light of Epaphroditus's brush with death, Paul is all the more eager to send him back to Philippi.[26] The Philippians will rejoice again[27] at seeing Epaphroditus, and Paul will be less sorrowful. One must presume that the

---

the (reasonable) assumption that, if Epaphroditus had taken ill after reaching Rome, it would have taken a long time to convey that information back to Philippi and then receive the Philippians' response in Rome (so, for example, Collange, *Philippians,* 19). While this is a serious consideration, it is not enough to outweigh the evidence that Paul was in Rome when he wrote Philippians. Here I would follow Fee's quite plausible scenario (*Philippians,* 278): Epaphroditus was delivering a substantial amount of money and so would not have traveled alone (cf. 1 Cor 16:3; 2 Cor 8:16-24; 11:9). On the way to Rome he took sick. One of his fellow travelers was sent home with this news while he and others carried on to Rome, even though this put his life at risk (cf. 2:30). See also C. O. Buchanan, "Epaphroditus' Sickness and the Letter to the Philippians."

24. Fee, *Philippians,* 279, goes to some length to note that some sort of miraculous healing cannot be ruled out here.

25. Chrysostom, *Homily* 9.

26. The adverbial form σπουδαιοτέρως/*spoudaioterōs* should not be taken to refer to a hasty and ill-conceived decision. Rather in the light of the way the comparative adjective σπουδαιότερος/*spoudaioteros* is used in a very similar context in 2 Cor 8:17, it is probably best to think of this word as expressing Paul's eagerness rather than haste. So Fee, *Philippians,* 280 n. 38.

27. The placement of "again" is somewhat ambiguous. Does it go with "rejoice" or "seeing"? Commentators all agree that Paul's normal usage is to put the adverb before the verb. In this case the adverb would modify "rejoice."

reduction in Paul's sorrow will be due to the Philippians' joy at seeing Epaphroditus.

In addition, Paul calls on the Philippians to welcome Epaphroditus in the Lord. The same phrase is also used in Rom. 16:1-2 for how the Romans should welcome Phoebe. The Romans are told that such a welcome is the response worthy of "the saints." It would appear, then, that the welcome that Paul calls for here is simply what Christians ought to do when servants of God come into their midst. By receiving them "in the Lord," Christians are simply receiving their brothers and sisters in the way that Christ would (cf. Rom 15:7). This should be the norm for Christians. Indeed, as *Didache* 12 indicates, such extensions of hospitality were the norm. Even the warnings about the abuse of hospitality in the *Didache* indicate that this was an unquestioned Christian obligation, and thereby open to abuse.[28]

Paul calls on the Philippians to welcome Epaphroditus "with all joy" and with the honor due such ones. There are several interesting points here. First, the use of the plural "such ones" indicates that Paul considers Epaphroditus part of a general class of people. The response due him is not simply the result of his connection to the Philippian congregation. Rather, he has fulfilled exemplary Christian duties, even putting his life in danger, and his reception should befit that. Second, in a culture that had very strong codes about the giving and withholding of honor, it is important to observe the types of activity Christians are to consider worthy of honor: attention to the needs of others rather than one's own (2:25) and doing the work of Christ (2:30). These are not activities for which Greco-Roman society normally offered honor. Successes in battle, large civic donations, and personal patronage were the primary ways to achieve honor in Greco-Roman society. Thus, Paul is reflecting some of the general structures of an honor-based culture but offering an alternative scale for measuring honor.[29] Our contemporary culture is less invested in matters of honor and shame than Paul's. Nevertheless, any extent to which Christians today think about the dispensing and acquiring of honor must be done on a scale that reflects the christological calibrations that Paul uses rather than any other cultural scale.

Paul continues expounding the reason for honoring Epaphroditus in v. 30. Epaphroditus risked his life in doing the work of Christ so that he might "fill up what was lacking" in the Philippians' service to Paul. While the notion

---

28. See also C. Pohl, *Making Room* for a readable history of hospitality as a Christian practice as well as an argument for reviving that practice in the present.

29. Bockmuehl, *Philippians*, 173, makes some similar points.

of putting one's life at risk to do the work of Christ will be a relatively familiar concept (if not practice), the notion of completing what was lacking in the Philippians' service to Paul will strike modern readers as odd.

Aside from this passage, the notion of filling a lack occurs four other times in Paul's letters.[30] In 2 Cor 9:12; 11:9 it refers to the meeting of material needs. In 1 Cor 16:17 it refers to the presence of certain friends, which makes up for the absence of others. In the obscure and contested Col 1:24, Paul uses the phrase to speak of how his sufferings bring to completion the sufferings of Christ. While the specific object changes, in each case the verb and noun together are used to speak of redressing a lack or absence. In this case the object is the Philippians' "service" (λειτουργία/*leitourgia*) to Paul. This echoes 2:25, where Paul characterized Epaphroditus as a minister (λειτουργός/*leitougos*) to Paul's needs, apparently the serious material needs Paul has as a prisoner. Some of these needs would have been met in a straightforward way by means of the financial gift Epaphroditus brought. In addition, he also provided the material presence of a brother in Christ (2:25).

What comes across with uncomfortable clarity here is that Paul has not taken on the persona of the supplicant. He has not begged the Philippians to spare what they can. Rather, he has assumed that his situation creates an obligation for them to offer service to him. Until they do so, there is a deficiency in their service to him, a deficiency that Epaphroditus has redressed.

Paul's language here points out some significant assumptions on his part about the obligations Christians have toward each other. While he is, of course, grateful for the Philippians' gift, his language here implies that when one Christian or group of Christians is in need and other Christians become aware of that need, a lack or deficiency is created that must be filled up or redressed. He is not talking here about sharing excess. The Philippians are obligated to fill up Paul's deficiency because of their connection in Christ.

The most obvious social structure in Paul's world that could have sustained such notions of obligation was the family. What seems to be the case here is that Paul has taken one of the structures of obligation that operated within Greco-Roman families and transferred it to the church. In this respect he was simply continuing the practice of Jesus. At the same time, Jesus made it clear that no human in the church occupies the position of *paterfamilias* (Matt 23:8-9). There is no father who would be the only one in a position to distribute goods to his children. This leaves Christians in a situation in which they are all brothers and sisters who can make claims on each other's re-

---

30. This construction uses the Greek verb ἀναπληρόω/*anaplēroō* along with ὑστέρημα/*hysterēma*.

sources.[31] Moreover, we should read Paul's claims here in the light of the parable of the sheep and the goats in Matthew 25. Jesus indicates there that when his followers encounter the least of Jesus' brothers and sisters in need (including imprisonment!), that very encounter establishes an obligation among disciples to fill up what is lacking in their service to the last and the least. In this light, it is not surprising that Paul says that Epaphroditus was doing "the work of Christ."

If we are offended by Paul's assumptions here, it is because we have been formed too deeply by ecclesiologies of individualism, patterns of Christian community which do not properly form us to recognize the obligations to others we incur by virtue of our baptism into Christ. It is not that we are stingy (though that may be true). We are relatively willing to give to supplicants whose requests assume that they are at the mercy of our excess and our generosity. We may even allow our blood relations to presume a certain claim on our charity. We seem fundamentally unwilling, however, to see ourselves as part of Christ's family. That is, we are unwilling to see that our baptism joins us to a "family" in which we inevitably will encounter "lack" which our familial connections oblige us to "fill up." Hence, we are put off by Paul's assumption that the Philippians, by virtue of their common bond in Christ, are obliged to fill up what Paul might be lacking in prison.

As I have already suggested, a properly Christian understanding of baptism is strongly at odds with an ecclesiology of individualism. It may well be that if we contemporary Christians are to unlearn the habits and practices that render Paul's language here so off-putting, we will have both to reinvigorate our practices of pre-baptismal catechesis and to reform congregations of the already baptized so that they may better understand the significance of their baptismal practices.

There is a correlative point to make here regarding the logic of Christian obligation in Paul. I could address this point at a variety of places in the epistle, but here seems as good a place as any. Paul's discourse here indicates that the needs of Christians implicate other Christians in a set of obligations. At the same time, his discourse undermines any notion that we are the sole arbiters of our own needs. Paul, Timothy, Epaphroditus, and even Christ are committed to caring for the Philippians' needs, but it is also clear that Paul assumes he has a relatively clear understanding of what the needs of the

31. In this regard see also Lohfink, *Jesus and Community,* 39-50. See also Bartchy, "Undermining Ancient Patriarchy." Bartchy uses issues of honor between siblings in ancient Mediterranean cultures as a way of viewing Paul as undermining the patriarchal family without instating a form of egalitarianism.

Philippian congregation are, needs that the Philippians might never recognize and name for themselves. His primary understanding of the Philippians' needs seems to stem from his account of how he and they fit into God's economy. If this is the case, at least two further points follow.

First, this notion does not prohibit Christians, either individually or within communities, from articulating their own needs. Of course, Paul does just this throughout the epistle. Rather, it implies that expressions of need are not self-authenticating. Instead, our thinking and speaking about needs must be enlivened and disciplined by our abilities to fit those needs into an account of how God is at work both in us and in the world around us. In this light, it is certainly possible, if not always likely, that others might offer a better account of our needs than we can. This is not to say that others will always know better than we. At the very least, however, we are called to a discerning attentiveness to what others might have to say to us.

Second, on the one hand, it is clear that the claim that needs are not self-authenticating cuts against the grain of the assumptions of a great number of American Christians. On the other hand, however, opening the articulation of need, and of the obligations thereby invoked, cannot simply be handed over to a central authority. Such a move would be a recipe for domination. Rather, Paul's abilities and willingness to speak about the Philippians' and his own needs assume an ongoing relationship between Paul and the Philippians. Paul can speak about the Philippians' needs as one who knows, loves, and prays for them (1:3-11). This relationship provides the trust that makes it possible for all parties to attend first to the concerns of others rather than their own without fear of domination.

As the counter-example of 1 and 2 Corinthians makes clear, Paul can accept a financial gift from the Philippians because their relationship is in good order.[32] The naming and meeting of needs in this case confirm and enhance the health of this relationship rather than distorting or destroying it. The Philippians' acceptance of Paul's account — an account both about his and their needs and about how that account can faithfully fit within a vision of God's economy — in large part depends on the strength of the bonds of trust between Paul and the Philippians. In the absence of such bonds of friendship, or when the friendship itself is in need of repair, speaking of needs and attempting to meet them can further disrupt and distort the friendship. Of course, this is not a call for rich Christians to withhold their wealth, but through confession, forgiveness, repentance, and reconciliation to repair the friendship.

---

32. For an account of how Paul's unwillingness to enter into a similar relationship with the Corinthians can create tension in a relationship see P. Marshall, *Enmity at Corinth*.

Timothy and Epaphroditus have specific duties to perform for Paul and the Philippians. It is also crucial for Paul's argument that Timothy and Epaphroditus function as exemplars of the habits, practices, and dispositions which Paul has displayed in regard to his own situation and which he has urged on the Philippians who find themselves engaged in the same struggle as Paul (1:30). Many interpreters approach this passage by reading behind the positive things said about each of these two coworkers and then assuming that they reflect some failure on the part of either Epaphroditus or the Philippians more generally. This approach depends on systematic arguments from silence. Moreover, such an approach will always fail to grasp the constructive importance of the specific things Paul says about each man and how Paul's account presents them as exemplars. As 2:21 implies, Christ's activity, especially as narrated in 2:6-11, is the primary exemplar for all of these habits, dispositions, and practices. Nevertheless, one cannot overestimate the importance of such live, concrete exemplars in helping Christians order their common life in a manner worthy of the gospel.

Although Paul would not have spoken in quite these terms, his rhetoric here reinforces both the importance of the communion of saints and the practice of narrating and attending to the lives of the saints. If we understand saints as those who have masterfully lived in a manner worthy of the gospel of Christ, those who have achieved excellence in the performance of Scripture, then their lives should play an important regulative and disciplining role in our lives. Neither the story of Christ nor Scripture in its fullness is self-interpreting. If Christians are to interpret and embody these texts in the concrete situations in which they find themselves (which is precisely what Paul wants the Philippians to do), then we must attend to those saintly lives around us as well as those saints preceding us who best embody those texts.

Thus, while Christians regularly confess their faith in the communion of saints in general, it is crucial to devote time to telling the specific stories of saints if those lives are to suggest in concrete ways how we might also live saintly lives. It is precisely this sort of narration that Paul offers in 2:19-30. He offers particular testimony about the lives of two fellow believers with whom the Philippians are soon to renew direct contact. In doing this, Paul situates their lives in relation to his own life, to the lives of the Philippians, and most importantly, within the ongoing story of God's action in the world. Both offering and wisely receiving such testimony allow the lives of the saints — those both well known and little known — to continue to exert a regulative function within a community of contemporary believers. Hence, while it is true that in this passage Paul is relating fairly mundane matters, particularly in comparison to 2:6-11, in doing so he is providing an example of a particular sort of theological practice. That is, he is narrating the lives of particular saints, making their lives imitable or exemplary for the Christians in Philippi.

3:1-11

1 Finally, then, rejoice in the Lord. I do not hesitate to write the same things to you because they will help you to be steadfast. 2 Avoid "the dogs," evil workers, and "mutilators," 3 for we are the circumcision, who serve by the Spirit of God, who boast in Christ Jesus and who put no confidence in the flesh. 4 If there are some who think they have reasons to have confidence in the flesh, I have more: 5 circumcised on the eighth day, a member of the people of Israel and of the tribe of Benjamin, a Hebrew of Hebrews. With respect to the Law, I was a Pharisee; 6 with respect to my zeal, I was a persecutor of the church; with respect to the righteousness found in the Law, I was blameless. 7 But these things that I used to consider to be assets, I now, because of Christ, consider to be losses. 8 Not only this, but what is more, I consider all these things to be "losses" due to the surpassing value of knowing Christ Jesus as my Lord. For his sake I have suffered the loss of all things, now considering them to be garbage, so that I may gain Christ 9 and be found in him, not having my own righteousness which comes from the Law, but that which comes through the faithfulness of Christ, the righteousness of God on the basis of faith. 10 My aim here is that I may know him, both the power of his resurrection and the sharing in his sufferings, 11 with the goal that I might somehow attain the resurrection from the dead.

Several scholars have taken Paul's remarks at the beginning of ch. 3 to indicate that Paul is closing off his letter. This, then, has led to various questions about the letter's unity. As I indicated in the introduction, the scholarly tide is now flowing firmly in the direction of treating the letter as a single composition.

This still leaves the question, "What is going on here in 3:1?" This verse is a sort of pivot on which the body of the letter moves. On the one hand, it provides a measure of closure to what has preceded. This happens on several levels. First, the imperative "rejoice in the Lord" is the last of a series of three imperatives that began at 2:29, all of which are related to the Philippians' reception of Epaphroditus: "welcome" Epaphroditus, "honor" Epaphroditus and such like him, and "rejoice in the Lord" at Epaphroditus's return to health and return home.[1] Second, with this final imperative Paul concludes

---

1. See Jeffrey Reed, *A Discourse Analysis of Philippians*, 259-60. Reed's work on 3:1-2 is one of the most persuasive accounts of the difficulties regarding these verses and of the overall unity of the letter.

his discussion of Timothy and Epaphroditus as exemplars to whom the Philippians should attend. Finally, this verse can be seen as the conclusion of the section which began in 1:12 with Paul's reflection on his circumstances, leading to his discussion of the Philippians' situation and how they should order their common life in a manner worthy of the gospel.

Paul claims here that not only does he not hesitate to write the same things to the Philippians, but such repetition will help them to remain steadfast.[2] What are these "same things" that Paul does not hesitate to write to the Philippians? We have no reason to think that this is a reference to previous written communication between Paul and the Philippians.[3] Moreover, the Greek indicates that Paul is, in some measure, apologizing for repeating himself here. This indicates that Paul's mentioning of "the same things" points to his command to rejoice. He has repeatedly discussed this topic earlier in the epistle (1:18; 2:17-18, 28, 29).[4] Hence, at the very least, Paul is claiming that he has no hesitation in again calling the Philippians to rejoice in the Lord.

In addition, Paul's assertion here that he has no hesitation in "writing the same things" to the Philippians opens up a new section in which Paul is about to engage in a more general sort of repetition in 3:2–4:20 of patterns and themes from 1:12–2:30.[5] One must not forget that Paul claims that writing

2. Reed's work demonstrates that the Greek word ὀκνηρόν/*oknēron* (often translated as "troublesome") is part of a well-attested Hellenistic epistolary convention known as the hesitation formula. After citing a diverse body of examples (*A Discourse Analysis of Philippians*, 231-38), Reed summarizes by saying, "the hesitation formula typically serves to remind the recipient that the sender is not being negligent, whether it be with respect to business matters, to their 'friendship,' or to the maintenance of contact. It is as if the sender is saying, 'I am not hesitating, thus you know that I am not being negligent or lazy'" (p. 238). Therefore, Reed rejects the typical claim that Paul here asserts that writing the "same things" is not troublesome to him. Rather, he asserts that he is not hesitant to write the same things to them. Moreover, as Reed shows, this hesitation formula is common in expressions of friendship (p. 251). Hence I have translated the phrase "I do not hesitate."

3. In this regard Lightfoot, *Philippians*, 140, and Bockmuehl, *Philippians*, 178-79, are quite right to subject all hypotheses about previous oral communication to the criticism that Paul is referring here to writing. Moreover, when he speaks of previous oral communication in 3:18 he uses a different verb.

4. See Reed, *A Discourse Analysis of Philippians*, 257-58; also Bockmuehl, *Philippians*, 180.

5. This is the view of Troels Engberg-Pedersen, *Paul and the Stoics*, 84-87. Engberg-Pedersen is developing observations from his own earlier work and from Wick, *Der Philipperbrief*. In making this claim, I want to be clear that I have no stake in asserting that there is an intentionally chiastic structure to the body of Philippians. It is too easy for commentators to let their views about structure shape and determine their views about the content of specific passages. I simply wish to suggest that in addition to closing out the previous section, 3:1 also opens up a new section in which Paul, while addressing different topics, addresses them in a manner similar to 1:12–2:30. For a thorough account of the conceptual inadequacies of accounts

the "same things" to the Philippians will help them remain "steadfast."[6] Thus here we see Paul reflecting on his own practice of letter writing. Even though he is (and will be) repeating things, Paul is willing to do this to render the Philippians more steadfast.

As 3:2 begins we find a fourth imperative clause. The first three spoke of Epaphroditus and other exemplary disciples. This one introduces a discussion of negative examples.[7] Most English versions translate the Greek word βλέπετε/*blepete*, which begins this verse, as "beware." While this is a possible translation of the Greek under certain conditions, those conditions do not apply here.[8] I have used the English word "avoid" rather than, say, "observe" because the context makes it clear that Paul is calling the Philippians to observe "dogs," "evil workers," and "the mutilators" with the aim of avoiding them.

Paul uses three terms to describe these characters to avoid, and most commentators take these terms as referring to a single group.[9] In Greco-Roman society dogs were considered despicable, unclean animals that scavenged for their food. Jews used the term insultingly to refer to Gentiles.[10] Moreover, "dogs" was used to derogate particularly unsavory Israelites.[11] As this seems to be a fairly common form of insult, we cannot really read behind it for any insight as to whom in particular Paul might have in mind. Any purchase we might find in this verse for identifying those spoken of here will have to come from the other two terms.

The phrase "evil workers" may play upon passages such as 2 Cor 11:13, 15; Matt 9:37-38; 10:10 which speak of various Christian missionaries. In Phil 3:2 then, Paul would be offering the judgment that their work is evil. More generally, this term may play off the Psalter's phrase "workers of iniquity."[12] Bockmuehl also suggests that this phrase may be an ironic evaluation of a Jew's or Jewish Christian's self-description as one who had taken on "works of the Law."[13]

Such judgments hang on the final term, "mutilation" (κατατομή/

of chiasm in Philippians and elsewhere in the NT see Porter and Reed, "Philippians as a Macro-Chiasm and Its Exegetical Significance."

6. Reed, *Discourse Analysis of Philippians*, 253; Engberg-Pedersen, *Paul and the Stoics*, 314 n. 10 show quite clearly that this is the best way to take ἀσφαλές/*asphales*, as opposed to "safe."

7. As Aquinas notes, "Above, he proposed the example they should follow; here he shows whose examples they should avoid" (94).

8. This has been demonstrated by G. D. Kilpatrick, "ΒΛΕΠΕΤΕ: Philippians 3:2."

9. Bockmuehl, *Philippians*, 183; Fee, *Philippians*, 293 n. 37; Hawthorne, *Philippians*, 124-25.

10. See 1 Sam 17:43; 24:14; 2 Sam 9:8; 16:9; 2 Kgs 8:13; Matt 7:6; 2 Pet 2:22.

11. Deut 23:18; Isa 56:10; Ps 22:16, 20.

12. LXX: Pss 5:5; 6:8; 13:4; 35:12; 52:4; 58:2, 5; 91:7, 9; 93:4, 16; 118:3; 124:5; 140:4, 9.

13. See Bockmuehl, *Philippians*, 188-89.

katatomē). This seems to be a rather clear and derisory play on the Greek word for circumcision, περιτομή/*peritomē*. Paul makes a similar sort of judgment in Gal. 5:12. The term is also related to the verb used in the LXX for pagan self-mutilation (see Lev 21:5; 1 Kgs 18:28; Isa 15:2; Hos 7:14).[14] Thus, the term "mutilation" seems to mark out this group as Jewish. Moreover, as this group seems to have a particular interest in the Philippian Christians, an interest of which Paul wants the Philippians to beware, these terms are most likely a reference to Jewish Christians rather than non-Christian Jews.

In this light, then, it would appear that all terms refer to believers who desire that Gentile Christians become Jews as a way of completing their faith in Christ. Paul, of course, addresses such Christians elsewhere. In Galatians Paul shows urgent concern for the fidelity of the Galatian congregations on just this point. In Philippians, however, Paul gives no evidence that the Philippians might be under pressure from "Judaizers" either within or outside the congregation. Further, to the extent that we can read backward from Paul's argument in Galatians, it appears that the Galatians were confronted with a theological argument, based in part on a reading of the life of Abraham, that Gentiles needed to supplement their faith in Christ by becoming Jews (Gal 3:6–4:31). All of this is absent in Philippians.

Since there does not seem be a party of Judaizers in Philippi who are making the sort of theological arguments that issue in responses similar to those Paul offers in Galatians, we should examine a couple other possibilities. One is that Paul is not referring to any particular group of Judaizers present in Philippi. Rather, he is making use of Judaizers as a sort of stock character, typifying behavior to be avoided by the Philippians in contrast to the behavior of Timothy and Epaphroditus.[15] Another possibility is that the primary attraction of Judaism for the Philippian Christians was not theological so much as social. That is, by becoming Jews the Philippian Christians would be seeking a measure of security from the Roman authorities in Philippi. To the extent that Judaism was a "tolerated" religion, Philippian Christians might find relief from pressure to participate in the imperial cult — which was so central to life in Philippi — by becoming Jews.[16] Precisely this sort of judaiz-

---

14. Bockmuehl, *Philippians*, 189; Fee, *Philippians*, 297; Hawthorne, *Philippians*, 126.

15. See, for example, N. T. Wright's views in "Paul's Gospel and Caesar's Empire." Wright argues that Paul refers here to Judaism as simply one form of paganism. This may have been a way of coding his subversive anti-imperial message to the Philippians.

16. This is suggested by M. Tellbe, "The Sociological Factors behind Philippians 3:1-11." Tellbe's view is also mentioned with cautious approval by Bockmuehl, *Philippians*, 191. Bockmuehl notes, however, that there is no direct documentary evidence that Christians were attracted to Judaism because of its official status.

ing behavior — judaizing for primarily social reasons — would stand in sharpest contrast to the behavior of Timothy, Epaphroditus, and particularly Paul himself.

There are several reasons to commend this suggestion over other possible scenarios. First, it establishes a greater measure of continuity between the discourse of 1:30–3:1 and the subsequent discussion in 3:2-11. Further, it is relatively clear how judaizing for these reasons might render one an enemy of the cross (3:18) and why Paul's own account of knowing Christ focuses on his fellowship in Christ's sufferings and becoming conformed to Christ's death as well as knowing the power of the resurrection (3:10). Second, it provides a concrete reason for the attractiveness of judaizing Christianity in the context of Philippians. If Luke's account of Paul's visit to Philippi is anything to go on, however, being considered part of a Jewish movement did not protect Paul and Silas from the anger of a Philippian mob (see Acts 16:19-24).

In the end, however, we must recognize that such speculations about why Paul says what he does are largely separable from explaining what Paul says.[17] In 3:2 it seems fairly clear that Paul is urging the Philippians to beware of judaizing Christians (whether present in Philippi or not), using language that judaizers might have used about themselves and turning it on its head so that, instead of signaling spiritual virtue, it designates worthless mutilation.

In 3:2 Paul uses terms designed to undermine "the mutilators'" pretensions to spiritual superiority. In 3:3 he contrasts those pretensions with the real state of the Philippian Christians. The latter "are the circumcision, who serve by the Spirit of God and who boast in Christ, not putting any confidence in the flesh." It is important to remember, however, that Paul's claim, "we are the circumcision," is not designed to contrast a true circumcision, associated with Christianity, with a now superseded Judaism, a false circumcision.[18] Rather, Paul's claim situates the Philippian believers already within the Abrahamic covenant apart from physical circumcision. By calling the physically uncircumcised Philippian Gentile Christians "the circumcision," Paul asserts that they are already children of the promises made to Abraham. They need to do nothing more in terms of taking on the yoke of Torah to situate themselves as heirs of Abraham. In this regard Paul draws on notions found

---

17. Commentators on these verses become interested in the *why* because *what* Paul says seems to be so discontinuous from what has preceded. The great temptation is to forget that speculations about the why are simply that, speculations that cannot provide decisive evidence for explicating the what. Hence, while I think Tellbe's proposal has some merit, it should not be used as the decisive element in adjudicating between competing interpretations of any particular verse.

18. See Bockmuehl, *Philippians*, 191; also Fee, *Philippians*, 298-99.

in Deut 10:16; 30:6; Jer 4:4; 9:25; and Ezek 44:9 that circumcision of the heart must accompany physical circumcision. Here as well as in Rom 2:26, however, Paul indicates that Gentiles with circumcised hearts are part of the Abrahamic covenant without being physically circumcised. Indeed, according to Paul's argument in Romans and Galatians, this was true of Abraham himself in that he was reckoned as righteous on the basis of his faith and prior to his circumcision. Paul's assertion in Phil 3:3 can be seen as part of a larger theological argument within the earliest church about how Gentiles are to join Jews in Christ as joint heirs of the promises to Abraham. In a sense, then, Paul's claim might be recast as "we are already the circumcision — there is nothing else we need to do."

The next three clauses characterize those who are "the circumcision." Nevertheless, we should be careful of assuming that every assertion Paul makes here is directly designed to counter some assertion made by "the mutilators." The first phrase claims that the Philippians serve by the Spirit of God.[19] The verb "to serve" (λατρεύω/*latreuō*) is used in the NT and LXX almost exclusively to speak of religious service to God or pagan gods. In this light, and in the light of Paul's warning about "the mutilators," it is interesting to note that in Lev 21:5 those sons of Aaron who have "mutilated" themselves are barred from performing service in the Temple. Again, however, Paul is not contrasting Jewish worship with Christian worship. Paul is quite clear that "the service" (along with the "sonship," "glory," "covenants," "Law," and "promises") all belong (irrevocably) to Israel (Rom 9:4). Rather, Paul's assertion seeks to locate the worship of the Christian community in Philippi already within the true worship of the God of Israel apart from circumcision and taking on the yoke of Torah.[20] This is the case because they worship by the Spirit, that is, by means of the Spirit's empowering and under the Spirit's direction.[21] In this respect there seems to be a parallel here between Paul's assertion and Jesus' assertions in John 4. In John 4 Jesus converses with the woman at the well in Sychar about where true worship of God is to be performed. Jesus shifts the terms of the argument, noting that since God is Spirit, those who worship God must worship in Spirit and in truth (John 4:19-24).

Because the Philippians "boast in Christ" they are further confirmed in their status as already fully participating in the Abrahamic covenants. Paul

19. Some mss. have "serve God by the Spirit," but these mss. are neither the earliest nor the most important.

20. Bockmuehl, *Philippians,* 192, is one of the few attentive to this issue.

21. Following most commentators and reading the Greek πνεύματι/*pneumati* ("by the Spirit") instrumentally, in line with Rom 8:13-14; 1 Cor 14:2; Gal 5:16, etc., Fee, *Philippians,* 300 n. 62, notes here the contrast between worship in the Spirit and confidence in the flesh.

immediately contrasts this boasting with a misplaced confidence in the flesh, which, presumably, characterizes "the mutilators." For Paul, boasting is not in itself bad. Instead, the crucial issue concerns the basis for the boasting. Under the guidance of Jer 9:23-24, Paul consistently admonishes the Corinthians to boast in what the Lord has done (cf. 1 Cor 1:31; 2 Cor 10:17). Thus the only acceptable boasting for Paul is boasting in God's works of redemption, foremost of which is the work of Christ. The prerequisite for such boasting, then, is the ability to understand properly God's economy of salvation.

In the absence of such wisdom, one can only put confidence "in the flesh." The term "flesh" (σάρξ/*sarx*) has a wide range of meanings, ranging from the physical to "human nature" to that realm opposed to God and so forth.[22] In this particular case, Paul may be playing upon several senses of the term. First, it may reflect a confidence in circumcision of the flesh, which Paul links with "the mutilators." Secondly, it may be part of a contrast between two realms, between worship by the Spirit and boasting in Christ on the one hand, and confidence in the flesh, on the other. Most importantly, as the following verses elaborate Paul's own basis for "confidence in the flesh," it may also reflect the same sort of fundamental misunderstanding of God's economy that previously characterized Paul himself. That is, "the flesh" comes to be a form of shorthand for a standard of judging God's desires for oneself and the world that is, ultimately, contrary to God's desires and purposes.

As will become clearer in the subsequent verses, Paul's dispute with the "mutilators" seems to be based on their failure to recognize two facts. First, the Philippian Gentile Christians are already fully participating in the Abrahamic covenant. There is nothing more they need to do in order to situate themselves within the ongoing drama of God's saving purposes. Secondly, to the extent that "the mutilators" desire the Philippians to "judaize" as a way of mitigating any persecution, they profoundly misunderstand the nature of God's salvation. As Paul has already manifested in his own life and through his account of Christ in 2:6-11, suffering willingly taken on in obedience to God, even to the extent of dying on the cross, is the way of God's salvation. To perceive this, however, the Philippians and we will need to become practiced at reading the drama of salvation properly. They also need to act in specific ways, as outlined in 1:30–2:4. Thus, a proper reading of the economy of salvation will enable them to situate themselves within that drama in the appropriate ways so that they will live, and continue to live, as "friends" of the cross.

In the verses that follow, vv. 4-6, Paul provides an example of this way of reading the economy of salvation by narrating his own life from the perspec-

---

22. See E. Schweizer, "σάρξ."

tive of one who is in Christ. As Paul notes, according to the standards provided by "the flesh," he has even more reason than most to be confident. From this assertion, Paul begins to offer an account of his past that allows him to demonstrate the way he has come to see himself within the scope of God's saving acts.

In 3:5-6 Paul lists his reasons for confidence according to fleshly standards. These are reasons that Jews or Jewish Christians would have to hold in high regard. He was "circumcised on the eighth day," that is, when he was eight days old. This is in conformity with Gen 17:12 and Lev 12:3. While this says more about his parents' observance of the Law than his own, it allows Paul to remind his audience that he is no proselyte. He was a member of the covenant people of God almost from birth. He is of the "race of Israel and the tribe of Benjamin" (cf. Romans 11). Benjamin, Rachel's younger son, was the only one of the twelve born in the Promised Land (Gen 35:16-18). Paul's namesake, Saul the first king of Israel, was a Benjaminite. Only Benjamin and Judah remained loyal to the Davidic house.

Paul's next self-designation is "Hebrew of Hebrews." Bockmuehl cites Acts 6:1; 2 Macc. passim; *4 Macc* 12:7; 16:15; Philo *Life of Moses* 2.32 to support the idea this means that Paul spoke or read Hebrew. Moreover, he notes that inscriptions from the Diaspora indicate that a "Hebrew" was a Jew who maintained close ties with Palestine and the Hebrew language.[23] Acts asserts that Paul was from Tarsus originally, but also that he studied under Gamaliel the Elder in Jerusalem (22:3; 26:4), where at least some of his siblings lived (23:16). At the same time this has to be squared with the fact that when Paul quotes Scripture, he seems always to rely on the Greek translation. In the end it is possible to read too much into this designation, though, at the very least, it indicates the purity of Paul's bloodlines.[24]

While these initial designations speak about Paul's deep connections to Israel, the next three claims describe the rigor of his personal devotion. In his approach to Torah Paul was a Pharisee. The Pharisees displayed a zeal for legal debate and emphasized the importance of purity laws, seeking to maintain in everyday life the standards of purity and holiness required for worship at the Temple. Josephus in particular stresses their rigor and strictness with regard to the law (*Antiquities* 15.288, 298; 17.42; 18.15). Paul's claim here echoes his assertion in Gal 1:14 that he assiduously attended to the traditions of his ancestors.

Paul then talks about his "zeal." While Paul can sometime use "zeal" to

23. Bockmuehl, *Philippians*, 196.
24. Fee, *Philippians*, 307 n. 14, adopts this minimalist approach.

refer to a vice (Rom 13:13; 1 Cor 3:3; 2 Cor 12:20; Gal 5:20), he can also use it approvingly of vigorous pursuit of an object of desire (cf. 1 Cor 12:31; 14:1, 39; 2 Cor 9:2; 11:2; Tit 2:14). In this particular case Paul cites his persecution of the church as a mark of his devotion to Judaism. No doubt few could match the claim that their love for God led them to persecute those seen to be heretics. Paul does not flinch in mentioning this; neither is he consumed by guilt because of it. From the perspective of his prior life it was a mark of virtue; from his current perspective it is a mark he is willing to dispose of.[25]

Finally, Paul claims that, according to the righteousness in the Law, he was blameless. This phrase more than any other has been invoked to undermine the notion that prior to his encounter with Christ on the road to Damascus Paul was a man consumed by guilt, tortured by an introspective conscience, and in search of a gracious God to free him from a legalistic and oppressive Judaism. Not only does this notion badly misrepresent Judaism, it simply is not an accurate account of Paul's self-perception. The pre-Christian Paul, like all other Pharisees, understood that the Law could indeed be kept. When one sinned, there were clear and direct ways for seeking and receiving forgiveness. "The Law as a way of life was widely thought to be feasible and practical: for most faithful Jews it would have been absurd to think that God had given a revelation that could not in fact be lived out."[26] In fact, when judged according to this standard Paul calls himself "blameless," the same word he uses in 2:15 when he calls the Philippians to be "blameless and innocent children of God."

As the contrast with 3:9 makes clear, Paul's point is neither about the possibility of keeping the Law nor about his particular success in this regard. Rather, it is to note that according to the standards of "the flesh," according to the righteousness "in the Law" he was blameless.[27] Of course, when using the wrong set of standards, the actual measurements do not really matter. A perspective driven by "the flesh" may give one a very clear account in fleshly terms. Paul has come to see, however, that this is the wrong perspective from which to render an account of his life. As 3:9 indicates, he now seeks to have that righteousness grounded in Christ's faithfulness. Now that Christ has taken hold of him, he is able to fit his life into the narrative of God's economy of salvation properly. This changes both the *telos* of his account and the standards by which he measures success and failure.

25. In 1 Cor 15:9 Paul notes that this activity renders him "the least of the apostles, unfit to be called an apostle."

26. Bockmuehl, *Philippians,* 202.

27. V. Koperski makes the point that in this context "relying on the law is one kind of relying on the flesh." See *The Knowledge of Jesus Christ My Lord,* 228.

What has changed is Paul's vantage point for considering himself and his past. "[But] these things which I used to consider assets, I now, through Christ, consider losses."[28] Paul's language of gain and loss invokes images of financial audit. Bockmuehl nicely displays this in his paraphrase: "In relation to God's audit in Jesus Christ, these things appear to be liabilities."[29] While this is correct, it is equally important to emphasize that Paul had to learn to see or consider things in this way. The difference between a liability and an asset here is not self-evident to all. Rather, it depends on learning to perceive things from a perspective in Christ.[30] This is a habit that had to be formed in Paul. Moreover, he wants the Philippians to have similar perceptual habits formed in them.

Just as in 1:12-26, Paul's account of himself and his circumstances has multiple aims. First and most straightforwardly, he wants the Philippians to see him in a particular way. Second, and more importantly for the long-term health of the Philippian congregation, Paul displays the perceptual habits, skills, and ways of life that allow him to fit himself into the ongoing drama of God's salvation. These are the habits, skills, and ways of life he desires to see formed in the Philippians. Indeed, this is in large part what he means in 2:5 when he urges the Philippians to adopt the particular pattern of practical reasoning appropriate to those in Christ.

The next sentence, which runs from v. 8 through v. 11, is a detailed elaboration of the point made in v. 7.[31] It begins, "Not only this, but what is more."[32] Although the Greek is a bit obscure, the phrase clearly introduces an elaboration of the previous point. It is not simply the case that Christ has altered Paul's perceptions about his past achievements. Rather, he now considers "all these things" losses from the perspective of being in Christ. The next clause makes it quite clear that Paul's ability to see things this way is due to the "surpassing value of knowing Christ Jesus my Lord."[33]

---

28. Many ancient mss. omit "But" (ἀλλά/*alla*). Omitting it is also the more difficult reading. Nevertheless, even if it is not original, the passage makes the contrast in Paul's pattern of reckoning clear.

29. Bockmuehl, *Philippians*, 204. See also Hawthorne, *Philippians*, 135.

30. As Koperski, *The Knowledge of Jesus Christ My Lord*, 232, suggests, "The entire context of Phil indicates that there is a basic question of correct perception at issue."

31. Although this is a single sentence in Greek, I have used several English sentences so that the translation is clearer and more fluid.

32. This is the translation Fee, *Philippians*, 317, offers.

33. The Greek participle, τό ὑπερέχον/*to hyperechon*, appears in different forms here and in 4:7 and 2:3. The verb means "to surpass or excel" (see BAGD, 840-41). In each case context adds further specificity. Here, with the financial metaphors of loss and gain, I have translated the term as "the surpassing value" of knowing Christ. See Bockmuehl, *Philippians*, 205; Fee, *Philippians*, 317 n. 19; Hawthorne, *Philippians*, 137.

In the light of the comments Paul makes in v. 10, it is clear that "the knowledge of Christ Jesus my Lord" in v. 8 cannot be seen in terms of amassing data about Christ. Rather, it refers to the "fundamental reality of Paul's life, the relationship which suffuses all that he is and does."[34] This "knowledge" of Christ allows him to perceive his prior life in a new and transformed way. Further, Paul's identification of Christ Jesus as "my Lord" may well play on the granting of the name to the exalted Christ in 2:11. Indeed, Paul is narrating himself into the story of salvation that begins, climaxes, and will end with Christ, particularly as related in 2:6-11.

Paul further shapes this thought by claiming that for Christ's sake he has suffered the loss of all things, now considering them rubbish, in order to gain Christ and be found in him. Again Paul invokes the language of profit and loss, asset and liability, but this clause makes two particular additions. First is the claim that Paul considers all of what he has lost as "rubbish." The term used here is sometimes used of discarded food and even human excrement.[35]

The second way in which Paul adds to the notion of "gaining Christ" is by the addition of the idea of "being found in him." This marks a decisive shift in the images Paul has just been using. In vv. 7-8 the financial metaphors of profit and loss, gain and liability usefully describe the sharp change in Paul's perceptions of his past "achievements." As v. 8 closes with the notion that Paul considers all things to be rubbish in order that he might "gain Christ," the problems latent in pursuing this line of financial metaphors become immediately clear. Christ is not simply some blue chip stock Paul has added to his portfolio. To stay with the financial metaphors at this point in the argument risks both making Christ into a commodity and allowing Paul to remain the subject of this narrative of transformation. Instead, Paul considers his past achievements to be rubbish so that he "might be found in Christ." Christ is no longer a commodity to be gained but a place, a home where the lost Paul is found. Paul speaks of "gaining" Christ in the sense that Christ is the *telos* toward which Paul now directs his life as opposed to those inferior things toward which he formerly directed his life. Moreover, by shifting to a passive verb Paul makes it clear that he does not find Christ; Christ

---

34. Bockmuehl, *Philippians*, 206.

35. See citations in Lightfoot, *Philippians*, 149. In this light Hays's translation "crap" may be most appropriate (see *Echoes of Scripture in the Letters of Paul*, 122). If, as was thought in the Middle Ages, the Greek word used here, σκύβαλα/*skybala*, is a contraction of τό τοῖς κυσὶ βαλλόμενον/*to tois kysi ballomenon*, "that which is thrown to the dogs," then we may have a further play on v. 2. This is suggested by Bockmuehl, *Philippians*, 207, following Lightfoot, *Philippians*, 149.

finds him. As we have seen elsewhere in Philippians (e.g., 1:12-26), Paul subtly shifts from being the subject of his own story to being part of a story in which Christ is now the subject.

The following clauses indicate what is involved in "being found in Christ." Paul initially describes this in negative terms, "not having my own righteousness, that is, the righteousness that comes from the Law." At once Paul is reminding us of his claim in v. 6, where he notes that he was both blameless according to the righteousness found in the Law and zealous in his devotion to the Law. This is similar to Rom 10:3, where Paul accuses the Jews of having "zeal without knowledge" as they pursue "their own righteousness" instead of God's. There is concern not with Jewish pride or exclusiveness but with a fundamental misperception of the *telos* of the Law. Here he now ascribes to himself, prior to his encounter with Christ, the same error of perception, which can be remedied only by Christ.[36] Christ's faithful obedience to God, most directly narrated in 2:5-11, reveals God's true righteousness. In the light of the transformations Christ has worked in his life, Paul now confidently and faithfully pursues this righteousness of God.

3:9 is one of the occasions where a form of the phrase "faith of Christ" (πίστις Χριστοῦ/*pistis Christou*) appears. This phrase has become a hotly contested battle zone in Pauline studies over the past twenty-five years. Some argue that we should understand "Christ" as a subjective genitive so that the phrase refers to Christ's obedient fidelity to the will of the Father. Others argue that the genitive is objective and that the phrase refers to the Christian's response of faith in Christ. The scholarly debate is quite contentious.[37] Each interpretation is grammatically possible and can make sense of the relevant passages. But we do not need to resolve it on a large scale to make judgments about this one verse because here both perspectives seem to be included. The righteousness of God is revealed and established "through the faithfulness of Christ" (διὰ πίστεως Χριστοῦ/*dia pisteōs Christou*) to which believers respond on the basis of faith (ἐπὶ τῇ πίστει/*epi tē pistei*).[38]

---

36. This is similar to Koperski's position, *The Knowledge of Jesus Christ My Lord*, 235-37. Fee, *Philippians*, 323 n. 39, also notes similarities with Rom 10:3.

37. See for example the recent article by R. Barry Matlock, "Detheologizing the ΠΙΣΤΙΣ ΧΡΙΣΤΟΥ Debate."

38. This is basically Bockmuehl's position, *Philippians*, 211. Fee, *Philippians*, 324-25 and n. 44, seems to take both occurrences of πίστις/*pistis* in this verse as saying the same thing. It would seem more likely that the different prepositions as well as the use of "Christ" to modify the first occurrence would indicate that Paul is making a distinction here rather than simply repeating himself.

In 3:10 Paul indicates that the purpose of gaining Christ and being found in him is "to know Christ."[39] This both reiterates Paul's point in v. 8 and expands on it through the following clauses: to know Christ is to know both "the power of his resurrection and the fellowship of his sufferings."[40]

Throughout 3:1-11 Paul has spoken of ways in which his knowledge of Christ has led him to perceive his past achievements in a new light. Moreover, his knowledge of Christ leads him to see his present situation and his future direction in new ways. These verses are in several respects an example of Paul manifesting the sorts of practical reason that is available to one in Christ and that he has urged the Philippians to adopt in 2:5.

In this light, we should take Paul's comments about knowing the power of Christ's resurrection and the fellowship of his sufferings as drawing their force from 2:6-11. Thus, when Paul speaks of the power of the resurrection, we should interpret this through the lens provided by 2:9-11. Although the resurrection is not explicitly mentioned in 2:9, it is clear that the power of the resurrection is the power that God displays in exalting the obedient crucified Christ. Moreover, this fits well with other passages where Paul speaks of God's power displayed in raising Christ (Rom 1:4; 8:11; 1 Cor 6:14; 2 Cor 13:4). God raised the obedient, crucified Jesus, so the power of the resurrection is definitively revealed in Christ's willed self-emptying and obedient suffering narrated in Phil 2:6-11. Thus, Paul cannot speak here of knowing Christ apart from speaking of sharing in Christ's sufferings.

As Paul speaks of it here, knowledge of Christ is ultimately cruciform. Is this the only way to "know Christ"? On the one hand, one has to say no. There are numerous ways in which believers come to know Christ. On the other hand, any understanding of Christ that ruled out or contradicted the knowledge of Christ displayed through fellowship in his sufferings and the power of God who raised Christ from the dead could not be true.[41]

Paul attains knowledge of Christ, including both the power of his resurrection and fellowship of his sufferings, by becoming "conformed to his death."[42] How might one be conformed to Christ's death? If it simply meant

---

39. The grammar here is a bit obscure. I follow Fee, *Philippians*, 326-27, and Bockmuehl, *Philippians*, 213, in taking the Greek infinitive "to know" as expressing the purpose of the preceding clauses.

40. The definite articles before "fellowship" and "sufferings" in some mss. are not in the earliest mss. and are probably later additions. See Fee's argument, *Philippians*, 311 n. 2.

41. In this respect I find Michael Gorman's *Cruciformity* exemplary.

42. I am taking the participle συμμορφιζόμενος/*symmorphizomenos* ("conformed") to indicate the mode in which Paul gains knowledge of Christ, with Fee, *Philippians*, 333; Bockmuehl, *Philippians*, 215. I think, however, that one should not draw too many connections between this

crucifixion at the hands of the Romans, then Paul did not conform to Christ's death and we cannot. But we should continue to let the story of Christ in 2:6-11 determine what conformity to Christ's death should mean. Three interrelated characteristics of Christ's death emerge from that story. First, it is the result of seeking the benefit of others. Christ did not use his equality with God as something for his own advantage. Second, it is the result of willed self-emptying. Third, it is the result of obedience to God. If we allow these characteristics to shape an understanding of conformity to Christ's death, then we can see the ways in which Paul's manner of life and our own might be ways of sharing in Christ's sufferings and, thus, being conformed to Christ's death.

Several things follow from this. First, not all suffering is sharing in Christ's suffering, and not all death is conformity to Christ's death. The story of Christ's willed self-emptying and obedience even to death on the cross provides an exemplar for directing one's life so that Christ is magnified, whether in life or in death (1:20). This is not a way of making all suffering intelligible. When Fee states that "through our suffering the significance of Christ's suffering is manifested to the world" he gets the matter backward.[43] Christ's suffering, which comes as a result of willed self-emptying and obedience to God, provides a standard of intelligibility for Paul's suffering and the suffering of other Christians resulting from their obedience. Paul is not offering a generalized account of suffering and death here. He is using the Christ-focused patterns of perception that he has developed over the course of his life to provide an account of his past and his present circumstances and to display his disposition toward the future. Moreover, part of his reason for displaying these patterns of perception is to help the Philippians develop similar patterns. To the extent that suffering has and may continue to come his way as the result of his commitments to Christ, Paul is able to make that suffering intelligible. Should the Philippians or other Christians develop similar abilities for fitting their lives into the ongoing story of God's redemption, they, too, will have resources for making the suffering that comes their way as the result of their commitments to Christ intelligible. Nevertheless, we should always recognize the possibility, and even likelihood, that some suffering may simply reduce us to silence. Hence, we should be wary of using this or any passage to explain too much.

Second, conforming to Christ's death is not really about the manner of Paul's death or ours. Instead, this sort of fellowship in Christ's sufferings pro-

---

word and μορφή/*morphē* ("form") in 2:6, 7. Of course, the same term does appear in 3:21, where the connections to this verse seem much clearer.

43. Fee, *Philippians*, 332.

vides a way of ordering Paul's life and our lives so that we seek the benefit of others in willed self-emptying and obedience to God. Rather than describing a manner of death, the phrases "sharing in Christ's sufferings" and "being conformed to his death" work as a shorthand expression of a standard of fidelity.

The final clause here, "if I might somehow arrive at the resurrection from the dead," is puzzling on several counts. First, the construction εἴ πως/*ei pōs*, rendered here as "if I might somehow," seems to imply a degree of contingency and even doubt on Paul's part. Paul's other uses of this construction are Rom 1:10; 11:14. Although the subject matter is different, the phrase does not in those places convey doubt so much as a strong hope or ardent desire for something that will happen, although God must bring it about.[44] Of course, it would be odd for Paul to make such strong assertions in 1:6 and 2:13 about God's providential working in the lives of the Philippians and at the same time have significant doubts about God's working in his own situation. Moreover, to the degree that there is a measure of contingency involved here, it would seem to be of the sort that Paul takes up in the next several verses. In particular, Paul makes the point that he has not arrived at his ultimate end yet. Rather, having had his desires and attention redirected by the resurrected Christ, as narrated in 3:4-8, Paul presses on to attain his proper end. In this journey he is full both of the ardent desire that comes from the conviction that his end is true and appropriate and of the hope that the God who raised Jesus from the dead will also do so in his case.[45]

The second puzzle lies in Paul's use of the Greek term ἐξανάστασις/*exanastasis* to refer to resurrection from the dead. This is the only NT occurrence of this word.[46] Presumably, Paul is not referring to a general resurrection of the just and unjust together such as is hinted at in 1 Cor 15:12-23; Rom 11:15; or Acts 24:15. This would account neither for the contingency expressed in this verse nor for Paul's ardent desire to attain this resurrection. Another alternative proposed by modern scholars is that Paul uses this term with its intensifying prefix to refute opponents who either doubted the Christian's participation in Christ's resurrection or thought that such participation had already been accomplished.[47] In each case, however, one must assume a good deal of knowledge about opponents whose very presence, much less their teaching, is not clearly expressed in the text.

44. See J. M. Gundry-Volf, *Paul and Perseverance*, 257-58.

45. See also Bockmuehl, *Philippians*, 217-18.

46. Ἀνάστασις/*anastasis* without the prefix is the common way of speaking of resurrection.

47. See Bockmuehl, *Philippians*, 219, for a defense of this former option, and H. Koester, "The Purpose of the Polemic of a Pauline Fragment," 323, for a defense of the latter option.

Despite these puzzles, it is clear that Paul is speaking of the true and proper end of his knowledge of Christ, that is, resurrection. Moreover, Paul cannot achieve such an end apart from conformity to Christ's death. Further, his knowledge of Christ shapes the way he understands his past and lives in the present. In this respect vv. 10-11 present us with that stable point on which Paul now stands. From this point he is able to retell the story of his past and the transformations Christ has worked in his life. Moreover, this point provides Paul with a perspective from which he can offer an account of his present circumstances, as he did in 1:12-26. In addition, being in Christ provides Paul with a clear sense of his *telos*, his proper end, that toward which God is ultimately drawing him. Nevertheless, as the subsequent verses make clear, Paul's convictions about the shape and nature of his *telos* do not imply that he has already attained that end.

In the following verses Paul will assert the importance of seeing life in Christ as an ongoing journey of having our attention and affections transformed as we are drawn ever deeper into fellowship with Christ. This journey begins for Paul with a radical undermining of his past standards and manner of attending to God. His past is not so much negated and erased as it is transformed. In Rom 12:1-3 Paul urges followers of Christ to be transformed by the renewing of their minds so that they might discern the will of God. Here in the course of Phil 3:1-11 Paul speaks of the renewing of his own mind as he is captivated by Christ. Paul's attention and affections are redirected so that he comes to understand God and God's ways with the world in profoundly different ways.

As 3:12-14 will confirm, being transformed by the renewing of one's mind is not a one-time achievement. Rather, it is a life-long process of having our desires and affections and attention continually redirected and refocused by our knowledge of the crucified and resurrected Christ. Moreover, failure to engage in this process of transformation will not leave Christians in some neutral, unformed state. Rather, our affections and attention will be drawn to and shaped by other factors. If, as some research indicates, we are confronted with up to 16,000 advertisements and media messages each day, it will not take long before our attention and ultimately our desires are drawn away from God and toward any number of enticements. We will no longer be friends of the cross. At best we will become strangers to it. At worst we will become enemies of the cross of Christ.

3:12-21

12 It is not that I have already attained this, nor have I reached my end. Instead I press on to take hold of that for which Christ took hold of me. 13 My brothers and sisters, I do not consider that I have already attained this end; but this one thing I do, forgetting what lies behind and straining forward toward what lies ahead, 14 I press on toward the finish line so that I might win the prize of the heavenly call of God in Christ Jesus. 15 Let as many of us as are mature display this way of thinking, feeling and acting. If any of you are inclined to adopt a different pattern of thinking, feeling, and acting, God will reveal to you the proper mindset to adopt. 16 In any case, let us keep in step with the common standard we have already attained. 17 Join together, brothers and sisters, in becoming imitators of me and attend to those who walk according to the example you have in us. 18 For, as I have often told you and now tearfully reiterate, there are many who walk as enemies of the cross of Christ. 19 Their end is destruction, their God is their belly, and their glory is in their shame. Their pattern of thinking, feeling, and acting is guided by earthly considerations. 20 For our commonwealth is in heaven, from whence we eagerly await a Savior, the Lord Jesus Christ. 21 He will transform our humiliated bodies so that they conform to his glorious body according to the power that enables him to subject all things to himself.

In the previous section Paul offered a narrative account of his past, emphasizing the ways in which his convictions about Christ led him to reconceive his past achievements. These Christ-focused convictions also provide him with a new direction and end-point for his life. Paul now perceives everything — his past, his present circumstances, and his future — in the light of his new ends and purposes in Christ. This pattern of perception will, of course, generate new patterns of living and acting in the world. Much of the first two chapters of Philippians reflects many of the practices that stem from these Christ-focused and Christ-directed patterns of perceiving and acting.

In the initial part of this section, vv. 12-14, we see how Paul's convictions about his ends and purposes in Christ direct his dispositions toward the present and the future.[1] While Paul's claims here are forceful, it seems far easier and preferable to fit them into a constructive rather than a polemical agenda. There is little evidence to think that Paul's vigorous assertions here, along

---

1. As Fee, *Philippians*, 338, notes, ". . . Paul's story takes a final turn, which simultaneously looks back to vv. 4-8 (forgetting the past), embraces the present (he is neither fully conformed to Christ's death nor has he arrived at the goal; vv. 10-11), and emphasizes his present pursuit of the final goal."

with his call to the Philippians to think and act likewise in vv. 15-21, indicate particular systemic problems, failures, or fractures within the Philippian congregation.[2]

Verse 12 begins by noting that Paul has not yet reached his goal or true end. In vv. 9-11 he has already articulated his goal.[3] The phrasing of vv. 10-11 might have led some to infer that Paul had reached his goal. Instead of emphasizing when he will attain his true end, Paul focuses on the way he comports himself in the present in the light of his future hopes. His disposition toward the future is one of striving, of pursuing of a worthy goal. He claims, "I press on to take hold of that for which Christ took hold of me."[4] Thus, Paul does not further articulate the contours of his final goal. Rather, he asserts that he strives for this goal because this is the goal Christ has for him.

This provides a sharp contrast between Paul's present and his past. In vv. 4-8 it is clear that Paul understood his Judaism to provide him with a set of ends and purposes toward which he should strive. By his own account he was largely successful in this. Being in Christ provides Paul with a different set of ends and purposes. In striving for these, Paul is conforming himself to the ends and purposes Christ has for him.

Paul emphasizes the change in perspective, perception, and action that Christ has worked in him. In addition, he focuses on developing, displaying, and passing on to the Philippians this specifically Christ-focused pattern of practical reasoning. In other epistles, however, Paul is at pains to argue that despite the fact he now conceives of his ends and purposes from the perspective of one who is in Christ, he has not in any way abandoned his Judaism. In fact, the upshot of the arguments in Romans and Galatians is that the ends and purposes he now has in Christ have always been the ends and purposes God has desired for the people of Israel. To develop this claim and its implications as fully as it ought to be would take a separate monograph. For my purposes, it is primarily important to remind Christians that Paul's claims here

---

2. Fee, *Philippians*, 341 n. 15, covers a variety of speculative attempts to read a perceived polemical agenda in these verses and uncover the identity of Paul's opponents.

3. In the light of the claim the Paul has not yet reached his goal, the verb τετελείωμαι/ *teteleiōmai* should be taken to indicate that Paul has not yet reached his proper end or *telos*, rather than indicating that he is not yet perfect.

4. In my account here I have followed J. A. Fitzmyer's argument that here in 3:12 the elliptical Greek phrase ἐφ' ᾧ/*eph' hō* should be read consecutively as the object of the verb. See Fitzmyer, "The Consecutive Meaning of ΕΦ' Ω in Romans 5.12," 321-39, especially 330. On Fitzmyer's account, then, the idiom is an elliptical form of τοῦτο ἐφ ᾧ/*touto eph' hō*. This is instead of the causal reading, which is translated as "I press on to make it my own because Christ Jesus has made me his own" (see RSV, NRSV).

in Philippians 3 bespeak a transformation in *his* perceptions about his Judaism, not a transformation in God's intentions and plans for the people of Israel. Paul's claims here do not imply that he ever stopped thinking of himself as a Jew or that God's plans and purposes for the people of Israel changed.

In 3:13 Paul reiterates that he does not consider that he has reached his goal yet. His point here is not to draw a contrast between himself and those who have reached this goal. Rather, the contrast is between Paul's current situation and where he plans to end up. He does not want simply to note this contrast but to show how it directs his current ways of thinking and acting. Having conformed his convictions about the ends and purposes of his life to those which Christ has for him, he now has a way of thinking about his past, of living in the present, and of directing his hopes and convictions in the light of his final end, his "heavenly calling."

To make these points in vv. 13-14 Paul employs athletic imagery similar to that found in 1 Cor 9:24-27, although to a different end.[5] For example, in 1 Cor 9:24 Paul emphasizes that only one of the competitors in a race wins the prize. In Phil 3:13-14 the issue is not winning or losing but how one ought to run the race. The image of a race displays the way Paul strives to live in the light of the story of his life as he has just told it. He pays no attention to his past and strains forward to what lies before him.

There are two interesting things to note about this claim. The first concerns this idea of "forgetting what lies behind." Although ἐπιλανθάνομαι/ *epilanthanomai*, "forget," appears only here in Paul, it occurs seven other times in the NT. In Matt 16:5; Mark 8:14; Luke 12:6; and Jas 1:24 the verb clearly indicates forgetting in a relatively straightforward sense of a failure of memory. The occurrences in Heb 6:10; 13:2, 16 all carry the sense of neglect. Here Paul must mean something more. Given that he parallels forgetting with "straining forward" in v. 14, it is clear that he wants to assert that he does not allow his past to encumber him as he strives for what lies ahead.

Nevertheless, it is also clear from 3:2-11 that Paul has not "forgotten" his past. He has reconceived it from the perspective of one who is now in Christ, but it is not forgotten. In fact, it is quite clear that it is only now, from the perspective of being in Christ, that Paul can offer a truthful account of his past. His ability to "press on toward the goal" can be sustained only by the truthful account of his past he is now able to narrate.

Understanding this distinction would seem to be particularly impor-

---

5. Further, Bockmuehl, *Philippians*, 222, notes that σκοπός/*skopos* (which only occurs here in the NT) denotes "a finish line which a runner has in view." In addition, it appears in the LXX of Job 16:12; Lam 3:12 to describe a target.

tant for contemporary Christians. Rather than advocating a pattern of spiritual life in which one constantly reinvents oneself, Paul uses an account of his past, narrated from the perspective of being in Christ, as a sort of springboard from which he propels himself forward toward the goal for which Christ has laid hold of him. Rather than having forgotten or erased the past, Paul has been offered a truthful vision of his past. It is only from the perspective of this truthful vision that he has any hope of directing his present and future in ways that will bring him to the goal for which Christ laid hold of him.

The second issue concerns the nature of the "prize" for which Paul is straining. "The prize" is specified as that of the "heavenly" or, more literally, "upward" call of God in Christ Jesus. The question for most modern commentators appears to be how this clause modifies one's understanding of the prize. For example, is the call itself the prize? Does it refer to a calling to be with Christ in heaven (cf. Heb 3:1; 9:15; Col 3:3-4; Eph 2:6)? "While this understanding of the 'upward call' could be compatible with Paul's thought elsewhere, it seems at this stage to disrupt the metaphor in which the goal is a prize not a calling. What is more, it is worth underlining that for Paul the word 'calling' (klēsis) normally denotes the divine act of calling itself rather than that to which one is called."[6]

Bockmuehl argues that the prize is the one "which *pertains* to the calling, i.e. to which the divine call invites and which it promises."[7] In this case "upward" (ἄνω/anō) indicates the divine origin and nature of the call. Hence, I have translated the term as "heavenly." "It is God who calls in Christ Jesus, and he calls the believer into eternal fellowship with him. This is the prize for which Paul is still contending."[8] The fact that this call of God is "in Christ Jesus" emphasizes that Christ is the one who is the source of God's call and the means by which that call is heard.

Although modern commentators are primarily interested in the figuring out what Paul means by "the prize of the upward call of God in Christ Jesus," they seem relatively uninterested in some of the theological implications of an answer to that question. This was not so in the patristic period. Modern commentators seem to assume that at some point in the eschatological future Paul would take possession of his prize. This, of course, is implied by Paul's language here. Such a claim, however, raises several other questions that are generally ignored but theologically important. For example, would

6. Bockmuehl, *Philippians,* 222.

7. Bockmuehl, *Philippians,* 223.

8. Bockmuehl, *Philippians,* 223. Fee, *Philippians,* 350, also notes, "This has been the aim of God's call right along, to lift them 'heavenward' to share in his eternal presence."

Paul's possession of his prize mean that his desire for God would be satisfied? Would he stop reaching out toward what lies ahead because he had finally reached it? If the answer to these questions were yes, it might, among other things, seriously compromise one's doctrine of God and God's economy of salvation. It would indicate that somehow God could be absolutely comprehended in such a way that one might become sated with God. In this light, patristic authors developed a very particular account of the importance of continually stretching out toward God, even after the *eschaton*. Indeed, by the fourth century Paul's notion of continually straining forward provided a significant image to describe the spiritual life, from the present into eternity.

Gregory of Nyssa, developing themes found initially in Origen, made particularly extensive use of this idea in his *Life of Moses*. As Gregory describes it, the proper end of the Christian life is not represented by the attainment of a particular state. Rather it is continual growth in virtue and the desire for God. In reflecting on Moses' insatiable capacity to desire God and to grow in virtue, even though he had already achieved great intimacy with God, Gregory notes that a soul once set on its upward course "will always make its flight yet higher — by its desire of the heavenly things *straining ahead for what is still to come*, as the Apostle says."[9] Growth in virtue, which includes an ever-enhanced desire for God, is an activity which "causes its capacity to grow through exertion; this kind of activity alone does not slacken its intensity by the effort, but increases it."[10] Drawing on Paul's image, Gregory seeks to display the spiritual life as ever-deepening communion with the triune God in a way that shows how we can never be sated in our desire for communion with God. The more one attains, the more one desires. Although such a notion clearly says more than Paul does, it ought to be taken as a faithful extension of Paul's claims, addressing crucial questions that Paul's own language puts on the agenda.

In 3:4-14 Paul manifests a Christ-focused form of practical reasoning in the way he speaks about his past, his present aspirations, and his future hopes. In this account vv. 10-11 provide the climactic cruciform key to how Paul thinks and acts in the world. Verses 12-14 display his outlook in relation to the present in the light of his final end. Finally, in vv. 15-21, at the close of this chapter, Paul urges the Philippians to adopt in their situation the same pattern of thinking, feeling, and acting that he has just displayed for them.

In the second part of this section, 3:15-21, Paul develops and expands the

9. See Gregory's *Life of Moses* 225.
10. *Life of Moses* 226.

account of his own life, urging the Philippians to adopt the perceptual and practical habits he has displayed in 3:4-14 as they seek to order their common life in a manner worthy of the gospel of Christ (cf. 1:27). Paul both points to himself and to others like him as constructive examples to be imitated and urges the Philippians to avoid those who are enemies of the cross of Christ, those who manifest a disordered, earth-bound practical reasoning.

Paul begins by talking about those (including himself) who are "mature."[11] As Paul sees it, maturity is manifested in those demonstrating the specific form of practical reasoning Paul has just displayed. He uses the verb φρονεῖν/*phronein*, as he did in 1:7; 2:5. Instead of using a more technical translation such as "practical reasoning," I have used phrases related to patterns of "thinking, feeling, and acting." His account of his own life beginning in 3:4 includes both coming to see his past and present from a particular point of view (which might in itself echo back to 1:12-26) and comporting himself in the present and the future in such a way that he could be counted a "friend of the cross" as described in 3:9-11. Reading Paul's admonition in this way not only holds vv. 4-14 together with vv. 15-21, but it makes a stronger connection to the subsequent admonition to the Philippians to become imitators of Paul rather than "enemies of the cross."

Following his admonition to display the practical reasoning of the "mature," Paul anticipates that some of the Philippians might have a different attitude.[12] He claims that if anyone is inclined to "think otherwise," to adopt a different pattern of practical reasoning (again using φρονεῖν/*phronein*), God will reveal the proper mindset to adopt. Whether Paul anticipates that some may come to think otherwise or that some already do (cf. 4:1-3) is less important than his response.

In epistolary literature the notion of "thinking otherwise" or in a contrary manner indicates discord in a friendship. Being of one mind or think-

---

11. There is some debate about what Paul means by this term. The Greek word is τέλειοι/*teleioi*. Having just claimed in v. 12 that he is not yet perfected τετελείωμαι/*teteleiōmai*, Paul now describes himself (and others) as τέλειοι/*teleioi*. Some take this as an ironic designation designed to undermine a group in the congregation who thought of themselves as "perfect" (Hawthorne, *Philippians*, 155-56; Lightfoot, *Philippians*, 153, and those listed by Fee, *Philippians*, 353 n. 10). There are several reasons against taking τέλειοι/*teleioi* in this way. First, Paul includes himself in this group. Secondly, it is not unusual to find related words used in different contexts to mean different things. Moreover, one can make good sense of the passage by taking τέλειοι/*teleioi* in its straightforward sense of "mature" as in 1 Cor 2:6; 14:20; Eph 4:13.

12. Hawthorne, *Philippians*, 156, argues that καὶ εἴ/*kai ei* indicates that they already do have a different attitude in some respects. Fee, *Philippians*, 358 n. 27, 359, on the other hand, contrasts this phrase with 1 Cor 14:37-38, where Paul also anticipates that some might not share his view of things, to argue that this is not a sign of concrete opposition.

ing the same way indicates concord.[13] In letters where discord has occurred, correspondents are usually at great pains both to show their concern for the state of the friendship and to do what is needed to repair the rupture. Paul does not directly do either. Rather, he has faith that God will reveal to those who think otherwise the proper mindset to adopt. This indicates first that Paul is not greatly concerned about discord between himself and the Philippians. Instead, he implies that adopting a different form of practical reasoning than the one Paul has just outlined will damage the Philippians' friendship with God. Hence, he trusts God to reveal to the Philippians the form of practical reasoning they will need to display to live faithfully before God (cf. 1:27), thus keeping their friendship with God in good order. Here we get a further example of how Paul both follows epistolary conventions of friendship letters while also directing those conventions to his larger theological purposes.

Paul does not explain how this revelation will take place. Presumably, the working of the Spirit in bringing the Philippians to embody the forms of thinking, feeling, and acting advocated by Paul happens in many and various ways. Paul's claim here in 3:15 reflects the same view he demonstrated in his earlier confident assertions of God's providential care of and commitment to the Philippian congregation in 1:6 and 2:13. It also fits with Paul's dispositions toward those who preach Christ from selfish motives in 1:18. This disposition of patient waiting on God's providence has something significant to say to those Christians pained by the manifest divisions within the body of Christ. God clearly wills that the church be one. Likewise, Paul sees that the unity of the Philippian congregation is crucial to their ability to form a common life worthy of the gospel and to be a vital witness to the reconciling power of God. It is important also to note that here and elsewhere in Philippians, Paul's patience in the face of those who think and act "otherwise" reflects neither confidence in his own rhetorical power nor in the reasonable nature of those he is addressing. Rather, it reflects a confidence in God's promises in Christ to maintain the church, which is itself a gift from God, until that time when Christ will perfect it.

In v. 16 Paul shifts from the second person plural back to the first person plural with which he began v. 15. Having conceded that the Philippians may have yet to adopt his perspective fully, he redirects their attention to what he and they have already attained, urging them to "keep in step" with this pattern of thinking, acting, and feeling. This notion of "keeping in step" draws

---

13. See Reed, *Discourse Analysis*, 268, for a thorough accounting of the evidence in the papyri.

on the military image of keeping in line or in step.[14] It speaks of a common pattern of behavior, conformed to a particular standard.[15] Paul is calling the Philippians to manifest a particular pattern of practical reasoning. Moreover, to the extent that he and they have yet to manifest it fully, they should at least continue to hold fast to what they have already attained.[16] Paul's use of the first person plural here indicates that the standard of thinking, feeling, and acting to which he calls the Philippians is the same standard to which he himself is called. "What he is therefore calling them to is to live in conformity to the gospel as that has been spelled out repeatedly in their hearing, and as it has now been repeated in the Christ narrative in 2:6-11 and in his own that has just preceded (vv. 4-14). What he and they have already 'attained' is an understanding of the gospel in which the life of the Crucified One is the paradigm for those who would be his followers. . . ."[17] This admonition to keep in step with the pattern they have already attained nicely leads to Paul's directive to the Philippians to join together in imitating him. Thus, in v. 17 Paul is primarily explicating how one keeps in step with what one has already attained.

Elsewhere Paul also calls congregations to be imitators of him (1 Cor 4:16; 11:1), of him and his colleagues (1 Thess 1:6; cf. 2:13). All these are exemplars to be imitated because they properly manifest a Christ-focused pattern of life.[18] Here Paul calls on the Philippians to "join together" in imitating him. This continues the tone established in chs. 1 and 2 and most recently in 3:16, in which Paul and the Philippians are seen as fellow participants in the life of discipleship, struggling toward a common goal.

While a call to "imitate me" may strike modern ears as arrogant, the imitation of exemplars is a crucial element in the life of discipleship. It would

---

14. See a similar usage in Gal 6:16. Also see Bockmuehl, *Philippians,* 228; Fee, *Philippians,* 360.

15. Indeed, the Majority text makes this notion of a common standard explicit when it inserts "Let us keep in step with the same standard, adopting the same pattern of thinking, feeling, and acting (φρονεῖν/phronein)." While this seems to be a correct understanding of the passage, it is doubtful that such an addition represents the original.

16. In 2 Cor 10:14 the same Greek verb translated here as "attained" is used to refer to reaching a certain geographical point. In Rom 9:31 the same verb refers to attaining a certain level of conduct.

17. Fee, *Philippians,* 361. This agenda seems so obviously constructive in its intent that one does not have to follow Fee in suggesting that some in the congregation had "lost their focus."

18. Elsewhere in the Pauline corpus imitation language appears in 2 Thess 3:7, 9 where the Thessalonians are urged to imitate Paul's pattern of working for a living. In Eph 5:1 the Ephesians are called to be "imitators of God." Such language also appears in Heb 6:12; 13:7; and 3 John 11.

have been particularly so for those early Christians, such as the Philippians, who could not simply have opened their New Testament to see what Jesus would have done. Even having a textual account of Jesus' words and deeds does not always provide a self-evident guide to what we should do. For Paul to write a brief memo to the Philippians calling them simply "to order their life in a manner worthy of the gospel of Christ" (cf. 1:27) would have been of little help. We have every indication that the Philippians already were disposed toward such a life. They needed further guidance on what such a life might look like in their particular context. The best way to see this would be by observing Paul and others like him who were involved in the same struggle as the Philippians (cf. 1:30).

According to Paul's description of such a life, both here in ch. 3 and earlier in the epistle, it is clear that such a life demands the acquisition and display of a variety of skills, disciplines, and habits of thinking, feeling and acting. As with any complex practice we can only hope to acquire these skills, disciplines, and habits to the extent that we submit ourselves to the example of those more advanced in the practice. Hence, for Paul and for all Christians, the only arrogance surrounding the language of imitation would be the arrogance of those so formed by the ethos of individualism that they think they can walk the path of discipleship without observing, learning from, and imitating those who are already farther down that path.[19]

Recently, scholars such as Elizabeth Castelli have voiced more significant concerns with the language of imitation.[20] Castelli examined Paul's discourse of imitation from the perspective of the French philosopher Michel Foucault. In that light, she makes two interrelated points about imitation language in Paul. First, it works as part of a discourse of power, reinscribing and naturalizing certain configurations of power within the Pauline congregations. Second, the logic of imitation moves to eliminate difference as one party moves toward becoming the same as or identical with the imitated party: "The favored movement is from difference toward similarity — or, ideally, and absolutely, toward sameness. Sameness itself becomes a more highly valued quality, and it is a quality which automatically inheres in the model in the mimetic relationship of model-copy."[21] Castelli worries that this version of imitation works as part of a process of homogenization in which the less powerful are forced into the likeness of the more powerful.

19. Stanley Hauerwas makes this same case in his essay, "The Politics of Church: How We Lay Bricks and Make Disciples," in *After Christendom,* 93-112.

20. See E. Castelli, *Imitating Paul.*

21. Castelli, *Imitating Paul,* 21.

Those familiar with the life of almost any contemporary institution will recognize the force of Castelli's argument. It is important to remember, however, that Paul's language about imitation fits within his larger purpose of forming particular types of thinking, feeling, and acting. His explicit language about imitation in 3:17 as well as his more implicit calls to imitate Christ, himself, Timothy, and Epaphroditus in chs. 1 and 2 all demand the exercise of practical reasoning. In fact, in regard to human action and belief, language about imitation cannot really operate without practical reasoning. This is because the sort of behavior called for can never be strictly identical with the exemplar to be imitated. Practical reasoning requires the discerning of similarities and differences between the exemplar and the particular contexts in which one tries to live in a manner appropriate to that exemplar. Practical reasoning allows one to discern the various ways one can be both in continuity with an example to be imitated and also different from the example. What one strives for is non-identical repetition based on analogies one draws between the exemplar and the context in which one finds oneself.[22]

For example, in 1:19-26 Paul offers his own reflections about his choice of life over death as a case of putting the needs of others before his own desires. He also presents Timothy's and Epaphroditus's actions as distinct, yet similar examples of that same disposition. Even the brief comments directed at Euodia and Syntyche offer an example — by means of antithesis — of this pattern of life. Of course, all these different examples are directed by and receive their intelligibility from the story of Christ in 2:6-11. The dispositions and pattern of life Paul desires for the Philippians can be displayed in a variety of ways that are both directed by Christ and conform to particular identities and contexts. There are both analogical continuity between these characters and individual and communal differentiation. Rather than a difference obliterating sameness, Paul's language of imitation in Philippians is designed to produce an ordered, harmonious diversity.

In the light of the sorts of challenges posed by scholars such as Castelli, it is clear that issues of imitation cannot be addressed apart from questions of ecclesiology. The particular nature and shape of Christian communities need to provide the context in which Paul and other saints can function in exemplary ways without at the same time requiring a stultifying homogeneity.

The peaceable self-donation characteristic of the inner life of the triune God provides a model for such harmoniously ordered diversity. The self-

---

22. Those familiar with John Milbank's *Theology and Social Theory* will recognize the debt I owe to that work in formulating the issues in this way. See also Catherine Pickstock's *After Writing*.

giving love of the three "persons" of the trinity establishes their difference while at the same time constituting their singular identity. This harmoniously ordered diversity is also dramatically displayed throughout the economy of salvation. For example, early in Genesis it becomes clear that God has always sought the blessing of all nations (Gen 12:1-3). Indeed, one of the marks of Israel's redemption would be the pilgrimage of the nations to the "mountain of the Lord, to the house of the God of Jacob; that he may teach us his ways and that we may walk in his paths" (Isa 2:2-3). Jesus uses the image of the messianic banquet in which many come from the east and west to sit at table with Abraham (Matt 8:5-11). Paul himself vociferously argued for the inclusion of Gentiles in the first Christian communities without requiring them to become Jews. Grafting the Gentiles into these local manifestations of redeemed Israel made two distinct peoples into one new body without requiring them to abandon their distinctiveness. The presence of these two diverse peoples, who were traditionally hostile toward each other, in the body of Christ was seen by theologians as diverse as Origen and Irenaeus as a concrete fulfillment of Isa. 2:1-4. Even though Christian communities from the first century to the present have often failed to embody rightly this aspect of the drama of salvation, the church is called both to bear witness to God's desire to draw the world back to God and to manifest this desire through word and deed in its common life.

In addition, the Pauline image of the church as the body of Christ provides further conceptual tools for imagining how the church might manifest a common life that cultivates imitation of the saints without simply requiring a difference-obliterating sameness. The diversity of the members of Christ's body is essential to its proper working. Yet if the head, Christ, does not discipline and coordinate the parts of the body, they become dysfunctional. To the extent that Christian communities provide not only a witness to God's redemption of the world but a foretaste of that redemption, they will be capable of manifesting a diversity marked by the peaceable harmony of those who have been made into one body in Christ. To the extent that they fail to display God's redeeming purposes for the world, any diversity they sustain within their common life will tend to look like the violent struggle of disconnected individuals, each struggling with and policing each other.

As I noted above, the sorts of imitation Paul calls for in v. 17 requires multiple acts of discernment and practical reasoning. As vv. 18-19 go on to show, one crucial act of discernment is to distinguish between those like Paul, Timothy, and Epaphroditus who walk according to a particular pattern and those who walk as "enemies of the cross of Christ." An enormous amount of print has been devoted to identifying these "enemies." Typical questions have focused on whether these were members of the congregation or outsiders. Were they related to the "dogs" warned against in 3:2? Are they foreshadowed by the discussion of those who preach from false motives in ch. 1?

Presumably, the Philippians knew to whom Paul was referring, but we are left to speculate if we wish to identify these characters with any precision. The need to identify these characters with a specific group that was troubling the Philippians increases in direct proportion to the degree to which one treats the epistle as a mirror, seeing constructive claims as direct responses to particular problems in the Philippian church. Nevertheless, whether Paul has specific characters in view or is just offering a friendly warning against certain courses of action, it is relevant to try to tease out the implications and inferences in Paul's description here. I will, however, try to keep speculation to a minimum.

The characters Paul talks about "walk" as enemies of the cross. Their practical reasoning is based on earthly things (again, using φρονεῖν/ *phronein*).[23] These two descriptions would seem to indicate that Paul is not talking so much about false teaching (as in Galatians) as a false pattern of thought and action.[24] We also know that Paul has noted the existence of characters like this many times to the Philippians. This would seem to indicate third parties who are not obviously part of the Philippian congregation. Further, the reference to "weeping" here indicates Paul's grief at the presence of such characters.[25] That Paul would weep over such people would indicate that he expected them to know better. That is, these are people who bear the name "Christian" yet are enemies of the cross of Christ.[26]

In the context of Philippians as a whole, being an "enemy of the cross of Christ" would imply that one rejected or opposed the claims made in 2:6-11. For example, it seems improbable that an enemy of the cross could recognize that the character of God was revealed in the self-emptying of the one who was equal to God or that the resurrection is God's vindication of Christ's obe-

---

23. Fee, *Philippians*, 368 n. 26, rightly takes this clause as modifying "many" in v. 18 against Lightfoot, *Philippians*, 156, and others who see this clause as having no grammatical connection to its context. Compare also the admonition in Col 3:2 to "set your minds (φρονεῖτε/ *phroneite*) on the things above" rather than on "earthly things."

24. So Fee, *Philippians*, 367. Obviously, it would be unwise to draw too sharp a distinction between "teaching" and "practice" in this respect. Paul's concerns here do, however, differ from his concerns in Galatians.

25. The reference to "tears" here should not be taken as an indication that Paul is speaking about non-believing Jews as in Rom 9:2. Rather, it is an image Paul uses elsewhere to describe his sorrow over various matters (cf. 2 Cor 2:4; 2 Tim 1:4; also Acts 20:19, 31).

26. See Acts 20:30-31, where Paul warns "with tears" of believers who will distort the truth.

dient life and his death on the cross. Further, if one reads this designation, "enemy of the cross of Christ," in the light of 1 Cor. 1:18–2:10, it indicates that "to be an enemy of the Cross means to trust in human wisdom and power rather than in God's redemption accomplished through apparent weakness and folly of the crucified Messiah. It is to adopt a stance, in other words, which is precisely the opposite of the one that Paul outlined in verses 4-14."[27] Moreover, such characters would probably reject the view that Paul, Timothy, and Epaphroditus are exemplars to be imitated. Indeed, cruciform living would be anathema to "enemies of the cross." In practice, one would expect that enemies of the cross would seek to avoid suffering that might come their way as the result of their convictions about Christ.

Paul then goes on to claim that "their end is destruction, their God is their belly, their glory is their shame." Scholars interested in providing a comprehensive identification of these enemies of the cross devote a great deal of space to explicating nuances and overtones of each of these designations. Much of the speculation has had to do with the terms "belly" (κοιλία/*koilia*) and "shame" (αἰσχύνη/*aischynē*). A common interpretive move going back as far as the patristic period is to take these terms as euphemistic references to Jewish food laws and circumcision.[28] Bockmuehl notes, however, that "the immediate context suggests no other connection with Jewish Christians; Paul never equates Judaizing dietary observance with idolatry; and the respective terms are used nowhere else in this allusive sense."[29] Moreover, Paul never refers to circumcision as shameful even if he thinks Gentile believers ought not be circumcised.[30] In addition, these terms can equally, if not better, refer to idolatry, gluttony, and illicit sexual activity, vices typically ascribed to pagans.[31]

Rather than referring to a narrow set of practices, it seems better to take these three designations as a whole to refer to the disordered perceptions and pursuits to be expected from those who are enemies of the cross, whose practical reasoning is guided by earthly concerns. Presumably, since these characters identify themselves as believers, they would claim that their proper end is salvation, that they worship the one true God in spirit and in truth, that they ascribe glory to the same things Christ would find glorious. Paul counters that they fundamentally misperceive their true end, the nature of God, and that to which glory should be ascribed. Rather than manifesting a pattern of

27. Bockmuehl, *Philippians,* 230.

28. See Fee, *Philippians,* 372 n. 39, for a list of some of the ancient and modern adherents of this view. To that list one can also add Aquinas.

29. Bockmuehl, *Philippians,* 231.

30. See de Vos, *Church and Community Conflicts,* 273.

31. De Vos, *Church and Community Conflicts,* 273,

practical reasoning guided by the heavenly call of God, their practical reasoning is earthbound. The problem is not that they lack practical reasoning, that they are not mindful of their true end, or that they are indifferent to God and matters of glory. Instead, recognizing the importance of these things, they fail to order them properly in the light of the cross.[32] Although they are not the same characters, they manifest the same flawed perceptions as the opponents mentioned in 1:28-29.

Whoever these believers are, we must assume that as Christians they did not set out to become enemies of the cross, neither would they have characterized themselves that way. Rather, Paul claims that because of the way they "walk," because of their distorted patterns of thinking, feeling, and acting, they have become enemies of the cross. Through a set of decisions and actions unknown to us, which probably seemed benign (if not good) to them, they now find themselves in a position where they are no longer capable of rightly recognizing God or God's purposes for them. It is crucial for contemporary Christians to recognize the ease with which this can happen. If we think of these characters as people who woke up one morning and simply decided to become enemies of the cross, we will not be concerned with Paul's admonition because it could not conceivably apply to us.

Instead, we should understand that these Christians were seeking to live faithful lives. Through various practices, lack of proper attention to the ways in which seemingly good decisions misdirected their lives, through a failure to have their thoughts, feelings, and actions appropriately directed by Christ, they slowly and imperceptibly became enemies of the cross. It is only when we see these people in this light that we can begin to imagine how easily friends of the cross can be transformed into enemies of the cross and to see how Paul's admonitions here could apply to us.

In v. 20 Paul contrasts[33] his account of those who are enemies of the cross with a characterization of those who live according to the pattern laid out by Paul and others like him. If the enemies of the cross are characterized by a pattern of practical reasoning directed by earthly concerns, Paul and those like him recognize that their allegiance is to a heavenly commonwealth.

---

32. Though this passage operates more by implication and inference than 1 Cor 1:18–2:16 does, the logic seems to work the same way.

33. The γάρ/*gar* here is problematic. The context gives every indication that Paul is introducing a contrast between the account in vv. 18-19 and vv. 20-21. Hence, many English versions translate γάρ/*gar* as "but." As Fee, *Philippians*, 375 n. 1 and 377 n. 13, is at pains to show, there is little lexical evidence for this. The solution seems to be to translate γάρ/*gar* as "for" and explain that its force is both contrastive and explanatory. Bockmuehl, *Philippians*, 223, and Hawthorne, *Philippians*, 169, concur.

The central term here, "commonwealth" (πολίτευμα/*politeuma*), has a variety of senses. Two particular ways in which the term is used are relevant for this passage. First, the word was often used to refer to a colony of relocated veterans.[34] The Philippians would have been particularly attentive to this in the light of their own local history. Secondly, Philo uses similar language to note that Jews are native citizens of the heavenly promised land and merely sojourners on earth.[35] Both uses help us understand this passage. Paul invites the Philippian Christians to see that they, too, are part of a commonwealth. They, too, have a distinct political identity, which provides a focus for their allegiance and commitments. Unlike their neighbors, however, their allegiance is to a polity completely outside the reaches of the Roman Empire, even though they remain spatially located within it.[36]

Those who are part of this heavenly commonwealth eagerly await a Savior, the Lord Jesus Christ. Paul normally uses the verb translated "we eagerly await" (ἀπεκδεχόμεθα/*apekdechometha*) of eschatological matters (cf. 1 Cor 1:7; Gal 5:5; Rom 8:19, 23, 25). This leads many commentators to focus on eschatological concerns about when the Savior will come. I think these concerns, while important, are secondary to the significant christological and political implications of the clause. In terms of coming to grips with the christological issues it is interesting to note that Paul rarely uses the term "Savior" (σωτήρ/*sōtēr*). Outside the Pastorals, it appears only here and in Eph 5:23. In general, the word was used to refer to one who delivers from adversity whether material, military, or spiritual.

In order to bring out some of the christological implications of Paul's terminology here it will be useful to reflect on a passage such as Isa 45:20-25, part of which is quoted in Phil 2:10-11 and applied to the Lord Jesus Christ. The noun "Savior" and the verb "save" play a significant role in the Isaiah passage, where God calls Israel to abandon all idols and to recognize that only God can save the nation. Only in God will Israel triumph, and God will, indeed, bring

---

34. See G. Lüderitz, "What Is the Politeuma?"

35. See *De Confusione linguarum* 78 and *De Gigantibus* 61.

36. Fee, as in his earlier comments on 1:27, reads Paul as asserting a dual citizenship. "Paul is not herewith renouncing their common citizenship in the earthly 'commonwealth' of Rome; on the contrary, that citizenship is what will make the present sentence ring the changes for the Philippians" (379). Even if γάρ in this verse does not grammatically indicate a sharp contrast, the thought here is clearly of a decisive contrast, calling the Philippians to a counter-politics, not a dual set of allegiances. In this case, Bockmuehl, p. 234, is more to the point, "Paul's aim here is to call the Philippians to *forget* the human status and achievements that lie behind and to shape their lives and aspirations in keeping with the heavenly counter-commonwealth of Christ to which they now belong."

about such triumph. In fact, there will be a universal recognition that there is no one like the God of Israel. All will ultimately submit to the Lord.

I do not mean to argue that Paul necessarily had Isaiah 45 in mind when he wrote Phil 3:20. Rather, I point to this passage in Isaiah because it has already played a role in Paul's discourse about Christ and because its claims about God, the Savior, are widely repeated in the OT. Hence, whether or not Paul has Isaiah 45 in mind, it is clear that by identifying "the Lord Jesus Christ" as "the Savior" he is ascribing to Jesus a role and status which the OT reserves for God alone. Paul's emphasis here is not so much on *when* the Savior appears, but *who* the Savior is.

The rich christological assertions here also serve to reinforce the political claims of the first part of the verse. Although Paul is not particularly fond of the term "Savior," in the Roman Empire the emperor was sometimes referred to as "savior."[37] This would not have been lost on the Philippians. The Christian commonwealth also has a Savior, the Lord Jesus Christ. Just as the heavenly commonwealth serves as a counter to the commonwealth provided by Rome, so Christians seek and anticipate salvation from a different source. Thus Paul further invites the Philippians to see the sharp alternative their commonwealth provides to that of their neighbors. As a gloss on this verse, the fifth chapter of the *Epistle to Diognetus* nicely articulates the differences that Paul is getting at. "Yet while living in Greek and barbarian cities, according as each obtained his lot, and following local customs, both in clothing and food and in the rest of life, they show forth the wonderful and confessedly strange (παράδοξαν/*paradoxan*) character of the constitution of their own citizenship."[38]

As ch. 3 closes Paul articulates the nature of the salvation which Christ will bring and which citizens of the heavenly commonwealth eagerly await. Like the salvation described in Isa 45:20-25, Paul indicates that Christ, the Lord and Savior, will ultimately subject all things to himself. His dominion will be unchallenged and universally recognized.[39] This verse reiterates the claims made about Christ in 2:10-11. Moreover, Paul's claims here echo 1 Cor 15:27; Eph 1:22; and Heb 2:6-9, all of which Christians have traditionally taken as christological explications of Ps 8:4-6. What Caesar and all his modern analogues seek to do, Christ will actually do. It is equally important to recog-

---

37. For a brief introduction to this matter see the excursus in Witherington, *Friendship and Finances*, 99-102.

38. *Diognetus* 5:4.

39. "All things" (τὰ πάντα/*ta panta*) is a common Pauline formulation to refer to the whole of the created order. See 1 Cor 15:27-28, with which this passage has many conceptual parallels; 1 Cor 8:6 (two occurrences); Rom 11:36.

nize, however, that the subjection of all things to Christ is not some added benefit bestowed on the resurrected one. Rather, it is fitting for all things to be subject to Christ because he is their creator. The subjection spoken of here is not the imposition of a new and more powerful force upon an ultimately recalcitrant creation. Rather, this is the reconciliation of all things to their proper Lord, a reconciliation for which all creation expectantly longs (Rom 8:18-25).

Not only will all things be subjected to Christ, but the same power that allows him to do that will also lead him to "transform" our bodies so that they "conform" to his glorious body.[40] In much briefer terms than we find in 1 Cor 15:42-57, Paul articulates what appears to be a very similar account of the resurrection body. Both passages leave us with many questions about how and when these things will take place and what these bodies will be like. Aquinas gives one of the best and most succinct accounts: "The body of Christ, of course, is glorified by the glory of His divinity; and He merited this by His passion. Therefore, whoever shares in the power of the divinity by grace and imitates the passion of Christ shall be glorified."[41] It is this integral connection between Christ's glorification and his passion that makes being an enemy of the cross so dangerous to one's position before God. This account notwithstanding, at this point Christians face a mystery. That is, they can and must affirm that this will happen without being able to explain fully how it will happen.

If we read this passage in the light of Paul's claim about magnifying Christ in his body in 1:20, it also reinforces the view that, despite the efforts of the Roman Empire and all other empires to control the bodies of their subjects, they cannot do so with Christian bodies. Any humiliation an empire might place on the bodies of the faithful will be transformed and redeemed by the power of the resurrected Christ.

By the end of this passage it is clear that Paul wants the Philippians to adopt a very particular pattern of thinking, acting, and feeling in their common life. Moreover, the Philippians clearly have a choice between the pattern displayed by Paul and those like him and the pattern displayed by the enemies of the cross. This is not simply a choice between abstract theological constructs. Paul calls on the Philippians to recognize that the patterns of thinking, feeling, and acting he desires for them are constituent parts of an alterna-

---

40. It is common for scholars to note what they take to be linguistic parallels between v. 21 and the language of 2:6-8 (e.g., Fee, *Philippians*, 382; Bockmuehl, *Philippians*, 235-36). If one looks at how these words actually work in these passages as well as the very obvious semantic differences between the relevant terms, it is clear that 3:21 is not picking up the language of 2:6-8 in any significant way.

41. Aquinas, 109.

tive culture or an alternative politics. He does not call the Philippians to a dual citizenship. Rather, he calls them out of a false politics ruled by a false savior and directed by an earthbound practical reason into a new political body ruled by the Lord Jesus Christ, the true Savior. This is a politics governed by a practical reason shaped by Christ's own person and work as exemplified in the life and practice of Paul and those who live according to that Christ-focused pattern.

4:1-3

1 So then, my brothers and sisters whom I love and long for, my joy and my crown, in this way stand firm in the Lord, my beloved. 2 I implore Euodia and I implore Syntyche to adopt a common pattern of thinking, feeling, and acting in the Lord. 3 Yes, and I ask you, my true companion, to help these women who have contended for the gospel with me along with Clement and the rest of my coworkers, whose names are in the book of life.

This short section of the epistle marks a slight shift in the argument. In 1:27–3:21 Paul has in various ways urged the Philippians to order their common life in a manner worthy of the gospel of Christ. There has been little basis in these admonitions for the assumption that the Philippians had abandoned the gospel or were on the verge of doing so. Rather, Paul both advocates and displays a set of habits and dispositions which will help the Philippians in their struggle to live faithfully before God in a context that is hostile to them. These habits and dispositions receive their intelligibility from the story of Christ narrated in 2:6-11. They are exemplified for the Philippians in the lives of people like Timothy and Epaphroditus and, most significantly, in the ways Paul comports himself as one who is engaged in the same struggle as the Philippians. As ch. 4 begins we find Paul offering expressions of deep affection for the Philippians. From this basis of affection, Paul moves to admonish directly two members of the congregation. Thus he moves here from a specific argument to an application of that argument (note the similar structure in 2:12-30).

Before he begins any application Paul characterizes his relationship with the Philippians in terms of great affection. He calls them "beloved" (twice!) and expresses his longing for them. This expression of longing for the Philippians echoes 1:8. Such expressions of longing are common among separated friends.[1] As Paul continues he calls the Philippians his "joy and crown."

---

1. See Stowers, "Friends and Enemies," 109.

This language closely parallels 1 Thess 2:19, in which Paul refers to the Thessalonians as his "hope, joy, and crown of boasting before Jesus at his coming." For Paul to speak of the Philippians as his joy seems appropriate enough given the overall tone of the letter. When Paul speaks here of them as his crown, he is picking up the thought, first expressed in 2:16, that Paul's status on the day of Christ will be shaped by the ways in which the Philippians succeed or fail in "holding fast to the word of life." In 2:16 Paul addressed the possibility that the Philippians might not succeed in this. Here he is supremely confident. Indeed, as Bockmuehl aptly states, "Verse 1 admirably captures the spirit of Paul's relationship with the Philippians throughout this letter and should in itself suffice to caution against theories of serious problems either within the church or in their friendship with Paul."[2] In the midst of this confidence, however, we modern readers can miss the strong sense in which Paul and the Philippians are accountable to each other. As I mentioned earlier with regard to 2:16, Paul's stance before Christ seems inextricably bound up with the state of the Philippian congregation. If we shared this sense of accountability we would also share in Paul's concerns over divisions within the body of Christ. We are far too indifferent to divisions within the body that do not directly involve us. If we saw our stance before God as bound up with the lives of others as strongly as Paul does, we would also share in Paul's concerns over divisions within the body.

Paul calls on his beloved Philippians to "stand firm." This admonition reaches back to 1:27. The adverbial phrase, "in this way," may point back only as far as 3:20-21,[3] or it may indicate all that follows from 1:27.[4] In any case, it is clear that the preceding admonitions have been about "standing firm." Hence, in some respects 4:1 really wraps up the preceding section before Paul moves to address a particular issue in the Philippian community.

At the same time the summary admonition of 4:1 to stand firm also leads into Paul's direct admonitions to two specific characters, Euodia and Syntyche, in 4:2. There is much scholarly debate about how central the dissension between Euodia and Syntyche is to the epistle as a whole.[5] While addressing Euodia and Syntyche clearly is one of Paul's purposes, taking this as his primary purpose makes it difficult to account for so much of the epistle that is either explicitly or implicitly directed to the entire congregation.

---

2. Bockmuehl, *Philippians*, 237.

3. So Bockmuehl, *Philippians*.

4. So Fee, *Philippians*, 389, and this seems to be the implication of Lightfoot's position (*Philippians*, 158). This is against Hawthorne, *Philippians*, 178, who sees the adverb as a reference to what follows.

5. See views in Fee, *Philippians*, 389.

Moreover, there is no indication that Euodia and Syntyche are either connected with those who preach from improper motives (1:15-18), the "dogs" (3:2), or the "enemies of the cross" (3:18).

Paul's plea to these two women to "adopt a common pattern of thinking, feeling, and acting in the Lord" (again using the phrase τὸ αὐτὸ φρονεῖν/ *to auto phronein*) indicates that there has been some sort of rupture in their relationship that needs attention.[6] Moreover, although language about adopting a common pattern of thinking, feeling, and acting is conventional in addressing the state of a friendship, it also directly repeats Paul's general admonition to the community in 2:2. That is, this is not simply a call to "be friends again." Rather, Paul is calling these two to display a set of habits and dispositions that he considers to be basic to living faithfully before God. The common pattern of thinking, feeling, and acting that Paul advocates here is shaped and directed by Euodia's and Syntyche's common connection to the Lord. Theirs is a friendship constituted and formed by a common friendship with Christ. Hence, a rupture in the friendship between Euodia and Syntyche also affects their friendship with Christ.

Further, even though we know very little about these two characters, they seem to have been influential members of the community.[7] Therefore, discord in their relationship would also have repercussions for the life of a community whose prospects for ordering their common life in a manner worthy of the gospel are directly tied to their adoption of unified patterns of thinking, feeling, and acting (1:27–2:4).

While Paul does not take sides in this dispute himself, he does ask his "true[8] comrade" to aid Euodia and Syntyche in reconciling themselves in the Lord.[9] While we do not really know who this character is, we should not be

6. As Reed, *Discourse Analysis*, 268, indicates, this language is typically used to talk about the health of a friendship. See also 2 Cor 13:11. Fee, *Philippians*, 390, suggests that the repetition of "implore" with each name indicates that Paul himself is not taking sides in the dispute.

7. Bockmuehl, *Philippians*, 238, suggests that these women might have had oversight of such crucial matters as hospitality, finances, or allocation of money for poor. Several authors note that women in Macedonia seem to have exercised an unusually large amount of influence. Moreover, in Acts 16 it is Lydia who seems to be the central figure in the founding of the church in Philippi, and in Thessalonica (another Macedonian city) Luke claims that some of the initial members of the church included "not a few of the leading women" (Acts 17:4, 12).

8. The Greek term γνήσιε/*gnēsie* deals with legitimacy, so "loyal" and "faithful" are not really appropriate translations. Rather, we should use "genuine" or "true." See the use of γνησίως/ *gnēsiōs* in 2:20; and Fee, *Philippians*, 392 n.40.

9. There is no evidence that σύζυγος/*syzygos* ("companion") was ever used as a proper name. Sometimes ἡ σύζυγος/*hē syzygos* is used to refer to a wife (e.g., *Testament of Reuben* 4:1). This led some early commentators to argue that Paul is here addressing his wife (e.g., Clement,

diverted by our speculations to such a degree that we forget that Euodia and Syntyche are the focus here. Paul's comrade is simply asked to assist them. Paul then suggests why he values Euodia and Syntyche and seeks their reconciliation. They have been partners with him in contending for the gospel. In 1:27 Paul used a similar athletic metaphor to indicate the ways in which the Philippians as a community might "stand firm." Moreover, as 1:27 makes clear success in "contending for the faith of the gospel" is closely tied to standing united in one spirit. In the light of Paul's earlier comments in 1:27 then, one must assume that the success that Euodia and Syntyche have enjoyed in their common struggle for the gospel alongside Paul, Clement, and Paul's other co-workers can only continue if they are reconciled and come again to share a common pattern of thought and action.

While we do not know who Clement and "the rest of my coworkers" are, we do learn that their names — along with Euodia's and Syntyche's — are written "in the book of life."[10] While this is an unusual image for Paul to use, it is not uncommon elsewhere in Scripture to find the image of a book used to describe one's membership among those who will inherit eternal life (cf. Exod 32:32-33: "the book you [God] have written"; Ps 69:28: "book of the living"; Dan 12:1; Luke 10:20: "your names have been written in heaven"; Rev 3:5; 13:8; 17:8; 20:12, 15; 21:27).

It is very easy to recognize how little we know of the details of this situation and of the characters involved and to stop at that. But several significant matters underlying this brief section ought to be mentioned. We see here an example of a member of Christ's body admonishing two other members to be reconciled with each other. This may count as the earliest glimpse of the pattern, described by Jesus in Matt 18:15-20, of how Christians who have sinned against each other are to engage in the process of reconciliation. Whether this is historically the case or not, we see here that for Paul as for Jesus the unity of the body of Christ is not dependent on the moral perfection of disciples. Rather, it depends on the commitment of Jesus' followers to the hard work of confession, the seeking and offering of forgiveness, and the practices of rec-

---

Stromateis 3.53.1). Fee, *Philippians,* 394, takes this person to be Luke on the basis of Acts, where the "'we' narrative takes Luke to Philippi in Acts 16, where it leaves off, until Paul's return to Philippi some four to six years later in 20:1-5." I am happy enough to follow this line of speculation as long as we recognize that it is highly speculative and that judgments here cannot be used as the basis for further judgments about the text of Philippians or the situation of the Philippian congregation.

10. Fee, *Philippians,* 395, asserts but does not show that "the context demands that they are fellow-Philippians." Without further evidence, it appears that all the context demands is that Clement was someone known to the Philippians.

onciliation. It should not be surprising to read that Christians and Christian leaders in particular fall out with each other. Paul does not seem shocked by this, nor does he assume that their disagreements are unjustified. Nevertheless, they must be reconciled; they must recapture a common pattern of thinking, feeling, and acting. This is essential for their own friendship, for their friendship with Christ, and for the continuing health of the Philippian congregation. Paul's admonition assumes that practices of forgiveness and reconciliation in the Philippian congregation are in good working order. Otherwise he would have no basis for calling these two to be reconciled and would have no reason to expect his "true companion" to be able to help them. Rather, his entire admonition here depends on the proper working of these practices in the Philippian congregation.

What we see in this brief section is that despite the fact that Euodia and Syntyche are at odds with each other, Paul assumes that the common life of the Philippian church is capable of surviving this disagreement and generating the practices needed to reconcile these two leaders. In addition, Paul's tone of urgency here reinforces the importance of the unity of the body of Christ. For Paul, and for all Christians, the unity of the church is not an optional extra to be pursued if time allows. Christian division is a serious wound to the body of Christ. We should feel its sting in the same way Paul does. At this point, having offered here a very specific admonition, Paul will now move on to offer some more general admonitions and exhortations to the congregation as a whole.

4:4-9

4 Rejoice in the Lord always, again, I say rejoice. 5 Let your forbearance be known to all people. The Lord is near. 6 Do not be anxious over anything, but in everything, by prayer and supplication with thanksgiving, let your requests be made known to God. 7 And the peace of God, which surpasses all understanding, will guard your hearts and minds in Christ Jesus.

8 Henceforth, brothers and sisters, whatever is true, whatever is noble, whatever is just, whatever is pure, whatever is pleasing, whatever is admirable, if there is anything morally excellent and anything praiseworthy, focus your attention on these things. 9 Continue to do the things you have been taught and you have received and have heard and seen in me, and the God of peace will be with you.

In this section Paul presents a set of imperatives directed toward specific dispositions and actions he wishes the Philippians to display. The clipped, almost terse, style here is similar to that found in the concluding sections of 1 Corinthians (16:13) and 2 Corinthians (13:11) and most resembles 1 Thess 5:16-22. It is tempting to treat Paul's remarks here as an almost offhand invocation of conventional standards of piety. Indeed, on the surface, vv. 4-7 reflect standards of piety with which almost no Christian (or Jew) would disagree. Moreover, an initial account of the exhortations in vv. 8-9 might seem perfectly acceptable to most Greco-Roman readers concerned with virtuous living. While I do not wish to deny the apparent conventionality of Paul's desires for the Philippians here, a closer look at these exhortations in the light of what has preceded in the epistle will show that Paul is advocating something much more substantial, demanding, and even subversive for the Philippians.

Paul's call to "rejoice in the Lord always" formally echoes the language of 3:1. By this point in the epistle, however, he has already indicated that the Philippians' commonwealth stands as an alternative political body, ruled by a different Lord, to that body constituted by the citizens of Philippi under the dominion of Caesar. Hence we may expect that Paul is directing the Philippians' joy in a way that will be different from that followed by their pagan neighbors.

Further, if one looks at the way Paul speaks about joy and rejoicing in the epistle as a whole, it becomes clear that he shapes the notion of joy in fairly precise ways. For example, in 1:18 he rejoiced in the fact that the gospel is preached despite the suspect motives of some. In 2:17-18 he spoke of the mutual joy that he and the Philippians will have in the midst of suffering if they hold fast to the word of life. In 4:10 Paul will express joy for the Philippians' gift because of what this gift will do for the Philippians, not for him. Further, Epaphroditus is to be welcomed with joy because he has risked his life for the work of Christ (2:28-30). In all these cases, joy is not so much a spontaneous emotion as a response formed in those who can read the economy of God's activity in particular ways and are able to act in conformity with that unfolding story. Joy is the appropriate response when one rightly perceives the unfolding of God's drama of salvation even in the midst of suffering and opposition.[1] Hence, Paul can claim in 2:2 that the Philippians will fulfill his joy if they come to adopt a common pattern of perceiving and acting, a pattern exemplified by the story of Christ in 2:6-11. Indeed, it is Paul's conviction in 1:25 that one of the points of remaining in this life is for the Philippians' advancement and joy in the faith.

---

1. Barth, *Philippians*, 120, writes that "joy in Philippians is a defiant 'Nevertheless!' which Paul sets as a full stop against the Philippians' anxiety." Whether the Philippians were anxious or not, Barth rightly captures Paul's rather unconventional understanding of joy here.

Thus, one can grant that it is conventional for friends to rejoice in each other. As Paul describes matters in the course of the epistle, however, the sorts of things in which the Philippians should rejoice in the Lord are the sorts of misfortunes that might terminate most friendships. Rejoicing in the Lord requires that one be formed to perceive things in very particular ways, ways that run counter to the conventional patterns of perception. Further, it would appear then that rejoicing is not something that Christians will simply do as a matter of course. Instead, it results from a disciplined formation of our ways of thinking and acting in the world. For Paul, then, rejoicing in the Lord always is not so much a spontaneous eruption of emotion as the sign that the Philippians are being formed in the ways he has advocated.

Paul's discussion here should remind Christians that joy, one of the fruits of the Spirit enumerated in Gal 5:22, is not an end in itself but a byproduct. In particular it is what results when one is able to recognize the presence and movement of God in specific circumstances. Joy can then testify to a person's or a community's achievement of the appropriate ways of thinking, feeling, and acting in the world. Such joy is focused not on the achievement but on the recognition of God's abiding presence even in the midst of suffering.

Paul's subsequent exhortation, "Let your forbearance be known to all people," would indicate that the formation that enables Christians to rejoice in the Lord always manifests itself to those outside the community in terms of "forbearance." The term "forbearance" appears in Paul only here and in the Pastorals. In 1 Tim 3:3 and Tit 3:2 it is contrasted with being "quarrelsome" to indicate a gentle agreeableness. That may be what Paul has in mind here. Alternatively, given that Paul has just called the Philippians to rejoice, and that Paul seems to tie the practice of rejoicing to a proper perception of God's presence in the midst of suffering and opposition, I think it more likely that here Paul is using the term in the way it appears in Wis 2:19.[2] There those who are persecuting the righteous say, "Let us test him with insult and torture so that we might find out his forbearance and test his patience." In this light, then, "forbearance" is directly tied to the ways in which the world perceives Christians who are facing opposition.[3]

Having urged the Philippians to rejoice in the Lord and to make their forbearance known to all, Paul then asserts, "the Lord is near." This might

2. Elsewhere in the LXX the term is most commonly used to describe the manner in which God deals with human failings (e.g., Ps 86:5, Baruch 2:27; Dan 3:42).

3. It is, no doubt, true that Christ is the primary example of this attribute. Nevertheless, I do not think that the use of the nominal form of this term in 2 Cor 10:1 points this way (against Bockmuehl, *Philippians*, 245). In this case, Paul is not talking about Christ's gentleness in the face of external opposition.

mean that the Philippians should rejoice and make their forbearance known because the Lord is near. This relies on a spatial image, echoing the claim in the Psalms that the "Lord is near those who call on him" (145:18; cf. 119:151). Alternatively, the claim that the Lord is near might introduce the call to prayer and thanksgiving in v. 6. This would result in a temporal image, echoing the NT idea (which has OT precedents) that the day of the Lord is near (see Rom 13:12; cf. Jas 5:8; Rev 1:3; 22:10).[4] There seems to be little reason to force this passage in one of these two possible ways, since it works well both ways. As Bockmuehl notes, ". . . Paul's affirmation that the Lord is near, both spatially and temporally, is the assurance that underpins the exhortations in 4.4-6 to joy and gentleness, to prayer and freedom from worry."[5]

Because the Lord is near, the Philippians are not to "be anxious about anything." Many commentators argue that this brief exhortation stems from the Jesus traditions reflected in Matt 6:25-34 and Luke 12:22. In the Gospels Jesus seems primarily concerned with disciples' concerns over material goods. He calls his followers to live without such anxiety because the Father cares for them. In Philippians Paul's call to be free from anxiety seems more directed toward anxiety that results from living in a world hostile to Christianity.

The Philippians can be free from such anxiety because the Lord is near. They can call on God in prayer and with thanksgiving. Just as the command to be free from anxiety extends to all things, the Philippians are to make their requests known to God "in all things." In this context, there appears to be little discernible difference between the various terms Paul uses for prayer. Most English translations use comparable terms such as prayer, supplication, and petition.

One of the most striking things about the command to be free from anxiety is that, by connecting it to the command to pray, Paul makes it clear that freedom from anxiety is not a matter of self-mastery. Stoics, although they used a different vocabulary, also sought freedom from anxiety. This, however, could really be achieved only through a self-mastery which rendered one indifferent to the ups and downs of fortune. In contrast to this, Paul ties the Philippians' prospects for freedom from anxiety to their commitment to bringing their requests to God in prayer. Rather than seeking freedom from anxiety through self-mastery, Paul's admonition presumes that freedom from anxiety comes only through prayerful, grateful acknowledgment of dependence on God.

---

4. I am less persuaded that this text is similar to the plea "come, our Lord" found in this form in 1 Cor 16:22 and "come, Lord Jesus" in Rev 22:20. These utterances are pleas. Paul here in Philippians is making an assertion.

5. Bockmuehl, *Philippians*, 246.

This becomes clear in the subsequent verse where the peace of God is proposed as the alternative to anxiety. This peace of God "surpasses all understanding." Paul is probably not asserting here that God's peace transcends all human comprehension. If so, it is hard to understand how something humans cannot comprehend would provide a direct alternative to anxiety. Moreover, those commentators who see a link here with Eph 3:19 miss something crucial. There the love of Christ is said to surpass knowledge. This correctly assumes that human love can imitate incompletely the love of Christ without comprehending the full dimensions of that love. The Philippians are not called to imitate the peace of God. Rather the peace of God is offered to them. Paul is indicating that the peace of God surpasses the unbelieving mind, which, as Fee notes, "is full of anxiety because it cannot think higher than itself."[6] Aquinas understood this issue and noted, "As it [the peace of God] exists in heaven, it surpasses all the knowledge of the angels; but as it exists in the saints on earth, it surpasses all the knowledge of those who lack grace."[7] God's peace is the gracious antidote to anxiety. Such peace is not the result of increased force or the coercive imposition of one power's will on another. Rather, it results from prayer.

The peace of God, which comes through prayer, counters anxiety because it "guards believers' thoughts and hearts in Christ." The notion of guarding would have resonated with the Philippians because the garrison stationed there was charged with guarding the interests of the empire.[8] Throughout the epistle Paul's aim has been to form the Philippians' habits of thinking, perceiving, and acting in a particular way, a way appropriate to those who are in Christ. Having one's thoughts and hearts in Christ will generate a pattern of thought and action that will be distinctly different from (and often opposed to) the lives, expectations, and perceptions of those whose political allegiance is not to Christ. Paul's assertion here at the end of the epistle that the peace of God will protect their thoughts and hearts stands in sharp contrast to the coercive force which guards the citizens of Philippi in the name of the *pax Romana*. That peace can never be a true peace because it is not founded in the God of peace.

The next two verses serve to fill out the contours of the preceding demands.[9] Bockmuehl rightly conveys the connection with the previous verses

---

6. Fee, *Philippians*, 410. See also Lightfoot, *Philippians*, 161.

7. Aquinas, 115.

8. Bockmuehl, *Philippians*, 248; Fee, *Philippians*, 411 n. 58.

9. As Reed has pointed out, in epistolary literature τὸ λοιπόν/*to loipon* tends not to introduce the conclusion of a letter, but to close off a series of imperatives, as in 3:1. It is better, then, to translate the word as "henceforth" rather than "finally." See the discussion of 3:1 above as well as Reed, *Discourse Analysis*, 259 nn. 385-86.

when he writes, "Having just introduced the important but unanticipated notion that the peace of God will guard their 'hearts and thoughts' in Christ, it is entirely appropriate for Paul to expand a little further as to the practical implications of this moral and intellectual guardianship for Christian life in Roman Philippi."[10]

Paul calls the Philippians to consider a series of praiseworthy things: "whatever is true, noble, just, pure, pleasing, and admirable." These words would have described things, or actions, which, presumably, all people would favor. Who, for example, would be against truth? The subsequent clause, however, qualifies the preceding six terms, making it clear that not all applications of these terms refer to things which are truly "morally excellent" or "praiseworthy."[11] Paul, in effect, calls on the Philippians to discern from among the many ways words like "true," "just," and "pure" might be used that which is truly excellent or praiseworthy and to make those things the focus of their attention.[12]

It is useful to cover the discrete vocabulary used here, and I will do so. It is much more important to try to understand that Paul could have used six other equally positive terms to make exactly the same point. The terms in themselves are not self-interpreting. It is their application in specific ways in particular circumstances that reveals something significant about them.

As we will see, each of these terms has a fairly wide range of meaning. For Paul, God is the one who measures what is "true" (cf. Rom 1:18). Indeed, denying the truth about God is the basis for all idolatry. Earlier in Phil 1:18 Paul contrasts those who preach the gospel under false pretenses with those who preach it in truth (cf. Prov 22:21). Upholding the truth is basis for justice (Isa 59:14).

"Noble" was used widely in a variety of literature. In the Pastorals it designates that gravity which good leaders ought to exhibit (1 Tim 2:2; 3:8; Tit 2:7). In Prov 8:6 it designates the nobility that wisdom displays. There it is used in conjunction with "truth" and "justice." Aristotle used the term to describe the mean between obsequiousness and stubbornness.[13]

Paul uses the term "just" repeatedly for the righteousness of God. In Phil 1:7 he uses it to claim that his particular attitude toward the Philippians is

---

10. Bockmuehl, *Philippians*, 249.

11. Fee, *Philippians*, 416 n. 13, makes a very strong case for taking "moral excellence" and "praiseworthy" as qualifiers of the previous six attributes.

12. Of course, virtually all ancient moralists would have considered discerning what is actually good from what is only apparently good as a crucial task for anyone seeking to be virtuous.

13. *Ethica Eudemia* II.III.4.

just or right or fitting. In Greek literature the word had a very wide range of application.[14]

In the LXX "pure" is used of both ritual purity[15] and God's or an individual's integrity (Ps 11:6; Prov 20:9). In the NT it signifies both moral uprightness (2 Cor 7:11; 1 Tim 5:22, etc.) and chastity (2 Cor 11:2).

"Pleasing" occurs only here in the NT. In Esth 5:1 it is used to describe Esther's physical beauty. In Sir 4:7; 20:13 it refers to behavior and speech which would make one well loved by one's peers.

Finally, "admirable" occurs only here in the NT and is the only term of these six that does not appear in the LXX. In 2 Cor 6:8 Paul uses the nominal form of this word to speak of having a good reputation.

The widespread contexts in which these words were used in Paul's world make it clear that using them in regard to some person, thing, or action is to regard that person, thing, or action favorably. That is simply the way these words function in Greek. To call something "just," for example, is, at least, to approve of it. Failure to use the word this way would simply indicate that one did not know how to use the word. The problem is not with what the words mean but to what persons, things, or actions they are applied. Here one could expect a fairly large measure of disagreement. By suggesting that not all applications of these terms refer to things that genuinely are "morally excellent" and "praiseworthy," Paul is calling the Philippians to discern between persons, things, and actions which appear to be favorable and those that really are.

On the one hand, this qualification is significant in that it assumes that these six terms can be applied in theologically incorrect or at least highly contestable ways. Hence, in calling the Philippians to be discerning in regard to these things, Paul is not calling them to "take into account the best of their Greco-Roman heritage."[16] Neither is he speaking as a public theologian, "prepared to countenance Christian truth as *public* truth, relevant to a Christian ethic that can at least in part be formulated in openly accessible terms."[17] Rather, Paul recognizes that these terms can be used in diverse and sometimes incompatible ways. Take, for example, a hypothetical Christian martyr in Philippi. To her brothers and sisters in the Lord, she displays an exemplary attachment to the truth. Her death has a sort of nobility to it. Moreover, in these circumstances, hers is the only just action for a believer to take. To the Roman magistrates who execute her, she is a liar (or is deceived), stubborn, and un-

---

14. See BAGD, 195-96.

15. This is not the normal term for cultic purity, but it is used this way in 2 Macc 13:8; 4 *Macc* 5:37; 18:7-8.

16. So Fee, *Philippians*, 414.

17. Bockmuehl, *Philippians*, 250.

reasonable, and the course of action they follow is the only just one. In a less direct way, Paul is reminding the Philippians of a point he makes more explicitly to the Corinthians. In 1 Cor 1:18–2:16 Paul is keenly aware that although everyone is in favor of being wise, Christians and pagans will have irreconcilable differences on what counts as wisdom.

It must be added, however, that if Paul simply urged the Philippians to discern what is genuinely worthy among these things he would not be advancing the issue all that much. This is because terms like "morally excellent" and "praiseworthy" are no more self-interpreting than the others. In phrasing things as he does in v. 8 Paul indicates that there is a distinction between the truly good and that which is only apparently so. Moreover, he calls the Philippians to make just such discerning distinctions. To do this they need some sort of framework which will provide them with conceptual, practical, and linguistic resources for using these terms in a manner appropriate to those whose who are in Christ. In the context of these few verses Paul offers them a twofold framework for rightly applying these terms to persons, things, and actions.

The first aspect is located in v. 7, where Paul notes that through prayer and supplication, the peace of God will guard their hearts and minds in Christ. Paul provides the second aspect of this framework in v. 9. The Philippians are to do the things they have "learned, received, heard, and seen" in Paul. This claim summarizes and assumes both Paul's exemplary account of his circumstances in 1:12-26 and his account of himself in 3:4-14, which culminated in his call to become fellow imitators of him in 3:17. Of course, we have already seen that if the Philippians are conformed to Paul's example and the example of those who follow the pattern like Paul's, they will be conforming to the pattern of life called forth and exemplified in Christ (2:6-11). More particularly, they will be able to make the necessary judgments that will allow them to attend to those persons, things, and actions that are truly excellent and praiseworthy. Rather than translating his exhortations into a "public" language of pagan virtue, Paul has throughout the epistle been providing the Philippians with the resources they need to deploy that language within the context of a Christ-focused, cruciform common life.

Paul concludes this section by noting that the end result of all this is that the God of peace will be with them. Hence, the claims that began in v. 8 as a further elaboration of the ways in which the peace of God will guard the thoughts and hearts of the Philippians, conclude here with the affirmation that the God of peace will be with the Philippians. This final assertion serves as a reminder that imitating Paul is not an end in itself. Rather, it is a means by which one can maintain and deepen one's communion with the God of peace.

In this short section, Paul's admonitions recognize the possibility that the Philippians may use and apply terms like true, just, and pleasing in ways different from their pagan neighbors. In a situation where the Philippian Christians are in a minority, they need to understand that their notions of moral excellence will be different from the conventional notions operative in the dominant culture in which they find themselves.

Christians both in Philippi and today need to remember, however, that moral excellence in Christ does not usually stand in blunt contrast to moral corruption. Instead moral excellence in Christ works to expose and stand as an alternative to false or merely apparent excellence in the surrounding world. Learning how to discern what is truly excellent in God's eyes as opposed to what merely appears excellent according to common convention is a crucial task in creating a Christian discourse. This discourse is not closed off from more conventional ways of speaking. Moreover, this discourse is, in theory, accessible to any who will learn the central convictions and practices that underwrite it. This implies that if Christians order their common life in a manner worthy of the gospel, if they master the convictions and practices appropriate to life in Christ, they will be able to discern what is truly excellent. Thus, it would appear that the ability to make sustained discriminations between excellence and its simulacra depends on the presence and good working of a community whose common life is appropriate to the gospel of Christ.

If in this passage Paul is plundering conventional language and refocusing it in the light of the economy of salvation in order to establish a Christian discourse, Christians today face an additional challenge. That is, once Christians develop their own Christ-focused ways of using terms such as "true," "just," and "pure," it is always possible that actors within the dominant culture will plunder Christian discourse and images for their own purposes. The two places where this happens most often are in the marketplace and in politics. For example, one need only look at how the cross has gone from being an image of torture and state-sponsored execution to being a form of personal decoration. Although I am sure that there are numerous factors behind this transformation, one of the central factors must be the fact that Christian language about the cross has all too often been detached from the practices and convictions which made it such a potent image for someone like Paul. When Christian communities do not form and enable people to live cruciform lives, the cross can become a piece of jewelry. In politics the state has a long history of using Christian terminology to justify its use of violence and its claims on the bodies of its citizenry. Again all too often, instead of vigorously opposing such plundering of its central terminology, the church has simply fallen into line and marched to Caesar's drum.

As Paul moves to conclude his epistle in 4:10-20 it will become clear that one of his central tasks is not only to recast the language of virtue which had such conventional currency, but also to recast the common practice of giving and receiving money.

4:10-23

10 I rejoice greatly in the Lord because now, at last, your normal disposition of care and concern for me has bloomed again. In fact, you have always been so disposed toward me, but you have lacked opportunity for showing it. 11 To be sure, I am not claiming that I lack anything. I have learned to be content with whatever I have. 12 I know what it is to be in want, and I know what it is to have plenty. In any and in all circumstances I have learned the secret of being well fed and hungry, of having plenty and of being in want. 13 I can do all things through the one who strengthens me. 14 In any case, you have done well to become partners in my tribulation. 15 For you Philippians know that from the first days of the gospel when I went out from Macedonia, no church shared with me in giving and receiving except you alone. 16 Even when I was in Thessalonica you sent gifts to meet my needs on several occasions. 17 I do not seek the gift itself but I do seek the fruit that accrues to your account. 18 I have received all that you sent and I am filled to overflowing, having received from Epaphroditus the gifts you sent, a fragrant odor and pleasing sacrifice to God. 19 My God will satisfy all your needs according to his glorious riches in Christ Jesus. 20 To our God and Father be glory now and forever, amen.

21 Greet all the saints in Christ Jesus. The brothers with me greet you. 22 All the saints greet you, especially those of Caesar's household.

23 The grace of the Lord Jesus Christ be with your spirit.

We turn now to what many take to be the most puzzling passage in the letter. Why does Paul wait until the end of the epistle to thank the Philippians for their financial gifts to him explicitly, especially if, as some believe, expressing his thanks is the primary purpose of the epistle? Why does he seem to hedge his expressions of gratitude? Does this reflect some level of discord between Paul and the Philippians? As biblical scholars reflect more and more on the conventions that underwrite social interaction in the Greco-Roman world, it has become clearer that many of these questions arise because scholars impose modern conceptions of giving and gratitude onto Philippians.[1]

---

1. One of the earliest accounts was J. Paul Sampley's *Pauline Partnership in Christ*, which argued that Paul and the Philippians had a quasi-contractual relationship. He preached; they paid. The epistle is in part a "formal receipt tendered by Paul to the Philippian Christians for

Perhaps the best recent discussion of these issues in regard to Philippians is G. W. Peterman's *Paul's Gift from Philippi*. Peterman shows that language about giving and receiving such as we find in Philippians is quite common in the Greco-Roman world. It is intimately tied to a host of conventions regarding social interactions between people and groups. To summarize Peterman's most relevant findings: The giving of a gift or favor can establish a relationship. If that gift is accepted and reciprocated, then a lasting relationship is formed. Failure to accept a gift can result in enmity (as in 1 Corinthians). Receiving a gift obliges the receiver to reciprocate in word or deed. In fact the counter-gift itself serves to express gratitude for the initial gift. A gift-giver is socially superior to the recipient, so parity in giving and receiving simply maintains the relative status of each party. To grow in status one must exceed in giving. Because this aspect of interpersonal relations is based on transactions among interested parties, language and images from the commercial sphere are sometimes used to describe these social relationships. Hence, one should not infer that such commercial language refers solely to commercial relationships.[2] Peterman's study nicely displays that giving and receiving of gifts is one part of the structure of the relationship between two parties. Further, it is a complex practice governed by a series of fairly well observed social conventions. Moreover, issues of giving and receiving gifts are directly related to issues of the relative power and status of the parties involved.

Understanding these issues helps put several of the questions regarding 4:10-20 in their proper perspective. While the Philippians' gift to Paul might be the most direct material reason for Paul writing the epistle, it is by no means the only or even primary reason. As with standard letters of friendship, Paul has shared news and solicited news from the Philippians. It is also clear that the friendship between Paul and the Philippians is based on their partnership in the gospel. Hence, the friendship between Paul and the Philippians cannot be evaluated apart from their common friendship with Christ. This will substantially alter conventions regarding reciprocity and the relative status of giver and receiver.

Since the practice of giving and receiving gifts is so deeply bound up with issues of power, status, and relations among people, it is not surprising that Paul treats this issue with some care. Whether he likes it or not, the offering and accepting (or rejecting) of financial gifts is such a socially significant action that it

---

their gift payment in response to his need-request" (p. 55). Sampley is followed by Brian Capper, "Paul's Dispute with Philippi." For the most part, however, scholars have been sharply critical of Sampley's argument.

2. See Peterman, *Paul's Gift from Philippi*, 88-89.

will play a significant role in the relationship between Paul and the Philippians. Because the dominant culture views giving and receiving in particular ways, Paul must set the Philippians' gift into the right sort of Christ-focused context if it is not to shape his relationship with the Philippians in deleterious ways.[3] This accounts for Paul's rather circumscribed expression of thanks better than does speculation about a rupture in his relationship with the Philippians.

As to the placement of this expression of thanks at the end of the letter, it is important to note that at several points in the epistle Paul has (at least indirectly) expressed his gratitude to the Philippians. Paul has thanked God for their partnership in the gospel (1:4-5). He has expressed joy in his relationship with them in Christ (2:16-18). In particular, the Philippians sent Epaphroditus to Paul, for whom Paul is especially grateful (2:25). 2:25 might have been an occasion for Paul to thank the Philippians more directly, but the discussion about Epaphroditus focuses on his exemplary practice of seeking the benefit of others. An extended period of thanks here would have distracted from Paul's purposes. Moreover, because in the course of thanking the Philippians, he is also implicitly and explicitly instructing them about the nature of giving and receiving in Christ, he could not simply have appended brief words of direct thanks here at this point.

In addition to these considerations, it is striking how many ideas from 1:3-11, where Paul expresses his affection and concern for the Philippians, are reflected in 4:10-20, where Paul speaks about their care and concern for him. For example, he thanks God every time he remembers the Philippians (1:3). In 4:10 he rejoices in the Lord that the Philippians have renewed their concern for him. In 1:5 Paul rejoices in their "partnership" (κοινωνία/ *koinōnia*) with him in the gospel. In 4:15 he both remembers and rejoices in how the Philippians initially entered into partnership (ἐκοινώνησεν/ *ekoinōnēsen*) with him in the gospel. In 1:6 Paul expresses confidence in God's continued care of the Philippians. In 4:13 he confidently asserts that God will strengthen him to do all things. In 1:7 and 4:14 he notes that they have joined with him in his trials and tribulations. Further, in 1:7 Paul expresses a disposition to think, feel, and act in a particular way in regard to the Philippians. In 4:10 Paul expresses joy at the Philippians' expression of their disposition to think, feel, and act in a particular way toward him. In both cases Paul employs the same Greek construc-

3. As Peterman, *Paul's Gift from Philippi*, 121, notes, "Paul must confront and correct some of the accepted Greek and Roman social conventions regarding the exchange of gifts and favours." Indeed, throughout Philippians Paul addresses the congregation with a variety of constructions using the prefix συν/*syn* (1:7; 2:17-18, 25; 3:17; 4:14). The closest English parallel would be the prefix co-. This allows Paul to sidestep usual forms of praising one's benefactor in favor of a relationship governed by cooperation.

tion using the verb φρονεῖν/*phronein*. Moreover, there are a variety of other linguistic parallels between these two passages. It should be noted, though, that in many cases the vocabulary shared between the two passages is relatively common and that some words are used in different ways in the two passages.[4]

Whether this makes the issue of the Philippians' gift the central issue, the issue to which the entire epistle has moved, is, I think, doubtful. Alternatively, it does show a couple things. First, it indicates that the expression of thanks in 4:10-20 is not an afterthought. Second, it is clear that 1:3-11 and 4:10-20 form a well-crafted frame within which the entire epistle fits quite nicely.

In v. 10 Paul begins by rejoicing greatly in the Lord because the Philippians have at last renewed their concern for him. Clearly, expressing joy is not the same as expressing thanks. In fact, as many have noted, Paul never uses any Greek word for "thanks" here. He is not offering a straightforward assertion of thanks for a financial gift. A straightforward expression of thanks would invoke the very social conventions about status and reciprocity that Paul seeks here to circumscribe, if not undermine. By the time we get to vv. 17-18 Paul makes claims that indirectly convey gratitude, but only indirectly. Here in 4:10 we should read Paul as expressing joy rather than thanks. As Peterman notes, in several papyri "[s]uch expressions of joy serve to confirm the bond between the parties, and are typically used at the receipt of a letter, not at the receipt of a gift."[5]

Moreover, an expression of joy fits the immediate context. Having exhorted the Philippians to rejoice in the Lord always in 4:4, here in 4:10 Paul himself rejoices greatly in the Lord. Not only does this clause echo 4:4, but also Paul is able to insert God as the crucial third party in his relationship with the Philippians. No doubt Paul is grateful to the Philippians. Nevertheless, by phrasing the issue this way at the outset, Paul makes it clear that he and the Philippians are not in a conventional relationship of reciprocity. Because issues of giving and receiving are also bound up in issues of power and status, it is crucial for Paul to make it clear to the Philippians that they and he are common partners in God's work. Their care for each other always has this element in view. As vv. 17-20 explicitly note, while the Philippians' gift to Paul helps him, it also deepens their relationship with God, who supplies their needs and who is, finally, the recipient of glory. Hence, giving and receiving between the Philippians and Paul does not profoundly alter their status in relation to each other. They are slaves of Christ Jesus (cf. 1:1).

---

4. Peterman, *Paul's Gift from Philippi*, 91-92; also others. In these cases the parallels are noted without really noting the differences.

5. Peterman, *Paul's Gift from Philippi*, 129.

The cause of Paul's joy in the Lord is that the Philippians have renewed their concern for him. Although English words like "care" and "concern" are common and appropriate translations of the Greek, such translations can miss two important elements. First, 4:10 is one more occasion where Paul relies on the Greek verb φρονεῖν/*phronein*. Throughout Philippians Paul has used this verb to indicate a particular disposition toward a Christ-focused pattern of thinking, feeling, and acting. This cannot be well expressed by words like "care" and "concern." Secondly, Paul is not invoking a therapeutic notion of care such as is common in most American churches. The cruciform patterns of thinking, feeling, and acting Paul desires to see formed in the Philippians may at times generate a warm and fuzzy emotional state, but that is not really at the heart of Paul's concerns. In 1:7 Paul uses the same construction to display a very specific set of dispositions to think and act in a particular way in regard to the Philippians in the light of their trials. We should take the use of this construction here in the same way. That is, Paul rejoices because the Philippians have again displayed a disposition to think and act in a particular way toward him in the light of his tribulations. Specifically this involved, among other things, sending Epaphroditus to him with a financial gift.

It appears, however, that some time has elapsed since the Philippians had last displayed these dispositions in regard to Paul. Paul uses a botanical image, "to bloom again,"[6] and the phrase "now, at last" to speak about the Philippians' renewal of a disposition to act in certain ways toward Paul that had lain dormant. This assertion of some sort of hiatus immediately raises the prospect that Paul is rebuking the Philippians either for tardiness or unwillingness in regard to expressing their concern for him. Such a situation could only have been intended to insult Paul. In the next clause Paul moves to head off this misunderstanding, noting that the Philippians were hindered in displaying their concern for him. Their concern was consistent, but they lacked opportunity to display it.[7] Paul does not say how they were hindered. Given his account of the poverty of the Macedonian churches in 2 Cor 8:1-3, the Philippians may have been hindered by lack of money.[8] While the reason for the Philippians' lack of opportunity must remain at the level of speculation, the important point here is that Paul does not blame them.

---

6. See Sir 1:18 ("The fear of the Lord is a crown of wisdom, causing peace and health to bloom again") and 11:22 ("The blessing of the Lord is the reward of the godly, and the Lord shall cause his blessing to bloom again quickly"). Also Fee, *Philippians*, 429 n. 24.

7. I am following Fitzmyer, "The Consecutive Meaning," 330 (also Fee, *Philippians*, 430 n. 28), and my earlier arguments in regard to 3:12 that ἐφ᾽ ᾧ/*eph' hō* should not be taken causally but consecutively (i.e., "to which end").

8. Peterman, *Paul's Gift from Philippi*, 134, suggests this.

In v. 11 Paul seeks to clarify any possible misunderstanding regarding his expression of joy in v. 10. First, he makes it clear that he is not writing because he lacks anything. That is, Paul's joy is not the result of having a need that the Philippians have met. As Peterman makes clear, citing Seneca's *De Beneficiis* 2.2.1-2; 7.24.1-2, merely mentioning one's lack of something could imply a request for that very thing. Paul is making no such request. Indeed earlier in the epistle Paul spoke of his own needs in 2:25 (see also 4:16). In sending Epaphroditus to attend to these needs, Paul makes it clear that the Philippians were addressing not Paul's lack but their own (2:30). Moreover, the point here is not to deny that Paul experiences deprivations. Rather, Paul wants to make it clear that in mentioning such things he is not implicitly requesting aid. As v. 11 continues, Paul explains that he can hold this position because he has learned to be content in all circumstances.[9]

Much has been made of the Stoic overtones of the term "contentment" (αὐτάρκης/*autarkēs*). Fee expresses it well when he claims, "On the surface, his [Paul's] explanation looks like a meteor has fallen from the Stoic sky into his epistle."[10] Many commentators note Seneca's similar-sounding claim in *De Vita Beata* 6.2 that "the happy man is content with his present lot, no matter what it is, and is reconciled to his circumstances."

For the Stoic, contentment was found in virtue alone. Virtue was found within oneself independent of others. Paul's contentment comes from without, from God's strengthening. Hence, at the very least, Paul's contentment has a different source than that of the Stoic person of virtue. It is also the case, however, that the nature and scope of Paul's notion of contentment differs from that of a typical Stoic. In the passage quoted above Seneca defines contentment as being reconciled to one's circumstances. As becomes clear in the rest of *De Vita Beata*, being reconciled to one's circumstances depends on recognition that one can do little to alter them. Hence, virtue and contentment lie in mastering one's fears and desires so that one becomes indifferent (and thus reconciled) to whatever fate throws one's way. "No matter what happens he is able to maintain his happiness since he is his own master. This emotional calm, or detachment (ἀπαθής) cannot be separated from αὐτάρκης."[11]

This notion of contentment is very different from Paul's. As is clear

9. I follow Fee, *Philippians*, 431 n. 36, in taking the Greek ἐν οἷς εἰμι/*en hois eimi* as "in the situations in which I find myself." As vv. 12-13 make clear Paul is referring to all circumstances, not simply his current imprisonment.

10. Fee, *Philippians*, 431. See also Collange, *Philippians*, 150; Hawthorne, *Philippians*, 198; Lightfoot, *Philippians*, 163.

11. Peterman, *Paul's Gift from Philippi*, 136. On 137 n. 93 Peterman gives other references to show that Seneca's views on this matter are typically Stoic.

from the entire epistle, Paul never seeks detachment from his circumstances. Rather, he has learned to narrate them as part of the story of God's economy of salvation. As a result, he is not an independent rational soul buffeted here and there by fortune. Rather, he is a passionate participant in a divinely ordered drama. Throughout the epistle Paul has sought to display not self-mastery but the various ways in which the gospel calls for a life which seeks the benefits of others. Rather than being independent, Paul and the Philippians share in a common life founded on the gospel. Further, Paul is passionately concerned that the Philippians come to see, think, and act in the ways that he does. He sheds tears for those who think and act otherwise (3:18). All these considerations make it clear that Paul's expression of contentment has less in common with Stoic notions than one might initially think.

Paul can thrive in want and in plenty because he is strengthened by God, not because he has achieved a measure of detachment. In v. 12 he presents a series of opposed pairs of words to display the extremes of want and plenty. He begins by noting that he has known both "want" and "abundance." While these two terms can describe a variety of types of want and abundance, the subsequent mention of hunger and being well fed indicates that Paul is speaking of material circumstances. His attitude toward his material circumstances is more important than the nature of his experience of want and abundance. He has learned the secret of contentment in any and all circumstances. Read in the light of 1:20, plenty and need are both circumstances in which Paul seeks to magnify Christ in his body.

Material lack poses challenges for Paul, but so also does abundance. If one is possessed by anxiety (cf. 4:6), material abundance does not alleviate the anxiety. Abundance simply shifts one's focus from getting things to keeping the things one has. The peace of God gained through prayer (4:6-7), which stands as the alternative to anxiety, allows Paul to know contentment in whatever circumstances he finds himself.

The power that enables Paul's contentment does not come from within. He is strengthened by the Lord to do all things. Although the Lord is not mentioned explicitly in 4:13 as the one who strengthens Paul, at the beginning of this passage Paul began by rejoicing "in the Lord."[12]

Christians have often taken 4:13 as providing what Fee calls "an eternal 'gnomic' promise of Christ's help for anything and everything."[13] In its own

---

12. The later manuscripts (א², D² F, G, Y, and the Majority text) which insert "Christ" (Χριστῷ/*Christō*) here must also have taken it this way.

13. See Fee, *Philippians*, 434 n. 50.

context, the verse provides a powerful enough assertion that in all things Christ has strengthened Paul by initiating him into the secret of Christ-focused contentment. Nevertheless, while this verse should not be read in ways that make it seem that Paul has a sort of spiritual magic wand, the contentment Paul knows presumably goes beyond just material circumstances, even though that is the focus of the discussion here.

In v. 14 Paul shifts attention back onto the Philippians, commending them for being fellow sharers in his tribulation. His assertion that they have done well indicates that there really is no hint of rebuke here. Nevertheless, this commendation is not an expression of thanks, which would also entail Paul's recognition of a social debt to the Philippians.[14] This is made evident by the fact that Paul does not commend their gift. Rather, he commends them for sharing in his affliction. That is, they have demonstrated a disposition to think about and act toward him in his affliction in a particular way.

Paul's "affliction" is apparently his imprisonment. In 1:7 he spoke of his "chains," and in 1:17 he explicitly links tribulation and imprisonment. Hence, he commends the Philippians here for demonstrating their concern for him by sharing in his imprisonment. No doubt this involves the financial gift sent with Epaphroditus. But it also involves a public display of solidarity with one who is in prison (cf. Matt 25:36). In doing so the Philippians, and Epaphroditus in particular, brought some measure of shame on themselves. By risking bringing suspicion on himself, Epaphroditus may have risked imprisonment as well. It was not hyperbole to say that Epaphroditus risked his life to minister to Paul (2:30).

Moreover, since Paul's imprisonment was for "the defense and establishment of the gospel," the Philippians have become fellow sharers in Paul's ministry as well. Of course all these claims were initially expressed in 1:7, when Paul justified the disposition he had to think and act in a particular way toward the Philippians. Here in 4:10 Paul commends the Philippians for displaying their dispositions to think and act in a particular way toward him as they share in his afflictions even in the midst of their own (cf. 1:28-30).

While there were many aspects to the Philippians' solidarity with Paul in his afflictions, they primarily expressed this solidarity by sending him financial gifts. In vv. 15-16 Paul explicitly commends their concern for him as it was expressed in their financial partnership with him in "giving and receiving," one of several terms and phrases in this passage that were often used to speak of commercial transactions. Peterman, however, has nicely shown that

14. See Peterman, *Paul's Gift from Philippi*, 145.

such terms were also used to refer to a much larger network of social practices regarding the giving and receiving of gifts and services.[15]

As I have already noted, the giving and receiving of gifts and services was loaded with social expectations and assumptions. Paul devotes 4:10-20 to putting this matter of the Philippians' partnership with him in giving and receiving into its proper theological perspective and showing how this partnership should not be understood in terms of Greco-Roman social conventions. Peterman lists six ways in which this is the case. First, there is no notion of debt. Paul never acknowledges a debt to the Philippians either for this gift or for past ones. Second, there is no hint of repayment (if there is no debt, how could there be repayment?). God repays. Third, the Philippians will reap spiritual benefits from their giving. God will give these benefits. Greco-Roman conventions allowed for non-material repayment in terms of honor given to the benefactor by the recipients. Fourth, the Philippians' gift brings them into solidarity with Paul's affliction. Fifth, this partnership furthers the gospel. Sixth, their gift is a spiritual sacrifice pleasing to God.[16] In addition, the central conviction which works to counter Greco-Roman social conventions around giving and receiving is that Paul and the Philippians share a friendship founded, directed, and sustained by Christ. Their giving and Paul's receiving happens in and through Christ. This subverts conventional notions about reciprocity and about the relative status of giver and receiver. Indeed, from this Christ-focused perspective it is not always clear who is giver and who is receiver. Further, because friendship with and in Christ is a friendship with the crucified and resurrected Lord of 2:6-11, Christian friends may encounter tribulations in the course of defense and confirmation of the gospel. Such affliction, however, does not break friendships. Rather, it evokes solidarity and partnership.

As Paul talks about this partnership in giving and receiving, he explicitly notes the Philippians' past practice of supporting his apostolic work. Several details here are worthy of note, particularly in the light of Paul's well-documented practice of not accepting financial support from the Corinthians while he was preaching and teaching in Corinth. In 1 Corinthians 9 and 2 Corinthians 11–12 Paul makes it clear that even though he had a right to expect the Corinthians to support him, he did not ask for or accept money from them. Rather, he practiced his trade of tent-making. This appears to have generated a number of problems and misunderstandings. Here in 4:15-16 Paul

---

15. See Peterman, *Paul's Gift from Philippi*, chapter 3 and 149-51.

16. See Peterman, *Paul's Gift from Philippi*, 149-50, to see these points spelled out in greater detail.

notes that the Philippians gave and he accepted financial gifts after he had left Macedonia.[17] It is only then that they, and only they, entered into a partnership of giving and receiving to advance the gospel. It thus appears that Paul is unwilling to accept payment from those he ministers to while he is ministering to them. In doing this he hopes to skirt a variety of issues regarding status and power between those who work and those who pay the worker, issues which could easily have undermined his ability to carry out his apostolic mission. The financial support he does receive "is giving and receiving while absent from the church geographically, yet working alongside the church to forward a common cause."[18]

No doubt the Philippians were hospitable to Paul while he was with them. The giving and receiving mentioned here, however, shows that they displayed their concern for the apostle even when he was absent. Moreover, this seems to be different from the contributions sent by Macedonians (including the Philippians, presumably) to the saints in Jerusalem. In Rom 15:22-29 Paul makes it clear that this contribution was owed as a sort of debt to the mother church in Jerusalem. Here in Phil 4:15-16 Paul never mentions a debt the Philippians owe to other churches. Rather, they are his partners in mission and share in his tribulations.

In 4:17 Paul further qualifies his previous remarks in order to set them in their proper context. Paul praises the Philippians for their giving while at the same time insisting that he is not seeking their gifts. He has learned the secret of contentment; he has the peace of God; he is freed from anxiety; he does not need support. This is true even though he admits the obvious in v. 16 that he had (and has) needs. Rather than seeking the Philippians' gifts, he desires the fruit that accrues to them from God due to their giving. The idea that God blesses the one who gives to those in need is well attested elsewhere in the NT (e.g., Matt 6:4; 19:21 and parallels; Luke 6:38; 7:4-5; 14:12-14). Moreover, this notion is evident in the OT as well.[19] In particular, Prov 19:17

---

17. The Greek phrase καὶ ἅπαξ καὶ δίς/*kai hapax kai dis* seems to be an idiomatic way of saying "more than once." See L. Morris, "ΚΑΙ ΑΠΑΞ ΚΑΙ ΔΙΣ." Although it does not designate a precise number of times, it suggests two or at the most three. See also Fee, *Philippians,* 445 n. 28.

18. Peterman, *Paul's Gift from Philippi,* 150. This is against Perkins, "Heavenly Politeuma," 103, who argues, based on Acts 16:14-15, that Paul was supported by Lydia and did not work while he was in Philippi. Even though Acts 16:40 still has Paul staying with Lydia, this does not imply that he was supported by her. For example, Acts 17:7 has Paul staying with Jason in Thessalonica. In addition, 1 Thess 2:9 indicates that Paul worked for a living while he was with the Thessalonians.

19. See Peterman, 23-27, for an account of this theme.

notes that "whoever is kind to the poor, lends to the Lord and will be repaid in full."

In the midst of setting the Philippians' gifts to him in their proper theological context, Paul confirms receipt of the specific gift they sent to him with Epaphroditus in v. 18. He acknowledges that he has received everything they sent. Given the distances involved and the insecurities of travel, it was common for someone receiving something to acknowledge receiving it in full. In 1:5 and 2:25 Paul has mentioned the gift, but the language here is much more direct and formal. Indeed, in many papyri receipts the Greek verb ἀπέχω/ *apechō*, translated as "I have received," is often used as a technical term. As Peterman notes, however, this language can also function in a less technical ways to acknowledge all sorts of social exchanges.[20] Paul himself uses the term in this less technical way in Phlm 15. Having received the Philippians' gift, Paul expansively goes on to note that he is filled and even abounds.

By the midpoint of v. 18 Paul has returned to a theological evaluation of the Philippians' gift. He calls their gift "a fragrant odor" and "a pleasing sacrifice, pleasing to God." This language is used in the LXX in such passages as Gen 8:21; Exod 29:18; and Lev 4:31 of animal sacrifices which are pleasing to the Lord. It also appears in Eph 5:2, referring to Christ's self-offering to God on behalf of the church. Moreover, Heb 13:16 expresses similar sentiments: "Do not neglect to do good and share what you have, for such sacrifices are pleasing to God."

In the light of the Philippians' sacrificial offering to God, Paul goes on to assert that God will meet all of their needs "according to his glorious riches in Christ Jesus" (4:19).[21] As he has done several times before, here he explicitly reintroduces the three-way relationship between the Philippians, himself, and God. This serves an important role in his attempts to situate the Philippians' gift in its proper theological context.

In the Greco-Roman world, acknowledging receipt of a gift would commit the receiver to some sort of reciprocal act. He would need to repay the gift or offer something else in return according to his means and status. Given

20. Peterman, 142.

21. I find Fee's account (*Philippians*, 453-54 n. 16) of the difficult Greek phase ἐν δόξῃ ἐν Χριστῷ ᾽Ιησοῦ/*en doxē en Christō Iēsou* (translated above as "glorious riches in Christ Jesus") the most convincing. That is, ἐν δόξῃ/*en doxē* ("in glory") is locative and modifies τὸ πλοῦτος αὐτοῦ/*to ploutos autou* ("his [God's] riches"). The phrase does not mean something like "in heaven." Rather, it defines the context in which God's riches are bestowed on humanity. This context is further qualified as "in Christ Jesus," which indicates "both where and how the riches that belong to God's own ineffable glory are made available to his people" (Fee, *Philippians*, 454 n. 16).

that Paul and the Philippians are partners and fellow sharers, Paul might well have been expected to pay the Philippians back in kind. But he never commits himself to do so. As vv. 18b-19 indicate, this is in part because the money the Philippians sent to Paul was also a sacrifice offered to God, a sacrifice pleasing to God. As Paul describes it here, the Philippians are acting appropriately primarily toward God and not Paul. As a result, God and not Paul will meet their needs.[22] Indeed, given Paul's unlikely prospect of ever being in a position to pay the Philippians back, the Philippians will reap far greater benefits from the one whose glorious riches are bestowed on humanity in Christ Jesus.

As he has done throughout these verses, Paul continues to set the Philippians' gift-giving in a theological context. This context implicitly recognizes the Greco-Roman social conventions inherent in giving and receiving while at the same time subverting these conventions in the light of the three-way relationship that obtains between Paul, the Philippians, and God.

Given the three-way relationship which lies at the root of this entire passage, it is appropriate for Paul to conclude this section with a doxology to God (4:20). Interestingly, Paul claims in v. 19 that "*my* God will meet all your needs. . . ." By v. 20 Paul directs his doxology to "*our* God." Because the Philippians entered into solidarity with Paul by manifesting a disposition to think and act in particular ways toward him (4:10), he promises that his God will meet the Philippians' needs (4:19). As this circle is closed, the passage finishes with a common expression of praise to "our God."[23]

On the surface, this passage has appeared to be a very awkward or reserved expression of thanks. Very few of the common expressions of thanks, need, and obligation appear in this passage. Those that do are explicated in ways that show Paul is attempting to counter many of the social conventions associated with giving and receiving in the Greco-Roman world. Thus it would appear that this passage has a dual aim. One of these aims is to express Paul's joy at and commendation of the Philippians' demonstration of the sort of dispositions to think and act in ways Paul has been urging throughout the epistle. They have shown the sort of concern toward him that he calls them to display toward each other in earlier parts of the epistle. That this concern involved financial gifts to Paul is, in a sense, secondary. Of course, in Paul's circumstances both Epaphroditus and the gifts he brought were welcome (cf. 2:25-30). Nevertheless, finances here simply provide one context in which

22. As Peterman explains in *Paul's Gift from Philippi,* chapter 2, this pattern of reasoning is similar to patterns found in the OT and extrabiblical Jewish literature. The paradigmatic verse here is Prov 19:17.

23. The wording of this doxology is similar to those found in Rom 16:27; Gal 1:4-5; Eph 3:21; 1 Tim 1:17; 2 Tim 4:18.

Christian *phronesis* or practical reasoning can be displayed. It is this expression of practical reasoning for which Paul rejoices and commends the Philippians.

In addition, Paul is also displaying for the Philippians and us how friendship in Christ transforms the way one approaches even mundane material practices such as the giving and receiving of financial gifts and support. In Paul's world (and in our own) giving and receiving gifts (and money in particular) is implicated in a host of widely recognized expectations governing the relationships between giver and receiver. Unless Paul had commented on this practice, the Philippians quite naturally would have understood their giving and Paul's receiving in the terms laid out by the dominant culture. Doing so would have substantially altered their friendship with Paul. In this passage, however, Paul sets the giving and receiving of financial gifts into a different context.

Both the quality of the common life of the Philippian Christians and the nature of their partnership with Paul in the gospel depend on Paul's ability to describe the material practices of giving and receiving in ways that are congruent with the gospel, in ways that recognize that the friendship Paul and the Philippians enjoy is founded, enabled, and maintained in Christ. Hence, Paul regularly invokes "the Lord" as the crucial third party in this friendship. This redirects the standard assumptions about reciprocity and relative status that were intricately embedded in Greco-Roman conventions regarding giving and receiving. Fitting the practices of giving and receiving into a different Christ-focused scheme enables Paul to give an alternative account of the context in which he and the Philippians find themselves. By accounting for this context in this different manner, both Paul and the Philippians are enabled to order their common life in a manner worthy of the gospel (1:27). Moreover, Paul implicitly invites the Philippians and all subsequent Christians to continue this sort of discerning of the conventional social contexts in which they find themselves long after the epistle has been read and digested. It is precisely this sort of ability to discern and account for one's situation that is the mark of the Christ-focused practical reasoning Paul has advocated throughout Philippians.

The epistle closes with a brief set of greetings. First, every one of the saints is greeted in Christ Jesus (4:21). There is an ambiguity in the phrase "in Christ Jesus." Does it refer to the sort of greeting to be conveyed, or does it modify "the saints"? In 1:14 there was a similar ambiguity in the phrase "in the Lord." Many scholars consider the reading "saints in Christ Jesus" an unnecessary redundancy.[24] In 1:1, however, the Philippians are addressed as "saints

---

24. Fee, *Philippians,* 458.

in Christ Jesus who are in Philippi." In that case I argued that phrasing the matter this way relativized the church's connection to the Roman colony. As Paul has consistently argued throughout the epistle that the Philippian Christians are part of an alternative polity to Caesar's, it seems that, rather than introducing a redundant phrase, Paul is simply indirectly reminding the Philippians of a point he has made earlier. Alternatively, the analogous phrasing in 1 Cor 16:19 indicates that here Paul may be conveying greetings "in Christ." It is not clear that a great deal hangs on choosing one of these options at the expense of the other. It is probably just as well to let the phrase point in both directions.[25]

A more puzzling matter concerns who is to do the greeting. The second person plural verb here seems to require someone other than Paul to convey greetings to the Philippians. Paul may simply be urging the Philippians to greet each other, but he is certainly capable of saying that more directly (1 Cor 16:20; 2 Cor 13:12). Some have argued that Paul is asking the deacons and overseers mentioned in 1:1 to convey greetings to the church as a whole.[26] This assumes that they (perhaps including the leaders mentioned in 4:1-3) received the letter and then had it read to the entire congregation. While this must remain a speculative suggestion, it does make sense of the text.

We then learn more about those who are sending the greetings. These include "the brothers (and sisters) with Paul," "all the saints," and "especially those of Caesar's household." The initial designation seems to refer to Paul's immediate coworkers.[27] Though he does not mention anyone by name, this list would at least include Timothy. We have no idea how many others would be included in this group. The intriguing phrase here is the mention of saints who are part of "Caesar's household." As Lightfoot notes at the beginning of his excursus on this phrase, it has "given rise to much speculation and formed the groundwork of more than one capricious theory."[28] He showed that the phrase does not refer to Caesar's relatives. Rather it would include imperial clients, civil servants, slaves, and freed slaves in the emperor's service.[29] While this certainly supports claims that Paul was writing from Rome, it was also the case the members of the imperial household would have been found throughout the empire. Indeed, a public inscription shows that three of Augustus' freedmen, members of his household, were present in Philippi in 36 or 37 CE.[30]

---

25. So Beare, p. 157, followed by Bockmuehl, *Philippians*, 268.
26. Hawthorne, *Philippians*, 214.
27. Fee, *Philippians*, 458; Bockmuehl, 269.
28. Lightfoot, *Philippians*, 171.
29. Lightfoot, *Philippians*, 171-72.
30. Cited in Bockmuehl, *Philippians*, 270.

The naming of names is not the important point here. Both those Christians in Philippi, who were suffering opposition from Roman citizens of Philippi, and Paul, who suffered at the hands of the empire both in Philippi and now in Rome, could draw encouragement and hope from movements in God's economy of salvation which had brought the gospel into Caesar's household.[31]

The epistle then concludes in a typically Pauline manner with a benediction.[32] Paul expresses the wish that the grace of the Lord Jesus Christ will be with the Philippians' spirit. Galatians, Philemon, and 2 Timothy all end in this way. Interestingly, Paul speaks here to the common, single spirit of the Philippian Christians. While this language is not unique to Philippians, it does echo Paul's desire for their common life expressed in 2:1-4. This is a useful reminder that this is not an epistle written to isolated individuals. To us contemporary American Christians, surrounded as we are by a culture of individualism, Paul leaves us with a final reminder that our primary task is to order the common life of our churches in a manner worthy of the gospel of Christ (1:27).

---

31. Fee, *Philippians*, 459; Bockmuehl, *Philippians*, 271, and Witherington, *Friendship and Finances*, 136, make similar sorts of claims.

32. Many ancient mss. add "Amen" to the end of the benediction in v. 23.

Theological Horizons of Philippians

Introduction

There are a variety of ways to write theologically about Philippians (or any other scriptural text). In the course of commenting on Philippians, I have tried to offer theological reflections, observations, and judgments on particular verses and passages when it seemed appropriate. Hence, I do not consider this part of this volume to be the place where I finally do theology. In the preceding pages the movements of the argument and the language and rhetoric of Philippians shaped when and how I would offer theological reflection and judgment. Here I offer a more synthetic sort of theological reflection and judgment. The theology here is driven more by the desire to unpack a set of themes and issues rather than by the text of Philippians. I am not, however, primarily offering a theology of Philippians in the sense that I am presenting the theological assumptions and convictions out of which Paul writes Philippians. I have tried to incorporate those judgments into the section-by-section commentary. Some of those judgments are relevant to my discussion here. I will try to develop them without repeating myself too much.

My comments here are more like an attempt to do theology as one who has read Philippians closely, but also in the light of other scriptural and theological considerations. With this end in mind I have decided to focus on a single topic. My choice of topic (friendship), the manner in which I approach it, and my choice of examples are all fairly directly generated out of a reading of Philippians. In this respect, one might say that the reflections on friendship which follow display some of the distinctive themes of Philippians among other NT epistles. There are other ways of approaching this topic, other scriptural texts to address, and different examples to draw from. I have no desire to foreclose those other avenues. Instead, I have a twofold aim here. First, and

largely by implication, I want to develop the pattern of theological interpretation of Scripture, which is partially exemplified in the commentary above
and, I hope, fruitfully furthered here. Second, and explicitly, I want to offer at
least the contours of a theology of friendship which draws deeply and vari-
ously from Philippians. I will begin, then, with a brief discussion of the role of
Christian formation and its importance for theological interpretation. Then I
will move to a more direct discussion of friendship.

Formation, Philippians, and Theological Interpretation

It is difficult to talk about or exemplify a form of theological interpretation of
Scripture apart from speaking briefly about issues of Christian formation.
Among other things, Paul wants to see the Philippians formed to be a community whose common life is worthy of the gospel (1:27), a people who are
steadfastly faithful in the face of opposition and even suffering (1:28-29), a
people pure and blameless, shining as stars in the midst of the world (1:10;
2:15), and a people capable of joy (1:18; 4:4). As we have seen, all these ways in
which Paul wants to see the Philippians formed and transformed depend on
the formation of Christ-focused practical reasoning.

Paul wants the Philippians (and us) to develop the capacity for and
habit of seeing things in the light of God's drama of salvation (especially as
displayed in 2:6-11). As Christians develop this capacity and habit, we will be
able to think, feel, and act in ways that enhance our communion with God
and each other. Thus, the quality of the friendship that Paul and the
Philippians share in Christ depends on all of them being able to fit themselves
and each other into this drama and to live accordingly.

Thus far, all I have said about formation largely summarizes discussions
in the "Commentary" section of this volume. Before moving to develop a theology of friendship, I want to extend this emphasis on formation to the reading of Scripture in Christian communities. Although the Philippians did not
have access to Scripture in the same ways we today do, I am confident that if
they had had such access then Paul would have also noted the importance of
formation for reading Scripture theologically. The primary reason for this is
that Scripture is the first of God's providentially ordered vehicles by which we
learn of and are drawn into the economy of salvation. Indeed, there is a happy
circular movement here: At its best, the reading of Scripture (under the
Spirit's direction) teaches us both the contours and depths of God's drama of
salvation. This increases our capacity for and habit of thinking, feeling, and
acting in ways that enhance our communion with God and each other. Being

thus formed, we are able to read Scripture in deeper and richer ways so that we become like Augustine's perfectly wise person who, "supported by faith, hope, and charity, with an unshaken hold upon them, does not need the Scriptures except for the instruction of others."[1] Augustine seems to indicate that there were such people in his world. I have not met such people. I am less troubled by this than by the fact that most churches I know do not see the close ties between formation, Scripture, and faithful life and worship. As a result, churches do not see that one of their primary and essential tasks is the formation of saints. As Michael Budde (among others) has trenchantly noted, there are a myriad of forces at work in our modern culture of hyper-consumption that frustrate attempts at disciplined Christian formation.[2] Thoughtful, faithful attempts at formation cannot hope to succeed against such external forces until the church recovers this sense that its mission, its worship, and its abilities to read and embody Scripture depend on forming Christians in ways such as those Paul advocates in Philippians. Minus such formation, we may find that our capacities for Christ-focused practical reasoning are not up to the task of leading us to order our common life in a manner worthy of the gospel.[3] Moreover, we will find that we are not able to sustain the sorts of friendships in Christ which Paul sought to develop with the Philippians.

A Brief Theology of Friendship Arising from Philippians

Using Philippians as a springboard into a theology of friendship seems quite fitting. First, scholars often call Philippians a letter of friendship.[4] When saying that, they usually mean that Philippians fits well within an ancient epistolary genre characterized by the letters friends sent to each other. This seems to be correct. Moreover, as far as it goes, such a finding helps solve some of the exegetical and formal puzzles of Philippians. Such genre classifications, however, are less helpful when it comes to thinking about the particular ways in which Philippians might display the nature and practices of friendships in Christ.

---

1. Augustine, *On Christian Doctrine* 1.43.

2. For an account of the necessity and difficulties of Christian formation in late capitalist America see Budde, *The (Magic) Kingdom of God.*

3. For a more extended account of the relationships between formation, interpretation, and practical reasoning, see Fowl, *Engaging Scripture,* chapter 7.

4. See the essays in *Friendship, Flattery and Frankness of Speech,* especially Fitzgerald's essay, "Philippians in the Light of Some Ancient Discussions of Friendship."

I would like here to extend that notion of friendship. I have already noted several times that Paul and the Philippians are friends in Christ. Several elements of the epistle are directly designed to address and direct that friendship.[5] Moreover, I believe that a theological reading of Philippians can help generate a rich theology of friendship. With the aim of sketching out the contours of such a theology, I will discuss four topics here. First, a theology of friendship must be based on the character of the triune God as decisively displayed in the life, death, and resurrection of Jesus. Phil 2:6-11 will be crucial here. That text needs to be read in the light of trinitarian concerns that were probably not overt concerns of Paul or the Philippians. I will try to explain briefly why I consider that a necessity and not a problem. I will also need to bring in factors arising from Christian convictions about creation. The second topic is related to understanding the character of God as displayed in narratives such as 2:6-11. In particular I want to focus on the notion of seeking the benefit of others as a decisive way in which Christ displays the form and glory of God to us. I take the mutual cultivation of this disposition to be one of the primary practices of Christian friendship. I have already said a good deal about this in the "Commentary" section of this volume.

The third topic addresses practices of friendship in Christian community. From Aristotle to Oprah, friendship has been a significant topic of reflection.[6] It is also clear that Aristotle and Oprah mean very different things when they talk about friendship. One of the ways these differences become clearer is by examining the practices which are constitutive of friendships and particularly friendships in Christ. One of the primary practices of Christian friends is helping each other narrate their lives within the larger drama of God's economy of salvation. This is a practice Paul clearly exemplifies for the Philippians. It is a practice that requires the formation of Christ-focused patterns of thinking, feeling, and acting (i.e., practical reasoning) if it is to be done well. While Paul exemplifies this practice for his Christian friends in Philippi, he also seeks to have the requisite practical reasoning formed in them so that they, too, may fit their lives into the drama of God's saving purposes. The aim of this is that they order their common life in a manner worthy of the gospel (1:27). Christian friends so formed will also need to think

5. Fitzgerald, using Aristotle's categories of friendship, conjectures that Paul is trying to elevate the Philippians' understanding of their friendship from one based on utility to one based on virtue. We have no reason to think that Paul and the Philippians had radically different notions of the nature of their friendship. Further, if Aristotle's basic categories are used, it also needs to be said that Paul would significantly revise Aristotle's account of the virtues.

6. Those interested in a detailed survey of ancient views of friendship should turn first to Konstan, *Friendship in the Classical World.*

about the material aspects and practices of their lives differently from the dominant cultures in which they find themselves. As Paul shows in 4:10-20, if he and the Philippians are not able to reconceive the practice of giving and receiving monetary gifts, than there is a great danger that they will view such giving and receiving in the same way that their pagan neighbors would have. As Paul understands, viewing the Philippians' financial gifts to him in this way would have had a corrosive effect on their friendship.

Finally, I must offer an account of the extraordinary emphasis on joy and rejoicing in Philippians. I will do that within the scope of my discussion of friendship. In Paul's world, even the best sorts of friends were engaged in a "friendly" competition for honor. I want to argue that for Paul and all Christians the result of the proper working of Christian friendships is joy.[7]

To begin, then, I want to lay out the relatively non-controversial view that friendship with God is our ultimate end because friendships of love are constitutive of the very life of the triune God.[8]

Friends of the Triune God

Thomas Aquinas reminds us that we are created for friendship with God.[9] This is the purpose for which humans were initially created. Friendship with God is also the end for which God redeems and renews us. Friendship with God is our ultimate end because such friendships of love constitute the very life of God, and God will give us nothing less. Hence, we must begin any account of Christian friendship with God, more specifically the triune God. In this regard Phil 2:6-11 plays a dual role. First, it sets out a series of claims which can really be properly ordered and understood only in the light of the doctrine of the trinity. Second, read in the light of that doctrine, 2:6-11 sets out a concise and authoritative account of God's character and of the sort of friendship God desires for us and with us. Moreover, this focus on 2:6-11 is

---

7. In these ways, a theology of friendship draws together traditionally distinct theological loci such as soteriology, ecclesiology, and ethics.

8. Although Aquinas uses language of friendship, language about "communion" is equally appropriate here and may be more familiar to readers.

9. See *Summa Theologiae* I-II.65.5 where Thomas says, "Charity signifies not only the love of God, but also a certain friendship with Him; which implies, besides love, a certain mutual return of love, together with mutual communion. . . . Now this fellowship of man with God, which consists in a certain familiar colloquy with Him is begun, in this life, by grace, but will be perfected in the future life by glory." See also II-II.23.1 for similar views. See also the very helpful discussion in Paul Wadell's *Friendship and the Moral Life*, chapter 5.

important in the light of the epistle as a whole. The patterns of thinking, feeling, and acting which Paul takes to be essential for his friendship with the Philippians and the Philippians' friendships with each other draw their force and intelligibility from this story of Christ narrated in 2:6-11. The characters Paul points to as exemplars of such patterns of thinking, feeling, and acting (Timothy, Epaphroditus, and Paul himself) are exemplary precisely because they embody those patterns definitively displayed by Christ in 2:6-11. Thus, any theological discussion of friendship that takes its bearings from Philippians must focus primarily on 2:6-11.

I have no intention of making the historically improbable argument that Paul wrote with knowledge of the doctrine of the trinity. Nevertheless, as David Yeago among others has recently shown, it is equally incorrect to argue that Nicene dogma of the triune God is somehow an imposition of alien (i.e., Greek) philosophical categories onto Scriptural texts such as 2:6-11.[10]

Phil 2:6-11 strongly, and without hesitation, locates Christ within the identity of the God of Abraham, Isaac, and Jacob. This is the upshot of such claims as: Christ is "in the form of God," thereby sharing in God's eternal glory, and Christ is "equal to God." Most significantly, Christ is "granted the name above all names" and confessed by all creation as Lord. This designation "Lord" is the way in which the LXX identifies Yahweh, the God of Israel.

This is a radical claim on several levels. First, and foremost, it is radical in that those making that claim were simultaneously also committed to the singularity of the God of Israel. The same people who confess Jesus as LORD are also committed to Deut 6:4, "Hear, O Israel, the LORD your God, the LORD is one." They are committed to the worship of the one God to the exclusion of all others. The question is how these seemingly conflicting convictions can be rightly ordered.

In the light of these apparently opposed claims, much modern NT scholarship has followed a history-of-religions approach to try to relate the NT's claims about Christ to conceptions of monotheism current in early Judaism. According to this approach, the more strict the monotheism of the Second Temple period, the more difficult it becomes for the first Jewish followers of Jesus to attribute real divinity to him. By attending to the numerous semi-divine figures that appear in Jewish literature of this period, a history-of-religions approach argues that early Judaism did not conceive of monotheism as strictly as one might think. This allowed the first Christians to rely on views about these intermediary figures for the conceptual and theological tools they would need to fashion their accounts of Jesus' connection to God.

10. Yeago, "The New Testament and Nicene Dogma."

In this light, the NT's claims about Jesus' divinity, then, are not all that radical. They represent a sort of ratcheting up of the already existing notion of semi-divine intermediary figures. Thus, rather than offering the radical assertion that Jesus is to be included within the unique identity of the God of Israel, Phil 2:6-11 is more of an incremental adjustment relative to Jewish claims about, say, Wisdom.

Recently, however, Richard Bauckham has offered a sharp deviation from this way of approaching NT texts about Christ.[11] Rather than focus on intermediary figures, Bauckham addresses the way God's identity was perceived in Second Temple Judaism. He notes, "What has been lacking in the whole discussion of this issue has been an adequate understanding of the ways in which Second Temple Judaism understood the uniqueness of God. By acquiring such an understanding, we shall be able to see that what the New Testament texts in general do is take up the well-known Jewish monotheistic ways of distinguishing the one God from all other reality and use these precisely as ways of including Jesus in the unique identity of the one God as commonly understood in Second Temple Judaism."[12]

As Bauckham presents the problem of relating Jesus and Jewish monotheism, the key issues have little to do with intermediary figures. Rather, the crucial first step is to characterize the unique identity of the God of Israel. Such an examination yields two distinct features as constitutive of God's identity, that "the one God is sole Creator of all things" and that "the one God is the sole Ruler of all things."[13] Since intermediary figures are clearly created and subject, they are unambiguously distinct from God's identity. They can in no way provide a bridge over which New Testament thinking about Christ can inch its way toward divinity. Alternatively, if one understands texts about Wisdom or Logos as personifications of divine attributes or characteristics, these obviously can be included within God's identity without ever compromising the singularity of that identity. Consequently, these characteristics cannot be shared with Christ if Christ is conceived of as separate from God's identity. Thus, "The decisive step of including Jesus in the unique identity of God was not a step that could be facilitated by prior, less radical steps. It was a

---

11. See Bauckham, *God Crucified*. While Bauckham's work is distinctive in a variety of ways, it is also deeply intertwined with the claims of others such as Hurtado, *One God, One Lord,* and *Lord Jesus Christ.*

12. Bauckham, *God Crucified*, 4.

13. Bauckham, *God Crucified*, 26. Those wishing to find a more detailed scholarly argument on this point can find it in Hurtado, *One God, One Lord,* and his magisterial *Lord Jesus Christ*, 32-50. One of the particular strengths of Hurtado's work is his emphasis on the practices of devotion relative to God and Christ.

step which, whenever it was taken, had to be taken simply for its own sake and *de novo.*"[14]

When Phil 2:9-11 ascribes to Christ the same sort of sovereignty over all things which is constitutive of God's identity, Paul is not simply associating Christ with God — a move that would compromise the singularity of God's identity. Rather, he includes Christ within that identity. This does not compromise the singular identity of the God of Israel, but claims such as we find in Phil 2:6-11 put intense pressure on that singularity. It is one thing to note that personifications of divine attributes such as Wisdom and Logos can be included within God's identity without compromising monotheism. When those personifications are applied to Christ, the Son of the living God, it is clear that Phil 2:6-11, and the NT as a whole, includes Christ within God's singular identity. It is less clear how this inclusion avoids fracturing the singularity of that identity.[15] The NT itself never really solves this problem. What is required and what subsequent developments of trinitarian dogma provide is a more developed, scripturally regulated grammar of divine singularity which includes Christ within God's identity. The subsequent formulation of trinitarian dogma is the appropriate way to order Christian scriptural claims about God. What Phil 2:6-11 first asserts in dramatic narrative form, and what later trinitarian dogma punctuates in a more formalized way, including reflection on the Spirit, is the claim that the identity of the one God of Israel is constituted by a trinity of persons, distinct yet undivided.[16]

As generations of Christians thought about, prayed to, and worshiped the triune God it became increasingly important to characterize God's life as constituted by the set of relationships between Father, Son, and Holy Spirit. As Basil of Caesarea put it, "But there is to be apprehended among the persons a sort of indescribable and inconceivable simultaneous communion. . . ."[17] While this is not all there is to say about the trinity, this notion of God's identity being constituted by a perfect and uninterrupted communion between Father, Son, and Spirit (a communion which does not compromise the singularity of God) forms a central conviction for Christian thinking

14. Bauckham, *God Crucified*, 28.

15. Hurtado, *Lord Jesus Christ*, 151-52, notes this. This was not simply a matter of dispute between early Christians and their Jewish interlocutors. It was also a matter of intense debate within Christianity. See, for example, Gregory of Nyssa's *To Ablabius: On Not Three Gods.* Also Lewis Ayres, "On Not Three People."

16. Obviously, there is no distinct mention of the Spirit in Phil 2:6-11.

17. See *Letter* 38. Many now attribute this letter to Gregory of Nyssa. See, for example, Sarah Coakley, "'Persons' in the 'Social' Doctrine of the Trinity."

about God.[18] This divine common life is God's identity. The basis of this communion is the love that binds all three persons of the trinity. It is this love which Thomas characterizes as the friendship which constitutes God's life.

When Christians confess that this God, whose life is constituted by communion, is the creator, they recognize first that creation is gratuitous. Creation does not address a lack or loneliness in God. It is, rather, the result of the overflowing of love that characterizes the common life of the triune God. Further, in the light of Gen 1:26-27, recognizing that humans are created in the image and likeness of the triune God, Christians assert a further act of God's grace. While humans as creatures are distinct from God, in creating humans in the image of God, God both wills and enables humans to enter into friendship with God. Being created in the image of God enables and points to our ultimate end of friendship with God. Indeed, we bear the image of God because God graciously wills to draw us into an ever-deeper friendship of love. As David Yeago puts it, "The gracious fulfillment towards which human nature is ordered must be described in Trinitarian terms. All creatures exist because they are *objects* of conversation within the Holy Trinity. They come to be because the Father and Son imagine them together in the freedom of the Spirit. The human creature, however, exists not only to be an *object* of the divine conversation but also to join as a *subject* in the divine conversation. God not only speaks *about* the human creature; God speaks *to* the human creature and waits for an answer. The human creature is created to be a partner, a participant, in the divine life."[19]

In this light, it would be extremely odd if we were growing into ever-deeper friendship with the triune God and at the same time not growing into deeper friendship with those who also bear the image of God and are on the same journey. God wills to draw us into ever-deeper communion with God. At the same time, the fact that all humanity bears God's image suits us for

18. The extremely influential work of J. Zizioulas, *Being as Communion*, attempts to take this notion of communion among the divine "persons" in Basil and the other two Cappadocians, Gregory of Nyssa and Gregory of Nazianzus, as the basis for a theology of human "persons." This, then, forms the basis of a particular way of living in the world. Volf, *After Our Likeness*, goes on to argue that this should also be the basis of ecclesiology as well. There have been numerous reexaminations of trinitarian "personhood" in recent years, and Zizioulas's work in particular (see Ayres, "On Not Three People," Coakley, "'Persons' in the 'Social' Doctrine of the Trinity," and Turescu, "'Person' versus 'Individual'"). I am not in a position to comment further about the subsequent constructions of Zizioulas. It is clear, however, that his foundational account of human personhood cannot be sustained by a "Cappadocian" account of divine personhood.

19. Yeago, unpublished manuscript on Christian doctrine, 2:15. See also Jenson, *Systematic Theology*, 58-60.

friendship with each other in God. This is reflected in Jesus' assertion that loving God with heart, mind, and soul *and* loving our neighbors as ourselves is the first and foundational commandment (Matt 22:36-40). As a way of explicating this, Dorotheos of Gaza, one of the desert fathers, used this illustration: "Suppose we were to take a compass and insert the point and draw the outline of a circle. The center point is the same distance from any point on the circumference. . . . Let us suppose that this circle is the world and that God is the center; the straight lines drawn from the circumference to the center are the lives of [humans]. . . . But at the same time, the closer they are to God, the closer they become to one another; and the closer they are to one another, the closer they become to God."[20] Or as Caroline Simon put it, "Knowing and loving our neighbors and friends is caught up in a sacred tangle of knowing and loving God."[21]

While an account of creation lays out God's desire for friendship with us, the fact of human sin threatens to leave that desire unrequited. This is why a Christian account of friendship must ultimately be founded in Christ. Christ is the one who reconciles us to God, heals us, and restores to us the prospect of friendship with God. Christ, through the Spirit, also fits us for true friendship with each other. Thus, Philippians, as well as all Christian accounts of friendship, assumes a three-way relationship in Christ.[22]

I do not want to drive a wedge between the persons of the godhead. God is the one who both begins a good work in the Philippians and in Paul and brings that good work to its proper end. The Spirit sustains and directs this friendship, guiding both parties to their proper *telos*. Centrally, however, it is Christ who is the cause of Christian friendships and provides their form and intelligibility. Paul and the Philippians are drawn into a relationship with each other because of their common Christ-focused convictions and practices.

It is not simply that Paul and the Philippians share a set of convictions and practices regarding Jesus. Rather, the very nature of these convictions and practices directly calls them and us into friendship with Christ and each other. As Rowan Williams puts it, "The event of Jesus' life, death and resurrection is not (or not only) an external model to be imitated. The important thing about it is that it has created a different sort of human community; professing commitment to Jesus as Lord connects us not only to Jesus but to one

20. Cited in Roberta Bondi, *To Pray and to Love,* 14-15. Similar sentiments can be found in the letters of Catherine of Siena; see *Catherine of Siena: Passion for the Truth, Compassion for Humanity,* especially 34-35, 39, 48.

21. "Inquiring After God through Our Neighbor," in Charry, *Inquiring After God,* 122.

22. Aelred of Rievaulx makes a similar point in his *Spiritual Friendship,* in Charry, *Inquiring After God,* 112.

another in a new way."[23] Entering into friendships in Christ such as Paul, the Philippians and we do is not simply an added benefit of the Christian life; it is constitutive of the Christian life.

Seeking the Benefit of Others:
The Character of God and Christian Friendships

Deepening our friendships with God and each other is both the task and goal of the Christian life because friendship is at the very heart of God's identity. Moreover, the possibility, nature, and shape of Christian friendships are christologically driven. Any theology of friendship, then, must rely on an understanding of the life, death, and resurrection of Jesus. For Paul and the Philippians, this understanding is focused on the account found in 2:6-11. For Christians today, this account can be equally normative for their thinking about friendship. This passage displays the identity and character of the one who calls Paul and the Philippians and us into a life of friendship. This points to the second way in which Phil 2:6-11's inclusion of Jesus within the identity of God is crucial for a theology of friendship. Here, especially in vv. 6b-8 we see the dispositions and actions of the one who is equal with God. Jesus, the one who is equal with God and never stops being equal with God, does not use this equality for his own advantage. Rather, seeking the benefit of others, he willingly empties himself. He becomes obedient; he takes human flesh. In unstinting obedience he becomes subject to the world's inability to abide the presence of the perfectly obedient Son. Christ's obedience is cruciform.

Willed self-emptying, cruciform obedience, seeking the benefit of others — these become the ways in which the glory of God is revealed to humans as God becomes human. The glory of the one who is in the "form of God," is, in part, constituted by this desire not to exploit that glory for his own benefit but to display it bodily in word and deed for the benefit of others. Because it reflects the character of God revealed in Jesus' life, death, and resurrection, this desire is also determinative for friendships in Christ. This characteristic of God is often referred to as God's benevolence. God's gracious benevolence toward us is to mark our friendships with each other. "Benevolence implies not only that the friend is loved for herself, but also, because she is loved, the active seeking of her good is the sustaining project of the lover's life. This is what friendship is, mutual devotion to the good of the other because it is a good both share."[24]

23. Williams, *On Christian Theology*, 172.
24. Wadell, *Friendship and the Moral Life*, 131-32.

For the Philippians and for those who subsequently read the epistle, friendships in Christ should manifest the benevolent dispositions and actions of Christ as related in 2:6-11. Further, throughout Philippians, Paul points to numerous human exemplars of these dispositions and actions including himself, Timothy, and Epaphroditus. Moreover, in many and various ways, but especially in 2:1-5, he calls on the Philippians to let these dispositions form and direct their common life, their friendships with each other.

Humans are made for friendship with God. This is a consequence of being created in the image of the God whose very life is the inseparable communion of Father, Son, and Holy Spirit. While our sin alienates us from God, Christians recognize that by being joined to Christ in baptism they are reconciled to God. In Christ, and through the power of the Spirit, we enter a journey of ever-deepening friendship with God. We are called and enabled to pursue that journey in the company of other friends, engaging in a three-way friendship with them and Christ. Christ's life, death, and resurrection display the appropriate character of all Christian friendships.

This further indicates that in several respects Christian friendships will differ from contemporary notions of friendship. For example, it is quite common to assume that we choose our friends. Most of us could generate a list of characteristics describing the sorts of people with whom we prefer to associate. Indeed, for a fee, you can have a computer connect you with those who share those characteristics. Christian friends do not really choose each other. We are called into friendship with each other because of our common friendship in Christ. We do not choose each other; Christ chooses us. In Phil 3:12 Paul uses the image of being "grabbed hold of" by Christ to speak of this. Friends in Christ might never have associated with each other on other grounds. Factors such as compatibility in class, education, or ethnic or national background cannot be invoked as the basis for Christian friendships.

It is significant that this component of Christian friendship directly contradicts many contemporary strategies for increasing church attendance. So-called church growth experts agree that people prefer to associate with those like themselves. The theory is that homogeneity attracts like-minded newcomers. This presents contemporary Christians with a particular challenge. Ordering the common life of any Christian community with an eye toward homogeneity may well increase attendance. We also, however, have good reason to think that doing so will also frustrate the formation of Christian friendships. Such a strategy also fundamentally misunderstands the nature of the church of Christ.

The first followers of Jesus were Jews. They saw their convictions about the life, death, and resurrection of Jesus as fully compatible with their Judaism. They saw in Jesus the climactic point in God's actions to redeem Israel. They saw themselves and the communities they formed as outposts of redeemed Israel. Further, in the light of such texts as Isa 2:1-4, they expected that as Gentiles witnessed God's redemption of Israel, manifested in the common life of these communities, all nations would be drawn to God. In short, they understood Christianity as a Jewish movement to which God draws the Gentiles as they perceive God's work of redemption. Acts relates this most clearly. The early chapters of Acts focus on the reconstitution of Israel in the light of the death and resurrection of the Messiah. Most of these transformations take place in and around Jerusalem. In time, the first followers of Jesus spread out from Jerusalem. In halting, sometimes faltering ways these Jews are led by the Spirit to preach to Gentiles. Much to their surprise, Gentiles receive the gospel in large numbers. Even Paul always begins by preaching to Jews when he first enters a town. Acts, Romans, and Galatians in particular make it clear that Christianity is a Jewish movement into which Gentiles are drawn.

Nevertheless, these two groups are as unlike each other as groups can be. The only thing they might have shared was mutual antipathy toward each other. In spite of that, it is crucial for these first Christians that they come to understand themselves as a single body of Jews and Gentiles united in the body of Christ. Gentiles neither need to become Jews nor are second-class citizens in God's redeemed Israel. Nowhere in the NT is this more clearly asserted than Ephesians 2. It is also manifested in the friendship between the Jew, Paul, and the Gentile Christians in Philippi. As the NT decisively displays, one of the ways God's redeeming work is most clearly manifested is in the formation of Christian friendships across the chasm that divided Jew and Gentile in the first century. Thus, because Christian friendships are bound up in a common friendship with Christ, we should not seek to build churches around socio-economic, racial, or ethnic similarities. By contrast, Christian friendships will flourish where people recognize the call to friendship with God and each other entailed in their common baptism and commonly cultivate the dispositions and actions needed to deepen those friendships. Much of what Paul both displays and advocates for the Philippians is the cultivation of just these habits of thinking, feeling, and acting. In the next section I would like to examine both the appropriate social context for cultivating Christian friendships and some of the primary practices of Christian friendships.

Friendship in Christian Community

Contexts

Those dispositions and actions directed toward deepening our friendships with God and each other require a social context in which they can be nurtured and sustained. Isolated individuals cannot sustain such friendships. For Paul, for the Philippians, and for us, the primary social context for nurturing and sustaining Christian friendships is the church, the earthly witness to and manifestation of our "heavenly commonwealth." In this light, it is not surprising that in Philippians Paul spends so much time addressing the common life of the Philippian Christians. It is crucial that the Philippians and we order our various communities in a manner worthy of the gospel of Christ if our friendships with God and each other are to remain in good working order.

Philippians indicates several different ways in which this is so. First, Paul recognizes that, because the church is not the only context in which friendships might be formed and sustained, the church must have a clear sense of how friendship with God must shape the ways in which we order all of our other relationships. For example, it appears that the empire, particularly in the form of the civil authorities of Philippi, wants to exert a claim on the loyalties of the Philippian Christians. The empire wants to form people to be friends of Caesar, at least to the degree that social class and status allow. As Paul sees things, the empire is hostile to the church and ultimately corrosive of Christian convictions and practices. The Philippians cannot be both friends of Caesar and friends of the cross and the crucified one. There is no notion of dual citizenship here, no possibilities for split allegiances. Paul understands that Christian friendships and ordering our common life in a manner worthy of the gospel will generate hostility from those who seek our allegiance if not our friendship. Of course Paul is not the only NT writer to make this point. James sharply reminds his readers, "Do you not know that friendship with the world is enmity with God? Therefore, whoever wishes to be a friend of the world becomes an enemy of God" (4:4). As Luke Johnson has made clear, "the world" here is not God's good creation but a pattern of perceiving, evaluating, and acting on things as if God did not exist. It reflects a politics — a way of ordering a common life — opposed to God.[25]

It may well be that Christians, at least in America, do not face hostility from the state in the ways that the Philippians did. What appear to be distinct alternatives to Paul may seem less clear to us. While there are obvious differ-

---

25. See also Luke T. Johnson, "Friendship with the World/Friendship with God."

ences between Paul's world and our own, we should be careful about dissolving the political bite of Paul's vision of the church as a society of cruciform friends standing as a contrast to other social arrangements. The fact that Christians in America do not face the hostility from the authorities that Christians in Philippi did may have little to do with the state's kind disposition toward Christianity. Rather, as scholars such as William Cavanaugh and Stanley Hauerwas have recently argued, in America (and many other places) the state is kindly disposed or indifferent to Christianity precisely to the degree that Christianity has become a religion.

Religion, in this sense, refers to a set of privately held beliefs and convictions disconnected from any set of public practices which might conflict with the state's claims to one's loyalty. It is possible to trace the rise of this notion of religion from the dissolution of the late medieval union of civil and ecclesial authority in which the ecclesial authority was dominant. As this union dissolved, various princes and kings struggled for dominance over ecclesiastical authorities in the fifteenth and sixteenth centuries. A centralized bureaucratic state emerged from this. As this newly emerging state sought to solidify its dominance over various populations, various political philosophers begin to speak of the role religion might play in this process, serving the needs of the sovereign. From Jean Bodin through Thomas Hobbes to John Locke, the state can become increasingly gracious and flexible toward religion as religion becomes an increasingly privatized affair that does not interfere with the day-to-day sovereignty of the state. Thus, by the time of the founding of the U.S., freedom of religion can be granted because religion, thus understood, cannot be a threat to the state.[26]

Such a notion of religion could not be further from the Christianity we see in Philippians. In particular, this disembodied notion of religion stands as a direct contradiction to Paul's bold assertion in 1:20 that whether he lives or dies he intends that Christ will be magnified in his body. The creation of religion as a set of privatized beliefs leaves our bodies under the control of the state or our employers or market forces. In life or death Paul belongs to Christ. Caesar may take Paul's life, yet even in this case Christ will be magnified. The empire can kill Paul, but because Paul has already offered his life back to God, the empire cannot take Paul's life. The empire cannot make Paul its victim. Paul's body is Christ's; Caesar cannot compel Paul's worship; Caesar cannot employ Paul's body in the empire's violence. Moreover, in calling the Philippians to be friends of the cross, Paul is calling on the Philippians

---

26. For a compelling account of this set of developments see W. T. Cavanaugh, "A Fire Strong Enough to Consume the House."

to think of themselves in the same way. The notion of religion as a set of privately held beliefs disconnected from both communal and individual practices would have been unintelligible to Paul. It ought to be so for us.

Just as the empire and its particular outpost in Philippi provide a social context for a certain sort of friendship, so also the church in Philippi provides a social context for the formation of friends of the cross. If such a notion seems inconceivable to Christians today, it may well reflect churches' unwillingness to call their members to cruciform friendship so that whether they live or die their bodies magnify Christ. If churches in America are not calling and enabling Christians to form and sustain such friendships with God and each other, the state has nothing to fear from us and no reason to be hostile toward us.

Practices

Secondly, in the light of Philippians, the church provides a context for what appears to be one of the foundational practices of Christian friendship for Paul. This is the practice of being able to narrate the story of one's own life into the ongoing story of God's economy of salvation. I realize that this is not what most people think of when they imagine what it takes to be someone's friend. Paul also understands that friendship involves other practices. In Philippians, however, Paul takes this ability of properly situating both oneself and one's friends within the drama of God's saving purposes to be foundational for all of the other practices of Christian friendship. Paul's first concern is to help the Philippians develop the perceptual skills and habits they will need to understand their circumstances, their past, and their future as episodes in that larger drama of God's purposes for creation. This may not be the most common practice of Christian friendship. It is, however, the practice on which all other practices of Christian friendship are based.

As with most complex practices, one best learns the skills, habits, and dispositions needed to fit one's own story into the larger story of God's purposes for creation by seeing it done by those accomplished in the practice. The Philippians see Paul doing this in two particular passages, 1:12-26 and 3:4-21. In 1:12-26 Paul provides the Philippians with news about himself and how he is faring in prison. This seems conventional enough. This, however, is not all that is going on. Rather, Paul narrates an account of his circumstances in prison in the light of his larger reading of God's economy of salvation. His account is not simply about episodes in his life but also about his life as an episode in the larger drama of God's saving purposes. Hence, he can begin by noting that contrary to expectation, his imprisonment has led to the advancement of the gospel. Moreover, by fitting his life within the larger story of God's s activity Paul is able, by means of inference and analogy, to see how he should comport himself in his particular situation.

In 3:4-14 Paul renders an account of his past and his future aspirations in this same light. He displays the ways in which his perceptions and dispositions toward his past have changed now that he is in Christ. Entering into friendship with Christ provided Paul with a perspective within the economy of salvation from which he could then look back on his past and renarrate it from the perspective of being in Christ. That perspective gave him a way of recasting his *telos* so that he now strains forward, reaching out to grasp that for which Christ first grasped him — friendship with God.

It may not yet be evident that being able to fit an account of one's life into the narrative of the economy of salvation is related to Christian friendships. The practice Paul illustrates here seems to be related to the individual's personal life with God. There is, however, more to say here. Paul does not stop at narrating his own circumstances. Because he knows something of the Philippians' situation, he is able to offer an account of that situation that shows the similarities between his circumstances and theirs. Hence, in 1:30 he can make the crucial claim that the Philippians are engaged in the same struggle as he is. Because they are in the same struggle, they, too, should see their story in the light of the divine economy. Thus, they should comport themselves in a manner similar to Paul. This pattern of argument becomes much more explicit in 3:4-21 and especially in 3:17 with the command to "join together in imitating me."

In several passages, but most clearly in 1:27-30, Paul briefly fits the Philippians' circumstances within the larger story of God's saving purposes. Paul wants the Philippians to order their common life in a manner worthy of the gospel so that they may remain steadfast in the face of opposition. He points out to them that their opponents will interpret this steadfastness as a sign of the Philippians' destruction. Paul assures them, however, that their steadfast fidelity even in midst of suffering will result in their salvation. He goes so far as to claim that suffering for the sake of their convictions about Christ is an opportunity that has been graciously offered to them. The only way these claims can have any force or intelligibility for the Philippians is if they appropriately fit themselves into the movements of God's economy of salvation. Ordering a community's common life in a manner worthy of the gospel presupposes that the members of the community rightly perceive the ways in which God's drama of salvation has developed, is now unfolding, and where it will ultimately end.

Paul's practice in Philippians indicates that one of the main activities of Christian friends is to help each other come to see our pasts, presents, and futures as part of God's drama of salvation. It is only when we do this that we can expect to order our common life in a manner worthy of the gospel of Christ. Such a common life will provide the best context for the flourishing of Christian friendships.

We also see in John 15:12-17 how friendship and the ability to fit oneself and others into the economy of salvation are related. Jesus begins there by commanding his followers to love one another as he has loved them. As a measure of this love he proclaims, "No one has greater love than this, to lay down one's life for one's friends." As Jesus further explains, friendship with him is tied to keeping this commandment. Then he goes on to explain that his disciples are no longer servants, since servants do not know what their master is doing. Instead, he says, "I have called you friends because I have made known to you everything I have heard from my Father." The difference between being a servant and a friend seems to be closely tied to learning God's plans. The transformation of Jesus' followers from servants to friends is closely tied to Jesus' making the economy of salvation known to them in word and deed.

Nevertheless, in the light of the whole of John, it is clear that there is a gap between Jesus making the economy of salvation known and the disciples' proper apprehension of this revelation. Given this gap, we might well doubt that the disciples will be able to maintain a friendship with Jesus if it depends on knowing and understanding the movements of God's saving purposes for creation. Within a few paragraphs of this passage, however, Jesus promises to send the Spirit, who will "testify" on Jesus' behalf (15:26). Further, "When the Spirit of truth comes, he will guide you into all the truth: for he will not speak on his own but will speak whatever he hears and will declare to you the things that are to come" (16:13). Hence, at least one of the Spirit's activities will be to help the friends of Jesus understand what Jesus has revealed about the economy of salvation. As 15:12 and 17 make clear, the end result of this is that the disciples should love one another just as Christ has loved them. In very laconic ways John here indicates the close connection between friendship, understanding the economy of salvation (with the Spirit's help), and loving as Jesus loved. In Philippians Paul offers a denser and more concrete account of how Christian friendship is tied to recognizing the workings of God's economy of salvation. Nevertheless, in both passages there is a close connection between friendships in Christian love and properly perceiving the economy of salvation.

Contemporary notions of friendship and intimacy are often measured by the ability of friends to tell each other anything and everything. Conversation becomes a central practice of friendship and a primary path to intimacy. There is a measure of truth to this. It will be important to note, however, that Christian friendships are primarily focused around a specific sort of conversation. This is a conversation in which friends help each other fit their lives into the ongoing drama of God's salvation. This is not to say that Christian friends only talk about this, but these particular conversations are constitutive of Christian friendship because they help us order our common life in a manner worthy of the gospel of Christ and they enhance our prospects of deepening our communion with God and with others.

There are numerous aspects to this practice. A variety of assumptions underlie it, and there are several ways in which this aspect of Christian friendship differs from more common notions of friendship. I will try to unpack these issues here.

First, the abilities of Christian friends to fit each other's lives into the economy of salvation depend on several things. Friends must learn and teach each other the various movements of this drama of God's saving purposes. Obviously, long and sustained attention to Scripture is essential here. In fact, Paul's use of Isaiah 45 and Job 13 has already worked to situate the Philippians within the movements of God's saving drama as revealed in the OT.[27] Although the Philippians did not have access to Scripture in the same ways that we do today, their material lack should not be the justification for our ignorance. While Christians clearly interpret Scripture in various ways and in the light of differing circumstances, they all recognize that God's economy of salvation is definitively and authoritatively displayed in Scripture. Hence, as Augustine reminds us, one speaks more or less wisely to the extent one has become more or less proficient in Scripture.[28] Augustine's personal example is also instructive here. Like Paul in Philippians 3, Augustine in his *Confessions* renarrates his life from the perspective of being in Christ, properly fitting himself into the movements of God's saving purposes. It also becomes clear that Augustine's perspective is gained through deep attention to Scripture. If the basic conversation of Christian friends is directed to more and more clearly and actively fitting their lives into the narrative of God's saving purposes, an understanding of the biblical story is essential.

Those who are either professional biblical scholars or familiar with such work will immediately want to raise questions about this notion of "the bibli-

27. Of course, other Pauline letters and the Gospels do this more extensively than Philippians.

28. *On Christian Doctrine* 4.5.

cal story" — and rightly so. Let me say a bit more about what I do and do not mean here. First, I do not mean to imply that there is a single narrative substructure to the entire Bible that is perfectly evident to all reasonable people of good will. Further, I see no point in arguing that individual biblical authors understood themselves to be contributing to this grand story. As Christians study and teach Scripture with and to each other, we must be careful to avoid reading from such a great height that we end up unable to see the details of any particular text. Christians have a theological obligation to read closely. This is true with regard to all texts, but especially Scripture. Hence, I do not take the notion of presenting "the biblical story" as a way of denying the obvious diversity of Scripture or its textual richness. Rather, "the biblical story" is a shorthand way to refer to the interpretive results of ordering the diversity of Scripture in the light of the economy of salvation as articulated in such ordering principles as the Rule of Faith or the creeds.

The question is not whether there is diversity in Scripture. This fact is really too obvious for comment. The question is, how can and should one order that diversity?[29] As I have already indicated, there appears to be a sort of circularity here. Christian friends read Scripture so that they can engage each other about how to fit their stories into the economy of salvation. At the same time, they must learn to order and direct their reading of Scripture in the light of the economy of salvation. In fact, this circle is really a spiral. The deeper one drinks from Scripture's well, the better one is equipped to fit one's own life and the lives of one's friends into the ongoing drama of God's saving purposes. The better one grasps the movements of this drama in its past, present, and future episodes, the better one can then read Scripture. One need not conclude that there is only one meaning or possible interpretation for a specific passage. Rather, reading in the light of the Rule of Faith can generate a plurality of interpretations, so long as they conform to the Rule. Done well, this sort of theological interpretation of Scripture produces a harmoniously ordered diversity of readings.

In addition to reading Scripture in the light of the Rule of Faith, Christian friends can be formed to better attend to the economy of salvation through attentive participation in the worship of the church, most particularly the Eucharist.

29. This is not a new question. Irenaeus saw the question of how a diverse Scripture is to be ordered as the essential issue in his disputes with such characters as the Valentinians. In Irenaeus's day many felt that some sort of philosophical scheme such as the one offered by Valentinus provided the proper way of ordering Scripture's diversity. Today, most so-called biblical theologians argue that some sort of historical or social scientific scheme is the proper way to order Scripture's diversity.

The Eucharist is coextensive with the history of salvation. Just as on a clear morning the whole sky is reflected in a dewdrop on a bush so the Eucharist reflects the whole history of salvation.

The Eucharist, however, is present in this history in three different ways at distinct times, or stages: it is present in the Old Testament as a *figure*, in the New Testament as an *event*, and in our time of the Church, as a *sacrament*. The figure anticipates and prepares the event, the sacrament "prolongs" the event and actualizes it.[30]

The Eucharist presents in a more compressed, yet more dramatic way the drama of salvation that Scripture lays out. In accepting Christ's invitation to join as friends around the eucharistic table we find ourselves inserted into that drama, "prolonging and actualizing" it. Thus, through regular attentive participation in the Eucharist, Christian friends can develop the skills, habits, and dispositions required to fit the movements of their lives into God's economy of salvation.

Most significantly, however, Paul expects the Philippians to develop these skills, habits, and dispositions in and through their ongoing friendship with him and with each other. Paul not only fits his own circumstances into God's economy of salvation, he also presumes to be able to narrate the Philippians' circumstances in the same way. Because they know and are known to each other, Paul can presume to say to the Philippians something like, "Here is how your circumstances can be seen as part of this divine drama, and here is how you should act in that light."

If we are to take Paul's assumptions seriously, we also have to recognize the level of intimacy and accountability among Christian friends that provides the basis for the practice of trying to make a friend's life intelligible within the economy of salvation. We have to assume that the better one knows and is known by one's friends, the better one will be at narrating their lives as parts of the drama of God's salvation. On the one hand, because our ultimate end in Christ is friendship with the God whose inner life is constituted by a triune friendship, Christian friendship precedes knowing someone well. Christian friendship is founded on a common baptism, on common membership in Christ's body. It is not dependent on liking each other. On the other hand, if our friendships in Christ are to enhance our growth into ever-deeper communion with God and with each other, they will both require and foster the sorts of intimacy and accountability that seem to operate between

---

30. This elegant way of formulating the matter comes from Raniero Cantalamessa, *The Eucharist: Our Sanctification*, 6.

Paul and the Philippians. Thus, we can distinguish those acts of God that generate and found our friendships from those practices that are necessary for those friendships to thrive.

Given that distinction, it seems improbable that Christian friends can cultivate the required levels of intimacy and accountability simply by gathering together for an hour on Sundays. Theologians such as Augustine and Aelred of Rievaulx understood that Christian friends needed to spend time together in order to grow in their love of God and each other. Monasticism provided just such a context. Those of us for whom that is not an option must work hard to establish time and space in our lives for meeting, gathering, and praying with friends outside the limited time set aside for worship on Sunday. Thus, acts of hospitality and fellowship are crucial to the establishment of intimacy and accountability that will advance friendships in Christ.

In this light it seems odd that ministerial training currently stresses the need to establish boundaries between clergy and congregations. I have no doubt that the potential for abusive and distorting relationships between clergy and members of congregations calls us to exercise prudence in the ways we relate to other members of the body of Christ. It may be useful to distinguish various ways in which Christians may play therapeutic or managerial roles in the lives of other Christians and Christian friendships that are directed toward bringing us into deeper communion with God and with others. It may be that churches need to develop procedures to ensure the good working of these various roles. At the same time, Christian friendships not only depend on a common life worthy of the gospel, they are also constitutive of such a common life. The absence of such friendships will frustrate us as we move toward our ultimate ends in God.

Suffering Friends in Christ

If attempting to narrate their own and each other's lives within the drama of God's salvation makes Paul and other Christian friends appear presumptuous in the eyes of American Christians schooled in individualism, such individualist Christians are likely to be scandalized to recognize that, in the case of Paul and the Philippians, Paul is narrating both his circumstances and theirs in ways that make intelligible the suffering that has come their way because of their Christian convictions. We are all aware, particularly in the light of the horrors of September 11, of how foolish (or worse) Christian leaders can sound as they try to make such suffering intelligible as God's judgment on America and the world for particular sins. It is important to note that Paul is not attempting to account for any and all suffering the Philippians might encounter. Rather, both he and they are suffering because of their convictions about Christ. This is suffering that comes their way as the result of their willing obedience to God. It is a way of embodying the obedience Christ displayed according to 2:7-8. Having placed their lives within the narrative of God's saving purposes, they have become people capable of offering their lives back to God. The world's response to such an offering, whether it is indifference or the imposition of suffering or death, is largely out of their hands. Nevertheless, such suffering and even death receive a certain sort of intelligibility in the light both of the world's response to the life of the willed obedience of Christ and of God's vindication of that obedience.

Making this particular type of suffering intelligible will always be a contested matter. For example, from the perspective of those who worked for his arrest and crucifixion, Jesus' death confirmed that he was at best a deluded false prophet and at worst a heretic and danger to faithful Israel. From the perspective of the disciples walking on the road to Emmaus, he was that one who they hoped would redeem Israel (Luke 24:21). His death meant that their hopes were misplaced. Of course, the resurrection changes all that. God vindicates the obedient suffering one, raising him from the dead, altering all evaluations of his life and death. In the same way, Paul notes that the Philippians' steadfast obedience in the face of hostility will generate conflicting evaluations. To their opponents, the Philippians' steadfast fidelity to the gospel can only be read as stubbornness that brings justified destruction.[31] For those who are united with the God who raised Jesus from the dead, steadfast fidelity in the face of opposition is a sign of their salvation (1:28). The life, death, and resurrection of Jesus provide Christian friends with a framework for making the suffering they encounter as the result of their convictions about Jesus intelligible to each other. As friends they help each other to do this as they fit one another's lives into the drama of God's saving purposes with an eye toward God's vindication of just the type of suffering they have taken on.

Without question, there are times when the suffering of Christians and others cannot be made intelligible. Sometimes the silence that comes out of solidarity is the only way for suffering friends to speak to each other. Other times, suffering does seem to be the result of sin. In such cases friends may

---

31. We also see this in the conflicting possibilities Paul lays out in the way he will comport himself in prison. He expects to magnify Christ in his body whether he lives or dies. He recognizes, however, the possibility that he might be disgraced in either the manner of his death or the way in which he continues to live (cf. 1:20).

need to speak prophetically to each other, urging each other to repentance and reconciliation. At the same time, we must remember the "friends" of Job. That is, we must recognize that sometimes speaking prophetically needs to be followed by a confession that it was the "prophet" who was in error. Of course, as friends who now narrate their lives from the perspective of those in Christ, we have ways of truthfully narrating our sin, confessing it, and engaging in the processes of forgiveness, repentance, and reconciliation.

In these ways I have argued that one of the primary practices of Christian friendship is helping each other fit our lives into the drama of God's economy of salvation. This practice is difficult and demanding, and not always straightforward. Paul and the Philippians would readily recognize that it is sometimes difficult to trace the movements of the divine economy. One's eye has to be trained so as to discern both the ways in which the economy of salvation moves and the particular ways in which Christians might fit themselves into that economy in the light of their particular circumstances. To help train the Philippians' eyes, Paul relates the story of God's activity in Christ in 2:6-11. There is a deeply ironic structure to this story. The initial result of Christ's obedience and suffering appears to be death. God overcomes death, reversing one's initial reading of the human Christ's self-emptying. I have already pointed out that in the light of this story Paul tends to adopt an ironic point of view in Philippians. In several respects, however, this ironic point of view is different from the perpetual irony of our current age, an irony that infinitely defers judgment and commitment, an irony that cannot but lapse into cynicism. Rather, Paul's irony is christologically dense. It is an ironic perspective that is decisively shaped by a particular narrative, the narrative of God's economy of salvation that reaches its climax in the life, death, and resurrection of Jesus. Like the irony of our current age, Paul's ironic perspective allows him to see the temporal contingency of present circumstances and current configurations of power. Unlike the contemporary ironist, Paul comports himself in the midst of adverse circumstances in the knowledge that these circumstances are ultimately ordered by God's providential will, a will that ensures that all things will be subject to Christ (3:21).

Without question, the NT manifests a variety of points of view one might adopt to narrate both the story of God's saving work and how one fits into that story. Behind this ironic point of view, however, is something more significant. Because the movements of God's economy in any set of present circumstances can be hard to discern, Paul recognizes the need for a Christ-focused pattern of practical reasoning. Paul's patterns of thinking, feeling, and acting have been formed over the time of his life in Christ so that he can adopt the appropriate point of view for the appropriate circumstances. This then enables him to properly fit his life and the Philippians' into the economy of salvation.

If the Philippians and we are to fit ourselves into the narrative of God's economy of salvation, we will need to have our perceptual skills, our patterns of thinking, acting, and feeling, developed in such a way that we can discern the movements of God's economy in the present and act accordingly. If one of the primary activities of Christian friends is helping each other fit our lives into the ongoing story of God's salvation, the Philippians and we will need to have a Christ-focused practical reasoning formed in us so that we can best fulfill our commitments to our friends in Christ.

Thus far, I have argued that one of the central practices of Christian friendship entails friends helping each other appropriately fit themselves into the ongoing drama of God's salvation. This is primarily a conversational practice which to be done well requires that friends are deeply familiar with Scripture and active attentive participants in worship. When friends engage in this practice at its best, it can even help them make the suffering that comes their way as the result of their commitments to Christ intelligible to each other. At this point I want to move on to explore how a theology of friendship relates to more mundane aspects of the Christian life.

Material Life

In addition to presenting the practice of fitting each other's lives into the economy of salvation as a crucial activity of Christian friends, Philippians also indicates some of the ways in which material circumstances shape and are shaped by the nature of Christian friendships. The Philippians had responded to Paul's imprisonment by sending Epaphroditus with a financial gift. In addition, Epaphroditus helped minister to Paul in various ways during his time with Paul. On the one hand, this seems to be an exemplary case of the activity of "seeking the benefit of others" which Paul advocates so strongly in the epistle. On the other hand, since the practice of giving and receiving of gifts is shaped by such extensive social codes and expectations, Paul needs to give an alternative, theological account of the Philippians' gift if it is not to distort their friendship.

Without significantly repeating my comments on 4:10-20, I will sketch the contours of this alternative account. First, Paul never directly thanks the Philippians for their gift. To do so would invoke social conventions concerning reciprocity and the status of Paul and the Philippians. Givers are superior to receivers. Instead Paul expresses joy. This works to maintain a friendship in which Paul and the Philippians are fellow slaves of Christ, common partners in God's work. The Philippians' gift clearly benefits Paul. It also deepens their relationship with the God who supplies their needs and meets Paul's needs as well.

Paul does not rebuke the Philippians for failing to send more gifts, nor does he acknowledge any need (thereby implicitly requesting further gifts). God has strengthened Paul to do all things. Paul has thereby developed an attitude of contentment. The Philippians' gift deepens their sharing in Paul's afflictions. It reflects their disposition to think and act toward him (remember Paul's use of φρονεῖν/*phronein* here) as they share in his afflictions in the midst of their own.

In the Greco-Roman world, acknowledging and expressing thanks for a gift would bind the receiver to repay with some sort of reciprocal act or risk damaging the relationship with the gift-giver. Paul never commits himself to such a course of action, not because he wishes to insult the Philippians but because the money they sent to him is primarily a sacrifice offered to God. God, then, will repay the Philippians.

Rather than following the standard social conventions for acknowledging and expressing thanks for a gift, the point of this passage is to express Paul's joy and to commend the Philippians for demonstrating the dispositions Paul has been urging throughout the epistle. They have shown the sort of concern toward him that he calls them to display toward each other.

Thus, the fact that this concern involved financial gifts to Paul is, in one sense, secondary. Alternatively, because the giving and receiving of gifts is implicated in widely recognized expectations governing the relationship between giver and receiver, Paul needs to comment on this practice. If he did not, the Philippians might well have understood their giving and his receiving in terms of the dominant culture. This would have substantially altered their friendship with Paul.

Both the form and nature of their friendship and the quality of the common life of the Philippian Christians depend on Paul's ability to narrate the material practices of giving and receiving in ways that are congruent with the gospel, in ways that recognize that the friendship Paul and the Philippians enjoy is founded, enabled, and maintained in Christ. Hence, in this passage and elsewhere Paul regularly invokes the Lord as the crucial third party in his friendship with the Philippians. This enables him to redirect the standard assumptions about reciprocity and relative status that are embedded in Greco-Roman conventions regarding giving and receiving. Paul here fits one of the basic material practices of their relationship into a new Christ-focused setting, just as he has fitted himself and the Philippians into a narrative of the economy of salvation. Moreover, Paul implicitly invites the Philippians and us to continue this sort of discerning long after the epistle has been read and digested.

Two points follow from this and are relevant for understanding Christian friendship. First, we ought to expect that in the course of fitting each other's lives into the drama of God's saving purposes we will also need to give alternative accounts of the social and material contexts and practices in which we find ourselves. Those accounts will affect for good or ill the shape of our friendships in Christ. For example, consider how material practices related to giving and receiving financial support shape the common life of contemporary Christian communities, particularly the relationship between a minister and a congregation. Once that relationship becomes characterized as that of employee and employer, a certain set of conventions and narratives come into play shaping that relationship in terms of power, status, authority, and accountability. But if the minister and the congregation are seen as fellow sharers in the gospel, each exercising diverse gifts for the proper ordering of the body of Christ, a different set of conventions and narratives will govern the relationship.

I suspect that in many churches in America we will find that much of the rhetoric is devoted to thinking of the relationship between a minister and a congregation in terms of being fellow sharers in the gospel along the lines noted above. I further suspect that in practice the managerial model of employer and employee is what primarily shapes this relationship. In some cases, even the rhetoric has shifted to adopt the managerial model. This is not altogether surprising when one recognizes the centrality of this model both in the dominant culture and in the daily lives of most Christians. On the one hand, we should not underestimate the attractiveness of this way of shaping relationships within the body of Christ. When one accepts the model as appropriate, it provides clear processes for shaping a relationship. There are a certain clarity and security in this model. In theory both parties know where each other stands, and there is less opportunity for personal considerations and judgments to influence the procedures. If one performs certain tasks well then one is appropriately compensated. If one fails to perform certain tasks to an agreed-on standard, then there are consequences.

On the other hand, this model leaves several basic issues untouched. For example, it cannot address questions about whether the tasks assigned to the minister are those that will further enhance a community's prospects of ordering their common life in a manner worthy of the gospel. Further, this model pushes both parties to see the priestly or ordained ministry, and the Christian life more generally, as a set of tasks and exchanges because it is much easier to

231

quantify and assess the performance of neatly specified tasks. It provides, for example, a clear and culturally accepted way for characterizing the giving and receiving of money. Even on its own terms, however, a managerial model decisively distorts the dispersal of power and accountability within a congregation. For example, is the minister the only party who must perform certain tasks? What, beyond providing money, are the tasks of the congregation? Who evaluates whether those tasks have been met? What consequences are there for failing to perform adequately? That these questions do not appear to have adequate answers may indicate the basic unsuitability of a managerial model for shaping the relationship between minister and congregation. Rather than accounting for the giving and receiving of money in a way that replicates Paul's Christ-focused practical wisdom, there is tremendous temptation to supplement the managerial model with a consumerist model. Members of a congregation are not simply the minister's employers; they are also customers or consumers. They come to church with self-perceived and self-articulated needs. If those needs are met in terms that they recognize, they stay and contribute money. If not, they go elsewhere. This not only shapes the relationship between minister and congregation, it shapes relationships among congregations, making them competitors for market share.

Although Paul could not have anticipated the particular ways in which market economies in contemporary societies would shape Christian friendships, he understood in ways that most contemporary Christians do not that material practices such as giving and receiving money are not simply natural processes governed by clearly observable laws. He understood that unless these practices were accounted for and shaped by Christians' participation in God's economy of salvation, then the conventions and narratives of the dominant culture would govern the way Christians came to understand those practices. Further, once that had happened, the Philippians would come to see their gifts to Paul in ways that would corrode their friendship.

Second, Paul's discussion of giving and receiving money poses an immediate challenge to relatively wealthy Christians in America (like me). How do we conceive of our relations and obligations to the poor, particularly the poor we do (or, more likely, do not) encounter in the body of Christ? If we learned to renarrate the contexts in which we find ourselves in the light of Paul's practice in Phil 4:10-20, it probably would have serious consequences for our giving, including our expectations of how that giving will be received.[32] Indeed, the most challenging part of this passage for American

---

32. I am not an expert on the growing literature on the issue of faith and wealth. There are a number of good discussions on the role of possessions in specific texts (e.g., Johnson, *Lit-*

Christians may be to narrate (and enact) our relationship to the poor in the universal body of Christ, along with our wealth, and our patterns of consumption and giving in ways that indicate that we are fellow sharers in the gospel with the poor. Moreover, our baptism calls us into a common friendship in Christ within which we are called to seek the benefit of others rather than our own.

Conclusion: Joy and Christian Friendship

A theology of friendship in Christ that takes its bearings from Philippians must ultimately speak about joy. Paul thinks of the Philippians "with joy" (1:4); he is convinced that deciding to remain and pursue fruitful labor in the flesh will help lead to the Philippians' advancement and joy in the faith (1:25); if the Philippians adopt a common pattern of Christ-focused, other-directed practical reasoning, they will fulfill Paul's joy (2:2); Paul directs them to welcome the returning Epaphroditus with joy (2:29); finally, Paul refers to the Philippians as his joy (4:1).

In addition, there are several occasions when Paul speaks of his or the Philippians' rejoicing. He rejoices that the gospel is proclaimed, whether from good motives or bad (1:18); though he may be "poured out as a drink offering," he rejoices and calls the Philippians to rejoice together with him (2:17-18); he issues two calls to the Philippians to "rejoice in the Lord" (3:1; 4:4); and he rejoices in the Lord in the light of the Philippians' gift (4:10).

Given this abundance of references to joy and rejoicing in the epistle, it is not surprising that joy should play a significant role in Christian friendship. In the light of what I have already said, I would argue that joy and rejoicing are not so much ends in themselves as byproducts of the proper working of

---

erary Function of Possessions in Luke-Acts) as well as studies that synthesize a variety of NT texts on possessions (e.g., Wheeler, *Wealth as Peril and Obligation*). These are often helpful studies. Passages such as Phil 4:10-20 rarely, if ever, play a role in such discussions. This indicates something significant. As Christians seriously engage Scripture with an eye toward what Scripture "says" about wealth or possessions, there is a real possibility that wealth or possessions will become abstractions, things that stand on their own. A passage such as Phil 4:10-20 (among others) indicates that Christians also need to learn to see that wealth and possessions are integrally tied up in networks of practices and patterns of relating to others that can either frustrate or enhance our life with God and each other. Learning to see how our possessions fit into such practices and networks, confessing and repenting when necessary, and strengthening and sustaining faithful practices are the crucial tasks confronting the churches in America. See also Fowl, *Engaging Scripture*, especially chapter 6, and "Wealth, Property and Theft."

Christian friendships, what one should expect in the midst of a common life ordered in a manner worthy of the gospel of Christ.

One of the first things to note here is that joy is always linked to the attainment of some good. This can be a difficult and demanding good such as the formation of Christ-focused, other-directed practical reasoning or the more straightforward task of appropriately welcoming Epaphroditus, who has risked his life in Christ's service. Thus, one does not pursue joy. Rather, one pursues some good, the attainment of which results in joy.[33] This is one of the distinctive ways in which joy differs from pleasure. Pleasure can be pursued for its own sake, joy cannot.

In addition, and more specifically, it appears that joy is tied to goods related to another. Whether it is Paul's prayerful recollections of the Philippians, his decision to do that which is more beneficial for them, the Philippians' welcome of Epaphroditus, or simply the attention Paul directs to their common friendship, joy in each of these cases is closely connected to one's relationship to others. As Philip Kenneson writes, "Joy is simply one of the consequences of being open to that which is beyond one's self. To pursue joy for its own sake, in order to take delight in one's own delight, is to ignore this crucial 'other-directedness' of joy."[34]

Given these considerations even in the midst of certain types of suffering, one might experience joy. This is not because the pain and anguish associated with suffering are goods. Instead, if suffering is the result of one's steadfast fidelity in a hostile situation, then the deepened communion with God and others resulting from that fidelity might occasion joy. It is knowing and experiencing God's presence in the midst of suffering that leads to joy, not the pain itself. Of course this further distinguishes joy from pleasure. While one might experience joy in certain sorts of suffering, one would not derive pleasure from that suffering.

These same considerations also apply to the activity of rejoicing. One rejoices to the extent that one is drawn out of oneself in gratitude and thanks as some good is achieved. In many cases this is some good that God is achieving and is perceived by Paul or the Philippians. This is the case when Paul rejoices in the proclamation of the gospel regardless of motive. Considering the prospect of his own death in 2:17-18, Paul rejoices in what God will make of his self-offering and calls on the Philippians to join him in this. In the eyes of Paul's opponents in 1:16-18, their preaching is designed to annoy and frustrate Paul. In the eyes of those who might put Paul to death, that death would

33. See the comments to this effect in C. S. Lewis's *Surprised by Joy*, 168.
34. *Life on the Vine: Cultivating the Fruit of the Spirit in Christian Community*, 59.

never be seen in the sacrificial terms Paul uses. Rejoicing assumes that one perceives God, oneself, and others in particular ways. A failure of vision will result in either an absence of rejoicing or rejoicing in the wrong thing or in the wrong way.

In all these cases God is the object of the rejoicing. This would have to be true by implication even when Paul does not explicitly speak of rejoicing in the Lord. Thus, the practice of rejoicing is closely tied to the ability to perceive God's activity and to properly situate oneself in relation to that activity. This depends on being able to fit one's life and the lives of others into the economy of salvation. This also depends on being able to describe and redescribe various practices and activities (such as giving and receiving money) in the light of God's saving purposes. As I have already indicated, these are two of the central practices of Christian friendship as seen in Philippians. Joy and rejoicing in the Lord, then, are the fruits of Christian friendships in good working order.

Bibliography

Alexander, L. C. A. "Hellenistic Letter-Forms and the Structure of Philippians." *JSNT* 37 (1989) 87-101.

Anselm. "Why God Became Man." In *A Scholastic Miscellany: Anselm to Ockham*, edited by E. Fairweather. Philadelphia: Westminster Press, 1961.

Aquinas, Thomas. *Summa Theologiae*. Blackfriars edition, translated by Thomas Gilby et al. New York: McGraw Hill Book Co., 1963.

———. *Commentary on 1 Thessalonians and Philippians*. Translated by F. R. Larcher. Albany, NY: Magi Books, 1969.

Augustine of Hippo. *On Christian Doctrine*. Translated by D. W. Robertson. New York: Macmillan, 1987.

Austin, J. L. *How to Do Things with Words*. Oxford: Clarendon, 1962.

Ayres, L. "On Not Three People: The Fundamental Themes of Gregory of Nyssa's Trinitarian Theology as Seen in *To Ablabius: On Not Three Gods*." *Modern Theology* 18:4 (2002) 445-474.

Bakirtzis, C., and H. Koester, eds. *Philippi at the Time of Paul and after His Death*. Harrisburg: Trinity Press International, 1998.

Barclay, John. "Mirror-Reading a Polemical Letter: Galatians as a Test Case." *JSNT* 31 (1987) 79-93.

Bartchy, S. *MALLON CHRĒSAI: First-Century Slavery and the Interpretation of 1 Corinthians 7:21*. SBLDS 11. Missoula, MT: Scholars Press, 1973.

———. "Undermining Ancient Patriarchy: The Apostle Paul's Vision of a Society of Siblings." *BTB* 29 (1999) 68-78.

Barth, K. *Epistle to the Philippians*. 40th Anniversary Edition with Introductory Essays by B. McCormack and F. Watson. Louisville: Westminster/John Knox Press, 2002.

Basil of Caesarea. *Works of St. Basil*. Loeb Classical Library, translated by R. Deferrari, 4 vols. Cambridge: Harvard University Press, 1950.

Bauckham, R. *God Crucified: Monotheism and Christology in the New Testament*. Grand Rapids: Eerdmans, 1998.

———. "The Worship of Jesus in Philippians 2:9-11." In *Where Christology Began*, edited by R. P. Martin and B. Dodd. Louisville: Westminster/John Knox, 1998.

Beare, F. W. *A Commentary on the Epistle to the Philippians.* London: A & C Black, 1973.

Behm, J. "μορφή." *TDNT* IV: 742-52.

Berger, K. "Hellenistische Gattungen im Neuen Testament." *ANRW,* II, 25.2 (1984) 1032-1462.

Bernard of Clairvaux. *On the Song of Songs.* Translated by Kilian Walsh. Spencer, MA: Cistercian Publications, 1971.

Bloomquist, G. *The Function of Suffering in Philippians.* JSNTS 78. Sheffield: JSOT Press, 1993.

Bockmuehl, Marcus. "A Commentator's Approach to the 'Effective History' of Philippians." *JSNT* 60 (1995) 57-88.

————. "'The Form of God' (Phil. 2.6): Variations on a Theme of Jewish Mysticism." *JTS* n.s. 48 (1997) 1-23.

————. *The Epistle to the Philippians.* Black's NT Commentaries. London: A. & C. Black, 1998.

Bondi, R. *To Pray and to Love.* Minneapolis: Augsburg Fortress, 1991.

Bonhoeffer, D. *Life Together.* Translated by J. Doberstein. New York: Harper and Row, 1954.

Bormann, L. *Philippi: Stadt und Christusgemeinde zur Zeit Paulus.* Leiden: Brill, 1995.

Bornkamm, G. "Zum Verständnis der Christus-Hymnus Phil. 2,5-11." In *Studien zu Antike und Urchristentum,* 177-87. Munich: Kaiser Verlag, 1963.

Brewer, R. "The Meaning of *Politeuesthe* in Philippians 1:27." *JBL* 71 (1952) 227-31.

Buchanan, C. O. "Epaphroditus' Sickness and the Letter to the Philippians." *EvQ* 36 (1964) 260-84.

Budde, M. *The (Magic) Kingdom of God.* Boulder, CO: Westview Press, 1997.

Bultmann, Rudolf. *New Testament Theology.* Translated by Kendrick Grobel. 2 volumes. New York: Scribner, 1951.

Burtchaell, J. T. *From Synagogue to Church.* Cambridge: Cambridge University Press, 1992.

Byrskog, S. "Co-Senders, Co-Authors and Paul's Use of the First Person Plural." *ZNW* 87 (1996) 233-36.

Caird. G. B. *Paul's Letters from Prison.* Oxford: Clarendon, 1974.

Cantalamessa, R. *The Eucharist: Our Sanctification.* Revised edition. Collegeville: Liturgical Press, 1995.

Capper, B. "Paul's Dispute with Philippi." *ThZ* 49 (1993) 193-214.

Cassidy, R. *Paul in Chains: Roman Imprisonment in the Letters of Paul.* New York: Herder and Herder, 2001.

Castelli, E. *Imitating Paul: A Discourse of Power.* Louisville: Westminster/John Knox Press, 1991.

Catherine of Siena. *Catherine of Siena: Passion for the Truth, Compassion for Humanity.* Edited by Mary O'Driscoll. Hyde Park: New City Press, 1993.

Cavanaugh, W. T. "A Fire Strong Enough to Consume The House: The Wars of Religion and the Rise of the State." *Modern Theology* 11:4 (1995) 397-420.

————. *Torture and Eucharist.* Oxford: Blackwell, 1998.

Charry, E., ed. *Inquiring After God: Classic and Contemporary Readings.* Oxford: Blackwell, 2000.

Chrysostom, John. *Homilies on Philippians.* Translated by J. Broadus. *The Nicene and Post-*

Nicene Fathers, Series 1. Edited by Philip Schaff. 1886-1889. 14 vols. Repr. Peabody, MA: Hendrickson, 1994.

Coakley, S. "'Persons' in the 'Social' Doctrine of the Trinity: Current Analytic Discussion and 'Cappodocian' Theology." In *Powers and Submissions,* 109-29. Oxford: Blackwell, 2002.

Collange, J.-F. *The Epistle of St. Paul to the Philippians.* Translated from the first French edition by A. W. Heathcote. London: Epworth Press, 1979.

Deichgräber, R. *Gotteshymnus und Christushymnus der frühen Christenheit.* Göttingen: Vandenhoeck and Ruprecht, 1967.

Denis, A. "Verse en libation (Phil. 2,17) = Verse son sang? A propos d'une reference de W. Bauer." *RSR* 45 (1957) 567-70.

Denniston, J. D. *Greek Particles.* Indianapolis: Hackett, 1996.

deVos, C. S. *Church and Community Conflicts: The Relationships of the Thessalonian, Corinthian and Philippian Churches to Their Wider Civic Communities.* SBLDS 168. Atlanta: Scholars Press, 1999.

Droge, A., and J. Tabor. *A Noble Death.* San Francisco: HarperSanFrancisco, 1992.

Dunn, J. D. G. *Christology in the Making.* London: SCM, 1980.

———. "Christ, Adam and Preexistence." In *Where Christology Began,* edited by R. P. Martin and B. Dodd, 74-83. Louisville: Westminster/John Knox, 1998.

Engberg-Pedersen, Troels. *Paul and the Stoics.* Louisville: Westminster/John Knox Press, 2000.

———. "Radical Altruism in Philippians 2:4." In *Early Christianity and Classical Culture: Comparative Studies in Honor of Abraham Malherbe,* edited by John Fitzgerald, Thomas Olbricht, and L. Michael White, 197-204. Leiden: Brill, 2003.

Fee, Gordon D. "Reflections on Commentary Writing." *Theology Today* 46 (1999) 387-92.

———. *Paul's Letter to the Philippians.* NICNT. Grand Rapids: Eerdmans, 1995.

Fitzgerald, J. T. "Philippians in the Light of Some Ancient Discussions of Friendship." In *Friendship, Flattery and Frankness of Speech: Studies on Friendship in the Ancient World,* edited by J. T. Fitzgerald, 141-60. Leiden: Brill, 1996.

Fitzmyer, J. A. "The Consecutive Meaning of EΦ' Ω in Romans 5.12." *NTS* 39 (1993) 321-339.

Foucault, M. *Discipline and Punish.* Translated by A. Sheridan. New York: Vintage Books, 1979.

Fowl, S. "Some Uses of Story in Moral Discourse: Reflections on Paul's Moral Discourse and Our Own." *Modern Theology* 4:4 (1988) 293-308.

———. *The Story of Christ in the Ethics of Paul.* JSNTS 36. Sheffield: JSOT Press, 1990.

———, and L. G. Jones. *Reading in Communion.* Grand Rapids: Eerdmans, 1991.

———. *Engaging Scripture.* Oxford: Blackwells, 1998.

———. "Being Blessed: Wealth, Property and Theft." In *The Blackwell Companion to Christian Ethics,* edited by S. Hauerwas and S. Wells, 455-67. Oxford: Blackwell, 2003.

Gamble, H. *Books and Readers in the Early Church.* New Haven: Yale University Press, 1995.

Garland, D. E. "The Composition and Unity of Philippians: Some Neglected Literary Factors." *NovT* 27 (1985) 141-175.

Gloer, W. H. "Homologies and Hymns in the New Testament: Form, Content and Criteria for Identification." *Perspectives in Religious Studies* 11.2 (1984) 115-32.

Gnilka, J. *Der Philipperbrief.* Freiburg: Verlag Herder, 1968.

Gorman, M. *Cruciformity: Paul's Narrative Spirituality of the Cross.* Grand Rapids: Eerdmans, 2001.

Gregory of Nazianzus. *Lettres Théologiques.* Edited by P. Gallay. Sources Chrétiennes 208. Paris: Cerf, 1974.

Gregory of Nyssa. *The Life of Moses.* Translated by E. Ferguson and A. Malherbe. New York: Paulist Press, 1978.

———. *To Ablabius: On Not Three Gods.* Translated by H. A. Wilson. NPNF.

Gundry, R. *Sōma in Biblical Theology with an Emphasis on Pauline Anthropology.* Cambridge: Cambridge University Press, 1976.

Gundry-Volf, J. *Paul and Perseverance.* Louisville: Westminster/John Knox Press, 1990.

Gunkel, H. "Die Lieder in der Kindheitsgeschichte Jesu." In *Festgabe von Fachgenossen und Freunden Adolf Harnack zum 70. Geburtstag dargebracht,* edited by K. Holl, 43-60. Tübingen: Mohr, 1921.

———, and J. Begrich. *Einleitung in die Psalmen.* 2nd edition. Göttingen: Vandenhoeck and Ruprecht, 1966, 1st ed. 1933.

Hauerwas, S. *After Christendom.* Nashville: Abingdon, 1991.

Hawthorne, Gerald F. *Philippians.* WBC. Waco: Word, 1983.

———. "In the Form of God and Equal with God (Philippians 2:6)." In *Where Christology Began,* edited by R. P. Martin and B. Dodd, 96-110. Louisville: Westminster/John Knox, 1998.

Hays, Richard. *Echoes of Scripture in the Letters of Paul.* New Haven: Yale University Press, 1989.

Hendriksen, W. *Exposition of Philippians.* Grand Rapids: Baker, 1962.

Hengel, M. *Crucifixion.* Translated by J. Bowden. London: SCM, 1977.

———. "Hymn and Christology." In *Studia Biblica III,* edited by E. A. Livingstone, 173-97. Sheffield: JSOT, 1980.

Hofius, O. *Der Christushymnus Philipper 2,6-11.* Tübingen: Mohr, 1991.

Hooker, M. *Jesus and the Servant.* London: SPCK, 1959.

Hoover, R. W. "The Harpagmos Enigma: A Philological Solution." *HTR* 64 (1971) 95-119.

Hurst, L. D. "Christ, Adam and Preexistence Revisited." In *Where Christology Began,* edited by R. P. Martin and B. Dodd, 85-95. Louisville: Westminster/John Knox, 1998.

Hurtado, L. "Jesus as Lordly Example in Philippians 2:5-11." In *From Jesus to Paul: Studies in Honour of Francis Wright Beare,* edited by P. Richardson and J. C. Hurd, 122-32. Waterloo: Wilfrid Laurier University Press, 1984.

———. *One God, One Lord: Early Christian Devotion and Ancient Jewish Monotheism.* Philadelphia: Fortress, 1988.

———. *Lord Jesus Christ.* Grand Rapids: Eerdmans, 2003.

Jaeger, W. "Eine stilgeschichtliche Studie zum Philipperbrief." *Hermes* 50 (1915) 536-63.

Jenson, Robert. *Systematic Theology.* Volume 2: *The Works of God.* Oxford: Oxford University Press, 1999.

Jeremias, J. "Zu Phil. ii.7: ἑαυτὸν ἐκένωσεν." *NovT* 6 (1963) 182-89.

Jewett, R. "The Epistolary Thanksgiving and the Integrity of Philippians." *NovT* 12 (1970) 40-43.

———. "Conflicting Movements in Early Christianity as Reflected in Philippians." *NovT* 12 (1970) 362-90.

Johnson, Luke T. *The Literary Function of Possessions in Luke-Acts.* SBLDS 39. Atlanta: Scholars Press, 1977.

———. "Friendship with the World/Friendship with God: A Study of Discipleship in James." In *Discipleship in the New Testament,* edited by F. Segovia, 166-83. Philadelphia: Fortress, 1985.

———. *The Acts of the Apostles.* Sacra Pagina. Collegeville: Michael Glazier, 1992.

Käsemann, E. "Kritische Analyse von Phil. 2,5-11." *ZTK* 47 (1950) 313-60.

Kenneson, P. *Life on the Vine: Cultivating the Fruit of the Spirit in Christian Community.* Downers Grove: InterVarsity Press, 1999.

———, and J. Street. *Selling Out the Church.* Nashville: Abingdon, 1997.

Kilpatrick, G. D. "ΒΛΕΠΕΤΕ: Philippians 3:2." In *In Memoriam Paul Kahle,* edited by M. Black and G. Fohrer, 146-48, Berlin: DeGruyter, 1968.

Kim, S. *The Origin of Paul's Gospel.* Grand Rapids: Eerdmans, 1981.

Koester, H. "The Purpose of the Polemic of a Pauline Fragment." *NTS* 8 (1961-62) 317-32.

Konstan, D. *Friendship in the Classical World.* Cambridge: Cambridge University Press, 1997.

Koperski, V. *The Knowledge of Jesus Christ My Lord.* Kampen: Kok Pharos, 1996.

Krenz, E. "Epideiktik and Hymnody: The New Testament and Its World." *Biblical Research* 40 (1995) 50-97.

Kugel, J. *The Idea of Biblical Poetry.* New Haven: Yale University Press, 1981.

Levison, J. R. *Portraits of Adam in Early Judaism.* Sheffield: JSOT Press, 1988.

Lewis, C. S. *Surprised by Joy.* New York: Harcourt, Brace & World, 1955.

Lightfoot, J. B. *St. Paul's Epistle to the Philippians.* Revised and enlarged edition 1881. Repr. Lynn, MA: Hendrickson, 1981.

Lincoln, A. T. *Paradise Now and Not Yet.* Cambridge: Cambridge University Press, 1981.

Lindbeck, G. "The Eucharist Tastes Bitter in a Divided Church." *Spectrum* 19:1 (1999) 1-5.

Lohfink, G. *Jesus and Community.* Translated by J. P. Galvin. Philadelphia: Fortress, 1984.

Lohmeyer, E. *Kyrios Jesus.* Sitzungsbericht der Heidelberger Akademie der Wissenschaften Phil.-hist.Kl. Jahr 1927-28.

———. *Die Briefe an die Philipper, an die Kolosser und an Philemon.* Göttingen: Vandenhoeck & Ruprecht, 1929.

Losie, L. A. "A Note on the Interpretation of Phil. 2,5." *Expository Times* 90 (1978) 52-54.

Lowth, R. *De Sacra Poesi Hebraeorum Praelectiones Academicae.* Oxford: Clarendon, 1821.

Lüderitz, G. "What Is the Politeuma?" In *Studies in Early Jewish Epigraphy,* edited by J. W. van Henten and P. W. van der Horst, 183-225. Leiden: Brill, 1994.

MacIntyre, A. "Positivism, Sociology and Practical Reasoning: Notes on Durkheim's *Suicide.*" In *Human Nature and Natural Knowledge,* edited by A. Donagan, A. N. Perovitch Jr., and M. V. Wedin. Dordrecht: D. Reidel, 1986.

Marshall, P. *Enmity at Corinth.* Tübingen: Mohr, 1997.

Martin, Dale. *Slavery as Salvation: The Metaphor of Slavery in Pauline Christianity.* New Haven: Yale University Press, 1990.

―――. *The Corinthian Body.* New Haven: Yale University Press, 1995.

Martin, R. P. "Some Reflections on New Testament Hymns." In *Christ the Lord,* Festschrift for D. Guthrie, edited by H. H. Rowland, 37-49. Leicester: Inter Varsity Press, 1982.

―――. *Carmen Christi.* Revised edition. Grand Rapids: Eerdmans, 1983.

―――, and B. Dodd, editors. *Where Christology Began.* Louisville: Westminster/John Knox, 1998.

Matlock, R. Barry. "Detheologizing the ΠΙΣΤΙΣ ΧΡΙΣΤΟΥ Debate: Cautionary Remarks from a Lexical Semantic Perspective." *NovT* 42 (2000) 1-22.

McCabe, H. *God Matters.* London: Geoffrey Chapman, 1987.

Meeks, W. "The Man from Heaven in Paul's Letter to the Philippians." In *The Future of Early Christianity: Essays in Honor of Helmut Koester,* edited by Birger Pearson, 329-36. Minneapolis: Fortress Press, 1991.

Metzger, B. M. *A Textual Commentary on the Greek New Testament.* London: United Bible Societies, 1971.

Milbank, J. *Theology and Social Theory.* Oxford: Blackwell, 1993.

―――. "Can a Gift Be Given? Prolegomena to a Future Trinitarian Metaphysic." *Modern Theology* 11:1 (1995) 119-61.

―――. "Can Morality Be Christian?" In *The Word Made Strange.* Oxford: Blackwells, 1997.

Moffatt, J. "Philippians II.26 and 2 Tim IV.13." *JTS* 18 (1917) 311-12.

Morris, L. "ΚΑΙ ΑΠΑΞ ΚΑΙ ΔΙΣ." *NovT* 1 (1956) 205-6.

Moule, C. F. D. "Further Reflections on Phil. 2:5-11." In *Apostolic History and the Gospel: Biblical and Historical Essays Presented to F. F. Bruce on His 60th Birthday.* Edited by W. W. Gasque and R. P. Martin, 264-76. Exeter: Paternoster Press, 1970.

Mullins, T. Y. "Disclosure: A Literary Form in the New Testament." *NovT* 7 (1964) 44-50.

Musurillo, H. ed. *The Acts of the Christian Martyrs.* Oxford: Clarendon, 1972.

Norden, E. *Der Antike Kunstprosa.* 2 vols. Leipzig: Teubner, 1898.

―――. *Agnostos Theos.* Stuttgart: Teubner, 1912.

Oakes, Peter. "Jason and Penelope Hear Philippians 1:1-11." In *Understanding, Studying and Reading: Essays in Honor of John Ashton.* Edited by C. Rowland. Sheffield: Sheffield Academic Press, 1998.

―――. *Philippians: From Letter to People.* SNTSMS 110. Cambridge: Cambridge University Press, 2001.

O'Brien, Peter. *Commentary on Philippians.* NIGTC. Grand Rapids: Eerdmans, 1991.

O'Neill, J. C. "Hoover on *Harpagmos* Reviewed, with a Modest Proposal Concerning Philippians 2:6." *HTR* 81 (1988) 445-49.

Perkins, P. "Philippians: Theology for the Heavenly Politeuma." In *Pauline Theology,* vol. 1, edited by J. M. Bassler, 89-104. Minneapolis: Fortress, 1991.

Peterlin, D. *Paul's Letter to the Philippians in the Light of Disunity of the Church.* Novum Testmentum Supplements 79. Leiden: Brill, 1995.

Peterman, G. W. *Paul's Gift from Philippi: Conventions of Gift Exchange and Christian Giving.* SNTSMS 92. Cambridge: Cambridge University Press, 1997.

Pickstock, C. *After Writing: On the Liturgical Consummation of Philosophy.* Oxford: Blackwell, 1998.

Plummer, A. *A Commentary on St. Paul's Epistle to the Philippians.* London: R. Scott, 1919.

Pohl, C. *Making Room: Recovering Hospitality as a Christian Tradition*. Grand Rapids: Eerdmans, 1999.

Porter, S., and J. Reed. "Philippians as a Macro-Chiasm and Its Exegetical Significance." *NTS* 44 (1998) 213-231.

Radner, E. *The End of the Church: A Pneumatology of Christian Division in the West*. Grand Rapids: Eerdmans, 1998.

Rapske, B. *The Book of Acts and Paul in Roman Custody*. Grand Rapids: Eerdmans, 1994.

Ratzinger, Joseph. "Anglican-Catholic Dialogue: Its Problems and Hopes." In *Church Ecumenism and Politics*. New York: Crossroad, 1988.

Reed, J. T. "The Infinitive with Two Substantival Accusatives: An Ambiguous Construction?" *NovT* 33 (1991) 1-27.

———. *A Discourse Analysis of Philippians*. JSNTS 136. Sheffield: Sheffield Academic Press, 1997.

Rese, M. "Formeln und Lieder im Neuen Testament: einige notwendige Anmerkungen." *Verkündigung und Forschung* 2 (1970) 75-95.

Reumann, J. "Contributions of the Philippian Community to Paul and to Earliest Christianity." *NTS* 39 (1993) 438-57.

Root, M. "Why Care About the Unity of the Church?" In *Why Are We Here?* edited by R. Thiemann and W. Placher, 98-111. Harrisburg: Trinity Press International, 1998.

Sampley, J. P. *Pauline Partnership in Christ*. Philadelphia: Fortress, 1980.

Sanders, J. *The New Testament Christological Hymns: Their Historical and Religious Background*. Cambridge: Cambridge University Press, 1971.

Schille, G. *Frühchristliche Hymnen*. Berlin: Evangelische Verlaganstalt, 1962.

Schmithals, W. "Die Irrlehrer der Philipperbriefes." *ZTK* 54 (1957) 297-341.

Schneider, J. "ὁμοίωμα." *TDNT* 5: 191-98.

Schweizer, E. "σάρξ." *TDNT* 7:125-51.

Seeburg, A. *Der Katechismus der Urchristenheit*. Leipzig: Teubner, 1903.

Segert, S. "Semitic Poetic Structures in the New Testament." *ANRW* II, 25.2 (1984) 1432-62.

Silva, M. *Philippians*. BECNT. Grand Rapids: Eerdmans, 1992.

Spicq, C. *Agape in the New Testament*. Translated by M. McNamara and M. Richter. 3 vols. St. Louis: Herder, 1965.

Stanley, C. *Paul and the Language of Scripture: Citation Technique in the Pauline Epistles and Contemporary Literature*. Cambridge: Cambridge University Press, 1992.

Steenburg, D. "The Case Against the Synonymity of *Morphē* and *Eikōn*." *JSNT* 34 (1988) 77-86.

Stowers, Stanley. *Letter Writing in Greco-Roman Antiquity*. Philadelphia: Westminster Press, 1986.

———. "Friends and Enemies in the Politics of Heaven." In *Pauline Theology*, vol. 1, edited by J. Bassler, 105-121. Minneapolis: Augsburg Fortress, 1991.

Tellbe, M. "The Sociological Factors behind Philippians 3:1-11 and the Conflict at Philippi." *JSNT* 55 (1994) 97-121.

Torrell, J-P. *Saint Thomas Aquinas*. Vol. 1. Translated by Robert Royal. Washington: Catholic University of America Press, 1996.

Turescu, L. "'Person' versus 'Individual' and Other Modern Misreadings of Gregory of Nyssa." *Modern Theology* 18 (2002) 527-40.

Volf, M. *After Our Likeness: The Church as Image of the Trinity.* Grand Rapids: Eerdmans, 1998.

von Balthasar, H. U. *The Glory of The Lord.* Vol. VII. Translated by B. McNeil. San Francisco: Ignatius Press, 1989.

———. *Mysterium Paschale.* Translated by Aidan Nichols, O.P. Grand Rapids: Eerdmans, 1990.

Wadell, P. *Friendship and the Moral Life.* Notre Dame: University of Notre Dame Press, 1989.

Wansink, C. *Chained in Christ.* JSNTS 130. Sheffield: Sheffield Academic Press, 1997.

Watson, D. "A Rhetorical Analysis of Philippians." *NovT* 30 (1988) 57-88.

Watson, W. *Classical Hebrew Poetry.* Sheffield: JSOT, 1984.

Weisheipl, James. *Friar Thomas D'Aquino.* New York: Doubleday, 1974.

Weiss, J. "Beiträge zur paulinischen Rhetorik." In *Theologische Studien für B. Weiss,* 165-247. Göttingen: Vandenhoeck and Ruprecht, 1897.

Wengst, K. *Christologische Formeln und Lieder des Urchristentums.* Gütersloh: Mohn, 1972.

Wheeler, S. *Wealth as Peril and Obligation.* Grand Rapids: Eerdmans, 1995.

Wick, P. *Der Philipperbrief: Der formale Aufbau des Briefs als Schlüssel zum Verständnis seines Inhalts.* Stuttgart: Kohlhammer, 1994.

Wilken, R. *The Christians as the Romans Saw Them.* New Haven: Yale University Press, 1984.

Williams, R. *On Christian Theology.* Oxford: Blackwells, 2001.

Witherington, Ben, III. *Friendship and Finances in Philippi: The Letter of Paul to the Philippians.* Valley Forge, PA: Trinity Press International, 1994.

Wright, N. T. *The Climax of the Covenant.* Minneapolis: Fortress Press, 1991.

———. "Paul's Gospel and Caesar's Empire." In *Paul and Politics,* edited by R. Horsley, 173-81. Philadelphia: Trinity Press, 2000.

Wuthnow, R. *Sharing the Journey.* New York: Free Press, 1994.

Yeago, D. "The New Testament and Nicene Dogma." In *The Theological Interpretation of Scripture,* edited by S. Fowl. 87-101. Oxford: Blackwells, 1997.

———. Unpublished typescript on Christian doctrine, 2 volumes, 1998.

Young, F. *From Nicea to Chalcedon.* London: SCM, 1983.

Zizioulas, J. *Being as Communion: Studies in Personhood and the Church.* Crestwood: St. Vladimir's Seminary Press, 1985.

Index of Modern Names

Index of Scripture and Other Ancient Writings